Towards Coherence in Criminal Justice

Jolanta Zajančkauskienė / Rima Ažubalytė /
Oleg Fedosiuk (eds.)

Towards Coherence in Criminal Justice

Challenges, Discussions And/Or Solutions

PETER LANG

Berlin - Bruxelles - Chennai - Lausanne - New York - Oxford

Library of Congress Cataloging-in-Publication Data

Names: Zajančkauskienė, Jolanta, editor. | Ažubalytė, Rima, editor. | Fedosiuk, Oleg, editor.
Title: Towards coherence in criminal justice : challenges, discussions, and/or solutions / edited by Jolanta Zajančkauskienė, Rima Ažubalytė, and Oleg Fedosiuk.
Description: New York : Peter Lang, 2025. | Includes bibliographical references and index.
Identifiers: LCCN 2025015805 (print) | LCCN 2025015806 (ebook) | ISBN 9783631929445 (hardcover) | ISBN 9783631935323 (ebook) | ISBN 9783631935330 (epub)
Subjects: LCSH: Criminal justice, Administration of. | Criminal jurisdiction. | Criminal law. | Criminal liability. | Evidence, Criminal. | Electronic evidence. | Convention for the Protection of Human Rights and Fundamental Freedoms (1950 November 5) | Fair trial.
Classification: LCC K5001 .T69 2025 (print) | LCC K5001 (ebook) | DDC 345—dc23/eng/20250403
LC record available at https://lccn.loc.gov/2025015805
LC ebook record available at https://lccn.loc.gov/2025015806

Bibliographic information published by the Deutsche Nationalbibliothek
The Deutsche Nationalbibliothek collects this publication in the Deutsche Nationalbibliografie; detailed bibliographic data are available on the Internet at .Nationalbibliografie; detailed bibliographic data are available on the Internet at http://dnb.d-nb.de.

MRU

Mykolas Romeris University

Reviewers:
Prof. dr. Edita Gruodytė (Vytautas Magnus University, Lithuania)
Prof. dr. hab. Wieslaw Plywaczewski (University of Warmia and Mazur in Olsztyn, Poland)

Copy-editor:
MB "Kopis"

Approved by Mykolas Romeris University Law School Council on 11 of June 2024 by resolution No. 1T-14 (1.12 E-20401).

ISBN 978-3-631-92944-5 (Print)
ISBN 978-3-631-93532-3 (E-PDF)
ISBN 978-3-631-93533-0 (E-PUB)
DOI.10.3726/b22750

PETER LANG Open

Published by Peter Lang GmbH, Berlin, Germany
info@peterlang.com - www.peterlang.com

Contents

Preface

The terms "coherence" and "sustainability" have firmly entered the vocabulary of modern official language and have become a kind of landmark on the path of social development in the 21st century. These signposts have also become significant in law, where the search for coherence is one of the most important goals of modern lawmaking. The presented publication is dedicated to the search for harmony in the field of criminal justice, so the texts of various authors address the questions of how to make the content of criminal laws and the practice of their application more rational, establish fairer rules for the criminal process, and harmonize the goal of protecting society from criminal acts with the imperative of human rights. The pursuit of harmony in criminal justice is fully in line with universally recognized legal principles, which must be followed when criminalizing and decriminalizing human behavior, defining and explaining the content of criminal acts, determining applicable legal measures for persons found guilty, regulating prosecution procedures, ensuring the real enforceability of procedural rights, etc. The search for coherence in the chosen field is aimed at transforming the usual principles of criminal law (legality, guilt, proportionality, legal certainty, ultima ratio, presumption of innocence, etc.) into a more rational model of criminal justice that meets the challenges of modern society and the achievements of the technological world.

Modern criminal justice in European countries is no longer solely a product of national law, it is inevitably influenced by international conventions, European Union legislation, the practice of the European Court of Human Rights and the Court of Justice of the European Union. Thus, the pursuit of coherence is also closely related to this external influence on national criminal justice. Therefore, the thoughtful implementation of conventional provisions considering the precedents of transnational courts is one of the most important directions in criminal justice development. The presented publication's content covers a wide range of substantive and procedural criminal law issues and judicial practice. The choice of the topic is primarily based on the actualities of Lithuanian criminal justice but is not limited to it alone. Areas of analyzed problems such as human trafficking, drug possession, stalking, criminal jurisdiction, electronic evidence, confiscation of criminal assets, and Human Rights Convention standards in criminal proceedings are believed to be relevant throughout Europe and should be of interest to legal researchers working in different countries.

We wish you meaningful reading.

Professor Dr. Oleg Fedosiuk,
Professor Dr. Rima Ažubalytė and
Professor Dr. Jolanta Zajančkauskienė

Jolanta Zajančkauskienė

Introduction: What is the Role of Coherence in Criminal Justice?

The Characterization of Coherence in Law

In modern society, the ever-increasing role of law as a basis for designing, adopting, expressing, and implementing social policy decisions and evaluating their consequences often overshadows the role of other social regulators. Thus, it is no coincidence that the legal system is one of the most important centers of social life in modern society. The legal system represents the totality of the legal reality – a phenomenon that embodies legal consciousness or ideology, legal psychology, objective law and the legal practice of any social group. In other words, the legal system is a concept that defines the characteristics of the legal reality of any social group – i.e., the totality of legal phenomena. This concept has both a broad and narrow interpretation. In the narrow sense, the legal system usually encompasses the system of law and legislation. In the broad sense, the legal system is not identical to the law system, as the content of the legal system may comprise more elements than law and legislation. The latter two elements are the normative basis of the legal system, acting as its central connecting link, on the basis of which the legal system encompasses legal theory, legal consciousness, and legal policy, i.e., theoretical elements and those that relate to worldview as well as legal practice (Šlapkauskas 2006, pp.21–22).

As mentioned above, from a functional perspective, law is considered a regulatory instrument for social affairs, and each country faces similar, if not identical, law problems. Various legal systems lead to the same system of functional complexes when applied in practice, despite their differences in historical development, theoretical and systemic structure, and style. The main functional subsystems of a legal system are legislation, jurisdiction, and jurisprudence (Galginaitis 2002, p.39).

The modern legal system and its functional subsystems are inextricable from coherence. A coherent legal system, presupposed by the principle of the rule of law, is one in which components are logically concerted and work together in harmony. Coherence emphasizes the need for a unified and integrated approach to the interpretation and application of the law to ensure the predictability and stability of legal outcomes. Overall, coherence is essential to maintaining a legal system that is fair to all stakeholders and fosters public confidence in its effectiveness.

For example, according to the doctrine of the Constitutional Court of the Republic of Lithuania (hereinafter – the Constitutional Court), the constitutional principle of the rule of law encompasses a large number of different interlinked imperatives. The content of this principle is revealed with respect to the various provisions of the Constitution of the Republic of Lithuania (hereinafter – the Constitution) by assessing the totality of the values enshrined therein and which are protected and defended under the Constitution (Resolution of the Constitutional Court of 13 December 2004). The constitutional principle of the rule of law must guide both the legislative and executive processes (Rulings of the Constitutional Court of 6 December 2000, 13 December 2004, 16 January 2006, 13 August 2007). The Constitutional Court has reiterated that the constitutional principle of the rule of law is inseparable from the principle of justice, and vice versa: the protection of legitimate expectations, legal certainty, and legal security are equally inseparable elements of the principle of the rule of law (Resolution of the Constitutional Court of 3 February 2010), as is the constitutional principle of proportionality (Rulings of the Constitutional Court of 29 December 2004, 29 September 2005, 10 April 2009). The Constitutional Court has also stated that public authorities must comply with the principle of the rule of law enshrined in the Constitution when drafting and adopting legal acts (Resolution of the Constitutional Court of 26 February 2010). Further, the Constitutional Court has established that an essential element of the principle of the rule of law enshrined in the Constitution is legal clarity, which implies certain mandatory requirements for legal regulation: it must be clear and coherent, and legal norms must be formulated precisely and not contain any ambiguities (Rulings of the Constitutional Court of 30 May 2003, 26 January 2004, 24 December 2008, 22 June 2009).

The particular significance of coherence has been emphasized in legal theory. Scholars have sought to demonstrate the importance of coherence as an ideal characteristic of law and a criterion for legal reasoning (Bertea 2005, pp.369–370). In the 20th century, some authors focused on what makes law coherent, while others debated whether law is coherent and, if so, why it should be thus (e.g., Levenbook 1984; Alexy and Peczenik 1990, as cited in Bertea 2005, p.370). For example, Dworkin (1986) described law as an integral system and its structure as an all-encompassing legal empire. Certainly, this structure is conflicting, as contradictions are bound to arise between different legal values expressed as principles. According to Dworkin, when deciding cases, judges do not possess the discretion to make law; instead, law ought only to be identified, discerned, and have its principles revealed (Dworkin 2005, pp.188–190). It should be noted that Dworkin made notions of law dependent on morality: law delegates to the court the power to implement its own notions of political morality (Dworkin 2004, p.200). On the other hand, different authors have treated the role of coherence in law in a different light. For example, Raz (1994) supported a rather critical view of the requirement for coherence in law. In 21st century legal scholarship, some iterations of a coherent law theory are already in development, such as "integrated coherentism," which postulates that law is "broadly coherent" (Hage 2004, p.101).

Without delving into a comprehensive analysis of the concept of coherence in legal literature, it may be noted that

> Coherence is generally held to be something more than logical consistency of proposition. But it is not clear exactly what this "something more" amounts to. Thus, coherence is often defined in figurative language as the equivalent of "hanging together," "making sense as a whole," "cohesion," "consonance," and "speaking with one voice." A coherent set might therefore be described as a "tightly knit unit." Which makes coherence a "kind of internal interconnectedness," a "plausible connection" that is not linear and asymmetrical, but circular and symmetrical: the elements of a coherent structure are mutually supporting and reinforcing. Coherence is argued on this basis to be a form of supportive rationality (Bertea 2005, pp.371–372).

These definitions allow for further internal distinctions to be made between types of coherence. "An important distinction is that between epistemic and constitutive coherence. Epistemic coherence is a condition of justified beliefs; constitutive coherence is a criterion of either correctness or truth" (Bertea 2005, p.372). Therefore, coherence in the context of "drawing inferences of fact from evidentiary facts" is referred to as "narrative"; when applied to matters of law, it is regarded as "normative coherence." The latter term may also be applied "to a normative system or to reasoning with norms" (Bertea 2005, p.372). Based on an approach involving a normative system, coherence is considered to be an ideal characteristic of any given legal system, i.e., it is recognised as a systemic category: "a legal system is coherent if its components fit together, either all of them (global systemic coherence) or a sub-part (in which case we have local systemic coherence)" (Bertea 2005, p.372). Normative coherence may also be applied in the assessment of legal arguments presented in support of specific decisions, i.e., whether each argument is consistent with the others, or whether a specific legal decision is in line with the fundamental principles of a given legal system (Bertea 2005, p.372).

Conversely, a more moderate view proposes that correct legal decisions are based on criteria other than coherence. To seek coherence means to accept the plurality of both evaluation/motivation criteria and the elements that make up the legal system without denying the multifaceted nature of coherence. Coherence, therefore, does not imply a commitment to ignore the complexity of the legal system and uphold an unrealistic ideal of the legal order (Bertea 2005, p.373).

In summary, while coherence is perceived as a minimum requirement for rationality, it is not itself superior to other values. For example, a sentencing system may appear coherent and harmonized, but in practice, sentences may be three times or one-third higher than they should be. Nonetheless, the prevailing belief is that any area of law should strive for coherence to avoid arbitrariness and injustice. As a minimum, the most obvious inconsistencies, errors, or discrepancies ought to be addressed despite the trouble or even impossibility of reaching a consensus as to what complete coherence actually means (Sunstein *et al.* 2002, p.1203). It is therefore no coincidence that the title of this monograph includes the words "towards coherence."

Coherence Between National, International, and EU Law

Globalization has had a profound effect on all areas of modern life, including law. In a globalized world, legal issues are increasingly becoming common to everyone. International transactions, business relations, and technological development, among other factors, are driving international, European Union (EU), and national legal systems to seek ways in which to align legal rules, institutions, and organizations with the implementation of the law and other components of the legal system to effectively address multinational issues.

The approximation of national law, international law and EU law is a key issue, especially for EU Member States. Member States have their own laws and legal systems, which reflect differences in national legal traditions. These differences can lead to certain challenges, including that of primacy – i.e., whether, in certain cases, EU law, international law or national law takes precedence. The coherence/harmonization process is meant to aid in such instances, as its purpose is to define a resolution mechanism for discordant legal systems and ensure their harmonized application.

The scientific literature has identified and continues to explore the various directions of the influence exerted by international and EU law: their impact on national legal systems (e.g., Bobek 2020; Brink 2017); their interaction (e.g., Hildebrandt 2020; Callewaert 2009); and the relationship between the case law of the European Court of Human Rights (hereinafter – ECtHR) and the Court of Justice of the European Union (hereinafter – CJEU) in the interpretation of the European Convention on Human Rights (hereinafter – ECHR) and EU laws, respectively (e.g., Kargopoulos 2015, as cited in Jočienė 2022, p.91). The issue of coherence in purely international or EU law has been raised further in scholarly discourse, accentuating the need for consistency across these legal systems, given that the "judicial category" is particularly dependent on an explicit and implicit legislative process (e.g., Trachtman 2011; Duic 2015).

The principle of constitutional supremacy is often explicitly enshrined in national constitutions, but provisions on the standing of international and EU law with regard to national legal systems are also included (Jočienė 2022, p.91). For example, in the constitutional law of the Republic of Lithuania, the principles of general law and *pacta sunt servanda* imply the commitment to fulfill in good faith the obligations of the Republic of Lithuania under international law alongside respect for international law, which is an integral part of the constitutional principle of the rule of law (Miliuvienė 2020, p.152). The Constitutional Court has ruled that minimum standards for the protection of human rights and freedoms in relation to national protection have been established by international legal norms and principles, and that, therefore, Lithuanian state institutions may not impose on the local population standards that are fundamentally different from those provided for by the norms of international law (Miliuvienė 2020, p.152).

The constitutional acceptance of international and EU law is also expressed by the geopolitical orientation of the Republic of Lithuania, which is rooted in the country's fundamental constitutional values – independence, democracy, and the country's status as a republic – and which implies the Republic of Lithuania's membership of the EU and NATO and the necessity of fulfilling the relevant international obligations that arise from these memberships (Miliuvienė 2020, p.153).

EU law has further constitutional "safeguards": the Constitutional Act "On Membership of the Republic of Lithuania in the European Union" is an integral part of the Constitution; therefore, Lithuania's membership in the EU is a constitutional value. This act *expressis verbis* provides a solution/rule regarding the question of applicable law: "The norms of European Union law shall be a constituent part of the legal system of the Republic of Lithuania. Where it concerns the founding Treaties of the European Union, the norms of European Union law shall be applied directly, while in the event of the collision of legal norms, they shall have supremacy over the laws and other legal acts of the Republic of Lithuania" (The Constitutional Act "On Membership of the Republic of Lithuania in the European Union" 2004).

Constitutional courts are mandated to ensure coherence between national constitutional provisions and international and EU law, and to adapt international and EU law to the national system. In other words, they must seek reconciliation between the two elements that comprise the rule of law: the supremacy of the national Constitution and respect for international and EU law. "While ensuring the supremacy of the Constitution, the Constitutional Court must find ways to bring it into accordance with another aspect of the rule of law – respect for international (and EU) law, and in fulfilling such an obligation, the Constitutional Court may apply all necessary measures – from harmonising interpretation, to pointing out the obligation to amend the Constitution or eliminating amendments to the Constitution that contradict international or EU law" (Žalimas 2018, p.67)

As further noted in the legal literature, the relationship between national constitutional law and international and EU legal systems is defined by the realist (coordination) theory, which does not recognize the primacy of any one of these legal systems. A key principle of this theory lies in "mutual comity," according to which constitutional courts interpret their national law in a manner that ensures maximum alignment with the provisions of international or EU law, while the pertinent international and EU courts interpret laws under their jurisdiction while remaining mindful of national constitutional jurisprudence. Therefore, hypothetical clashes between different legal systems and the jurisprudence of their representative courts are exceedingly rare, as both sides make a conscious effort to avoid them. The success of this theory is strongly contingent on the coordination and harmonization of international, EU, and national legal systems. The establishment of a global and universal legal order that comprises national, international, and EU legal systems operating on an equal footing rests on the acceptance of constitutional pluralism (Miliuviene 2020, pp.158–159).

Challenges to the Coherence of Criminal Law in the EU

The term *criminal justice system* "[…] describes the formal governmental institutions that aim to regulate human behavior and human morality in order to achieve social control through criminal legislation, law enforcement, courts, corrections, pardons and parole, and rehabilitation and treatment programs – as well as by understanding, predicting, and managing the occurrence of crime" (Friedman 2015, Abstract). Similar to other judicial systems, the criminal justice system currently faces challenges arising from, among other things, internationalization, digitization, and European integration.

This is particularly evident in the EU, where national substantive and procedural criminal law is covered by EU legislation to a significant extent. The dynamic interaction between EU law and criminal law (which broadly encompasses substantive, procedural, and sentencing law) is shaping and redefining their very foundations, principles, and concepts. This is done in pursuit of effective crime control and due process at the national, EU, and international levels, as well as to implement EU policies and to maintain the EU's standing as a global player in the fields of security and criminal justice.

> The Union is founded on the values of respect for human dignity, freedom, democracy, equality, the rule of law and respect for human rights, including the rights of persons belonging to minorities (Consolidated version of the Treaty on European Union, Article 2). These values are central to the functioning of the EU; upholding them is a prerequisite for accession, and they must not be infringed on afterwards (Mancano 2021, p.477).

In a sense, the EU values are the blood vessels, with EU and national law acting as the blood of the Union legal order: when the mechanisms to ensure that the values are respected throughout the EU fail, it is the whole legal organism that suffers the consequences (Mancano 2021, pp.477–478).

Based on these values, the EU aims to foster and develop an area of freedom, security, and justice, where fundamental rights and the different legal systems and traditions of the Member States are respected (Consolidated version of the Treaty on the Functioning of the European Union, Article 67). The EU respects the national identities of the Member States, which are inseparable from their fundamental political and constitutional structures (Consolidated version of the Treaty on European Union, 2020, Article 4, paragraph 2). The preamble of the Charter of Fundamental Rights of the European Union (2016); hereinafter – the EU Charter) also recognizes that the EU respects, among other things, the diversity of the traditions of the peoples of Europe. Traditionally, criminal law has been ascribed to national competence and therefore subject to "intergovernmental" governance at the EU and international level (Öberg 2021, p.409). Some criminal law issues, such as criminalization, sanctioning, procedural models, etc., often echo national traditions which vary considerably across Member States and are not immune to the effects of societal change. However, EU criminal policy employs a range of legal instruments that impact national criminal justice systems to a variable scope and degree. "In that regard, although it is true that the authors of the Treaties have ascribed only limited powers to the Union in criminal matters, it is nonetheless apparent from the case-law of the Court that EU law sets certain limits to the powers of Member States in such matters […]. Indeed, that power of the Member States must be exercised in line with not only the fundamental freedoms guaranteed by EU law […], but also EU law as a whole, in particular primary EU law" (*Ilmārs Rimšēvičs and European Central Bank v. Republic of Latvia* [GC] 2019, paragraph 57). As regards criminal matters, Member States must fulfill their obligations under EU law.

Firstly, both the improvement of the mutual recognition of convictions and other judicial decisions, and targeted legislative harmonization are necessary to facilitate cooperation between competent authorities in the field of criminal justice and to ensure the protection of individual rights. In accordance with Article 82 of the Treaty on the Functioning of the European Union (hereinafter – TFEU), "judicial cooperation in criminal matters in the Union shall be based on the principle of mutual recognition of judgments and judicial decisions and shall include the approximation of the laws and regulations of the Member States in the areas referred to in paragraph 2 and in Article 83." The principle of mutual recognition assumes that Member States trust their respective criminal justice systems. The CJEU has also ruled that the principle of mutual recognition is based on the mutual confidence of Member States in the ability of their respective national legal systems to ensure the equivalent and effective protection of fundamental rights recognized at the EU level. The principle of mutual trust requires each Member State to presume that, barring exceptional circumstances, all other Member States comply with EU law and, in particular, uphold the fundamental rights enshrined therein, and limitations on the principles of mutual recognition and trust between Member States may only be imposed in exceptional circumstances (*Pál Aranyosi and Robert Căldăraru v. Generalstaatsanwaltschaft Bremen* [GC] 2016, paragraphs 76–78, 82).

The extent to which the principle of mutual recognition is implemented hinges on a number of factors, including, among other things, the existence of harmonized mechanisms for the protection of the parties to criminal proceedings and standards for the admissibility of mutual evidence. Pursuant to Article 82(2) of the TFEU, directives may establish minimum rules to facilitate the mutual recognition of convictions and judgments and cooperation between the police and judicial authorities in cross-border criminal matters. The minimum rules apply to the areas laid down in Article 82(2) (a)–(d), and they have received considerable attention in the EU legislative agenda. The following areas are worthy of separate mention: common minimum standards for criminal proceedings; the fight against terrorism; the fight against corruption, cybercrime, fraud, and money laundering; the exchange of information between Member States and EU agencies; the protection of victims; and both agencies for judicial cooperation in criminal matters and other related bodies, such as the European Union Agency for Criminal Justice Cooperation (Eurojust) and the European Public Prosecutor's Office (Judicial Cooperation in Criminal Matters 2023; also, see Ouwerkerk 2019). It should be noted that although the competence of the EU is functional under Article 82(2) of the TFEU, the harmonization of the rights of defense applies not only to cross-border cases, but also to those of a domestic nature.

> Although the Treaty limits EU power to minimum harmonisation, the CJEU has already confirmed that the effectiveness of EU law applies fully to EU measures on defence rights, including the securing the effective exercise of rights on the ground. Although it has been argued that EU secondary law would be superfluous in this field, as the rights are already enshrined in the ECHR and the Charter, the adoption of secondary harmonising EU law has had the effect of amplifying these rights, and triggering the reach of a variety of enforcement mechanisms under EU law. The approach of the CJEU thus far has demonstrated that the interaction between EU secondary law and ECHR and Charter norms has not been problematic. With the CJEU relying on the ECHR to determine the content of specific Directive provisions when there is already Strasbourg case-law, reverting to general principles of EU law when called to balance the effectiveness of enforcement with the effectiveness of fundamental rights protection more broadly (Mitsilegas 2019b, p.141).

Second, the EU's competence in the area of substantive criminal law includes the establishment of minimum rules for offenses and sanctions in the areas of particularly serious crimes with a cross-border dimension, such as terrorism, trafficking in human beings and the sexual exploitation of women and children, illicit drug trafficking, illicit arms trafficking, money laundering, corruption, counterfeiting means of payment, computer crime, and organized crime (Article 83(1) of the TFEU). Furthermore, the CJEU has ruled that although in principle criminal law and criminal procedure rules fall outside EU competence, the EU legislator is not precluded from taking measures with regard to the criminal laws of Member States in situations where competent national authorities must impose effective, proportionate and dissuasive criminal sanctions in order to guarantee the effective implementation of an EU policy. This competence is expressly provided for in Article 83(2) of the TFEU (Opinion of Advocate General Pitruzzella, delivered on 27 April 2023, paragraph 32).

Despite considerable progress having been made in the functioning of the EU within the scope of Articles 82 and 83 of the TFEU, a number of challenging issues remain concerning the approximation of legislation and its subsequent interpretation, application and so on. For example, the scope of the EU's "functional criminalization" competence under Article 83(2) of the TFEU is considered ambiguous; the multi-layered system of the European Public Prosecutor's Office is considered to lack legal certainty (Mitsilegas 2019a, pp. 393, 394–395); and the legal justification for the formulation of EU criminal policy is viewed critically (Öberg 2021).

Research Object

Toward Coherence in Criminal Justice: Challenges, Discussions, and/or Solutions is a comprehensive study of coherence in various aspects of criminal justice. The research focuses on coherence as a principle that enhances the effectiveness of criminal justice and its individual components.

It critically examines practical issues of coherence in various areas of criminal justice. The monograph analyzes existing research, legal frameworks, case law, and empirical evidence to identify the level of coherence in various areas of criminal justice. It also examines whether a degree of coherence is compatible with the objectives of justice and public safety, as well as possible tensions or trade-offs between coherence and other values, such as flexibility and responsiveness to a changing social environment.

In summary, this monograph aims to examine the coherence of legal regulation and the application of individual elements of criminal justice. The authors of the monograph aim to contribute to scientific progress in the field of criminal justice and to the improvement of its policy and practice by presenting the most important theoretical and practical views on the coherence of individual areas of criminal justice, identifying existing problems, potential challenges, and proposing solutions.

Research Aim and Objectives

The aim of this study is to identify the main challenges or problems and to offer possible solutions, or at least to initiate a scholarly debate on how to achieve greater coherence in the various areas of criminal justice.

Research objectives:

1. An examination of the coherence of legal regulations and their interpretation, application, and practical implementation in the following areas of substantive criminal law:
   (a) criminalization or decriminalization, the legal framework and its interpretation, and practice within individual offenses (e.g., human trafficking, drug possession, offenses against justice, and unlawful stalking);
   (b) compatibility between the application of administrative and criminal liability; and
   (c) the uniform application of criminal jurisdiction principles to offenses committed abroad by Member State nationals and residents.

2. An examination of the coherence of legal regulations and their interpretation, application, and practical implementation in the following areas of criminal procedural law:
   (a) the movement of electronic evidence between EU Member States and the assessment of its reliability;
   (b) the standard of proof in a confiscation procedure not predicated on a conviction and its compatibility with human rights, particularly the presumption of innocence; and
   (c) subjective threats to the free evaluation of evidence;
   (d) separate issues relating to the right to a fair criminal trial – whether written procedures are an absolute limitation on the right to an oral hearing before an appellate court, and the limits of the integration of technology into criminal procedure.

Research Methodology

This monograph has been prepared in response to the *Rule of Law, Sustainability, Technologies* 2022–2026 research program approved by Mykolas Romeris University in 2021. The program includes a fourth research axis: *Research for more effective justice*. Improving the criminal justice system is crucial to achieving more effective justice. This can be achieved through measures such as criminalizing or decriminalizing offenses, exploring new methods of investigating or assessing evidence, and finding solutions to the challenges posed by remote criminal proceedings, etc.

The relationship between the coherence and effectiveness of the criminal justice system and its components is complementary. A coherent criminal justice system ensures that all its components work smoothly together, avoiding contradictions or incompatibilities that could hamper its effectiveness. When legislation is coherent, and its application and implementation are consistent, this can increase the efficiency of the system by streamlining processes, reducing delays and maximizing resources.

This monograph is the result of a collaborative effort among researchers to improve the coherence of criminal justice. Criminal justice scholars were invited to participate in the study and answer the following questions: Why is legal coherence relevant to your proposed criminal justice research? How might your research be developed through the prism of legal coherence? What developments in legal coherence have influenced the development of your proposed criminal justice research? What are the main barriers to legal coherence in your field, and how can they be overcome?

Limitations

This edited volume has a limited geographical scope, covering mainly Lithuanian and European legal perspectives. Some parts of the monograph deal with Lithuanian issues in a European context, in some cases using non-European examples. Other parts focus solely on the Lithuanian aspect, while some parts go beyond Lithuania to include examples from Latvia, for example. The authors' coverage of a wide range of topics is crucial for presenting specific issues of legal coherence in Lithuania and highlighting problems and challenges both within and outside the region.

The Structure of the Book

The structure of this monograph is divided into two parts. The first part, *The Search for Coherence in Substantive Criminal Law*, addresses several key issues. These include criminalization or decriminalization, the legal framework and its interpretation, and practice within the areas of individual offenses (human trafficking, drug possession, offenses against justice, and unlawful stalking). It also examines the compatibility of administrative and criminal liability and the consistent application of criminal jurisdiction principles to offenses committed abroad by nationals and residents of a Member State.

The second part of the monograph, *The transformation of Criminal Procedure Law in the Context of Coherence*, focuses on several issues, including: the movement of electronic evidence between EU Member States; the concept of electronic evidence and the assessment of its reliability; subjective threats to the free assessment of evidence; and the standard of proof in a confiscation procedure not predicated on a conviction and its compatibility with human rights, particularly the presumption of innocence. It also addresses specific issues related to the right to a fair criminal trial, such as whether the written procedure of a case constitutes an absolute restriction on the right to an oral hearing before an appellate court and the limits of the integration of technology into criminal procedure.

The edited volume also contains conclusions and a summary.

References

Alexy, R., and Peczenik, A., 1990. The Concept of Coherence and Its Significance for Discursive Rationality. *Ratio Juris*, 3, 130–147.

Bertea, S., 2005. The Arguments from Coherence: Analysis and Evaluation [Online]. *Oxford Journal of Legal Studies*, 25 (3), 369–391. Available from: https://www.jstor.org/stable/3600675 [Accessed 27 June 2023].

Bobek, M., 2020. The Effects of EU Law in the National Legal Systems [Online]. In: C. Barnard, and S. Peers (eds.), *European Union Law*, 3rd edn. Oxford University Press, 154–190. Available from: https://doi.org/10.2139/ssrn.3726872 [Accessed 28 July 2023].

Brink, T., 2017. The Impact of EU Legislation on National Legal Systems: Towards a New Approach to EU – Member State Relations [Online]. *Cambridge Yearbook of European Legal Studies*, 19, 211–235. Available from: https://doi.org/10.1017/cel.2017.2 [Accessed 14 August 2023]

Callewaert, J., 2009. The European Convention on Human Rights and European Union Law: a Long Way to Harmony [Online]. Reprinted from *European Human Rights Law Review*, 6, 768–783. London: Sweet & Maxwell. Available from: https://d-nb.info/1133493823/34 [Accessed 1 August 2023].

Charter of Fundamental Rights of the European Union [Online]. Available from: https://eur-lex.europa.eu/legal-content/EN/TXT/PDF/?uri=CELEX:12016P/TXT&rid=3 [Accessed 7 June 2016].

Consolidated version of the Treaty on European Union, 2020 [Online]. Available from: https://eur-lex.europa.eu/legal-content/EN/TXT/?uri=CELEX:02016M/TXT-20200301 [Accessed 3 August 2023].

Consolidated version of the Treaty on the Functioning of the European Union, 2020 [Online]. Available from: https://eur-lex.europa.eu/legal-content/EN/TXT/?uri=CELEX:02016E/TXT-20200301 [Accessed 4 August 2023].

Duic, D., 2015. The Concept of Coherence in EU Law [Online]. *Zbornik Pravnog Fakulteta u Zagrebu*, 65 (3–4), 537–554. Available from: https://hrcak.srce.hr/clanak/219964 [Accessed 1 July 2023].

Dworkin, R., 1986. *Law's Empire*. London: Fontana.

Dworkin R., 2004. *Rimtas požiūris į teises [Taking Rights Seriously]*. Vilnius: Lietuvos rašytojų sąjungos leidykla.

Dworkin R., 2005. *Teisės imperija [Law's Empire]*. Vilnius: Lietuvos rašytojų sąjungos leidykla.

Friedmann, R.R., 2015. Criminal Justice System. Abstract [Online]. *The Encyclopedia of Crime and Punishment*. Available from: http://doi.org/10.1002/9781118519639.wbecpx153 [Accessed 17 July 2023].

Galginaitis, J., 2002. Teisinė sistema ir pagrindinės jos subsistemos kaip lyginamosios teisėtyros objektas [The legal system and its main subsystems as an object of comparative legal studies]. *Law*, 44, 31–41.

Hage, J., 2004. Law and Coherence. *Ratio Juris*, 17 (1), 87–105.

Hildebrandt, M., 2020. International and Supranational Law [Online]. *Law for Computer Scientists and Other Folk.* Oxford: Oxford Academic, 75–96. Available from: https://doi.org/10.1093/oso/9780198860877.003.0004 [Accessed 14 August 2023].

Jočienė, D., 2022. Tarptautinės teisės ir Europos Sąjungos teisės įtaka Lietuvos Respublikos Konstitucinio Teismo oficialiajai konstitucinei doktrinai [The Influence of International Law and the Law of the European Union on the Official Constitutional Doctrine of the Constitutional Court of the Republic of Lithuania]. In *Kelyje su konstitucija: recenzuotų mokslinių straipsnių rinkinys [On the Road to the Constitution: a collection of peer-reviewed scholarly articles]*. Vilnius: Vilnius University Press, 91–117.

Judgment of the Court (Grand Chamber), 2019. Ilmārs Rimšēvičs and European Central Bank v. Republic of Latvia. European System of Central Banks — Action based on infringement of the second subparagraph of Article 14.2 of the Statute of the European System of Central Banks and of the European Central Bank — Decision of a national authority suspending the governor of the national central bank from office. Joined Cases C-202/18 and C-238/18 [Online]. Available from: https://eur-lex.europa.eu/legal-content/EN/TXT/?uri=celex:62018CJ0202 [Accessed 11 August 2023].

Judgment of the Court (Grand Chamber), 2016. Pál Aranyosi and Robert Căldăraru v. Generalstaatsanwaltschaft Bremen. Requests for a preliminary ruling from the Hanseatisches Oberlandesgericht in Bremen. Reference for a preliminary ruling — Police and judicial cooperation in criminal matters — Framework Decision 2002/584/JHA — European arrest warrant — Grounds for refusal to execute — Charter of Fundamental Rights of the European Union — Article 4 — Prohibition of inhuman or degrading treatment — Conditions of detention in the issuing Member State. Joined Cases C-404/15 and C-659/15 PPU [Online]. Available from: https://eur-lex.europa.eu/legal-content/EN/TXT/?uri=celex:62018CJ0202 [Accessed 12 August 2023].

Judicial Cooperation in Criminal Matters, 2023 [Online]. Available from: https://www.europarl.europa.eu/factsheets/en/sheet/155/judicial-cooperation-in-criminal-matters [Accessed 11 August 2023].

Kargopoulos, A. I., 2015. ECHR and the CJEU: Competing, Overlapping, or Supplementary Competences? [Online]. *Eucrim*, 3, 96–100. Available from: https://eucrim.eu/articles/echr-and-cjeu/ [Accessed 21 July 2023]

Levenbook, B. B., 1984. The Role of Coherence in Legal Reasoning [Online]. *Law and Philosophy*, 3 (3), 355–374. Available from: http://www.jstor.org/stable/3504658 [Accessed 23 June 2023].

Mancano, L., 2021. A Theory of Justice? Securing the Normative Foundations of EU Criminal Law Through an Integrated Approach to Independence. *European Law Journal*, 27 (4–6), 477–501. https://doi.org/10.1111/eulj.12442

Miliuvienė, J., 2020. *Soft law įtaka konstitucinės jurisprudencijos raidai* [The influence of soft law on the development of constitutional jurisprudence]. Doctoral dissertation, Mykolas Romeris University, Vilnius.

Mitsilegas, V., 2019a. The Constitutional Dimension of European Criminal Law [Online]. *University of Bologna Law Review*, 4 (2), 390–398. Available from: https://bolognalawreview.unibo.it/article/download/10426/10462/34863 [Accessed 13 August 2023].

Mitsilegas, V., 2019b. The Impact of Legislative Harmonisation on Effective Judicial Protection in Europe's Area of Criminal Justice [Online]. *Review of European Administrative Law*, 12 (2), 117–142. Available from: https://www.uitgeverijparis.nl/scripts/read_article_pdf?editie=206691&id=1001471743 [Accessed 12 August 2023].

Öberg J., 2021. Normative justifications of EU criminal law: European public goods and transnational interests [Online]. *European Law Journal*, 27 (4–6), 408–425. Available from: https://onlinelibrary.wiley.com/doi/10.1111/eulj.12451 [Accessed 7 June 2023].

Opinion of Advocate General Pitruzzella delivered on 27 April 2023 [Online]. Available from: https://eur-lex.europa.eu/legal-content/EN/TXT/?uri=CELEX:62021CC0655 [Accessed 12 August 2023].

Ouwerkerk, J., 2019. EU Competence in the Area of Procedural Criminal Law: Functional vs. Self-standing Approximation of Procedural Rights and Their Progressive Effect on the Charter's Scope of Application [Online]. *European Journal of Crime, Criminal Law and Criminal Justice*, 27 (2), 89–96, Available from: https://doi.org/10.1163/15718174-02702001 [Accessed 13 August 2023]

Raz, J., 1994. The Relevance of Coherence. In: J. Raz, *Ethics in the Public Domain*, Oxford: Clarendon, 277–326.

Ruling of the Constitutional Court of the Republic of Lithuania of 6 December 2000.

Ruling of the Constitutional Court of the Republic of Lithuania of 30 May 2003.

Ruling of the Constitutional Court of the Republic of Lithuania of 13 December 2004.

Ruling of the Constitutional Court of the Republic of Lithuania of 29 December 2004.

Ruling of the Constitutional Court of the Republic of Lithuania of 26 January 2004.

Ruling of the Constitutional Court of the Republic of Lithuania of 29 September 2005.

Ruling of the Constitutional Court of the Republic of Lithuania of 16 January 2006.

Ruling of the Constitutional Court of the Republic of Lithuania of 13 August 2007.

Ruling of the Constitutional Court of the Republic of Lithuania of 24 December 2008.

Ruling of the Constitutional Court of the Republic of Lithuania of 10 April 2009.

Ruling of the Constitutional Court of the Republic of Lithuania of 22 June 2009.

Ruling of the Constitutional Court of the Republic of Lithuania of 26 February 2010.

Ruling of the Constitutional Court of the Republic of Lithuania of 3 February 2010.

Šlapkauskas, V., 2006. Teisinės sistemos disfunkcija – silpnos socialinės politikos požymis [Dysfunctional legal system – a sign of weak social politics] [Online]. *Social Work*, 5, 21–29.

Sunstein, C. R., Kahneman, D., Schkade, D., and Ritov, I., 2002. Predictably Incoherent Judgments. *Stanford Law Review*, 54 (6), 1153–1215. https://doi.org/10.2307/1229618

The Law Supplementing the Constitution of the Republic of Lithuania with the Constitutional Act "On Membership of the Republic of Lithuania in the European Union" and Supplementing Article 150 of the Constitution of the Republic of Lithuania (No. IX-2343) of 13 July 2004, *Valstybės žinios* [*Official Gazette*], 2004, No. 111–4123.

Trachtman, J. P., 2011. Fragmentation, Coherence and Synergy in International Law [Online]. *Transnational Legal Theory*, 2 (4), 505–536. Available from: https://doi.org/10.2139/ssrn.1908862 [Accessed 17 June 2023].

Žalimas, D., 2018. Konstitucijos viršenybės užtikrinimas: kai kurie konstitucinio teismo implicitinių įgaliojimų aspektai [Ensuring the supremacy of the Constitution: certain aspects of the implied powers of the Constitutional Court]. *Jurisprudence*, 25 (1), 38–68.

Part I
The Search for Coherence in Substantive Criminal Law

Oleg Fedosiuk

The Gray Area in the Concept of Human Trafficking: Between the Text of the Law and the Purpose of Criminalization

Human Trafficking as a Legal Concept

The modern concept of human trafficking as a criminal offense is the result of long-term international efforts to curb the enslavement and exploitation of vulnerable people (primarily for prostitution and forced labor). In this context, the White Slave conventions (1904, 1910), Slavery conventions (1926, 1956), Forced Labor conventions (1930, 1957), and Trafficking convention (1949) should be mentioned. However, the concept of human trafficking was finally formed in international and European Union law only at the beginning of the 21st century. Its content today is determined by the following three legal acts: the United Nations Protocol to Prevent, Suppress, and Punish Trafficking in Persons Especially Women and Children (2000, hereinafter – the Palermo Protocol); the Council of Europe Convention on Action against Trafficking in Human Beings (2005); and the European Union Directive 2011/36/EU on preventing and combating trafficking in human beings and protecting its victims (2011). These legal acts, based on international agreements, define trafficking in humans the same way, which leads to the uniform content of national criminal laws. As for the Republic of Lithuania, the concept of human trafficking was transposed into national criminal law identically and implemented in two norms: one criminalizes trafficking in adult victims (Article 147 of the Criminal Code), the other trafficking in children (Article 157 of the Criminal Code).

The unified concept of human trafficking undoubtedly represents a big step toward coherence in the fight against modern slavery around the world. The need for such a legal remedy was determined by the fact that the concepts of other known crimes against a person proved powerless against modern slavery, which is usually based not on capture and kidnapping, but on agreements between vulnerable victims and their exploiters. This led to the need for a more effective legal instrument that would cover the so-called "voluntary involvement" of victims in exploitation and allow countries to significantly intensify the fight against the phenomenon known as human trafficking.

Without repeating the rather long and complex definition presented in the relevant international and European Union legislation, the concept of human trafficking is usually explained by emphasizing three key elements that must be present for a situation of trafficking in adult persons to exist: action, means, and purpose (Gallagher 2010, p.29; Stoyanova 2013, p.66; Chuang 2014, p.616; Office of the High Commissioner 2014, p.3).

The first element of human trafficking (action) refers to a certain transaction, the object of which is a human being. The following types of transaction are specified in this concept: recruitment, transportation, transfer, and the harboring or reception of persons, including the exchange or transfer of control over those persons. Note that the transactions can take place between the perpetrator and the exploited person (e.g., recruitment) or between the perpetrator and a third party (e.g., transfer). It is also important to note that human trafficking does not require the crossing of an international border:

> The definition covers internal as well as cross-border trafficking. That is, it is legally possible for trafficking to take place within a single country, including the victim's own. Trafficking does not always require movement. The definition of trafficking identifies movement as just one viable way that the "action" element can be satisfied (Office of the High Commissioner 2014, p.3).

The second necessary element of the concept (means) refers to a malicious effect on the victim, which can be coercive or non-coercive. Coercive means include the threat or use of force or other forms of coercion and abduction. Fraud, deception, and the abuse of power or of a position of vulnerability are indicated as non-coercive alternative ways of enslaving the victim. An important detail is that the consent of the victim to become an object of enslavement is not legally significant if this consent is obtained using the malicious influence (means). Moreover, an enslavement transaction involving a child is recognized as human trafficking even if there was no malevolent effect listed above.

Among the methods of operation of human traffickers, the concept mentions one that is not related to the impact on the victim – that is: "the giving or receiving of payments or benefits to achieve the consent of a person having control over another person." Adding this type of modus operandi to the structure of human trafficking does not seem logical, as it is more appropriate to name the element of the action than the means. For example, in the Lithuanian version of human trafficking, the buying and selling of the victim is directly indicated as an element of the action, so there is complete overlap with the element of giving or receiving payments or benefits to the person controlling the victim. This obviously undermines the clarity of the definition.

The third necessary element of human trafficking (purpose) indicates that said acts are intended to involve the exploitation of the victim. The concept directly names such commonly known areas of exploitation as: prostitution of others or other forms of sexual exploitation; forced labor or services, including begging, slavery, or practices similar to slavery; servitude; the exploitation of criminal activities; and the removal of organs. Illegal adoption and forced marriage are also mentioned in the preamble of the EU directive on human trafficking as areas of exploitation. It should be noted that this list is not exhaustive, so countries can identify a wider list of exploitation areas. For example, in the definition of human trafficking established in Lithuanian criminal law, fictitious marriage is additionally specified as an area of exploitation. The Lithuanian version also provides for the possibility of recognizing any other exploitation, the content of which may be revealed in a specific case.

International and European Union legislation also imposes some additional requirements on the national law of states related to the need to establish the criminalization of incitement, complicity, and attempt, stipulating a certain severity of the punishment and its differentiation according to some criteria of dangerousness. According to Directive 2011/36/EU (para. 14 of the Preamble), European Union Member States must also establish the exception of persecution—namely, that victims of trafficking in human beings should, in accordance with the basic principles of the legal systems of the relevant Member States, be protected from prosecution or punishment for criminal activities, such as the use of false documents or offenses under legislation on prostitution or immigration, that they have been compelled to commit as a direct consequence of being subject to trafficking. The aim of such protection is to safeguard the human rights of victims, to avoid further victimization, and to encourage them to act as witnesses in criminal proceedings against perpetrators. For example, in the articles of the Lithuanian Criminal Code on human trafficking, this exception is directly indicated.

In assessing the added value of the unified concept of human trafficking for criminal justice, it should first be noted that it covers a wide range of exploitation areas, including so-called "voluntary slavery," in which victims are recruited by non-violent methods primarily because of their vulnerability. These elements of the concept (there is an extensive list of areas involving exploitation and the abuse of vulnerability) undoubtedly served to intensify the fight against diverse types of human trafficking and opened the possibility to prove this crime in court in general (in this aspect, Lithuanian criminal justice is quite effective). On the other hand, the above-mentioned legal elements are too flexible and subject to various interpretations. This view is echoed by Stojanova (2014):

> The international law definition of human trafficking contains elements ("exploitation," "deception," "abuse of position of vulnerability") which are ambiguous and, therefore,

> it might be difficult for a criminal court to convict an alleged perpetrator for human trafficking without entering into serious interpretation problems (p.433).

A situation of insufficient specificity risks the over-criminalization of some social ills, such as illegal work, poor working conditions, the legal sex industry and the pornography businesses, corrupt adoption, etc. Such practices would certainly not meet the needs of the coherent and targeted application of the concept of human trafficking. On the other hand, too much room for interpretation can sometimes lead to the inaction of law enforcement in investigating serious cases of human trafficking, thus causing the state to fail to fulfill its positive duty under Article 4 of the European Convention on Human Rights (the prohibition of slavery and forced labor). Stojanova (2014) expresses the following apprehension in this aspect:

> Therefore, national legislation which has incorporated the concept of "exploitation" as an element of the crime of human trafficking without further defining it, might not be compatible with the standards established in the ECtHR case law (p.433).

As an example, the author refers to ECHR cases (*Siliadin v. France* 2005; *CN and V v. France* 2012) in which it was established that the unsuccessful prosecution of exploiters and the violation of Article 4 of the Convention were partly caused by the fact that the national criminal law provisions on modern slavery were open to very different interpretations from one court to the next.

This study is specifically dedicated to the aforementioned "grey zone" in the concept of human trafficking – more precisely, to the proper interpretation of its ambiguous elements, thus promoting coherence in the application of this unique legal instrument in practice.

The Problem of Defining the Content of Exploitation

It has been mentioned that the concept of human trafficking covers a wide range of exploitation areas. Moreover, this list is not exhaustive, so the national law and jurisprudence of states may recognize other forms of exploitation. This is both a strength and a weakness of the concept. On the one hand, the concept of human trafficking becomes a universal tool in the fight against all forms of exploitation; on the other hand, the list of areas of exploitation does not resolve the question of what the essence and content of this phenomenon are. This, in turn, brings uncertainty and ambiguity to the very concept of human trafficking.

Such a situation encourages practices where the purpose of exploitation is determined formally according to the field in which the person was intended to be employed, regardless of how this person was treated, what interests and rights were violated, and whether they were violated at all. According to the formal point of view, even legal prostitution or participating in the filming of legal and well-paid pornography can be classified as exploitation, so in this sense the concept of human trafficking can even contradict economic legal regulation in one or another state where such activities are allowed. It is not surprising, therefore, that the drafters of the Palermo Protocol are often criticized in the legal literature for not having been able to properly define the content of exploitation. According to Noll (2007, pp.347–349), the meaning of exploitation is "painfully unclear" and "inoperable in a criminal law context with its demands on predictability flowing from the maxim of nullum crimen sine lege." A lot of criticism has been expressed regarding the failure to specify the content of sexual exploitation. Indeed, on this much-debated issue, the Interpretative notes to the Palermo Protocol permit a very flexible interpretation:

> The protocol addresses the exploitation of the prostitution of others and other forms of sexual exploitation only in the context of trafficking in persons. The terms "exploitation of the prostitution of others" or "other forms of sexual exploitation" are not defined in the protocol, which is therefore without prejudice to how States parties address prostitution in their respective domestic laws (§64).

Stoyanova (2013) expresses this reproach as follows:

> Ultimately, the phrase "sexual exploitation" may be interpreted for the convenience of either party to the dispute on prostitution. It could mean that any prostitution per se is exploitation and it could also mean that there should be force and coercion in the prostitution in order to be classified as "sexual exploitation." Thus, "sexual exploitation" is sufficiently elastic to cover different approaches to prostitution. However, this only enables further ambiguity in this field of law and flies in the face of the principle of legal certainty and specificity (p.69).

In this context, it is worth paying attention to the abolitionist approach to prostitution that has become established in Lithuanian law, where even legal work in this field in a foreign country is equated with exploitation. An excerpt from the ruling of the Supreme Court of Lithuania in criminal case no. 2K-487/2014 illustrates this:

> The fact that the victims were given to the owner of a legally operating brothel does not matter for the act's qualification. The composition of the crime of human trafficking does not require that engaging in prostitution or profiting from the prostitution of another person be prohibited in the state where it is intended to do so.

Such a strict interpretation is partly determined by the fact that prostitution is completely prohibited in Lithuania. Courts in countries where prostitution is not prohibited and is a matter of legal regulation could hardly be guided by this point of view.

Legal researchers also fear that the unresolved question of the definition of exploitation allows space for conflicting interpretations as to what does and does not constitute trafficking, including other sectors of exploitation than the sex industry (Anderson and O'Connell Davidson 2004, p.18). Indeed, there is a risk that spouses who pay bribes to facilitate the adoption of a baby with the intention of raising and loving the child will be charged with human trafficking, as illegal adoption is included in the list of areas of exploitation. A person who simply persuades another person to join a gang operating abroad can also be charged with human trafficking. It is also possible that the mere fact of engaging in a fictitious marriage for money or not providing good working conditions to workers can become a basis for accusations of human trafficking. Considering that the fight against human trafficking has become a kind of brand in the criminal justice system of the modern democratic world, an overly elastic concept of this crime may lead to its excessive application.

In addition, there is a tendency for the laws of various countries to include more areas of exploitation (some of which are quite exotic) in the definition of human trafficking (Allain 2019, pp.3–6). Thus, national laws are slowly enshrining broader concepts of human trafficking than those agreed upon under the Palermo Protocol, although the idea was to unify the world's perception of this crime. In such a situation, the proposal to move "from a consideration of the various types of exploitative practices to a conceptualization of exploitation" sounds truly relevant, thereby establishing "an effective transnational regime which ensures the prosecution of organized crime groups across borders for human trafficking" (Allain 2019, p.9). Unfortunately, the exploitation formula proposed by the author of the idea – "where A takes unfair advantage of B" – would hardly bring more accuracy to the concept of human trafficking.

In a general sense (according to the Cambridge Dictionary, n.d.), human exploitation can be understood as the act of using someone unfairly for one's own advantage. Summarizing the views expressed in the legal literature on exploitation as a legal category (Wilkinson 2003; Munro 2008; Campana and Varese 2016), three essential identification criteria can be distinguished. The first criterion (wrongful use) denotes the moral aspect; in other words, exploitation means that a person is being used solely as a means. The second criterion (disparity of value or unfair advantage) represents the economic aspect; in Wilkinson's (2003, p.173) words, where the distribution of benefit and harm between the exploiter and the exploited is unjust. In simpler terms, when the exploited is underpaid. The third criterion (invalid consent) reflects the legal aspect of human exploitation; namely that the deal is done under conditions that negate the individual's consent to be exploited. Of course, it is simply impossible to fit all of this into a universal legal definition of exploitation. In addition, the concept of human trafficking includes not only exploitation of an economic nature, but also, for example, illegal adoption, where the recognition of exploitation could not be based on said criteria. Marks' (2008, p.299) analysis of the content of the concept of exploitation in international law allowed her to conclude that this concept "relates to the exceptional contexts in which the word *exploitation* has been used." Considering that the concept of human trafficking is directed against all forms of human exploitation, creating a universal legal definition seems like an impossible task.

As always, this task that the legislature has failed to achieve is then left to the courts, which have their own tools to fill these gaps. In the current situation, there is no other way to solve the problem than to seek a certain standard of judicial interpretation according to which the goals of exploitation are determined not only according to the formal criteria of exploitation. Without forgetting the already mentioned criteria for identifying exploitation, in a specific case it is necessary to establish such facts that would indicate the dangerous and intolerable treatment of a person by, among other things, assessing it according to the generally known principles of criminalization of human behavior (harm principle, crime as a public wrong, *ultima ratio*, *Rechtsgüterschutz*, etc.). It should be remembered that the very concept of human trafficking is of international origin and serves as a uniform perception of this phenomenon in the world, so the interpretation of its elements in national law should not depart from the context of international agreements. For example, the Palermo Protocol directly links the need to criminalize human trafficking to the activities of international organized crime; while the preamble of the Council of Europe Convention declares that trafficking in human beings is a serious crime, often committed within the framework of organized crime, a gross violation of fundamental rights and explicitly prohibited by the Charter of Fundamental Rights of the European Union, and that special attention must be paid to the protection of victims who have already suffered the abuse and degrading treatment which trafficking commonly entails. This leads to the conclusion that, when admitting in a criminal case that the defendants acted with the aim of exploiting a person, it is simply necessary to consider the reasons for the adoption of the anti-trafficking acts. In this context, attention should also be paid to the description of the crime of human trafficking provided by the European Court of Human Rights in the case of *Rantsev v. Cyprus and Russia* (2010):

> The court considers that trafficking in human beings, by its very nature and aim of exploitation, is based on the exercise of powers attaching to the right of ownership. It treats human beings as commodities to be bought and sold and put to forced labour,

> often for little or no payment, usually in the sex industry but also elsewhere […]. It implied close surveillance of the activities of victims, whose movements were often circumscribed […]. It involved the use of violence and threats against victims, who live and work under poor conditions […]. It is described by Interights and the explanatory report accompanying the Anti-Trafficking Convention as the modern form of the old worldwide slave trade […]. There can be no doubt that trafficking threatens the human dignity and fundamental freedoms of its victims and cannot be considered compatible with a democratic society and the values expounded in the Convention (Paras. 281–282).

In the Lithuanian legal literature, human trafficking is also treated primarily as a restriction of personal freedom (Fedosiuk 2007, pp.57–59) and a violation of basic constitutional human rights, including the right to security (Sirgedienė 2014, p.232), the humiliation of a person's dignity, the manifestation of modern slavery (Gutauskas 2016, pp.193–195), etc. Thus, legal logic dictates that the criminalization of human trafficking is intended for extremely serious cases of human rights violations of a criminal nature, and the content of this crime should not be trivialized. Despite this self-evident knowledge, in the absence of a universal definition of exploitation, cases sometimes occur in Lithuanian legal practice where the purposes of exploitation are incriminated without substantiating the real danger and compliance with the general concept of human trafficking.

For example, in one case, two persons (one of whom was not a Lithuanian national) were convicted of human trafficking because they recruited a vulnerable woman (a citizen of Lithuania) to enter a fictitious marriage with one of them, paying her €100 each month. Both in the decisions of the court of first instance and the Court of Appeal, several arguments were presented substantiating the facts of the woman's vulnerability (health problems, tough economic situation), but the element of exploitation was established formally – since in the Lithuanian version of human trafficking, fictitious marriage is indicated as an area of exploitation. However, the Supreme Court of Lithuania did not agree with such arguments and, without establishing all the necessary elements of human trafficking, acquitted the mentioned persons primarily due to the absence of the purpose of exploitation. It was concluded that the woman's goal was to receive a monetary reward and the defendants' goal was to attain permission to temporarily live in the Republic of Lithuania for one of them, but not to control and exploit the woman (Ruling of the Supreme Court of Lithuania in criminal case no. 2K-1-1073/2023). Thus, the conclusions of this case support the thesis that naming any field of exploitation in the human trafficking norm should not automatically lead to the conclusion that a person being recruited in this field entailed the intention of exploitation under conditions that correspond to the general concept of human trafficking.

In this context, due to the risk of excessive criminalization, the preamble of EU Directive 2011/36/EU indicates how the forms of exploitation added to the concept of human trafficking, such as begging, illegal adoption, and forced marriage—are to be understood:

> Within the context of this Directive, forced begging should be understood as a form of forced labour or services as defined in the 1930 ILO Convention No 29 concerning Forced or Compulsory Labour. Therefore, the exploitation of begging, including the use of a trafficked dependent person for begging, falls within the scope of the definition of trafficking in human beings only when all the elements of forced labour or services occur. In the light of the relevant case law, the validity of any possible consent to perform such labour or services should be evaluated on a case-by-case basis. […] The definition also covers, […] for instance, other behaviour such as illegal adoption or forced marriage in so far as they fulfil the constitutive elements of trafficking in human beings (Clause 11 of the Preamble).

The notion of the narrowing interpretation is even more relevant when assessing the scenario of entering a fictitious marriage. In such cases, the incrimination of the purpose of exploitation should be even more cautious. Of course, there may be cases where a marriage of convenience will involve real exploitation, such as taking out bank loans in the spouse's name, seizing assets, etc., but these aspects must be proven and substantiated, otherwise human trafficking through recruitment into a fictitious marriage can become a crime, the danger of which is no different from simple forgery.

In another criminal case, a person was charged with human trafficking for recruiting vulnerable and job-seeking people to Germany where they would be exploited. However, during the investigation, it was not possible to determine exactly what the recruited persons had to do in Germany and under what conditions. From some aspects of the case, it could be concluded that upon arrival in Germany, it is likely that fictitious transactions would be concluded in the names of these persons during online trading, etc. The persons were promised a reward for the trip and a quick, safe return to Lithuania. Lithuanian courts of all instances rejected the accusation of human trafficking because the purposes of exploitation were based only on assumptions. However, the Supreme Court of Lithuania also emphasized the need to link the goals of exploitation with the context of the criminalization of human trafficking:

> It should also be noted that human trafficking is treated as a form of slavery in both international and European Union law and is recognized as a violation of basic human rights. Common forms of human exploitation associated with human trafficking include

> slavery, prostitution, and other forms of sexual exploitation, production of pornography, forced labor and services, begging, enslavement for debt, criminal status, illegal adoption, involvement in criminal activities, marital slavery, illegal transplantation of human organs. The definition of human trafficking provided in Article 147 of the Criminal Code leaves the possibility to recognize other less known or previously unseen forms as exploitation, on the other hand, such a conclusion must be harmonized with the general legal concept of this serious crime. Thus, only those forms of using another person that are sufficiently dangerous, grossly violate human rights and dignity, and are incompatible with the rules of a civilized society can be recognized as other forms of exploitation (Ruling in criminal case no. 2K-551-788/ 2015).

This clarification is believed to have had a positive effect on court practice in human trafficking cases, reducing the risk of artificial incrimination.

In another case, the Supreme Court presented a vision of the difference between exploitation for criminal activities and mere complicity:

> The purpose of exploitation for criminal activity is to be interpreted as an attempt to use another person so that he performs one or other criminal acts for the benefit of persons organizing criminal activities (commits theft, distributes, or transports drugs, transports cash of criminal origin, collects money from defrauded people, etc.). Usually, the use of such people reduces the risks and costs of the organizers of criminal activities. On the other hand, the mere fact that a person has accepted an offer to engage in criminal activity does not in itself mean that such a person is intended to be exploited. The purpose of exploitation as a constituent element of the concept of human trafficking is associated with such forms of unfair use of another human being that are sufficiently dangerous, grossly violate human rights and dignity, and are incompatible with the rules of civilized society [...]. Therefore, the conclusion about the purpose of exploitation for criminal activity can be made in cases where the context of the established circumstances makes it possible to state that the recruited persons, although they are at risk of being prosecuted, are not the main beneficiaries of the criminal activity, that is, they do not act on their own initiative, but according to the instructions of those who control them, as lawless executors of the will of other persons (Ruling in criminal case no. 2K-258-788/2022).

In conclusion, the incrimination of the goals of exploitation in cases of human trafficking must be based not only on the criteria of the field of exploitation, but also on arguments that justify that the determined treatment of a person grossly violates their rights and the norms of a civilized society, when there is a moral basis on which talk about modern slavery. For this, it is necessary to assess what damage or moral losses (such as discrimination, injustice, humiliation) the victim experienced or could experience as a result of the evaluated behavior, what part of their freedom or simply normal life they lost or would have lost, how much the criminals benefitted from it, whether such behavior correlates with traffickers' usual methods of operation and victim control, etc. Only then can we expect the proper application of the human trafficking norm in judicial practice.

The Limitlessness of the Concept of Abuse of a Position of Vulnerability

Of all the methods of non-violent human enslavement enshrined in the concept of human trafficking, the most problematic is the abuse of a position of vulnerability. This problem arises from the fact that in this way traffickers achieve the victim's conscious consent to be exploited. Human vulnerability is indeed the single largest premise of modern slavery. In this context, a study prepared by the United Nations Office on Drugs and Crime (2013, p.71) stated: "All those surveyed agreed that vulnerability is central to any understanding of trafficking: that abuse of vulnerability is an inherent feature of most, if not all, trafficking cases." On the other hand, the concept of human vulnerability is limitless and lends itself to various interpretations which are highly undesirable in criminal law. It can be assumed that the inclusion of abuse of vulnerability in the structure of human trafficking was undertaken in the name of its more effective application but sacrificing the principle of *nullum crimen sine lege*.

All conventions related to human trafficking pay special attention to the concept of abuse of vulnerability. However, all attempts to legally define this method only prove the limitlessness of this concept. Abuse of vulnerability is officially defined as "a situation in which the person concerned has no real or acceptable alternative but to submit to the abuse involved" (Interpretative notes 2000, § 63; Directive 2011/36/EU, Art. 2(2); Explanatory Report to the Council of Europe Convention 2005, para. 83). The preamble of EU Directive 2011/36/EU additionally states:

> In the context of this Directive, particularly vulnerable persons should include at least all children. Other factors that could be taken into account when assessing the vulnerability of a victim include, for example, gender, pregnancy, state of health, and disability (Clause 12).

The Explanatory Note to the Council of Europe Convention (2005) provides an even wider list of examples:

> The vulnerability may be of any kind, whether physical, psychological, emotional, family-related, social, or economic. The situation might, for example, involve insecurity or illegality of the victim's administrative status, economic dependence, or fragile health. In short, the situation can be any state of hardship in which a human being is impelled to accept being exploited (Clause 83).

Recognizing the uniqueness and importance of the concept of abuse of a vulnerable position, the United Nations Office on Drugs and Crime issued Guidance

Notes (2012) specifically for this issue. This document separately explains what vulnerability and abuse of a position of vulnerability mean, as can be seen from the following explanations:

> Personal vulnerability for instance, may relate to a person's physical or mental disability. Situational vulnerability may relate to a person being irregularly in a foreign country in which he or she is socially or linguistically isolated. Circumstantial vulnerability may relate to a person's unemployment or economic destitution. Such vulnerabilities can be pre-existing and can also be created by the trafficker. Pre-existing vulnerability may relate (but not be limited) to poverty; mental or physical disability; youth or old age; gender; pregnancy; culture; language; belief; family situation or irregular status. Created vulnerability may relate (but not be limited) to social, cultural or linguistic isolation; irregular status; or dependency cultivated through drug addiction or a romantic or emotional attachment or through the use of cultural or religious rituals or practices (Para. 2.3.).

Victims may not identify themselves as victims, particularly where they continue to remain dependent on or otherwise attached to those who have abused their vulnerability. (Para. 5.3)

Abuse of a position of vulnerability occurs when an individual's personal, situational, or circumstantial vulnerability is intentionally used or otherwise taken advantage of, to recruit, transport, transfer, harbor, or receive that person for the purpose of exploiting him or her, such that the person believes that submitting to the will of the abuser is the only real or acceptable option available to him or her, and that belief is reasonable in light of the victim's situation. In determining whether the victim's belief that he or she has no real or acceptable option is reasonable, the personal characteristics and circumstances of the victim should be taken into account. (Para. 2.5)

Given the possibility of such a broad understanding of this essential element of human trafficking, the Guidance Notes also identified the resulting risks:

> The lack of a clear definition of APOV and resulting ambiguities create certain risks that should be identified and managed. Misapplication of the concept could potentially compromise the rights of victims to be recognized as such, as well as the rights of accused persons to a fair trial. There is also a risk that misapplication could lead to an expansion of the concept of trafficking that detracts from its essential nature as an extremely serious crime and violation of human rights (Para. 6.1).

Attention should be drawn to certain clarifications of the Guidance Notes that reduce these risks:

> The mere existence of proven vulnerability is not sufficient to support a prosecution that alleges APOV as the means by which a specific "act" was undertaken. In such cases both the existence of vulnerability and the abuse of that vulnerability must be established by credible evidence (Para. 2.2).

APOV should not be more or less easily found in relation to certain exploitative purposes than in relation to others (Para. 4.2).

The use of "means" must be of a sufficiently serious nature and extent as to vitiate the consent of the victim. (Para. 5.2)

Trafficking in persons is a serious crime that carries severe penalties. Safeguards should be put in place to ensure that a commonsense approach can be taken to understanding and applying APOV, to promote an effective criminal justice response to trafficking and protect against the risks outlined above (Para. 6.3).

The reference to common sense is perhaps the most productive recommendation for the legal practitioner.

In Lithuanian criminal practice, accusations of human trafficking are often based on abuse of vulnerability, and attempts have been made to clarify this element in several rulings of the Supreme Court of Lithuania as follows:

> [...] The perpetrator must be aware of the victim's vulnerability; that is, it must be established that he, while carrying out certain criminal acts, realized or assumed the victim's tricky situation and took advantage of it. In addition, this element must be determined and individualized objectively according to the case data. Be it mental or psychological vulnerability, addiction to alcohol, drugs, material situation - these facts must lead to a limitation of the victim's ability to choose and provide the perpetrator with an obvious opportunity to manipulate the victim [...]. Often, the vulnerability of the victim is determined not by one, but at least several combined circumstances that significantly complicate the possibility of refusing to accept the perpetrator's offer to be exploited (e.g. difficult financial situation, early age, lack of social skills, etc.). In particular, the situation of the victim can be complicated by the situation when he is brought to a foreign country and does not have a legal status, does not speak the language of that country, etc. (Ruling in criminal case no. 2K-7-73-511/2021).

The fact that a difficult financial, social, or other existing situation is not the only reason for which a person accepts such an offer does not in itself eliminate the fact of abuse of vulnerability. At the same time, it must be recognized that the courts, when determining the facts of abuse of the victim's vulnerability, assess not only the factual circumstances of the victim's situation, but also the nature of the exploitation in which they are included and its consequences for their fate, as well as all other reasons that led to the acceptance of the malicious offer (Ruling in criminal case no. 2K-172-788/2021).

The latter assessment was provided by the Supreme Court of Lithuania in a case in which human trafficking was carried out by recruiting persons to act as drug couriers by organizing their flights to foreign countries and back and providing detailed instructions on where to acquire and hide narcotics. The drug couriers were paid enough money for such trips, so the defense denied the abuse of their vulnerability, saying that their consent was motivated by a desire to make good money, not a dire situation. One of the court's arguments in rejecting this position was that the recruiters purposefully sought out antisocial, low-income, and alcohol-dependent persons, and that the victims consented to be exploited in the extremely dangerous area of drug trafficking at a considerable risk of being arrested and imprisoned.

Such court reasoning leads to the conclusion that abuse of vulnerability is a highly contextual concept and its provability depends on various details, including the level of abnormality of the activity into which victims are recruited and the potential impact of this activity on their fate. It is because of this aspect that accusations based on abuse of the victim's vulnerability first emerged in cases of the recruitment of women for prostitution, because it is common knowledge that the sex service industry (especially when illegal) is very cruel to women and is hardly likely to be the result of their free choice. In other cases, accusations formulated in this way face a strong counterargument from the defense. Although the United Nations Office on Drugs and Crime (2012, para. 4.2) recommends the provision that abuse of vulnerability should not be easily found in relation to certain exploitative purposes than in relation to others, in practical human trafficking cases it is difficult follow this provision. In legal reality, a situation where an unemployed woman is recruited into prostitution is viewed by the judge as more favorable to the conclusion that the recruiters took advantage of her vulnerability than a situation in which such a woman is recruited to shoplift. In any case, when deciding whether a person's vulnerability has been abused, not only that person's life situation must be assessed. The recruiter's own behavior must also be evaluated according to the criteria of dangerousness, malice, treachery, indifference to the fate of the victim, etc. Only such an assessment allows us to answer the question of whether the victim's consent to engage in certain activities is in fact legally insignificant and is not the true will and choice of an adult but imposed on them in a malicious way.

Interim Findings

The lack of certainty regarding the essential elements of trafficking in humans, such as the purposes of exploitation and the abuse of a position of vulnerability, creates the risk of the incoherent and excessive application of this serious crime. Legal ambiguity in this area can lead to the over-criminalization of some social problems, such as illegal work, poor working conditions, legal prostitution and participation in pornography, corrupt adoptions, sham marriages, etc. Such practices would certainly not meet the needs of a coherent fight against human trafficking and would compromise the very idea. To avoid this, the determination of the legal elements in specific cases cannot be based solely on the text of the law and must correspond to the essence of the concept of human trafficking and the goals of its criminalization as declared in international law and European Union legal acts. Therefore, when recognizing the existence of real exploitation or such a purpose, it is necessary to assess not only the formal list of areas of exploitation, but also what real damage (discrimination, injustice, humiliation, disease) the victim has experienced or could experience as a result of the evaluated behavior, how much the exploiters benefited from it, whether this behavior correlates with the usual methods of traffickers' activities and control of victims, etc. Abuse of vulnerability as a legal element of human trafficking is also a very contextual concept, and its application must consider not only the life situation of the victim, but also other aspects of the case that allow the legal significance of the victim's consent to the malicious offer of traffickers to be negated.

References

Abolition of Forced Labour Convention, 5 June 1957 (No. 105). International Labour Organization [online]. Available from: https://www.ilo.org/dyn/normlex/en/f?p=NORMLEXPUB:12100:0::NO::P12100_ILO_CODE:C105 [Accessed 6 May 2023].

Allain, J., 2019. Conceptualizing the Exploitation of Human Trafficking. In: J. B. Clark and S. Poucki (ed.). *The SAGE Handbook of Human Trafficking and Modern Day Slavery*. SAGE Publications Ltd [online]. Available from: https://www.researchgate.net/publication/325846087_Conceptualizing_the_Exploitation_of_Human_Trafficking [Accessed 6 May 2023].

Anderson, B., and O'connell Davidson, J., 2004. *Trafficking – A Demand Led Problem? Part 1: Review of Evidence and Debates*. Save the Children Sweden, Stockholm. Available from: https://resourcecentre.savethechildren.net/pdf/2402.pdf/ [Accessed 6 May 2023].

Cambridge Dictionary, n.d. Exploitation [online]. Available from: https://dictionary.cambridge.org/dictionary/english/exploitation [Accessed 6 May 2023].

Campana, P., and Varese, F., 2016. Exploitation in Human Trafficking and Smuggling. *European Journal on Criminal Policy and Research*, 22, 89–105 [online]. Available from: https://core.ac.uk/download/pdf/42339082.pdf [Accessed 6 May 2023].

Chuang, J., 2014. Exploitation Creep and the Unmaking of Human Trafficking Law. *The American Journal of International Law*, 108 (4) [online]. Available from: https://www.jstor.org/stable/10.5305/amerjintelaw.108.4.0609?seq=2#metadata_info_tab_contents [Accessed 6 May 2023].

Convention concerning Forced or Compulsory Labour, 28 June 1930 (No. 29). International Labour Organization [online]. Available from: https://www.ilo.org/dyn/normlex/en/f?p=1000:12100:0::NO::P12100_ILO_CODE:C029 [Accessed 6 May 2023].

Convention for the Suppression of the Traffic in Persons and of the Exploitation of the Prostitution of Others, 2 December 1949 [online]. UNTS 96. Available from: https://treaties.un.org/doc/Publication/UNTS/Volume%2096/v96.pdf [Accessed 6 May 2023].

Convention to Suppress the Slave Trade and Slavery, 25 September 1926. Available from: https://lawphil.net/international/treaties/patcsg.html [Accessed 6 May 2023].

Council of Europe Convention on Action against Trafficking in Human Beings, 16 May 2005. CETS 197 [online]. Available from: https://rm.coe.int/168008371d [Accessed 6 May 2023].

Directive 2011/36/EU of the European Parliament and of the Council of 5 April 2011 on preventing and combating trafficking in human beings and protecting its victims, and replacing Council Framework Decision 2002/629/JHA. OJ L 101/1 [online]. Available from: https://eur-lex.europa.eu/legal-content/en/TXT/?uri=CELEX%3A32011L0036 [Accessed 6 May 2023].

Explanatory Report to the Council of Europe Convention on Action against Trafficking in Human Beings, 16 May 2005. CETS 197 [online]. Available from: https://rm.coe.int/16800d3812 [Accessed 6 May 2023].

Fedosiuk, O., 2007. Prekybos žmonėmis nusikaltimo normos naujosios redakcijos (2005 m. birželio 23 d.) aiškinimo ir taikymo problemos. (The Problems of Explanation and Application of the New Edition (June 23, 2005) of the Norm on Crime of Trafficking in Human Beings). *Jurisprudencija*, 98 (8), 54–61.

Gallagher, A. T., 2010. *The International Law of Human Trafficking*. Cambridge: Cambridge University Press.

Gutauskas, A., 2016. Diagnozė – šiuolaikinė vergovė: ar įmanoma ją sustabdyti? Vyraujančios teismų praktikos tendencijos [Diagnosis – Modern Slavery: Is it Possible to Stop it? Prevailing Trends of Judicial Practice]. *Jurisprudencija*, 23 (2).

International Agreement for the suppression of the "White Slave Traffic," signed at Paris, 18 March 1904 [online]. League of Nations Treaty Series, 1 (1). Available from: https://treaties.un.org/doc/Publication/UNTS/LON/Volume%201/v1.pdf [Accessed 6 May 2023].

International Convention for the Suppression of the White Slave Traffic, signed at Paris on 4 May 1910, amended by the Protocol signed at Lake Success, New York, 4 May 1949. UNTS 98. [online]. Available from: https://treaties.un.org/doc/Publication/UNTS/Volume%2098/v98.pdf [Accessed 6 May 2023].

Interpretative notes for the official records (travaux préparatoires) of the negotiation of the Protocol to Prevent, Suppress and Punish Trafficking in Persons, Especially Women and Children, supplementing the United Nations Convention against Transnational Organized Crime. United Nations General Assembly, 3 November 2000, A/55/383/Add.1 [online]. Available from: https://www.unodc.org/pdf/crime/final_instruments/383a1e.pdf [Accessed 6 May 2023].

ECtHR, *Siliadin v. France*, application no. 73316/01, 26 July 2005.

ECtHR, *Rantsev v. Cyprus and Russia*, application no. 25965/04, 7 January 2010.

ECtHR, *CN and V v. France*, application no. 67724/09; 11 October 2012.

Marks, S., 2008. Exploitation as an International Legal Concept. In: S. Marks, ed. *International Law on the Left Re-examining Marxist Legacies*, Cambridge University Press, 281–307 [online]. Available from: https://legalform.files.wordpress.com/2017/08/marks-exploitation-as-an-international-law-concept-2008.pdf [Accessed 6 May 2023].

Munro, V. E., 2008. Exploring Exploitation: Trafficking in Sex, Work and Sex Work. In: V. Munro and M. della Giusta, (eds.), *Demanding Sex: Critical Reflections on the Regulation of Prostitution*. Abingdon, Oxon: Ashgate, 83–98.

Noll, G., 2007. The Insecurity of Trafficking in International Law. In: V. Chetail, (ed.). *Mondialisation, migration et droits de l'homme: le droit international en question*. Brussels: Bruylant [online]. Available from: https://lucris.lub.lu.se/ws/portalfiles/portal/8160914/The_Insecurity_of_Trafficking_in_International_Law.pdf [Accessed 6 May 2023].

Office of The High Commissioner, 2014. *Human Rights and Human Trafficking*. Fact Sheet No. 36. United Nations, New York and Geneva [online]. Available from: https://www.ohchr.org/sites/default/files/Documents/Publications/FS36_en.pdf [Accessed 6 May 2023].

Ruling of the Supreme Court of Lithuania in Criminal Case No. 2K-487/2014.

Ruling of the Supreme Court of Lithuania in Criminal Case No. 2K-551-788/2015.

Ruling of the Supreme Court of Lithuania in Criminal Case No. 2K-7-73-511/2021.

Ruling of the Supreme Court of Lithuania in Criminal Case No. 2K-172-788/2021.

Ruling of the Supreme Court of Lithuania in Criminal Case No. 2K-258-788/2022.

Ruling of the Supreme Court of Lithuania in Criminal Case No. 2K-1-1073/2023.

Sirgedienė, R., 2014. *Kovos su prekyba žmonėmis koordinavimo problemos administracinėje teisėje* [Problems of Coordination of the Fight Against Trafficking in Human Beings in Administrative Law]. Thesis. (PhD). Mykolas Romeris University.

Stoyanova, V., 2013. The Crisis of a Definition: Human Trafficking in Bulgarian Law. *Amsterdam Law Forum*, 5 (1), 64–79.

Stoyanova, V., 2014. Article 4 of the ECHR and the Obligation of Criminalising Slavery, Servitude, Forced Labour and Human Trafficking. *Cambridge Journal of International and Comparative Law*, (3) 2, 407–443.

Supplementary Convention on the Abolition of Slavery, the Slave Trade, and Institutions and Practices Similar to Slavery. Geneva, 7 September 1956 [online]. Available from: https://treaties.un.org/doc/Publication/UNTS/Volume%20266/v266.pdf [Accessed 6 May 2023].

United Nations Office On Drugs and Crime, 2012. Guidance Note on 'abuse of a position of vulnerability' As a Means of Trafficking in Persons in Article 3 of the Protocol to Prevent, Suppress and Punish Trafficking in Persons, Especially Women and Children, supplementing the United Nations Convention Against Transnational Organized Crime. [online]. Available from: https://www.unodc.org/documents/human-trafficking/2012/UNODC_2012_Guidance_Note_-_Abuse_of_a_Position_of_Vulnerability_E.pdf [Accessed 6 May 2023].

United Nations Office On Drugs and Crime, 2013. *Abuse of a Position of Vulnerability and Other "Means" Within the Definition of Trafficking in Persons*. Issue Paper. United Nations, New York [online]. Available from: https://www.unodc.org/documents/human-trafficking/2012/UNODC_2012_Issue_Paper_-_Abuse_of_a_Position_of_Vulnerability.pdf [Accessed 6 May 2023].

United Nations Protocol to Prevent, Suppress and Punish Trafficking in Persons Especially Women and Children, supplementing the United Nations Convention against Transnational Organized Crime. General Assembly Resolution 55/25, Palermo, 5 November 2000 [online]. Available from: https://www.ohchr.org/en/instruments-mechanisms/instruments/protocol-prevent-suppress-and-punish-trafficking-persons [Accessed 6 May 2023].

Wilkinson, S., 2003. The Exploitation Argument against Commercial Surrogacy. *Bioethics*, 17 (2), 169–187.

Linas Žalnieriūnas

The Search for Legal Coherence in the Criminalization or Decriminalization of Drug Possession

Factors Influencing Drug Use

Drug use can be traced back through centuries of human experience. Humans have an innate curiosity and a desire to explore their environment. This instinct extends to our interactions with the natural world, especially in terms of discovering the potential of different plants: different plants and the materials they produce may have provided advantages for survival (Sullivan *et al.* 2008, p.1237); may have led to the discovery of valuable resources for nourishment, healing, or for forging community bonds; may have provided adaptive benefits (Naranjo 1981, p.164); and may have brought a calm altered consciousness that brings a state of happiness. It is well known that people have long sought ways to alter their conscious state with natural substances such as coca leaves, cannabis, and opium poppies (Schultes *et al.* 2001). Ancient Hindu Vedic texts mention a substance called Soma, a ritual drink believed to provide spiritual experiences. Evidence suggests that the Sumerians were already familiar with opium by 3400 BC. They called it the "plant of joy," alluding to its recreational or medicinal use (Gootenberg 2022). Tribes in the New World used the hallucinogenic drink ayahuasca for centuries. Many South American cultures, such as the Maya and the Aztecs, used plants such as peyote and ayahuasca for spiritual and shamanic practices (Gootenberg 2022). As a result, scholars have emphasized the importance of drugs in ancient spiritual practices (McKenna 2004).

Today, drug use is a widespread phenomenon worldwide. The question is whether this phenomenon is natural to human nature or whether it is a need that has been artificially shaped by human beings themselves for different purposes throughout history. The search for pleasure is an important focus for understanding drug use, as people instinctively seek pleasure and avoid pain (Freud 1920, p.8). Drugs interact with the brain's reward circuitry to induce euphoric feelings, which is why some people find them highly desirable. In addition, drugs provide an "escape," i.e., a temporary break from the difficulties of life. For some, they help them to overcome mental health problems, trauma or stress (Khantzian 1985, p.1312). In addition, substances such as psychedelics have historically been used for self-knowledge and spiritual exploration, as they can induce profound experiences and provide insights into one's psyche and the universe (Smith 2000, p.45). Modern lifestyles, characterized by rapid urbanization and technological advances, can lead to states of isolation, stress, and detachment, which can lead to drug use as a coping mechanism (Galea *et al.* 2005, p.1013).

If happiness is understood as an emotional and physiological response, often influenced by external events, internal cognitive processes, and biological factors, then from the perspective of biochemical science, it is possible that one of the primary reasons for drug use is the pursuit of obsession and the feeling of happiness. According to scientific sources, the natural level of happiness varies from one person to another, as it depends on different genetic markers in our bodies. For most people, the level of happiness is biochemically average, i.e., neither too high nor too low (De Neve *et al.* 2012, p.590). Therefore, it is possible that people with a naturally lower level of happiness tend to seek to increase their happiness through drug use, especially given that experiencing happiness due to environmental influences is quite difficult, as happiness-inducing factors such as receiving a promotion or a raise at work, winning the lottery, getting a new car, falling in love, having a child, overcoming pain, etc., are relatively rare events in our lives, or we quickly get used to them and stop enjoying them after a while. Meanwhile, the desire to feel happiness is more or less constant. Assuming that external events and circumstances make it increasingly difficult for people to experience permanent happiness, it is not uncommon to find ways to achieve pleasure and happiness by stimulating biochemical processes in the body with drugs.

In discussing these biochemical processes, it is noted that the neurochemical basis of happiness consists of three substances: serotonin, dopamine, and endorphins (Berridge and Kringelbach 2015). These chemicals are released during the perception of happy situations: pain relief, energy, mood elevation, falling in love, winning the lottery, getting promoted, winning a competition, having a baby, feeling physical closeness, etc., but they also occur during drug use. Serotonin, as a neurotransmitter, is important for its mood-regulating properties. Elevated levels of serotonin are often associated with mood elevation, while its deficiency can lead to depression (Young 2007). Dopamine, known as the "reward neurotransmitter," plays a key role in pleasure- and reward-seeking behavior. Happiness-inducing activities often stimulate dopamine release in the brain (Keighron *et al.* 2023; Wise 2008). Meanwhile, endorphins are the body's natural painkillers and mood enhancers. Many types of drugs stimulate the release of endorphins (Dietrich and McDaniel 2004). It is likely that the primary cause of drug use is the natural human desire to experience states of happiness and pleasure. Accordingly, narcotic substances can be divided into several main groups according to their effects on the human body and brain:

- *Stimulants* such as cocaine, amphetamines, MDMA (ecstasy), and Ritalin improve the mood, increasing alertness and energy. They also play a role in increasing levels of dopamine, a neurotransmitter that is vital for pleasure, motivation and motor function. For example, cocaine prevents dopamine from being reabsorbed, leading to increased feelings of euphoria (Volkow *et al.* 2019).
- *Depressants* such as alcohol, benzodiazepines and certain sleep medications such as zolpidem, Valium, Xanax, and barbiturates reduce (Central nervous system) CNS activity. These drugs induce feelings of relaxation, reduce anxiety, and slow down brain activity, leading to drowsiness or sedation (Bateson 2002).
- *Opioids* such as morphine, fentanyl, heroin, oxycodone (OxyContin), and hydrocodone (Vicodin) are primarily known for their painkilling properties. They can cause euphoria or drowsiness. Such drugs work by mimicking the body's natural endorphins and binding to opioid receptors in the brain, reducing pain perception (Volkow *et al.* 2020).
- *Hallucinogens* such as LSD, psilocybin (magic mushrooms), PCP (phencyclidine), and DMT (dimethyltryptamine) can dramatically alter perception, thoughts and feelings by acting on serotonin receptors in the brain. The changes caused by these drugs are often manifested as hallucinations – experiences in which people perceive things that are not really there (Nichols 2016).
- *Dissociative drugs* such as ketamine and dextromethorphan (found in some cough syrups) cause feelings of detachment from the environment and even from oneself. They work by inhibiting the NMDA receptor, which plays an important role in perception and consciousness (Zanos and Gould 2018).
- *Cannabinoids* – whether naturally occurring, such as THC (tetrahydrocannabinol in marijuana), or synthetically produced, such as Spice or K2 – interact with the brain's endocannabinoid system. This interaction can lead to changes in memory, mood and perception, and can result in the loss of anxiety and the relaxation of the body (Lu and Mackie 2016).
- *Inhalants* include a wide range of volatile substances, and substances such as nitrous oxide and amyl nitrate affect a variety of human mechanisms, for example by inhibiting neurotransmitter activity, which can lead to mental state-altering effects (Volkow *et al.* 2019).

Similarly to humans, many animals have neurotransmitter systems that can be modulated by a variety of substances, resulting in feelings of euphoria or altered states of consciousness. For example, Amazonian jaguars have been documented to consume parts of the *Banisteriopsis caapi* vine, resulting in a trance-like state

(Schultes and Raffauf 1990). In the insect world, ants catch and eat aphids not only because of their sweet secretions, but also because certain species of aphids produce chemicals that can help deter predatory ants (Detrain and Deneubourg 2008). These examples of human and animal behavior show beyond doubt that, in the early stages, drug use in the wild is in fact, a natural phenomenon, free of socio-cultural influence.

As a secondary cause of drug use, many drugs promote psychological and physical dependence due to the level and frequency of the release of the aforementioned happiness hormones and the constant need to maintain a state of happiness. Over time, higher and higher doses are needed to achieve the same level of happiness hormones. To deliberately stop using drugs and live with significantly lower levels of happiness hormones in the body is a challenge that is difficult to overcome. External factors can also be seen as a secondary cause of drug use, where well-developed drug supply chains make drugs easily and quickly available. In addition, globalization processes have led to the rapid spread of knowledge about countries where drugs are legalized, which creates an impression of justification in the mind and encourages people to try drugs in countries where they are legally traded. It is therefore undeniable that economic, cultural, and legal factors have also played a role in the spread of drugs in the more recent stages of human civilization. For example, the expansion of global trade and the development of sophisticated transport systems facilitated the movement of illicit drugs across national borders. Trade routes, especially those that are less controlled, provide opportunities for drug trafficking. Economic instability, poverty and the lack of employment opportunities in certain regions encourage individuals to choose drug trafficking as a source of income (UNODC 2018, 2023). Regions affected by political unrest or armed conflict are characterized by weak law enforcement, which creates a favorable environment for illicit drug cultivation, production and trafficking (UNODC 2023). The development of the internet and encrypted communication platforms has also facilitated a more discrete drug trade, leading to an increase in the number of online drug marketplaces on the dark web (Martin 2014). In some societies, the use of certain drugs is embedded in cultural or religious practices or is normalized, which has implications for their spread (Labate and Cavnar 2014). Different countries' drug policies can affect drug trafficking routes. For example, strict enforcement of drug control in one country may push drug trafficking to neighboring countries with more lenient policies (Bewley-Taylor 2012).

Drug use is essentially a dualistic phenomenon due to innate human tendencies and the influence of external factors. The primary causes of drug use are deeply rooted in human nature, but the secondary causes of drug use are determined by changing social, cultural, and legal factors.

While some countries around the world have liberal policies on drug use, the possession of drugs is banned and criminalized in many parts of the world. This situation leads to a lack of legal coherence in this area. However, the criminalization or decriminalization of drug use is an ongoing process, and the issue of legal coherence has not yet reached its final stage.

Causes of Drug Criminalization

The process of criminalization of drug use is a result of the interaction and interplay of social, political, economic, and cultural factors that have occurred throughout world history. In this process, public health issues have become intertwined with broader social, political, and legal issues.

The main rationale for banning certain drugs is their harmful effects on public health. Medical evidence supports the harmful consequences of drug abuse, which have led to the imposition of strict legal measures. The increase in knowledge of neurobiology and human behavior has increased our understanding of the health consequences of drugs, and the following research is relevant to the health risks of drugs.

Experiments carried out in Rat Park in 1978 confirmed the profound effects of drugs on the development of addictions (Alexander *et al.* 1978). The National Epidemiological Studies on Drunkenness and Related Conditions (NESARC) have helped to shed light on the links between drug use and mental health disorders, with an emphasis on the interaction between mental health and psychoactive substance dependence (Hasin *et al.* 2007). Trials of methadone maintenance therapy in the 1960s confirmed findings of severe opioid dependence (Dole and Nyswander 1965). Internationally, the Global Burden of Disease Study, launched in 1990, summarizes global health problems related to psychoactive substance abuse by linking global morbidity and mortality to the use of various drugs (Degenhardt *et al.* 2018). Although various data show that statistics on drug-related deaths are complicated by the fact that the causes of death are not always correctly identified, the inclusion of deaths that are not directly attributable to drugs, but are related to their use, in these figures is important. As of 2019, the United Nations Office on Drugs and Crime (UNODC) estimated that around 585,000 people died as a result of drug use in 2017, which included indirect deaths, such as those caused by HIV and hepatitis C acquired through unsafe use (UNODC 2019). The World Health Organization (WHO) reported in its 2015 estimates that more than 450,000 deaths worldwide were attributable to psychoactive substance use disorders, which include alcohol, tobacco, and illicit drugs (WHO 2015). In 2017, a high number of overdose deaths were observed (Wilson *et al.* 2020).

In addition, the link between drug use and mental disorders is increasingly well documented in contemporary literature. The therapeutic use of certain psychedelics contrasts sharply with the unpredictable consequences of their misuse (Smith *et al.* 2017; Di Forti *et al.* 2019; Hines *et al.* 2020). Studies specific to cannabis point to potential long-term mental health consequences, as chronic cannabis use has been associated with psychiatric disorders, particularly psychosis (Moffitt *et al.* 2007; Volkow *et al.* 2014).

In addition, drug abuse can be disruptive to society, leading to increased criminal activity, family disruption, and societal disintegration (Dhawan and Chopra 2020; Degenhardt *et al.* 2016). Substance abuse inevitably creates a significant workload on the healthcare infrastructure (Congressional Research Service 2020).

More recent research shows that the use of some substances contributes to recovery from post-traumatic stress disorder, and that such therapeutic use of narcotic substances (e.g., MDMA) has potential benefits, but that uncontrolled use, for example for recreational purposes, can have harmful effects. Therefore, studies support the benefits and necessity of controlled use of some substances (Mithoefer *et al.* 2018).

In summary, the main reason for drug prohibition is the harm to the health of individuals and society, based on various studies. Numerous empirical studies underline the multifaceted dangers of drug abuse and justify the strict legal regulation leading to drug prohibition.

A Brief History of Drug Prohibition

As described in the previous subsection, ancient civilizations have historically used drugs for a variety of purposes, including healing, pain relief, religious rituals, and spiritual quests. The pursuit of these goals has often facilitated the release of neurotransmitters such as dopamine, serotonin, and endorphins, leading to euphoric sensations. Over time, however, due to concerns about damage to human and public health, the use of specific drugs became restricted or banned altogether. On the other hand, the use of drugs in certain areas is legal in countries all over the world; for example, in the health treatment system, and the use of medicinal preparations with narcotic properties requires strict supervision and a doctor's authorization. However, the use of drugs for spiritual ceremonies and religion, as well as for recreational purposes or pleasure, is prohibited in many countries.

The original prohibitions on drug use were based on the exclusive ability of authority figures, such as tribal leaders or seers, to obtain or have access to drugs. Other individuals did not have access to them.

Interestingly, the forerunner of modern drug prohibition was China, which restricted opium possession in 1729. Although opium's therapeutic properties were recognized, the 18th century saw an increase in recreational use, which made people who used it unwilling to work, with a negative impact on the economy. Thus, in 1729 Emperor Yongzheng of the Qing Dynasty imposed prohibitions, which became increasingly severe until the trade was banned altogether in 1799 (Spence 1999). This means that for more than 1700 years, humanity did not see a pressing need to prohibit drugs.

One of the first known pieces of drug control legislation was enacted in Great Britain in 1868—the Pharmacy Act, which restricted the sale of opium (Berridge 1999). It aimed to curb the recreational use of opium and the then-common practice of sedating babies with opium-containing "sedative syrups" (Berridge 1999). The British Pharmacy Act was one of the first attempts to regulate the sale of certain dangerous substances, including opium and its preparations.

The International Opium Convention, signed in The Hague in 1912, was one of the first international drug control treaties and was later incorporated into the League of Nations (McAllister 2000). The countries participating in the International Opium Convention were primarily the major players in the global opium trade: Austria-Hungary, Belgium, France, Germany, Italy, the Netherlands, Portugal, and the United Kingdom (and its possessions, including India). In addition to these European countries, countries such as the United States of America, China, Japan, Persia (now Iran), and Siam (now Thailand) were also signatories to the Convention.

The 1931 Convention on the Control of the Production and Distribution of Narcotic Drugs and the 1936 Convention for the Suppression of the Illicit Traffic in Dangerous Drugs were adopted. These Conventions expanded the scope of controlled substances and established new regulatory mechanisms. The Convention on the Control of the Production and Distribution of Narcotic Drugs (1931) controlled not only opium, but also other drugs and their precursors. Many countries in Europe, North and South America, Asia, and other parts of the world, such as the United Kingdom, France, Germany, the United States of America, Japan, and others, signed or later acceded to this Convention. The Convention for the Suppression of the Illicit Traffic in Dangerous Drugs (1936) was the first to criminalize the possession and distribution of narcotics.

The WHO, established in 1948 after the Second World War, played a central role in drug-related issues. Its pain management guidelines (WHO 1986) have had a major impact on the global approach to opioid prescription.

China, India, Indonesia, Japan, Malaysia, Pakistan, the Philippines, South Korea, Thailand, and many other countries are signatories to the Single Convention on Narcotic Drugs (1961), which sought to bring together in a single instrument a large number of international treaties on drug control. It is the founding document of modern international drug control and aims to combat drug abuse by consolidating previous treaties and including more types of narcotic substances.

In the United Kingdom, the Misuse of Drugs Act 1971 categorizes drugs into three harm categories, with penalties for possession and distribution (Bean and Nemitz 2004). In the same year (1971), the United Nations Convention on Psychotropic Substances was signed to control psychoactive substances such as amphetamines, barbiturates, benzodiazepines, and psychedelics. This treaty was developed in response to the widespread recreational use of many new psychotropic substances in the 1960s and aimed to limit the abuse of these substances while ensuring that they are not available except for medical and scientific purposes. A few years later, the US Drug Enforcement Administration (DEA), established in 1973, began to combat drug trafficking and abuse. In 1974, the National Institute on Drug Abuse (NIDA) was established in the US, focusing on research into drug use and addiction.

The United Nations Convention against Illicit Traffic in Narcotic Drugs and Psychotropic Substances was adopted in 1988 and was intended to create additional legal mechanisms to enforce the 1961 and 1971 Conventions, and to introduce measures against money laundering and the disposal of precursors.

The United Nations has operated mainly through three international drug control conventions: the 1961 Single Convention on Narcotic Drugs, the 1971 Convention on Psychotropic Substances, and the 1988 Convention against Illicit Traffic in Narcotic Drugs and Psychotropic Substances. These Conventions have had a major impact and shaped the global trajectory of drug regulation. However, since 1988, there have been no new Conventions, but only a number of resolutions, declarations, and other agreements that built on the previous Conventions.

In the 20th century, especially in the 1980s, drug prohibition became a symbol of the "war on drugs." This policy emphasized the use of harsh mandatory sentences for drug possession, leading to a rapid increase in the number of prisoners. This tough stance was eventually adopted by many countries around the world (Nellis 2016). On the other hand, recent global trends are moving away from such strict policies, as it has become evident that strict drug policies have not solved the underlying problems and have not reduced harm, and the view that the war on drugs is over and the treatment of drug addicts has begun is coming to be accepted. This shift in thinking changes the course of legal coherence.

Factors Influencing Drug Categorization and Quantification in Europe

It is worth briefly discussing the content of drug criminalization in Europe. European drug prohibition policies, which have significant socio-economic health impacts, require careful study (Chatwin 2011) to justify which substances to criminalize and to set threshold values for illicit drug possession, which in many countries determine the nature and severity of legal consequences (EMCDDA 2020, 2023).

When discussing the criteria for drug prohibition, scientific bodies such as the European Monitoring Centre for Drugs and Drug Addiction (EMCDDA) conduct in-depth studies on substances to assess the nature of their harms, covering physical, psychological and societal aspects, and review detailed pharmacokinetic and toxicological data (EMCDDA 2011). Their analyses prioritize the biochemical interactions of drugs, the risk of overdose and long-term health effects. Policymakers consider societal consequences, such as propensity for drug-induced crime, economic, and other societal impacts. These considerations are heavily influenced by input from law enforcement agencies and socio-economic researchers (MacCoun and Reuter 2001). Many European countries are signatories to international treaties, such as the United Nations Convention on the Control of Drugs, which require Member States to criminalize specific substances.

Law enforcement authorities and courts are guided by these conventions and recommendations when interpreting and determining the quantities of specific drugs. A "small" quantity can generally indicate personal use, while "large" and "very large" quantities can indicate intent to distribute or traffic (Wouters *et al.* 2010). Regulators can use demographic analysis to identify prevailing patterns of drug use. Insights into the average daily or weekly intake of users can help to establish criteria for "low" levels (Caulkins and Pacula 2006). Medical bodies, such as the WHO's European Office and national health agencies, make recommendations based on health risks. Levels that approach potentially lethal doses or are likely to cause serious health complications are labelled "very high" (van Amsterdam *et al.* 2010). European countries often build on the practices of neighboring countries or apply a harmonized approach that is similar across the EU, thus ensuring a certain degree of legal coherence (EMCDDA 2019).

Based on available evidence and societal norms, national parliaments or equivalent legislative bodies consider and formalize the list of banned substances and the limits on their possession. European states use expert advisory committees of scientists, medical doctors, law enforcement officials, and sociologists to make informed recommendations on drug classifications and quantities (Hughes and Stevens 2010; Heidt 2021). Some jurisdictions, as part of their appreciation of the principles of participatory democracy, conduct public consultations to capture public sentiment and concerns, thereby ensuring that policies are in line with the realities of the situation (Holland *et al.* 2023).

Politicians can be influenced by the government's policy stance on drugs. For example, a conservative government may advocate stricter rules and definitions, while a more liberal government may lean toward decriminalization and softer definitions. Countries in certain regions, such as the European Union, may harmonize their drug policies to a certain extent so that similar definitions of quantities may apply, ensuring legal consistency. Policymakers may look at the drug policies of other countries, particularly neighboring countries or countries with similar societal structures, to make decisions.

The overall impact on public health – both direct health effects and secondary effects such as drug-related crime or hospital admissions – can also be important in determining quantities. It is worth noting that drug quantity determinations are not static; they can change in response to new scientific discoveries, societal changes, or changes in political or public opinion.

Determining what constitutes a small, large, and very large quantity of drugs requires a multifaceted decision. This process is based on scientific research, societal norms, political considerations and international treaties or agreements. These quantities are usually determined in different countries based on data on lethal doses and harmful effects in toxicology reports. By understanding how drugs work in the body, decisions can be made about what constitutes a quantity for "personal use" and what constitutes a quantity for distribution. Substances that are highly addictive may be subject to stricter rules, and governments thus need to analyze patterns of drug use in their populations. This may mean determining the average amount that a user consumes per day or week, which may help to define the amount for "personal use." It is thus very important to distinguish between possession for personal use and intent to distribute.

However, there is no single overarching law in Europe that sets drug levels in all European countries, as drug policy is largely a matter for individual Member States. Nevertheless, there are institutions and instruments at the EU level that provide guidelines, frameworks and recommendations on drug policy, including on drug quantity: the EMCDDA does not directly set legal thresholds, but provides analyses of drug trends that can be useful for national policies (EMCDDA 2019). The EU Drugs Strategy (2013–2020) and the EU Drugs Action Plan (2017–2020) do not set drug quantities, but provide an overarching policy framework. Council Framework Decision 2004/757/JHA sets out the imperative to apply minimum provisions on offenses and penalties related to drug trafficking. Although the Decision refers to quantities, it does not set specific thresholds, but emphasizes that offenses involving large quantities of drugs should be punished with more severe penalties. The precise definition of these quantities is left to the discretion of the Member States (Decision 2004/757/JHA, 2004). The United Nations drug conventions require signatories to regulate and control certain substances. However, the way in which each country defines quantities may vary (Chatwin 2011) because, as mentioned above, each EU Member State sets specific rules and limits in its national laws. For example, several countries have clear legal thresholds that distinguish between possession for personal use and trafficking. Portugal decriminalized the personal possession of all drugs in 2001. The law in Portugal allows the possession for personal use of up to 25 grams of cannabis, 5 grams of cannabis resin, 2 grams of cocaine, or 1 gram of MDMA. Possession of more than these quantities is prohibited (Hughes and Stevens 2010). In Spain, cannabis use and possession for personal use are allowed, but are regarded as administrative offenses if committed in public spaces. To differentiate personal drug use from trafficking, Spanish courts generally focus on the amounts seized. If these exceed the limits for each substance determined by the National Institute of Toxicology – 100 grams of marijuana and 25 grams of hashish – it is usually regarded as trafficking (Bąkowski, 2023). The Netherlands has a policy of tolerance toward cannabis possession, where possession of up to 5 grams of cannabis without intent to distribute is decriminalized. The cultivation of up to five plants is also decriminalized, but exceeding these quantities can lead to sanctions and possible prosecution (EMCDDA 2016). In 2010, the Czech Republic set the "legal" quantities of drugs for personal possession at 15 grams of cannabis or 1.5 grams of heroin. Quantities above these thresholds may be subject to legal sanctions and may be interpreted as intent to distribute (Belackova *et al.* 2017). Germany has a more ambiguous system. While there are no precise legal thresholds, the possession of a "small amount" for personal use may not be punishable, but this "small amount" varies depending on the federal state and the substance possessed, with up to 6 grams of cannabis generally considered legal in most territories (Werse and Morgenstern 2012). In Lithuania, possession of up to 5 grams of cannabis for personal use is considered to be a small amount.

Possession of more than 5 grams but less than 20 grams is considered to be a larger quantity, while possession of more than 20 grams is considered to be a large quantity, and more than 500 grams is considered to be a "very large" quantity and liability is incurred under the distribution article. It should be noted that in Lithuania, even possession of a "small quantity" is subject to criminal liability.

In conclusion, the complex policy of identification and quantification of illicit drugs in Europe calls for greater legal coherence, thus unifying the conditions for criminal liability and the structure of legal assessment. However, as the landscape of drug use and its consequences changes, so too must the regulatory frameworks to ensure that they remain sensitive, fair and coherent (Bühringer *et al.* 2014).

Consequences of the Criminalization of Narcotic Drugs

The criminalization of drugs, or the war on drugs, has a negative side in addition to its good intentions and results. From an economic point of view, the criminalization of drugs encourages the development of a black market, which deprives governments of potential revenues while reinforcing illicit revenues (Costa Storti and De Grauwe, 2009). The EMCDDA's European Drug Report provides a comprehensive overview of recent drug trends in Europe. The report estimates that the illicit drug market in the EU is worth around €30 billion annually (EMCDDA 2021). The UNODC estimates that the methamphetamine trade in South-East Asia generates \$30–\$61 billion annually (UNODC 2020). Meanwhile, an ONDCP report estimates that in 2010, Americans spent almost \$100 billion on substances such as cocaine, heroin, marijuana, and methamphetamine (ONDCP 2014). However, due to clandestine black-market operations, it is difficult to accurately calculate the revenue generated by the shadow drug trade (EMCDDA 2019). In addition, significant financial resources are devoted to drug interdiction, law enforcement investigations, trials, and incarceration for drug-related crimes (Hughes and Stevens 2010). As a result, huge financial resources are devoted to combating this problem.

The war on drugs can also be said to be linked to deaths and violence. In Central and South America, where drug cartels have gained immense power, large-scale violence has resulted, and aggressive anti-drug campaigns, such as in Mexico, have generated high homicide rates, a significant proportion of which are attributable to drug-related clashes (Bagley and Rosen 2015). In Europe, which is grappling with a drug crisis, overdose deaths among those aged 50–64 increased by 69% between 2012 and 2021 in 13 EU countries, and a Norwegian review found that drug users have a risk of dying that is between 3 and more than

20 times higher than their peers in the general population. This increased risk is not limited to overdoses, but also includes deaths due to accidents, violence, various diseases, infections such as HIV and viral hepatitis, and suicide (EMCDDA 2023). The report also indicates that over the last decade, HIV outbreaks linked to the injection of illicit synthetic stimulants have occurred in six major European cities in five EU countries. Stimulant use is associated with a potentially higher incidence of injecting compared to heroin use, and the crushing and dissolving of crack cocaine and other pills by injecting also poses additional health risks. Such consumption patterns raise questions, for example, about the type and suitability of needles and syringes provided in street-based open drug consumption areas, which are usually characterized by multi-drug use. An additional concern is that service restrictions through COVID-19 sites have negatively affected testing for drug-related infections such as HIV and HCV and access to care for more vulnerable and marginalized groups of drug users, including those experiencing homelessness (UNODC 2023).

Worryingly, these deaths are not exclusively linked to the drug trade, but involve civilians as well as law enforcement and security forces. The grim reality is that global efforts to combat the drug menace, aimed at protecting public health, appear to be causing deaths in numbers that do not keep pace with the direct toll of drug use. This is why the term "war on drugs" is no longer appropriate, because in every war someone is bound to die. The term "war" is therefore being replaced by "control, assistance, or treatment" (Reuter 2013).

The health impact of criminalizing drugs is therefore debatable. Although criminalization is intended as a protective measure, it can unexpectedly increase health risks. For example, illicit drug users may avoid health services for fear of legal consequences, making it more difficult to access necessary treatment or preventive measures (Cook and Kanaef 2008). Such dynamics can lead to increased health complications, as seen in the increased prevalence of blood-borne diseases among injecting drug users in several European countries (EMCDDA 2023). Although some countries around the world have criminal codes that provide for exemption from criminal liability if a person goes to a treatment facility and voluntarily and without coercion transfers substances, in the absence of social programs to encourage this, few people take advantage of this norm and opportunity.

It should not be forgotten that, particularly in view of the prevalence of drugs, the vast majority of those arrested are young people who have a criminal record when prosecuted. This makes a large (and growing) proportion of society criminal, and this proliferation of convictions in society changes attitudes toward criminal responsibility, making it a normal outcome. As a result, criminal responsibility is no longer an exceptional life event that is shameful and hidden, but on the contrary a widespread phenomenon, especially among young people. This results in a high number of convictions, especially in view of the opinion that the penalties for drug possession are very severe. In Lithuania, for example, this opinion is shared by legal scholars working in the judiciary.

In summary, while the criminalization of drugs is aimed at the public good, it has many negative consequences. Policymakers therefore need to consider these consequences when designing regulatory frameworks. However, countries such as Portugal, Spain, Switzerland, Belgium, the Netherlands, the Czech Republic, Uruguay, Mexico, Georgia, Luxembourg, Estonia, Colombia, Jamaica, Argentina, Costa Rica, Peru, Bolivia, and some states in the United States of America have advocated for some form of decriminalization, underlining the view that drug addiction is a public health challenge rather than a criminal offense (Hughes and Stevens 2012).

The Health-Oriented Decriminalization of Drugs

The decriminalization of drugs is a hot topic in contemporary global public health discourse and jurisprudence. The decriminalization of narcotic drugs essentially means the abolition of criminal liability for the personal use and possession of drugs.

The concept of the decriminalization of drugs should be linked to a legislative reorientation away from treating the disposal of drugs for personal use as a crime or a misdemeanor, and instead as an administrative offense (Chatwin 2011). This construction differs sharply from legalization – the deregulation of the prohibition of drug use, production and distribution (Hughes and Stevens 2010).

The general movement toward decriminalization in some countries can be explained in large part by greater awareness of the multiple health consequences associated with the use of psychoactive substances, as well as the perceived inefficiencies and harms associated with the fight against drug trafficking. Some authors argue that penal systems sometimes reinforce negative health effects without intending to do so, and facilitate the spread of pathologies such as HIV and hepatitis C among drug-using groups (Degenhardt *et al.* 2017, p.1201). As a result, contemporary policy is increasingly focusing on a health-centered approach. This includes initiatives such as syringe exchange services, controlled substance use sites and opioid substitution treatment interventions (Rhodes and Hedrich 2010), treating rather than judging users. The WHO and the EMCDDA have reaffirmed the importance of these health-oriented strategies, favoring them over punitive drug policies (WHO, 2014). The changing drug situation in

Europe poses new challenges for harm reduction interventions. Illicit drug use is recognized as contributing to the global burden of disease. Interventions to reduce this burden include prevention activities aimed at reducing or slowing down the rate of onset of drug use and offering treatment to those with drug problems. This complementary set of approaches is referred to by the generic name of harm reduction. This emphasizes non-judgmental work with drug users in order to reduce the risks associated with behaviors that are commonly associated with negative health consequences and to promote health and well-being more generally. Over time, such approaches have contributed to the fact that the number of new HIV infections related to injecting drugs in Europe is now relatively low compared to international standards.

The European Drugs Report 2023 states that harm reduction services have become increasingly integrated into the mainstream of drug users' health-care delivery in Europe over the last two decades. Initially, the focus was on expanding access to opioid agonist treatment and needle and syringe programs as part of the response to high-risk drug use, primarily targeting injecting heroin use and the HIV/AIDS epidemic (EMCDDA 2023). The report also indicates that over the last two decades, in some EU countries, the harm reduction approach has been extended to other responses, including supervised drug consumption rooms and take-home naloxone programs to reduce fatal overdoses. Some countries also have drug testing centers set up to give people a better understanding of the substances in the illicit drugs they buy. For example, tablets purchased as MDMA may also contain adulterants and other drugs such as synthetic cathinones. As many synthetic stimulants and new psychoactive substances are currently available on the illicit market in the form of similar-looking powders or tablets, users may be increasingly at risk of being unaware of the specific stimulant or mixture of substances they are taking. A ban in this place would only increase the risk and danger to public health.

The latest report (EMCDDA 2023) also points out that although some harm reduction measures remain controversial in some European countries, the concept that evidence-based harm reduction measures are an important part of a balanced drug policy is generally accepted. Therefore, the context in which harm reduction services operate, the evidence base underpinning them and what constitutes quality standards of care in this field remain key areas for policy consideration. Looking ahead, the evolving health threats posed by Europe's dynamic illicit drug markets highlight the increasing need to assess new and evolving models of service delivery that may be needed to protect the health of people at risk of adverse outcomes arising from more complex patterns of use, new substances and mixtures, or those associated with particular subgroups or environments.

Various interventions aimed at health promotion rather than prohibition have been effective in reducing the negative consequences associated with psychoactive substances, and countries have embarked on a transformative journey by combining their decriminalization principles with these health-oriented measures. Portugal is becoming a model for drug decriminalization. In 2001, faced with rising drug use mortality and HIV prevalence, the country took the bold step of universal drug decriminalization (Laqueur 2015). This transformative measure entailed a strategic departure from the use of punitive policies and a shift toward the development of public health and harm reduction systems. The reconceptualization of drug use within the public health spectrum was intended to create an environment conducive to the therapeutic and rehabilitative tendencies of drug users (EMCDDA 2011).

At the same time, the Netherlands has adopted a distinctive strategy. Although drugs were not fully decriminalized, at the end of the 1960s a "*gedoogbeleid*" – a manifesto of tolerance for the possession of small amounts of cannabis – was introduced. This doctrinal position stemmed from the desire to separate the markets for light and hard drugs and to reduce the risks for enthusiasts of light drugs (e.g. cannabis), while easing the burden on the judicial apparatus (MacCoun 2011).

In 2010, the Czech Republic announced that it had decriminalized small quantities of most recreational drugs. For example, legal provisions allowed individuals to possess up to 15 grams of marijuana or 1.5 grams of heroin without facing criminal consequences (EMCDDA 2010). Subsequent observations have shown a reduction in drug-related fatalities and a reduction in HIV transmission among injecting drug users. Despite these favorable results, cannabis use has increased (Csete *et al.* 2016).

Canada has legalized the use of marijuana but refrained from decriminalizing other drugs. The legalization of cannabis has led to a decrease in drug-related offenses and an increase in government revenue. However, the full impact of this paradigm shift on society and health has yet to be fully assessed (Rotermann 2020).

In addition to the countries mentioned above, others have relaxed their legal frameworks in relation to drugs, decriminalizing in one way or another the disposal of drugs for personal use. These countries include Spain, Switzerland, Belgium, Uruguay, Mexico, Georgia, Luxembourg, Estonia, Colombia, Jamaica, Argentina, Costa Rica, Peru, Bolivia, and some US states. This has led to a general recognition that substance dependence requires interventions in the public health field rather than in the prosecution field (Hughes and Stevens 2012).

Although the overarching imperative of decriminalization aims to promote a more humane approach to drug users, this initiative remains unchallenged in European intellectual and legal circles (Montanari *et al.* 2022).

One of the main criticisms voiced by legal scholars is that decriminalizing drugs could lead to increased drug use. Although countries such as Portugal have not seen a significant increase in drug use after decriminalization (Laqueur 2015), this concern remains a topical debate, especially in the context of Central and Eastern Europe (Eastwood *et al.* 2016). The distinction between "personal use" and "intent to distribute" or "possession with intent to palliate" has been a persistent problem in several jurisdictions. This boundary is subject to *ad hoc* assessments in legal practice, which can lead to inconsistent legal decisions (Chatwin 2011).

International obligations, in particular the United Nations Drug Control Convention, often lead to legal disagreements and international implications when states' decriminalization policies are juxtaposed (Boister 2001). Some European health professionals and legal scholars argue that decriminalization can inadvertently lead to public health problems, including increased strain on health infrastructures and the potential spread of drug-related diseases if not properly managed (Rolles and Murkin 2013). On the other hand, public opinion may remain unchanged and dead set against decriminalization, so that stigmas associated with drug use may persist and entrenched attitudes may hinder the reintegration of drug users into society and undermine the decriminalization process itself (Ahern *et al.* 2007). It is necessary for legal scholars, policy makers, and society as a whole to understand, compare, and address the harms of drug criminalization and decriminalization. Only with this comprehensive understanding can robust and coherent legal frameworks be developed that are mutually consistent and focused on achieving the best possible outcome.

Various European examples, notably Portugal, the Netherlands, and the Czech Republic, have added the decriminalization of drugs to their legal frameworks in order to move from punitive measures to rehabilitative and public health-oriented strategies. One obvious benefit of decriminalizing drug use is the significant reduction in imprisonment for drug-related offenses. In Portugal, a decriminalization strategy implemented in 2001 led to a significant reduction in drug-related imprisonment, thereby easing the economic burden on the criminal justice system and significantly reducing the associated costs to society (Hughes and Stevens 2010).

Decriminalization, by its very nature, emphasizes that drug use is a health issue, not a criminal issue. In the Dutch context, the actual decriminalization of cannabis through the "coffee shop" system was associated with lower levels of heavy drug use, suggesting that decriminalization of light drugs may have led to a greater preference for these drugs and a greater refusal of heavier drugs, indicating a possible "separation effect" (MacCoun and Reuter 1997). In addition, in the Portuguese model, a focus on harm reduction, such as needle exchange programs and increased access to treatment, led to a significant reduction in drug-related deaths and HIV transmission rates (Greenwald 2009). Meanwhile, the Netherlands, which has partially legalized the cannabis trade, has generated substantial revenues from taxation of the cannabis sector. This financial flow not only boosts public coffers, but also takes control of the market away from illicit traffickers, thereby reducing the flow of related criminal offenses (Červený *et al.* 2017). Decriminalization also allows for a more rational use of law enforcement resources. For example, in the Czech Republic, where possession of small amounts of drugs was decriminalized in 2010, police efforts were directed toward more serious drug-related offenses rather than minor drug offenses, thereby optimizing the efficiency of the criminal justice apparatus (Eastwood *et al.* 2016). Accordingly, decriminalizing personal drug use weakens the social stigmas attached to it. This transformation fosters a more inclusive social environment in which rehabilitated drug users are more smoothly reintegrated, as observed in countries with rehabilitative and health-oriented approaches (Korf 2002).

In summary, the attempted decriminalization of drugs by European countries such as Portugal, the Netherlands, and the Czech Republic provides compelling empirical evidence that such legislative change can be beneficial from a legal, social, and economic perspective. For European countries considering similar paths, these success stories, which lead to tangible socio-economic gains, can be an important starting point.

Interim Findings

Drug use is determined by primary and secondary drivers of use. Primary drivers include natural human curiosity and the influence of biochemical processes in the human body, where drug users experience happiness and become addicted. Secondary factors are represented by drug supply systems and chains.

There are clear changes in the legal, cultural, and social processes around the world as decriminalization policies spread. The experience of countries that have decriminalized drugs shows that the consequences of such decriminalization practices are not inherently harmful, as previously thought. Countries with a strict prohibition stance show an increase in drug consumption, while countries with a consistent decriminalization approach show a decrease in drug use, although there are discrepancies between the two scenarios, which call for a more detailed analysis of these figures. However, there is growing global momentum toward a coherent approach, as countries introspectively assess their established drug policies and consider more coherent and sustainable alternatives.

The key to this dialogue is to achieve legal coherence between criminalization and decriminalization, while trying to understand the possible consequences of drug-related legislation on people's consumption habits, thereby achieving consistency. Legal frameworks need to be formulated in a way that is consistent with public health objectives, ensuring that they do not discourage drug use and do not disproportionately punish users, especially those who only occasionally use light drugs without causing harm. The biggest threat is the lack of legal consistency, which leads to criminal consequences and the dangers of unregulated drug markets. The legal community and policymakers must take into account the good practices of countries that have decriminalized drugs when setting the future trajectory of global drug policy.

References

Ahern, J., Stuber, J., and Galea, S., 2007. Stigma, Discrimination and the Health of Illicit Drug Users. *Drug and Alcohol Dependence*, 88 (2–3), 188–196. [Online]. Available from: https://doi.org/10.1016/j.drugalcdep.2006.10.014 [Accessed 1 December 2023].

Alexander, B. K., Coambs, R. B., and Hadaway, P. F., 1978. The Effect of Housing and Gender on Morphine Self-Administration in Rats. *Psychopharmacology*, 58 (2), 175–179. [Online]. Available from: https://doi.org/10.1007/bf00426903 [Accessed 27 May 2023].

Bagley, B. M., and Rosen, J. D., 2015. *Drug Trafficking, Organized Crime, and Violence in the Americas Today*. University of Florida Press.

Bateson, A. N., 2002. Basic Pharmacologic Mechanisms Involved in Benzodiazepine Tolerance and Withdrawal. *Current Pharmaceutical Design*, 8 (1), 5–21. [Online]. Available from: https://doi.org/10.2174/1381612023396681 [Accessed 28 May 2023].

Bean, P., and Nemitz, T., (eds.), 2004. *Drug Treatment: What Works?* London and New York: Routledge.

Belackova, V., Vacek, J., Janikova, B., Mravcik, V., Zabransky, T., Ivanovova, L., & Csemy, L., 2017. "Just Another Drug" for Marginalized Users: The Risks of Using Synthetic Cathinones among NSP Clients in the Czech Republic.

Journal of Substance Use, 22 (6), 567–573. [Online]. Available from: https://doi.org/10.1080/14659891.2016.1271034 [Accessed 27 May 2023].

Berridge, V., 1999. *Opium and the People: Opiate Use and Drug Control Policy in Nineteenth and Early Twentieth Century England.* London: Free Association Books.

Berridge, K. C., and Kringelbach, M. L., 2015. Pleasure Systems in the Brain. *Neuron*, 86 (3), 646–664. [Online]. Available from: https://doi.org/10.1016/j.peptides.2015.10.009 [Accessed 27 May 2023].

Bewley-Taylor, D. R., 2012. *International Drug Control: Consensus Fractured.* Cambridge: Cambridge University Press.

Boister, N., 2001. *Penal Aspects of the UN Drug Conventions. Brill Nijhoff.*

Bąkowski, P., 2023. Recreational Use of Cannabis: Legislation and Policy in Selected EU Member States. European Parliament Research Service briefing PE 749.792. [Online]. Available from: https://www.europarl.europa.eu/RegData/etudes/BRIE/2023/749792/EPRS_BRI(2023)749792_EN.pdf [Accessed 3 March 2024].

Bühringer, G., 2014. Addiction Research Centres and the Promotion of Creativity. *Addiction*, 109 (8), 1245–1251. [Online] Available from: https://onlinelibrary.wiley.com/doi/full/10.1111/add.12592 [Accessed 3 March 2024].

Caulkins, J. P., and Pacula, R. L., 2006. Marijuana Markets: Inferences from reports by the Household Population. *Journal of Drug Issues*, 36 (1), 173–200. [Online]. Available from: https://doi.org/10.1177/002204260603600108 [Accessed 16 September 2023].

Chatwin, C., 2011. *Drug Policy Harmonization and the European Union.* London: Palgrave Macmillan.

Congressional Research Service, 2020. Substance Abuse and Mental Health Services Administration (SAMHSA): Overview of the Agency and Major Programs. [Online]. Available from: https://crsreports.congress.gov/product/pdf/R/R46426 [Accessed 5 June 2023].

Convention for Limiting the Manufacture and Regulating the Distribution of Narcotic Drugs, 1931. *League of Nations Treaty Series*, Vol. 139. [Online]. Available from: https://treaties.un.org/pages/ViewDetails.aspx?src=TREATY&mtdsg_no=VI-8-a&chapter=6&clang=_en [Accessed 26 May 2023].

Convention for the Suppression of the Illicit Traffic in Dangerous Drugs, 1936. *League of Nations Treaty Series*, Vol. 198. [Online]. Available from: https://treaties.un.org/pages/ViewDetails.aspx?src=TREATY&mtdsg_no=VI-11&chapter=6&clang=_en [Accessed 26 May 2023].

Cook, C., and Kanaef, N., 2008. The Global State of Drug Harm Reduction 2008: Mapping the response to drug-related HIV and hepatitis C epidemics. [Online]. International Harm Reduction Association. Available from:

https://hri.global/wp-content/uploads/2022/10/GSHR-Report-2008-1.pdf [Accessed 26 October 2023].

Costa Storti, C., and De Grauwe, P., 2009. Globalization and the Price Decline of Illicit Drugs. *International Journal of Drug Policy*, 20 (1), 48–61. [Online]. Available from: https://doi.org/10.1016/j.drugpo.2007.11.016 [Accessed 20 October 2023].

Council Framework Decision 2004/757/JHA of 25 October 2004 laying down minimum provisions on the constituent elements of criminal acts and penalties in the field of illicit drug trafficking. OJ L 335, 11.11.2004, p. 8–11. [Online]. Available from: http://data.europa.eu/eli/dec_framw/2004/757/oj [Accessed 20 October 2023].

Csete, J., Kamarulzaman, A., Kazatchkine, M., Altice, F., Balicki, M., Buxton, J., … and Beyrer, C., 2016. Public Health and International Drug Policy. *The Lancet*, 387 (10026), 1427–1480. [Online]. Available from: https://www.ncbi.nlm.nih.gov/pmc/articles/PMC5042332/ [Accessed 11 November 2023].

Červený, J., Chomynová, P., Mravčík, V., and van Ours, J. C., 2017. Cannabis decriminalization and the age of onset of cannabis use. *International Journal of Drug Policy*, 43, 122–129. [Online]. Available from: https://pubmed.ncbi.nlm.nih.gov/28395168/ [Accessed 1 December 2023].

De Neve, J. E., Christakis, N. A., Fowler, J. H., and Frey, B. S., 2012. Genes, Economics, and Happiness. *Journal of Neuroscience, Psychology, and Economics*, 5 (4), 193–211. [Online]. Available from: https://www.ncbi.nlm.nih.gov/pmc/articles/PMC3858957/ [Accessed 24 May 2023].

Degenhardt, L., Peacock, A., Colledge, S., Leung, J., Grebely, J., Vickerman, P., Stone, J., … and Larney, S., 2017. Global Prevalence of Injecting Drug Use and Sociodemographic Characteristics and Prevalence of HIV, HBV, and HCV in People Who Inject Drugs: A Multistage Systematic Review. *The Lancet Global Health*, 5 (12), 1192–1207. [Online]. Available from: https://www.thelancet.com/journals/langlo/article/PIIS2214-109X(17)30375-3/fulltext [Accessed 11 November 2023].

Degenhardt, L., Charlson, F., Ferrari, A., Santomauro, D., Erskine, H., Mantilla-Herrara, A., and Sorensen, R., 2018. The Global Burden of Disease Attributable to Alcohol and Drug Use in 195 Countries and Territories, 1990–2016: A Systematic Analysis for the Global Burden of Disease Study 2016. *The Lancet Psychiatry, 5* (12), 987–1012. [Online]. Available from: https://doi.org/10.1016/S2215-0366(18)30337-7 [Accessed 29 May 2023].

Degenhardt, L., Whiteford, H. A., Ferrari, A. J., Baxter, A. J., Charlson, F. J., Hall, W. D., … and Burstein, R., 2016. Global Burden of Disease Attributable to Illicit Drug Use and Dependence: Findings From the Global Burden of

Disease Study 2010. *The Lancet, 382* (9904), 1564–1574. [Online]. Available from: https://pubmed.ncbi.nlm.nih.gov/23993281/ [Accessed 30 May 2023].

Detrain, C., and Deneubourg, J. L., 2008. Collective Decision-Making and Foraging Patterns in Ants and Bees. *Advances in Insect Physiology*, 35, 123–173. [Online]. Available from: http://dx.doi.org/10.1016/S0065-2806(08)00002-7 [Accessed 26 May 2023].

Dhawan, A., and Chopra, A., 2020. Does the Bane of "drugs" Have a Boon? A Review of the Mixed Results from the Psycho-Social Research on Substance Abuse. *Journal of Psychosocial Research, 15* (1).

Di Forti, M., Quattrone, D., Freeman, T. P., Tripoli, G., Gayer-Anderson, C., Quigley, H., … and Murray, R. M., 2019. The Contribution of Cannabis Use to Variation in the Incidence of Psychotic Disorders Across Europe (EU-GEI): A Multicentre Case-Control Study. *The Lancet Psychiatry*, 6 (5), 427–436. [Online]. Available from: https://doi.org/10.1016/S2215-0366(19)30048-3 [Accessed 25 May 2023].

Dietrich, A., and Mcdaniel, W. F., 2004. Endocannabinoids and Exercise. *British Journal of Sports Medicine*, 38 (5), 536–541. [Online]. Available from: https://bjsm.bmj.com/content/38/5/536 [Accessed 25 May 2023].

Dole, V. P., & Nyswander, M. E., 1965. A Medical Treatment for Diacetylmorphine (heroin) Addiction: A Clinical Trial with Methadone Hydrochloride. *JAMA, 193* (8), 646–650. [Online]. Available from: https://pubmed.ncbi.nlm.nih.gov/14321530/ [Accessed 30 May 2023].

Eastwood, N., Fox, E. and Rosmarin, A., 2016. *A quiet revolution: Drug decriminalisation across the globe. Release.* [Online]. Available from: https://www.release.org.uk/sites/default/files/pdf/publications/A%20Quiet%20Revolution%20-%20Decriminalisation%20Across%20the%20Globe.pdf [Accessed 2 December 2023].

EMCDDA (European Monitoring Centre for Drugs and Drug Addiction), 2010. *Czech Republic: Country Drug Report.* Lisbon: EMCDDA. [Online]. Available from: https://www.emcdda.europa.eu/html.cfm/index142348EN.html_en [Accessed 11 November 2023].

EMCDDA, 2011. 2011 Annual Report on the State of the Drugs Problem in Europe. Lisbon: EMCDDA. [Online]. Available from: https://www.emcdda.europa.eu/publications/annual-report/2011_en [Accessed 8 November 2023].

EMCDDA, 2016. *European Drug Report 2016: Trends and Developments.* Lisbon: EMCDDA. [Online]. Available from: https://www.emcdda.europa.eu/publications/edr/trends-developments/2016_en [Accessed 7 September 2023].

EMCDDA, 2019. *European Drug Report 2019: Trends and Developments*. Lisbon: EMCDDA. [Online]. Available from: https://www.emcdda.europa.eu/publications/edr/trends-developments/2019_en [Accessed 7 September 2023].

EMCDDA, 2020. *European Drug Report 2020: Trends and Developments*. Lisbon: EMCDDA. [Online]. Available from: https://www.emcdda.europa.eu/publications/edr/trends-developments/2020_en [Accessed 7 September 2023].

EMCDDA, 2021. *European Drug Report 2021: Trends and Developments*. Lisbon: EMCDDA. [Online]. Available from: https://www.emcdda.europa.eu/publications/edr/trends-developments/2021_en [Accessed 7 September 2023].

EMCDDA, 2023. *European Drug Report 2023*. Lisbon: EMCDDA. [Online]. Available from: https://www.emcdda.europa.eu/publications/european-drug-report/2023_en [Accessed 8 November 2023]

Freud, S., 1920. *Beyond the Pleasure Principle*. Internationaler Psychoanalytischer Verlag. [Online]. Available from: https://www.sas.upenn.edu/~cavitch/pdf-library/Freud_Beyond_P_P.pdf [Accessed 23 May 2023].

Galea, S., Nandi, A., and Vlahov, D., 2005. The social epidemiology of substance use. *Epidemiologic Reviews*, 27 (1), 36–52. [Online]. Available from https://doi.org/10.1093/epirev/mxh007 [Accessed 27 May 2023].

Greenwald, G., 2009. *Drug Decriminalization in Portugal: Lessons for Creating Fair and Successful Drug Policies*. CATO Institute. [Online]. Available from: https://www.cato.org/white-paper/drug-decriminalization-portugal-lessons-creating-fair-successful-drug-policies [Accessed 1 December 2023].

Gootenberg, P., 2022. *The Oxford Handbook of Global Drug History*. Oxford: Oxford University Press.

Hasin, D. S., Stinson, F. S., Ogburn, E., and Grant, B. F., 2007. Prevalence, Correlates, Disability, and Comorbidity of DSM-IV Alcohol Abuse and Dependence in the United States: Results from the National Epidemiologic Survey on Alcohol and Related Conditions. *Archives of General Psychiatry, 64* (7), 830–842. [Online]. Available from: https://doi.org/10.1001/archpsyc.64.7.830 [Accessed 29 May 2023].

Heidt, J., 2021. *Alternatives to the Criminalization of Simple Possession of Illicit Drugs: Review and Analysis of the Literature*. [Online]. International Centre for Criminal Law Reform. Available from: https://icclr.org/wp-content/uploads/2021/12/Heidt_Alternatives-to-criminalization-of-simple-possession.pdf?x56541&x96127 [Accessed 13 September 2023].

Hines, L. A., Freeman, T. P., Gage, S. H., Zammit, S., Hickman, M., Cannon, M., … and Heron, J., 2020. The association of high-potency cannabis use with mental health and psychoactive substance use in adolescence. *JAMA Psychiatry*, 77 (10), 1044–1051. [Online]. Available from: https://doi.org/10.1001/jamapsychiatry.2020.1035 [Accessed 15 September 2023].

Holland, A., Stevens, A., Harris, M., Lewer, D., Sumnall, H., Stewart, D., and Hickman, M., 2023. Analysis of the UK Government's 10-Year Drugs Strategy—a resource for practitioners and policymakers. *Journal of Public Health*, 45 (2), e215–e224. Available from: https://doi.org/10.1093/pubmed/fdac114 [Accessed 15 September 2023].

Hughes, C. E., and Stevens, A., 2010. What Can We Learn From The Portuguese Decriminalization of Illicit Drugs? *The British Journal of Criminology*, 50 (3), 999–1022. [Online]. Available from: https://doi.org/10.1093/bjc/azq038 [Accessed 13 September 2023].

Hughes, C. E., and Stevens, A., 2012. A Resounding Success or a Disastrous Failure: Re-examining the Interpretation of Evidence on the Portuguese Decriminalisation of Illicit Drugs. *Drug and Alcohol Review*, 31 (1), 101–113. [Online]. Available from: https://doi.org/10.1111/j.1465-3362.2011.00383.xhttps://onlinelibrary.wiley.com/doi/abs/10.1111/j.1465-3362.2011.00383.x[Accessed 14 June 2023].

International Convention on Opium, 1912. [Online]. *League of Nations Treaty Series*, Vol. 8. Available from: https://treaties.un.org/pages/ViewDetailsIV.aspx?src=TREATY&mtdsg_no=VI-2&chapter=6&Temp=mtdsg4&clang=_en [Accessed 27 May 2023].

Keighron, J. D., Bonaventura, J., Li, Y., Yang, J.W., Demarco, E. M., Hersey, M., … and Tanda, G., 2023. Interactions of Calmodulin Kinase II with the Dopamine Transporter Facilitate Cocaine-Induced Enhancement of Evoked Dopamine Release. *Translational Psychiatry*, 13 (1), 202. [Online]. Available from: https://pubmed.ncbi.nlm.nih.gov/37311803/ [Accessed 23 May 2023].

Khantzian, E. J., 1985. The Self-Medication Hypothesis of Addictive Disorders: Focus on Heroin And Cocaine Dependence. *American Journal of Psychiatry*, 142 (11), 1259–1264. [Online]. Available from: https://pubmed.ncbi.nlm.nih.gov/3904487/ [Accessed 27 May 2023].

Korf, D. J., 2002. Dutch Coffee Shops and Trends in Cannabis Use. *Addictive Behaviors*, 27 (6), 851–866. [Online]. Available from: https://doi.org/10.1016/S0306-4603(02)00291-5 [Accessed 3 December 2023].

Labate, B. C., and Cavnar, C., 2014. *Ayahuasca Shamanism in the Amazon and Beyond*. Oxford: Oxford University Press.

Laqueur, H., 2015. Uses and Abuses of Drug Decriminalization in Portugal. *Law and Social Inquiry*, 40 (3), 746–781. [Online]. Available from: https://doi.org/10.1111/lsi.12104 [Accessed 8 November 2023].

Lu, H. C., and Mackie, K., 2016. An Introduction to the Endogenous Cannabinoid System. *Biological Psychiatry*, 79 (7), 516–525. [Online]. Available from: https://doi.org/10.1016%2Fj.biopsych.2015.07.028 [Accessed 28 May 2023].

Maccoun, R., 2011. What Can We Learn From the Dutch Cannabis Coffeeshop Experience? *Addiction, 106 (11),* 1899–1910. [Online]. Available from: https://doi.org/10.1111/j.1360-0443.2011.03572.x [Accessed 8 November 2023].

Maccoun, R., and Reuter, P., 1997. Interpreting Dutch Cannabis Policy: Reasoning By Analogy in the Legalization Debate. *Science*, 278 (5335), 47–52. [Online]. Available from: http://dx.doi.org/10.1126/science.278.5335.47 [Accessed 1 December 2023].

Maccoun, R., and Reuter, P., 2001. *Drug War Heresies: Learning from Other Vices, Times, and Places*. Cambridge: Cambridge University Press.

Martin, J., 2014. *Drugs on the Darknet: How Cryptomarkets are Transforming the Global Trade in Illicit Drugs*. London: Palgrave Pivot.

Mcallister, W. B., 2000. *Drug Diplomacy in the Twentieth Century*. London and New York: Routledge.

Mckenna, D. J., 2004. Clinical Investigations of the Therapeutic Potential of Ayahuasca: Rationale and Regulatory Challenges. *Pharmacology and Therapeutics*, 102 (2), 111–129. [Online]. Available from: https://pubmed.ncbi.nlm.nih.gov/15163593/ [Accessed 27 May 2023].

Mithoefer, M. C., Mithoefer, A. T., Feduccia, A. A., Jerome, L., Wagner, M., Wymer, J., … and Yazar-Klosinski, B., 2018. 3,4-methylenedioxymethamphetamine (MDMA)-assisted psychotherapy for post-traumatic stress disorder in military veterans, firefighters, and police officers: A randomised, double-blind, dose-response, phase 2 clinical trial. *The Lancet Psychiatry, 5* (6), 486–497. [Online]. Available from: https://doi.org/10.1016/s2215-0366(18)30135-4 [Accessed 30 May 2023].

Moffitt, T. E., Harrington, H., Caspi, A., Kim-Cohen, J., Goldberg, D., Gregory, A. M., and Poulton, R., 2007. Depression and Generalized Anxiety Disorder: Cumulative and Sequential Comorbidity in a Birth Cohort Followed Prospectively to Age 32 Years. *Archives of General Psychiatry, 64* (6), 651–660. [Online]. Available from: http://dx.doi.org/10.1001/archpsyc.64.6.651 [Accessed 30 May 2023].

Montanari, L., Royuela, L., Hasselberg, I., and Vandam, L., 2022. *Prison and Drugs in Europe: Current and Future Challenges*. European Monitoring Centre for Drugs and Drug Addiction. [Online]. Available from: https://www.emcdda.europa.eu/publications/insights/prison-and-drugs-in-europe_en [Accessed 12 November 2023].

Naranjo, P., 1981. Social Function of Coca in Pre-Columbian America. *Journal of Ethnopharmacology*, 3 (2–3), 161–172. [Online]. Available from: https://doi.org/10.1016/0378-8741(81)90052-0 [Accessed 26 May 2023].

Nellis, A., 2016. *The Color of Justice: Racial and Ethnic Disparity in State Prisons.* The Sentencing Project. [Online]. Available from: https://www.sentencingproject.org/reports/the-color-of-justice-racial-and-ethnic-disparity-in-state-prisons-the-sentencing-project/ [Accessed 6 June 2023].

Nichols, D.E., 2016. Psychedelics. *Pharmacological Reviews*, 68 (2), 264–355. [Online]. Available from: https://doi.org/10.1124/pr.115.011478 [Accessed 28 May 2023].

ONDCP, 2014. *National Drug Control Strategy. Data Supplement 2014.* Office of National Drug Control Policy. [Online]. Available from: https://obamawhitehouse.archives.gov/sites/default/files/ondcp/policy-and-research/ndcs_data_supplement_2014.pdf [Accessed 21 October 2023].

Reuter, P. (2013) 'Why has US drug policy changed so little over 30 years?', *Crime and Justice*, 42(1), pp. 75–140. Available at: https://www.jstor.org/stable/10.1086/670818 [Accessed 1 March 2025].

Rhodes, T., and Hedrich, D., (eds.), 2010. *Harm Reduction: Evidence, Impacts and Challenges.* Lisbon: European Monitoring Centre for Drugs and Drug Addiction. [Online]. Available from: https://www.emcdda.europa.eu/publications/monographs/harm-reduction_en [Accessed 11 November 2023].

Rolles, S., and Murkin, G., 2013. *How to Regulate Cannabis: A Practical Guide.* Transform Drug Policy Foundation. [Online]. Available from: https://transformdrugs.org/publications/how-to-regulate-cannabis-3rd-ed [Accessed 11 November 2023].

Rotermann, M., 2020. *Analysis of Trends in the Prevalence of Cannabis Use and Related Metrics in Canada. Statistics Canada.* [Online]. Available from: https://www150.statcan.gc.ca/n1/pub/82-003-x/2019006/article/00001-eng.htm [Accessed 11 November 2023].

Smith, L. L., Yan, F., Charles, M., Mohiuddin, K., Tyus, D., Adekeye, O., and Holden, K. B., 2017. Exploring the Link Between Substance Use and Mental Health Status: What can we learn from self-medication theory? *Journal of Health Care for the Poor and Underserved*, 28 (2S), 113–131. [Online]. Available from: https://doi.org/10.1353/hpu.2017.0056 [Accessed 11 November 2023].

Schultes, R. E., and Raffauf, R. F., 1990. *The Healing Forest: Medicinal and Toxic Plants of the Northwest Amazonia.* Dioscorides Press.

Schultes, R. E., Hofmann, A., and Rätsch, C., 2001. *Plants of the Gods: Their Sacred, Healing, and Hallucinogenic Powers.* Healing Arts Press.

Single Convention on Narcotic Drugs, 1961. [Online]. United Nations. Available from: https://www.unodc.org/pdf/convention_1961_en.pdf [Accessed 3 June 2023].

Smith, H., 2000. *Cleansing the Doors of Perception: The Religious Significance of Entheogenic Plants and Chemicals*. Tarcher/Putnam.

Spence, J. D., 1999. *The Search for Modern China*. W. W. Norton & Company.

Sullivan, R. J., Hagen, E. H., and Hammerstein, P., 2008. Revealing the Paradox of Drug Reward in Human Evolution. *Proceedings of the Royal Society B: Biological Sciences*, 275 (1640), 1231–1241. [Online]. Available from: https://www.ncbi.nlm.nih.gov/pmc/articles/PMC2367444/ [Accessed 27 May 2023].

United Nations Convention Against Illicit Traffic in Narcotic Drugs and Psychotropic Substances, 1988. [Online]. United Nations. Available from: https://www.unodc.org/pdf/convention_1988_en.pdf [Accessed 4 June 2023].

UNODC (United Nations Office on Drugs and Crime), 2018. *World Drug Report 2018. Executive Summary: Conclusions and Policy Implications*. Vienna: UNODC. [Online]. Available from: https://www.unodc.org/wdr2018/prelaunch/WDR18_Booklet_1_EXSUM.pdf [Accessed 27 May 2023].

UNODC, 2019. *World Drug Report 2019*. Vienna: UNODC. [Online]. Available from: https://wdr.unodc.org/wdr2019/ [Accessed 27 May 2023].

UNODC, 2020. *World Drug Report 2020*. Vienna: UNODC. [Online]. Available from: https://wdr.unodc.org/wdr2020/index2020.html [Accessed 20 October 2023].

UNODC, 2023. *World Drug Report 2023*. Vienna: UNODC. [Online]. Available from: https://www.unodc.org/unodc/en/data-and-analysis/world-drug-report-2023.html [Accessed 4 March 2024].

Van Amsterdam, J., Opperhuizen, A., Koeter, M., and Van Den Brink, W., 2010. Ranking the harm of alcohol, tobacco and illicit drugs for the individual and the population. *European Addiction Research*, 21 (2), 202–207. [Online]. Available from: https://doi.org/10.1159/000317249 [Accessed 15 September 2023].

Volkow, N. D., Baler, R. D., Compton, W. M., and Weiss, S. R., 2014. Adverse Health Effects of Marijuana se. *New England Journal of Medicine, 370* (23), 2219–2227. [Online]. Available from: https://doi.org/10.1056/NEJMra1402309 [Accessed 30 May 2023].

Volkow, N.D., Michaelides, M. and Baler, R., 2019. The Neuroscience of Drug Reward and Addiction. *Physiological Reviews*, 99 (4), 2115–2140. [Online]. Available from: https://doi.org/10.1152/physrev.00014.2018 [Accessed 30 May 2023].

Volkow, N. D., Jones, E. B., Einstein, E. B., and Wargo, E. M., 2020. Prevention and Treatment of Opioid Misuse and Addiction: A Review. *JAMA Psychiatry*, 76 (2), 208–216. [Online]. Available from: https://doi.org/10.1001/jamapsychiatry.2018.3126 [Accessed 28 May 2023].

Werse, B., and Morgenstern, C., 2012. How to Handle Legal Highs? Findings from a German Online Survey and Considerations on Drug Policy Issues. *Drugs and Alcohol Today*, 12 (4), 222–231. [Online]. https://doi.org/10.1108/17459261211286636 [Accessed 25 May 2023].

Wilson, N., Kariisa, M., Seth, P., Smith, H. IV, and Davis, N. L., 2020. Drug and Opioid Overdose Deaths – United States, 2017–2018. *MMWR Morbidity and Mortality Weekly Report*, 69 (11), 290–297. Available from: https://www.cdc.gov/mmwr/volumes/69/wr/mm6911a4.htm [Accessed 30 May 2023].

Wise, R. A., 2008. Dopamine and Reward: The Anhedonia Hypothesis 30 Years On. *Neurotoxicity Research*, 14 (2–3), 169–183. [Online]. Available from: https://www.ncbi.nlm.nih.gov/pmc/articles/PMC3155128/ [Accessed 25 May 2023].

WHO (World Health Organization), 1986. *Cancer Pain Management*. Geneva: WHO [Online]. Available from: https://apps.who.int/iris/bitstream/handle/10665/43944/9241561009_eng.pdf [Accessed 27 May 2023].

WHO, 2014. *Consolidated Guidelines on HIV Prevention, Diagnosis, Treatment and Care for Key Populations*. Geneva: WHO. [Online]. Available from: https://iris.who.int/bitstream/handle/10665/128048/9789241507431_eng.pdf?sequence=1 [Accessed 11 November 2023].

WHO, 2015. *World Health Statistics 2015*. Geneva: WHO. [Online]. Available from: https://www.who.int/docs/default-source/gho-documents/world-health-statistic-reports/world-health-statistics-2015.pdf [Accessed 27 May 2023].

Wouters, M., Benschop, A., and Korf, D. J., 2010. *Local Politics and Retail Cannabis Markets: The Case of the Dutch Coffeeshops. The International Journal on Drug Policy*, 21 (4), 315–320 [Online]. Available from: https://doi.org/10.1016/j.drugpo.2010.01.003 [Accessed 7 September 2023].

Young, S. N., 2007. How to Increase Serotonin in the Human Brain Without Drugs. *Journal of Psychiatry and Neuroscience*, 32 (6), 394–399. [Online]. Available from: https://www.ncbi.nlm.nih.gov/pmc/articles/PMC2077351/ [Accessed 25 May 2023].

Zanos, P., and Gould, T. D., 2018. Mechanisms of Ketamine Action as an Antidepressant. *Molecular Psychiatry*, 23 (4), 801–811. [Online]. Available from: https://doi.org/10.1038/mp.2017.255 [Accessed 28 May 2023].

Tomas Girdenis

Coherence in Criminal Policy for Offenses Against Justice That Obstruct the Investigation of a Case

The System of Offenses Against Justice in the Criminal Code of the Republic of Lithuania and Its Coherence

The effective combating of crimes against justice is an indispensable element of every state's criminal policy. Only by ensuring a safe environment for participants in criminal proceedings can a smooth criminal trial be expected. Therefore, the effective combating of crimes against justice requires coherence, both in criminal law and in the case law implementing it. Importantly, coherence between the provisions of the special and general part of the Criminal Code is essential for effective criminal policy. A lack of coherence between criminal law rules can lead to highly ineffective criminal policy. This analysis of both criminal law rules and case law shows precisely how a lack of coherence between criminal law rules leads to an ineffective and, in some cases, totally non-deterrent criminal policy in the fight against crimes against justice.

Chapter XXXIV of the Criminal Code of the Republic of Lithuania (hereinafter – the CC) is devoted to crimes and misdemeanors against justice. Criminal offenses against justice can be broadly divided into two groups: 1) offenses that obstruct the investigation or trial of a case; and 2) offenses that obstruct the implementation of legal decisions. The following acts may be included among the offenses of obstructing the investigation or trial of a case: 1) obstructing the activities of a judge, prosecutor, pre-trial investigation officer, or advocate (Art. 231 of the CC); 2) contempt of court (Art. 232 of the CC); 3) influencing a witness, victim, expert, specialist, or translator (Art. 233 of the CC); 4) influencing a victim to reconcile with the perpetrator (Art. 234 of the CC); 5) false complaint, statement, report, testimony, conclusion, or translation (Art. 235 of the CC); 6) false accusation or report of an unlawful offense (Art. 236 of the CC); 7) concealment of the offense or of the perpetrator of the offense (Art. 237 of the CC); 8) failure to report the offense (Art. 238 of the CC); and 9) disclosure of data of a pre-trial investigation without authorization (Art. 247 of the CC). The following acts may be included among the offenses impeding the implementation of legal decisions: 1) obstruction of the activities of a bailiff (Art. 231 of the CC); 2) disorganization of the work of a custodial institution (Art. 239 of the CC); 3) release of a prisoner (Art. 240 of the CC); 4) escape of a prisoner

(Art. 241 of the CC); 5) evasion of the execution of a custodial sentence or of a prison sentence, or of the return to the place of custody (Art. 242 of the CC); 6) evasion of penal measures (Art. 243 of the CC); 7) failure to comply with a sentence imposed on a legal person (Art. 244 of the CC); 8) failure to comply with a non-punitive court decision (Art. 245 of the CC); and 9) transfer, concealment, destruction, or damage of inventoried or seized property or property subject to a temporary restraint of title (Art. 246 of the CC).

When analyzing the penalties for obstruction of justice offenses in the CC, it can be noted that the legislator does not consider these offenses to be particularly dangerous, as most of them are minor offenses, with the most severe penalty being imprisonment for up to 1 or 2 years. In exceptional cases, usually when coercion is used to commit these crimes or when other qualifying features are present, these crimes are of a minor nature, with the most severe penalty being imprisonment of up to 4 or 5 years. Criminal offenses of evading a court order are even less serious, are generally considered misdemeanors, which are not punishable by imprisonment or as a minor offense, and are punishable by up to 2 years' imprisonment. One exception is the offense of concealment of seized property, which can be punished by up to 7 years' imprisonment, depending on the value of the property. Only offenses involving obstruction of serving a custodial sentence are punishable by stricter penalties – up to a maximum of 3, 6, or 15 years of imprisonment, depending on the seriousness of the offense and the consequences caused.

Although the CC has as many as 9 articles devoted to the offenses of obstructing the investigation of a case, the main offenses in this category are: Art. 231 of the CC, i.e., obstruction of the activities of a judge, prosecutor, pre-trial investigation officer, or advocate; and Art. 233 of the CC, i.e., influence on a witness, victim, expert, specialist, or interpreter. The seriousness of these offenses in the eyes of the legislator is essentially identical. Simple obstruction of the subjects of the investigation or influence on other participants in the proceedings is punishable, among other penalties, by up to 2 years of imprisonment, and the penalty is increased to up to 4 years of imprisonment if the offense is committed by means of physical or other coercion. If physical injuries are caused during these crimes, this would lead to criminal liability under the norms for the qualified commission of the relevant injuries: minor bodily injury is punishable by imprisonment of up to 5 years, serious bodily injury is punishable by imprisonment of between 2 and 12 years, and murder is punishable by imprisonment of between 8 and 20 years, or life imprisonment.

Assessing whether such sanctions are sufficient and dissuasive is quite difficult. However, an analysis of the CC allows us to see how they fit in with other criminal offenses prohibited in Lithuania. Although the interpretation of a dangerous act is broader under Art. 231 of the CC than under Art. 233 of the CC, they both have in common that they prohibit any influence on the participants in the proceedings. The Supreme Court of Lithuania, when interpreting the element of obstruction under Art. 231 of the CC, stated that "obstruction as a criminal offense may consist of both active and passive acts [...], obstruction may take the form of a demand, request, advice, instruction, etc." (2K-350-693/2017, 2017). It is therefore logical to look at how the CC prohibits other unlawful influences on persons.

The closest norm for obstruction of the investigation of a case, which specifically relates to influencing the subjects of the investigation, is bribery (Art. 227 of the CC). Bribery is essentially the obstruction of an investigation where the subjects of the investigation are influenced by the payment of a bribe. Bribery is in fact a special norm in relation to Art. 231(1) of the CC. However, simple bribery by giving a bribe for a lawful act or omission in the exercise of authority is already punishable by up to 4 years of imprisonment, bribery for an unlawful act or omission in the exercise of authority is punishable by up to 5 years of imprisonment, and the giving of a large bribe is punishable by up to 7 years of imprisonment. So, we have a rather strange situation where influencing the subjects of an investigation by means of a bribe is punished almost twice as harshly as influencing them by means of coercion. An equally interesting picture emerges when we compare the effects of psychological violence on the subjects of an investigation or other participants in a case, with the norms prohibiting psychological violence based on other types of action. Here, the mere act of making an intense threat to any person is considered to be terrorizing a person and is punishable by up to 4 years of imprisonment – the same as if the threat involved influencing both the investigation and the other participants in the case. In other words, no additional, more severe liability is provided for if the threat is intended to influence the investigation. If a person uses coercion to enforce a real or perceived right, they are exercising self-willed conduct and can be sentenced to up to 5 years of imprisonment. The penalties are even stricter if psychological coercion is used to force a person to transfer property. For example, if psychological coercion is used to demand the performance of an act of a financial nature, it is considered extortion and is punishable by up to 6 years of imprisonment, and up to 10 years of imprisonment if the extortion of high-value property is involved. On a theoretical level, it is possible to envisage absurd situations where a person who uses psychological coercion against a victim directly and demands the transfer of a high-value asset should be punished 2.5 times more severely than if they were to use the same coercion against a judge demanding that they be awarded the same high-value asset, when perhaps the opposite should be true.

Thus, a comparison of these norms shows that the norms and sanctions in the special part of the CC and the penalties for them are not in line with the penalties for offenses against justice, and that the penalties for the offenses against justice under investigation are too lenient and do not reflect the potential seriousness of the offenses.

Criminal Liability for Offenses Against Justice in the United Kingdom and the United States of America

To paint a fuller picture of the adequacy of Lithuanian criminal policy in combating crimes against justice, it is necessary to look at the broader context, i.e., how other countries combat these crimes.

Since Lithuania is part of the continental legal system, it would be natural to analyze the criminal policy of the European Union (EU) countries on this issue. However, the EU countries are dominated by the rather abstract sentencing rules of the continental legal tradition. Therefore, to assess the fairness of the offenses in question not only in terms of formal criminality (the penalties laid down in the law), but also in terms of actual sentencing aspects, the EU countries become inappropriate for the purpose of the study without a separate analysis of the case law of those countries regarding the sentencing of penalties. The United Kingdom (UK) and the United States of America (USA) were therefore chosen for the analysis of foreign countries. The reason for this choice is that the criminal policy of these countries is moving toward a more detailed formalization of sentencing through the adoption of sentencing guides for the courts. It is the more detailed formalization of the sentencing process that allows for a more precise assessment not only of the possible sanctions provided for in their law, but also of the specific criteria for sentencing in the analysis of offenses against justice. The choice of these non-EU countries thus enables a more accurate assessment of the real criminal policy in the fight against crimes against justice, and not just that which is formalized in law.

Punishing crimes of perverting the course of justice in the UK

In the UK, in order to charge a person for perverting the course of justice, prosecutors must prove that an accused person committed an act or series of acts which has or have a tendency to pervert and which is or are intended to pervert the course of public justice (Crown Prosecution Service 2022). According to the guidance of the Crown Prosecution Service of the UK, the following types of act may constitute the offense of perverting the course of Justice:

> persuading, or attempting to persuade, by intimidation, harm or otherwise, a witness not to give evidence, to alter his evidence or to give false evidence; interference with jurors with a view to influencing their verdict; false alibis and interference with evidence or exhibits, for example blood and DNA samples; providing false details of identity to the police or courts with a view to avoiding the consequences of a police investigation or prosecution; giving false information, or agreeing to give false information, to the police with a view to frustrating a police inquiry; for example, lying as to who was driving when a road traffic accident occurred; lending a driving licence to another to produce to the police following a notice to produce, thereby avoiding an offence of driving whilst disqualified being discovered; agreeing to give false evidence; concealing or destroying evidence concerning a police investigation to avoid arrest; assisting others to evade arrest for a significant period of time; and making a false allegation which wrongfully exposes another person to the risk of arrest, imprisonment pending trial, and possible wrongful conviction and sentence (Crown Prosecution Service 2022).

According to the Charging Standard, prosecutors, in deciding whether or not it is in the public interest to proceed with charges of perverting the course of justice, must consider the nature of the proceedings with which the defendant was trying to interfere and the consequences, or possible consequences, of their interference (Crown Prosecution Service 2022). For example, it is likely that perverting the course of justice will be the appropriate charge when: "the acts wrongfully expose another person to risk of arrest or prosecution; the obstruction of a police investigation is premeditated, prolonged, or elaborate; the acts hide from the police the commission of a serious crime; […] concerted attempts to interfere with jurors; attacks on counsel or the judge; or conduct designed to cause the proceedings to be completely abandoned; a concerted attempt has been made to influence significant witnesses, particularly if accompanied by serious violence" (Crown Prosecution Service 2022) and so on.

Thus, under UK law, both unjustified prejudice to litigants and obstruction of justice in general, depending on the seriousness of the offense, can be regarded as representing the crime of perverting the course of justice. However, it should be noted that in less serious cases, tampering with a witness may also be punishable under Section 51 of the Criminal Justice and Public Order Act 1994. If the offense is not serious enough according to the factors outlined in the General Charging Principles to justify charges of perverting the course of justice, Section 51 of the Criminal Justice and Public Order Act 1994 is applicable, and this act can invoke up to 5 years of imprisonment (Crown Prosecution Service 2022). However, when a person is sentenced for perverting the course of justice, other rules apply.

In this case, the Sentencing Guidelines (Sentencing Council 2023) must be used. It is worth mentioning that the Sentencing Guidelines for Perverting the Course of Justice are effective only from October 1, 2023. According to the Guidelines, perverting the course of justice is punishable by anything from a community order to 7 years in custody. For the purposes of sentencing under the Guidelines, it is first necessary to determine the category of the offense, which depends on culpability and damage. Culpability can be high, medium, or low. For example, high culpability can be demonstrated by one or more of the following: "conduct over a sustained period of time; sophisticated and/or planned nature of conduct; underlying offence very serious; breach of trust or abuse of position or office" (Sentencing Council 2023), whereas low culpability can be observed if the offense was "unplanned and/or limited in scope and duration; unsophisticated nature of conduct; underlying offence was not serious; involved through coercion, intimidation or exploitation or as a result of domestic abuse; offender's responsibility substantially reduced by mental disorder or learning disability" (Sentencing Council 2023). Level of harm falls into three categories and can be assessed by a number of factors. For example, Category 1 harm (the most serious category) is determined when: "serious consequences for an innocent party as a result of the offense (for example time spent in custody/arrest); serious distress caused to an innocent party (for example loss of reputation); serious impact on administration of justice; substantial delay caused to the course of justice" (Sentencing Council 2023) and Category 3 is identified when all of the abovementioned factors had limited impact. So, in case of high culpability and serious harm (category 1), a person should be sentenced to 2–7 years of custody, with a starting point of 4 years of custody. In case of low culpability but serious harm (category 1) or high culpability but limited harm (category 3), a person should be sentenced from 9 months to 2 years of custody, with a starting point of 1 year of custody. Only low culpability with limited harm (category 3) could lead to the mildest punishment, ranging from a high-level community order to 9 months of custody, with a starting point of 6 months of custody. Of course, "once the starting point is established, the court should consider further aggravating and mitigating factors and previous convictions so as to adjust the sentence within the range" (Crown Prosecution Service 2023).

Punishing Obstruction of Justice Crimes in the USA

At the federal level in the USA, criminal acts are prohibited by the United States Code (USC). Obstruction of justice is considered as any act that involves interference with the orderly administration of law and justice (Chang *et al.* 2023).

Crimes related to obstruction of justice are prohibited by §§ 1501–1521 of Title 18 in the USC. These provisions guarding against obstruction of justice address very particular behaviors, but the criminal acts closest to our research are established in §§ 1503, 1505, 1510, and 1512. The central provision in this statutory arrangement is § 1503, which is known as the catch-all provision. This provision prohibits obstruction of justice, jury tampering, or any attempts to use force, threats, or coercion to influence, obstruct, or impede the due administration of justice (Roman *et al.* 2018). "Related sections include §§ 1505, 1510, and 1512, which prohibit the obstruction of proceedings before departments, agencies, and committees, the obstruction of criminal investigations, and tampering with a witness, victim, or informant" (Roman *et al.* 2018). Furthermore, § 1503 prohibits "influencing or injuring officer or juror generally," § 1505 "Obstruction of proceedings before departments, agencies, and committees," § 1510 "Obstruction of criminal investigations" and § 1512 "Tampering with a witness, victim, or an informant" (USC 2023). Due to the limited scope of this study, only §§ 1503 and 1512 will be further analyzed.

It is necessary to emphasize that § 1503 addresses conduct that obstructs justice in both civil and criminal judicial proceedings. Section 1503(a) can be viewed as having two parts. The first part of § 1503(a) protects jurors and judicial officers from threats, intimidation, and retaliation. The second part of § 1503(a) forbids corrupt endeavors to influence, obstruct, or impede the due administration of justice (Chang *et al.* 2023).

If obstruction of justice is not related to murder, it can be punishable by imprisonment for not more than 10 years, a fine under this title, or both (USC 2023). Additionally, according to § 1503, "if the offense under this section occurs in connection with a trial of a criminal case, and the act in violation of this section involves the threat of physical force or physical force, the maximum term of imprisonment which may be imposed for the offense shall be the higher of that otherwise provided by law or the maximum term that could have been imposed for any offense charged in such case" (USC 2023). "When the act of obstruction is a homicide, the maximum penalty for a § 1503 violation is life imprisonment or death. If the obstruction involves an attempted killing or an offense against a petit juror, the maximum punishment is twenty years of imprisonment and a fine" (Chang *et al.* 2023). The sentencing guidelines (United States Sentencing Commission 2021b) provide for more detailed sentencing.

"Defendants convicted under § 1503 are sentenced in accordance with § 2J1.2 of the United States Sentencing Guidelines ('Guidelines'), which carries with it a base offense level of fourteen" (Chang *et al.* 2023). The base offense level of 14 means that, depending on the criminal history of the defendant, this offense is punishable by 15–21 months of imprisonment in case of the 1st criminal history category, and up to 37–46 months of imprisonment in case of the sixth category of criminal history. It is also worth mentioning that a base offense level of 14 also means that this crime falls into Zone D. According to the sentencing guidelines, "if the applicable guideline range is in Zone D of the Sentencing Table, the minimum term shall be satisfied by a sentence of imprisonment" (United States Sentencing Commission 2021a). So, a fine or probationary sentence alone is not allowed by the sentencing guidelines, and real imprisonment is the only option.

"Under the Guidelines, if the obstruction offense causes physical injury or property damage (or threatens to cause either), the offense level increases by eight" (Chang *et al.* 2023). This means that the total offense level is equal to 22, and it is punishable by from 41–51 months of imprisonment to 84–105 months of imprisonment, depending on the category of criminal history (United States Sentencing Commission 2021b). Of course, there are more aggravating circumstances in the sentencing guidelines, but these are the closest to the main aggravating elements of a crime established in the Lithuanian CC, so they are the most suitable for comparison.

Section 1512 prohibits witness tampering and protects "any person," which is broadly construed to include potential witnesses, grand jury witnesses, excused witnesses, and state investigators (Chang *et al.* 2023). Section 1512(a) forbids tampering with a witness, victim, or an informant related to (a) (1) killing or attempting to kill another person and (a) (2) the use of physical force or the threat of physical force against any person or any attempt to do so (USC 2023). "To prove witness tampering under § 1512(b), the prosecution must show that the defendant: (i) knowingly (ii) engaged in intimidation, physical force, threats, misleading conduct, or corrupt persuasion toward another person (iii) with intent to influence, delay, or prevent testimony or cause any person to withhold a record, object, document, or testimony (iv) from an official proceeding" (Chang *et al.* 2023). Corrupt persuasion includes deterring or attempting to influence testimony through sheer persuasion with a corrupt purpose, and "corrupt persuasion" is defined as persuading someone not to fulfil a legal duty (Chang *et al.* 2023).

If witness tampering was committed while using physical force, as provided in § 1512(a), the punishment is based on the amount of physical harm inflicted by the crime. In the case of the threat to use physical force against any person under § 1512(a), or in case of witness tampering under § 1512(b), a person can be a subject to imprisonment for not more than 20 years. So, when sentencing for witness tampering under § 1512(b), as in the case of § 1503(a), § 2J1.2 2 of the United States Sentencing Guidelines applies, and determines a base offense level of 14. If the offense causes physical injury or property damage (or threatens to cause either), the offense level increases by eight (United States Sentencing Commission 2021a).

Obstruction of justice is also considered an aggravating circumstance and, under § 3C1.1 of the Guidelines, if a person commits other crimes then the applicable base offense level is increased by two. Section 3C1.1 acts independently of the obstruction of justice sections discussed earlier. As such, this two-level increase does not apply to convictions under § 1503 or § 1512 unless the defendant obstructed or attempted to obstruct the investigation or trial of an obstruction of justice count (Chang *et al.* 2023).

An analysis of the criminal policy of the UK and the USA in the fight against crimes against justice shows that these countries have a much stricter policy than Lithuania in this regard. In the UK, for example, the criminalization of the most serious cases of offenses against justice starts from 4 years of imprisonment, with the possibility of imposing up to 7 years of imprisonment, whereas in Lithuania, 4 years is the maximum penalty for an offense of a similar nature. In the USA, the criminal policy is even stricter, with a minimum guideline of up to 7 years of imprisonment for offenses of a similar nature, without additional circumstances.

Sentencing for Crimes Against Justice in Lithuanian Case Law

Having concluded that the Lithuanian criminal policy is not strict enough at the legislative level alone in combating the crimes against justice in question, it is necessary to look even deeper, i.e., at how this legislative policy manifests itself at the level of case law. Therefore, to assess the practical criminal policy of Lithuania in the fight against crimes against justice, a study of Lithuanian case law was conducted. The penalties under two articles of the CC, i.e., Art. 231 (Obstruction of the activities of a judge, public prosecutor, pre-trial investigation officer, lawyer, or bailiff) and Art. 233 (Influencing a witness, victim, expert, specialist, or translator), were examined. Sentencing policy was examined from two perspectives. Firstly, the sentences imposed separately for each of the offenses in question were examined. However, as the offenses against justice are related to the impact on the investigation of the case (on the investigators or on other participants in the case), it is clear that the offenses against justice that are being investigated are usually (but not always) committed with the aim of avoiding responsibility for other offenses committed previously. In such cases, the person is usually tried both for the previous offense(s) and for subsequent offenses against justice. Real accountability for crimes against justice is therefore achieved through the process of combining the sentences. To fully assess accountability for crimes against justice, it was therefore necessary to also carry out a study on the impact of the process of combining sentences on accountability.

In order to analyze the sentencing policy, all sentences and criminal orders (a criminal order is a sentence issued by a court without a hearing) handed down by the courts of first instance in the Republic of Lithuania in the last 5 years, i.e., from January 1, 2018, to December 31, 2022, were analyzed. The sentencing of the following offenses was therefore examined:

1) 7 convictions were investigated under Art. 231(1) of the CC (Obstruction of a judge, prosecutor, pre-trial investigation officer, lawyer or an official of the International Criminal Court or other international judicial authority in the performance of their duties related to the investigation or examination of a case of a criminal, civil, administrative, or international judicial authority. It should be noted that Art. 231 of the CC also criminalizes obstructing a bailiff in the execution of a judgment, but as this study focused only on offenses against justice related to influencing the investigation of a case, and obstructing a bailiff in the execution of a judgment does not normally affect the investigation of a case, convictions related to obstructing a bailiff were not investigated);
2) 4 convictions were investigated under Art. 231(2) of the CC (Obstruction of the aforementioned officials by means of violence or other coercion);
3) 51 convictions were investigated under Art. 233(1) of the CC (Influencing a witness, a victim, an expert, a specialist, or an interpreter);
4) 6 convictions were investigated under Art. 233(3) of the CC (Influencing a witness, a victim, an expert, a specialist, or a translator by means of violence or other coercion).

At the same time, it was also sought to investigate sentences for very similar offenses, i.e., influencing a witness, victim, expert, specialist, or translator to give false testimony to the Seimas Special Investigation Commission or the Seimas during the impeachment proceedings (Art. 233 (2) of the CC) and influencing the victim to reconcile with the perpetrator through physical, or other forms of violence (Art. 234 of the CC). However, no convictions for these articles in were found the abovementioned period. The verdicts were selected using the publicly available Liteko (Teismai.lt, n.d.) Lithuanian court information system. Cases were selected using the criminal case classifier. In the analysis of the sentences imposed, both repeated convictions of the same person for separate offenses and convictions of separate persons in the same case were considered as individual cases (convictions). Thus, a total of 68 convictions were examined.

Sentencing for Separate Crimes Against Justice

The offense provided for in Art. 231(1) of the CC is a minor offense, punishable by community service or a fine, or by the restriction of liberty or imprisonment for up to 2 years. Of the seven persons convicted under Art. 231(1) of the CC for obstructing the subjects of the investigation, 57% (4 convictions) were sentenced to imprisonment and 43% (3 convictions) to alternative penalties (2 fines and 1 community service). As a rule, alternative sentences to imprisonment were imposed on first-time offenders (2 out of 3 convictions, i.e., 67% of cases), whereas in all cases where a custodial sentence was imposed (4 out of 4 convictions, i.e., 100%), the persons were not on trial for the first time. In general (3 out of 4 convictions, i.e., 75% of cases), the sentences imposed were significantly lower than the average penalty provided for in the law (the average penalty provided for was 1 year and 1.5 months; the average sentence imposed was 5.6 months), and only once (25% of the cases) was a sentence imposed that was slightly higher than the average penalty provided for in the legislation (i.e., a prison sentence of 1 year and 2 months).

Art. 231(2) of the CC imposes a stricter liability for the obstruction of the subjects of an investigation by violence or other coercion. The offense therefore falls into the category of less serious offenses, punishable by a fine or arrest or imprisonment of up to 4 years. Of the four persons convicted under Art. 231(2) of the CC, in 50% of cases (2 convictions) a penalty involving imprisonment was imposed (in 1 case 1 year and 6 months' imprisonment, and in 1 case 15 days' arrest), and in the other 50% of cases (2 convictions) a fine of €1,883 was imposed. The abovementioned imprisonment was imposed on a person who had already been tried for the 15th time, and the actual sentence was reduced to 1 year of imprisonment because the case was dealt with under the simplified procedure. In all other cases, the persons were tried for the first time. However, it should be noted that the actual prison sentence imposed was also half the statutory average for this offense – i.e., 2 years and 1.5 months.

Art. 233(1) of the CC provides for liability for influencing participants in a case to give false testimony. This offense is minor and may be punishable by public works or a fine, restriction of liberty, arrest, or imprisonment for up to 2 years. Of the 51 persons convicted under this Article, 59% (30 convictions) were sentenced to a custodial sentence, 37% (19 convictions) to alternatives to imprisonment, and 4% (2 persons) were exempted from criminal liability. Imprisonment was imposed in 47 % of cases (24 convictions), of which 83% (20 convictions) were not the first time the person was tried. Arrest was imposed in 12% of cases (6 convictions), of which 83% (5 convictions) were not the first time the person was tried. Of the sentences imposed in connection with imprisonment, 37% (9 imprisonment and 2 arrest) were suspended. In 50% of these cases the sentence was close to the average statutory sentence of 1 year and 1.5 months of imprisonment (12 convictions were sentenced to between 9 months and 1 year and 1 month of imprisonment, with an average of 11.7 months), while in the other 50% of these cases the sentence was not close to the average statutory sentence (12 convictions were sentenced to between 4 months and 6 months of imprisonment, with an average of 5.2 months). In none of these cases was the sentence imposed higher than the average penalty of imprisonment provided for by law. The sentences of arrest were generally close to the statutory average, i.e., in 83% of cases (5 convictions) an average of 48 days of arrest was imposed, and in only 17% of cases (1 conviction) was the sentence imposed closer to the maximum limit of 72 days of arrest. As mentioned above, of the 19 convictions in which a non-custodial sentence was imposed, 47% (9 convictions) were fined (an average of €3,399), 37% (7 convictions) were sentenced to a restriction of liberty (an average of 6.9 months) and only 16% (3 convictions) were given a community service sentence (an average of 328 hours of work).

Art. 233(3) of the CC provides for liability for influencing participants in a case to give false testimony by means of violence or other coercion. This offense is classified in the category of less serious offenses and is punishable by arrest or imprisonment for up to 4 years. In all 6 convictions (i.e., 100% of the cases), a prison sentence was incurred, but in 2 (33% of the cases), a suspension of the execution of the sentence was applied. In all six convictions (i.e., 100% of the cases), this was not the first time these persons were tried. In 50% of these convictions (3 convictions), a sentence of arrest close to the average sentence provided for in the law was imposed (55 days of arrest on average against an average sentence of 52.5 days of arrest), while in the other 50 % of cases (3 convictions) the sentence was imprisonment. Of the custodial sentences imposed, all were slightly lower than the average sentence provided for in the law, i.e., an average of 1 year and 7 months of imprisonment, compared to an average of 2 years and 1.5 months of imprisonment.

Overall, the results of the sentencing practice show that the state's harshest response to crimes against justice, which can be considered as cases in which a real custodial sentence is imposed without suspension of sentence, is in fact rather limited. In the case of the analyzed acts against justice without physical or psychological violence, under Art. 231(1) of the CC, a real penalty of imprisonment was imposed in 57% of cases (4 convictions), with an average sentence of 7.8 months of imprisonment. Under Art. 233(1) of the CC, a real penalty of imprisonment was imposed in 29% of cases (15 convictions), with an average sentence of 8.7 months of imprisonment. If the influence on justice is exercised through physical or psychological violence, under Art. 231(2) of the CC, real imprisonment is imposed, as was the case in 25% of cases (1 conviction), with an average sentence of 1 year of imprisonment. Under Art. 233(3) of the CC, real imprisonment was imposed in 33% of cases (2 convictions), with an average sentence of 1 year and 7.5 months. Of all these cases, only once was the sentence imposed very slightly above the average penalty of imprisonment (under Art. 231(1) of the CC, a sentence of 1 year and 2 months was imposed against an average of 1 year and 1.5 months). However, according to the data from the investigation, some of the persons concerned had already been tried as many as 14 or 15 times.

The Impact of the Process of Combining Sentences on Punishing Crimes Against Justice

The CC provides for three methods of combining sentences:

1) a fully cumulative sentence (Art. 63(3) of the CC), whereby all the lesser sentences imposed are added to the most severe sentence imposed for one of the offenses committed;
2) a partially cumulative sentence (Art. 63(4) of the CC), whereby the more severe sentence imposed for one of the offenses committed is partially supplemented by the lesser sentences. The part of the sentence to be added may not, according to the law, be less than the minimum level of that type of sentence;
3) the consolidation of sentences (Art. 63(2) of the CC), where the more severe sentence is cumulated with the less severe sentences and the final combined sentence is equal to the most severe of the sentences imposed for the individual offenses.

In the study of the practice of combining sentences, it was found that criminal law does not oblige the court to indicate which part of the sentence is added for each individual offense, and that additional criteria have to be applied to determine exactly which part of the sentence is to be added for the crime against justice in question. Thus, of all the judgments and criminal orders of the courts of first instance of the Republic of Lithuania issued in the last 5 years analyzed above, i.e., those issued from January 1, 2018, to December 31, 2022, only those judgments where the sentence for the crime against justice in question was combined with the sentences imposed for another crime(s) committed before the conviction for at least one of them were selected. From these cases, only those where it was possible to identify the specific part of the added penalty for the crime against justice under analysis were selected. Thus, the following types of cases were used to analyze the part of the sentence that was added for the crimes against justice in question:

1) where only one other offense in addition to the offense against the administration of justice has been committed and the sentence imposed for that offense has been combined;
2) where, in addition to the offence against justice, several other offenses have been committed, but the punishment for these offenses has been imposed by a different judgment and, in effect, the already combined sentence has been combined with the offense in question in accordance with Art. 63(9) of the CC (according to this Article, the sentence shall be combined in cases where it is established, after the passing of a judgment, that a person has committed a different offense before the passing of the judgment in the first case);
3) where, in addition to the offense against the administration of justice, several other offenses have been committed, but where at least one of the other offenses differs substantially in seriousness, with the result that the sentences have been consolidated in accordance with Art. 63(5)(2) of the CC; and
4) where several offenses were committed in addition to the offense against justice, but the court, when imposing the sentence, indicated which part of the sentence imposed for the offense in question was added.

In total, 33 convictions met the above criteria, including 3 convictions under Art. 231(1) of the CC, 1 conviction under Art. 231(2) of the CC, 26 convictions under Art. 233(1) of the CC, and 3 convictions under Art. 233(3) of the CC. All of these cases can be grouped into three categories according to the part of the sentence that was added for the offense against justice:

1) cases where the full sentence imposed for an offense against justice was added to the combined sentence;
2) cases where part of the sentence imposed for an offense against justice was added as part of the combined sentence; and
3) cases where no part of the sentence imposed for an offense against justice was added as part of the combined sentence.

When combining the sentences imposed for obstructing the investigation (Art. 231(1) of the CC), in 67% of cases (2 convictions), 4 months of imprisonment was actually added to the average sentence of 6 months of imprisonment. In 33% of cases (1 conviction), the sentences were consolidated, and 5 months of imprisonment for the offense of obstruction of justice was not added.

When combining the sentences imposed for obstructing the investigation by physical or mental violence (Art. 231(2) of the CC), 5 months of imprisonment were added to the actual sentence of 1 year of imprisonment.

When combining the sentences imposed for influencing other participants in the case to make false statements (Art. 233(1) of the CC), the total sentence imposed for the offense of perverting the course of justice was added in 19% of cases (5 convictions), with an average of 10 months of imprisonment, or, in one case, by adding a total fine of €3,766. Partial cumulation was applied in 50% of cases (13 convictions). Of the average sentence of 7.7 months of imprisonment imposed (7 convictions), an average sentence of 4.3 months of imprisonment was actually added for the purposes of cumulation. In all cases where a restriction of liberty was imposed (5 convictions), only the legal minimum of 3 months of imprisonment was added from an average sentence of 6.8 months. In one case, where a fine of €3,000 was imposed, a significant amount of €2,500 was actually added to the combined sentence. In the remaining 31% of cases (8 convictions), no part of the average sentence of 8.4 months of imprisonment (5 cases) or the average sentence of 47 days of detention (3 cases) was added, because of the application of consolidation as a method of combining sentences.

When combining the sentences imposed for violent influence on other participants in the case with the purpose of forcing false statements (Art. 233(3) of the CC), the full cumulation of the sentences was applied in one case and the full sentence of 60 days of arrest was added. In the other case, partial cumulation of the sentences was applied, and only 20 days of arrest were actually added from the sentence of 45 days of arrest imposed. In the case of a third sentence, cumulation was applied, and 2 years of imprisonment for the crime of justice was not added.

After reviewing the entire practice of combining sentences during the period in question, it is necessary to take a deeper look at the reasons for this variety of combinations. The choice of the method of combining sentences is further analyzed below for all of the offenses examined, both for offenses under Art. 231 CC and Art. 233 CC together (33 cases).

In cases where the full sentence imposed for the offenses in question was added, only 3% of the cases (1 conviction) were subject to full cumulation, and this was in the case of a fine. In the remaining 15% of cases (5 convictions), the full sentence imposed for the offenses in question was added because it was the harshest of the sentences imposed, and the sentences for the other offenses were therefore added on top of the penalty imposed for that offense.

Partial cumulation of sentences was applied in 52% of cases (17 convictions), and in 33% of cases (11 convictions) a part of the sentence was added close to the minimum amount of the sentence required by law (in the case of imprisonment, the addition was always 3 to 4 months, in the case of deprivation of liberty, always only 3 months and, in the case of an arrest, 20 days of arrest). In 15% of cases (5 convictions), a slightly higher part of the sentence was added (in the cases of imprisonment, 5 to 6 months and in the case of a fine, €2,500 of the €3,000 imposed). It may therefore be concluded that, when applying partial cumulation of sentences and when selecting the size of the sentence to be added, the courts usually focus on the minimum amount of the sentence to be added as provided for by law.

The consolidation of sentences, whereby the punishment for the crime against justice was fully absorbed by the more severe penalty, was applied in 30% of cases (10 convictions). In only 6% of cases (2 convictions) the application of the consolidation of sentences was due to truly serious reasons. In one case, the application of consolidation of sentences was due to the fact that the person had been sentenced to life imprisonment for another offense. In a second case, consolidation of sentences was applied because the forcible coercion to give false testimony led to more serious consequences, which was considered to be an ideal concurrence of offenses (two offenses committed in a single act), for which consolidation of sentences was also applied. In the other 24% of cases (8 convictions), consolidation of sentences was applied based on the specific rule of consolidation of sentences laid down in Art. 63(5)(2) of the CC, which states that consolidation of sentences is also applicable when the offenses committed differ significantly in terms of seriousness and are classified in different types or categories of criminal offenses.

In accordance with Articles 11 and 12 of the CC, criminal offenses in Lithuania are classified according to their seriousness into the following types and categories: criminal misdemeanor, reckless offense, minor intentional offense, less serious intentional offense, serious intentional offense, and very serious intentional offense. Thus, in accordance with the practice of the Supreme Court of Lithuania, "if criminal offences are categorised as belonging to different categories over one or more (e.g., a minor offence and a serious offence), or one of the offences is a misdemeanour, and the other is a minor, serious, or very serious crime, the courts shall recognise the fact that they are significantly different in terms of their seriousness in the sense of subparagraph (2) of Art. 63(5) of the Criminal Code" (Teisės gidas 2007). The Supreme Court of Lithuania's reasoning allows courts to apply consolidation of sentences even if "the offences fall into adjacent categories (e.g., a minor offence and a petty offence), or if one of the offences is a misdemeanour and the other is a minor offence" (Teisės gidas 2007). In such a case, "the gravity of these acts is to be assessed by the courts on a case-by-case basis (i.e. by comparing the objects of the offence, the matter, the means of perpetration, the effects produced, etc.)" (Teisės gidas 2007).

Taking into account that the offenses in question are classified as minor (Art. 231(1), 233(1) of the CC) or less serious (Art. 231(2), 233(3) of the CC), the application of this rule leads to a paradoxical situation where, in the case of a serious or very serious offense and after application of the rules on the consolidation of penalties, the obstruction of the subjects of the criminal proceedings or coercion into making a false statement goes practically unpunished, while, in the case of a very serious offense, the application of the rules on the consolidation of penalties renders similar acts unpunished, even if they involve the use of physical or psychological violence. This is exactly what the case-law study shows. Here, the punishment for the influence on the participants in the case was included because the perpetrator, in addition to the offense against justice, had committed rape (1-232-348/2018, 2018; 1-50-620/2019, 2019; 1-56-1118/2021, 2021), the distribution of narcotics or psychotropic substances to juveniles (N1-11-282/2021, 2021), grievous bodily harm (N1-81-1021, 2022), and other offenses. Similar decisions can also be found in the practice of the Supreme Court of Lithuania (2K-222-511/2019, 2019; 2K-82-654/2023, 2023; 2K-11-697/2023, 2023). The only case found was one in which the court did not comply with the requirements of Art. 63(5)(2) of the CC and partially added the sentence for coercing a false statement to the sentence imposed for distribution of narcotic drugs or psychotropic substances to minors (i.e., a very serious offense) (N1-207-919/2021, 2021). However, since the court did not say anything at all in the judgment as to the reasons for not applying the requirements of Art. 63(5)(2) of the CC, it is more probable that this case involved the mistaken of application of law, rather than that it represents a different position of the court on the matter.

Clearly, a situation in which committing a serious or very serious crime makes it possible to commit crimes against justice with complete impunity is a dangerous situation. Such a regulation demonstrates a complete lack of coherence between the provisions of the CC, and may indirectly encourage perpetrators to exert an unlawful influence on both the subjects of the investigations and the other participants in the case, with a view to avoiding criminal liability. This lack of coherence can be addressed in two ways. The simplest way, of course, is to improve the CC – i.e., to amend the provisions of Art. 63(5)(2) of the CC so that this rule of consolidation of sentences is inapplicable to offenses against justice. However, the Supreme Court of Lithuania itself could resolve this problem, given that amending the law is not a simple procedure. Since the provision of Art. 63(5)(2) of the CC, according to which the consolidation of sentences is to be applied when the offenses committed differ significantly in terms of seriousness and belong to different types or categories of offenses, is rather abstract, it would be sufficient to clarify to the Supreme Court of Lithuania that offenses committed in the context of offenses against justice are closely linked to the offenses for which the attempt to evade responsibility was made. This interconnectedness therefore shows that these crimes are similar and do not differ greatly in their seriousness, even if they are classified as different types or categories of crime. Moreover, similar cases and similar decisions have already been made in the practice of the Supreme Court of Lithuania. In a number of cases (2K-570/2012, 2012; 2K-397/2014, 2014; 2K-233-511/2018, 2018; 2A-7-3-489/2019, 2019; 2K-7-71-458/2020, 2020) in which the offenses committed did not fall into adjacent categories, the Supreme Court of Lithuania did not apply Art. 63(5)(2) of the CC and combined the sentences by means of partial cumulation. The main motivation for these decisions was that the offenses were similar to one another, and thus did not differ significantly in terms of their dangerousness. Such a change in case law would therefore not even be considered a significant departure from existing case law and would be an excellent complement to the already established case law, ensuring greater coherence between the provisions of the CC.

Interim Findings

On the basis of research on sentencing for separate offenses against justice, it can be observed that courts usually impose non-custodial sentences for offenses against justice. The most severe state response to offenses against justice, which can be seen as the imposition of a sentence of actual imprisonment without suspension, is also quite limited, with courts usually imposing a sentence that is below the average sentence provided for in the sanction. This study also showed that by combining sentences, courts further dilute the penal policy against crimes against justice, usually by adding only a part of the sentence that is close to the minimum sentence required by law or via the over-application of consolidation of sentences.

A study of the laws and sentencing practices of foreign countries has shown that the criminal policy of Lithuania in the fight against crimes against justice, when obstructing the investigation or influencing the participants in the case, both at the level of legislation and case law, is considerably more lenient than that of the UK or the USA in this regard.

Thus, the CC, in the norms providing for criminal liability for crimes against justice when obstructing the investigation of a case, lacks coherence both with other norms of the special part and with the norms of the general part. The penalties for the offenses against justice in question are inconsistent with, and too lenient in relation to, the other provisions of the special part of the CC, which provide for liability for similar offenses. The rules on combining sentences provided for in the general part of the CC are not in accordance with the aims of the penalty and unjustifiably expand the use of the application of the cumulation of sentences, thus leading to a situation in which, in cases of serious or very serious offenses, offenses against justice are in fact not punished.

References

1-232-348/2018, 2018. Regional Court of Kaunas. Available from: https://liteko.teismai.lt/viesasprendimupaieska/tekstas.aspx?id=670f2aaf-6ce9-44d6-84ee-b1a929953dea [Accessed 14 September 2023].

1-81-1021-2022, 2022. Marijampolė District Court. Available from: https://liteko.teismai.lt/viesasprendimupaieska/tekstas.aspx?id=df721093-80bc-497f-8cb3-1c698a4230cb [Accessed 14 September 2023].

1-50-620/2019, 2019. Panevėžys District Court. Available from: https://liteko.teismai.lt/viesasprendimupaieska/tekstas.aspx?id=79526a1c-aaed-481b-9bfa-ddce34f900d1 [Accessed 14 September 2023].

1-56-1118/2021, 2021. Telšiai District Court. Available from: https://liteko.teismai.lt/viesasprendimupaieska/tekstas.aspx?id=af06fb45-baa3-451a-871f-22d2aa7811e5 [Accessed 14 September 2023].

2K-570/2012, 2012. Supreme Court of Lithuania. Available from: https://liteko.teismai.lt/viesasprendimupaieska/tekstas.aspx?id=fa982b39-1031-4a0c-a075-34ac6db5e8b6 [Accessed 14 September 2023].

2K-397/2014, 2014. Supreme Court of Lithuania. Available from: https://liteko.teismai.lt/viesasprendimupaieska/tekstas.aspx?id=f34d9852-a8ee-4f2c-9ea4-c5a9fc0355ef [Accessed 14 September 2023].

2K-350-693/2017, 2017. Supreme Court of Lithuania. Available from: https://liteko.teismai.lt/viesasprendimupaieska/tekstas.aspx?id=7a23d630-e0c3-4fb1-9afd-d79abe60c51a [Accessed 14 September 2023].

2K-233-511/2018, 2018. Supreme Court of Lithuania. Available from: https://liteko.teismai.lt/viesasprendimupaieska/tekstas.aspx?id=c72d8090-328f-4f9b-9cdd-a5e3fa28febc [Accessed 14 September 2023].

2A-7-3-489/2019, 2019. Supreme Court of Lithuania. Available from: https://liteko.teismai.lt/viesasprendimupaieska/tekstas.aspx?id=1068da4f-6304-46b5-9f57-d968aab0ec7f [Accessed 14 September 2023].

2K-222-511/2019, 2019. Supreme Court of Lithuania. Available from: https://liteko.teismai.lt/viesasprendimupaieska/tekstas.aspx?id=444d6f7f-cc52-49ee-9cea-1add8d7c2765 [Accessed 14 September 2023].

2K-7-71-458/2020, 2020. Supreme Court of Lithuania. Available from: https://liteko.teismai.lt/viesasprendimupaieska/tekstas.aspx?id=3cea9170-a6f8-4d4c-83b4-44b6d3b8e21f [Accessed 14 September 2023].

2K-82-654-2023, 2023. Supreme Court of Lithuania. Available from: https://liteko.teismai.lt/viesasprendimupaieska/tekstas.aspx?id=8e51c991-26c5-4299-871f-57be9ee41aad [Accessed 14 September 2023].

2K-11-697/2023, 2023. Supreme Court of Lithuania. Available from: https://liteko.teismai.lt/viesasprendimupaieska/tekstas.aspx?id=4df26486-2428-449b-8acd-058b3c98fe62 [Accessed 14 September 2023].

Chang, W., Ebert, R., Galst, J., and Khemani, A., 2023. Obstruction of Justice. *American Criminal Law Review*, 60 (3), 1093–1126.

Criminal Justice and Public Order Act 1994 (c.33). [online] Legislation.gov.uk. Available from: https://www.legislation.gov.uk/ukpga/1994/33/section/51 [Accessed 29 September 2023].

Crown Prosecution Service, 2022. Public Justice Offences Incorporating the Charging Standard. [online] Available from: https://www.cps.gov.uk/legal-guidance/public-justice-offences-incorporating-charging-standard [Accessed 29 September 2023].

Crown Prosecution Service, 2023. Sentencing – Overview, General Principles and Mandatory Custodial Sentences. [online] Available from: https://www.cps.gov.uk/legal-guidance/sentencing-overview-general-principles-and-mandatory-custodial-sentences [Accessed 29 September 2023].

N1-11-282/2021, 2021. Regional Court of Šiauliai. Available from: https://liteko.teismai.lt/viesasprendimupaieska/tekstas.aspx?id=bc3cb56b-6718-42dd-b436-bf964ce30574 [Accessed 14 September 2023].

N1-207-919/2021, 2021. Regional Court of Kaunas. Available from: https://liteko.teismai.lt/viesasprendimupaieska/tekstas.aspx?id=62e54d54-60d1-4bb6-9ed7-98d626b79388 [Accessed 14 September 2023].

Obstruction of Justice, 18 USC Ch. 73, §§ 1501–1521, 2023. [online] Available from: https://uscode.house.gov/browse/prelim@title18/part1/chapter73&edition=prelim [Accessed 29 September 2023].

Roman, E., Gonzalez, M., and Torres, D., 2018. Collusion, Obstruction of Justice, and Impeachment. *Journal of Legislation*, 45 (1), 9–59.

Sentencing Council, 2023. Perverting the Course of Justice. [online] Available from: https://www.sentencingcouncil.org.uk/offences/crown-court/item/perverting-the-course-of-justice/ [Accessed 29 September 2023].

Teisės Gidas, 2007. Review of Case Law on Sentencing (Articles 54-64 CC). [online] Available from: https://www.teisesgidas.lt/modules/paieska/lat.php?id=32351 [Accessed 29 September 2023].

Teismai.LT. (n.d.). LITEKO. [online] Available from: https://liteko.teismai.lt/viesasprendimupaieska/detalipaieska.aspx?detali=2 [Accessed 14 September 2023].

United States Sentencing Commission, 2021a. Guidelines Manual. Available from: https://www.ussc.gov/sites/default/files/pdf/guidelines-manual/2021/GLMFull.pdf [Accessed 29 September 2023].

United States Sentencing Commission, 2021b. Guidelines Manual Annotated. Available from: https://www.ussc.gov/guidelines/2021-guidelines-manual-annotated [Accessed 29 September 2023].

Jolita Šukytė

The Unlawful Stalking of a Person

Stalking is one of the most pressing issues today – not only in criminal law, but also in other disciplines such as criminology, psychology, psychiatry, and sociology. Unlawful stalking has been defined, from its earliest scientific analysis, as a type of behavior that usually manifests itself in a form of unwanted behavior by the perpetrator that harasses the victim (Čėsnienė and Čėsna 2006, p.27), and as behavior that creates a sense of fear and danger. According to researchers, stalking is interference with another person's psyche by repeated acts of intimidation, forcing the person to experience constant stress, fear, insecurity, and loss of control over the situation, leading to negative consequences that affect not only the person's mental health but also their physical health, well-being and quality of life (Michailovič 2018, pp.86, 89). However, it is extremely difficult to provide a clearly formulated and valid definition of stalking, as the term can be applied to a wide range of behaviors (Michailovič 2018, p.86). It should be noted that there are also very graphic representations of stalking in the literature; these include the cat-and-mouse game, where the cat, chasing its victim, initially plays with it for a while, and the game is nothing more than the cat tormenting the victim until the mouse loses its life (MacFarlane 1997, p.37). This description is intended to precisely convey the sense of terror, fear, insecurity, and loss of control that the person being stalked experiences. Thus, as can be seen, stalking requires a balanced and therefore coherent approach to this social concept and its legal assessment.

Stalking as a Dangerous Form of Human Behavior and the Justification for Its Criminalization

In demonstrating the distinctiveness of stalking, the academic literature notes that while criminal offenses traditionally refer to a specific, dangerous act or omission of a person that harms, or at least threatens to harm, a value protected by criminal law, stalking can refer not only to criminal conduct, but also to a range of non-criminal conduct. It should be noted that stalking often consists of individual acts performed by a person. However, while these acts, in themselves or individually, may be regarded as not dangerous, and, therefore, not punishable, when viewed as a set of factors causing fear, anxiety, and insecurity to the victim, there is a necessity to treat them as criminal, and, therefore, subject to criminal responsibility (National Center for Victims of Crime, n.d.). After all, acts such as sending flowers, texting, leaving messages (Mullen and Path 2002, p.293) or standing outside a workplace or home are not in themselves criminal, but this can change if they are related to the intention to make a person experience fear, insecurity, and loss of control. Of course, in the case of stalking, the commission of acts such as threats to kill, the disruption of health, the impairment of health, interference with physical liberty, the violation of a person's honor, and the violation of the inviolability of private life are also relevant. It is precisely because some forms of stalking have been criminalized as *delicta sui generis* that for a long time – even in the Western world – it was not seen as necessary to treat this criminal phenomenon as an independent criminal offense. It should be noted that in some of the above-mentioned categories, the application of criminal liability as a complete act is linked to the moment of causing damage to a value protected by criminal law, whereas the essence of the criminalization of stalking is to prevent the perpetrator's various behaviors that cause fear, anxiety and insecurity. It is worth noting that, according to the case law of the European Court of Human Rights (hereinafter – ECtHR), the abuse suffered by the victim, which may take the form of bodily harm and mental pressure, may be considered sufficiently serious to constitute inhuman treatment within the meaning of Article 3 of the European Convention on Human Rights, entitled "Prohibition of Torture" (*Talpis v. Italy* 2017). As stalking can be one of the expressions of domestic violence, it is relevant that, according to the case law of the ECtHR, depending on the seriousness of the offense and the risk of further offenses, the Convention may impose an obligation on the State to continue prosecuting domestic violence on the grounds of public interest, even if the victim drops their complaint. In such cases, it is necessary to consider the reasons for the victim's decision, the victim's situation (economic, psychological, and other aspects), and the possible unlawful influence of the perpetrator on the victim's decision (e.g., threats to kill or the use of mental violence, other forms of pressure). A particularly significant case for the development of the ECtHR's domestic violence jurisprudence was *Opuz v. Turkey* (2009), which almost set out these principles.

Scientific sources show that stalking was only criminalized as an independent offense at the end of the 20th century. However, this in no way implies that this phenomenon, in all its forms of expression, constitutes a new assessment of a person's deed. As Ilona Mikhailovich pointed out, stalking, although a new and rarely used word, is an excellent description of behavior that is as old as humanity itself (Michailovič 2018, p.87).

The actions that are today referred to as stalking, in its various forms of expression, are analyzed and referred to in different scientific contexts under different terms. For example, psychiatric science has dealt with erotomania, which is the behavior of a person who has an obsessive desire to be in a relationship, usually a close one, with a well-known, prominent public figure. These stalkers constantly follow individuals with whom they are simply obsessed (MacFarlane 1997, pp.43, 44). It should be noted that the phenomenon of stalking has become more visible and audible due to actions normally directed against well-known, prominent persons in society. For this reason, the term "star/celebrity stalking" has been increasingly used (Fahnestock 1993, p.784). The phenomenon of stalking is, of course, not limited only to people who are well known in society – it is also very widespread among people who are normally in a close relationship (MacFarlane 1999a, p.201.). Depending on the relationship between the stalker and the stalked person, different types of stalking can be identified in the literature, such as the star stalking of known persons mentioned above, familial stalking (the stalking of persons who are in a close relationship or who have been in a close relationship), and the stalking of persons who are in an employment relationship (Fahnestock 1993, p.784). This is an exemplary distinction of stalking types that demonstrates how widespread this phenomenon is. Over the years, the term stalking has come to be used to refer to a wide range of actions by individuals which, in isolation, often do not even qualify as a violation of the law, but which cause the victim a sense of fear, anxiety, insecurity, and loss of privacy and control.

As regards the origins of the criminalization of stalking as an unlawful act, the murder of the actress Rebecca Shaeffer in 1989 was the basis for the criminal law in the State of California (United States of America). This was the first time in the history of the Western world that a criminal law had been enacted to prevent this criminal phenomenon (Mullen and Path 2002, p.274). Thus, it was the version of the criminal law adopted in this state (California Penal Code 646.9) that first criminalized stalking, defining a person who commits stalking as an individual who "willfully, maliciously, and repeatedly follows or harasses another person and who makes a credible threat with the intent to place that person in reasonable fear for his or her safety, or the safety of his or her immediate family" (Blaauw *et al.* 2002, p.136).

This provision of the law eventually led the legislatures of the 49 other states to criminalize stalking by introducing their own norms. It should be emphasized that the stalking norms in different states have emphasized different types of unlawful and dangerous conduct. Interestingly, some definitions include the element of surveillance in the content of stalking, while others emphasize that stalking refers to the initiation and implementation of communication against a person's will, i.e., in the absence of the parties' mutual consent. Stalking is also often seen as "lying in wait" (MacFarlane, 1999a, p.48).

It should be noted that the diversity of definitions of stalking prompted the United States Department of Justice, in conjunction with the National Institute of Justice, to submit a document (the Model Anti-Stalking Code) to all US states a few years later (in 1993). The latter document not only laid down the basic guidelines for combating the crime of stalking, highlighting the dangerousness of the phenomenon and the multiplicity of its expressions, but also assisted in the criminalization of stalking, the drafting of the law, and the development and application of its coherence (Lamplugh and Infield 2003, p.860). It is important to note that this is one of the most important documents that laid the foundations for the development of criminal stalking policy.

Since the content of stalking reflects a variety of individual acts both within and outside the scope of the offense, the legal technique of this phenomenon, according to the authors of the Model Anti-Stalking Code, must be clear, allowing the determination of which acts, or the totality of acts, performed by a person are worthy of legal evaluation. An overly broad, vague and nebulous definition becomes the basis for restricting a person's freedom of expression, while an overly specific and defined concept opens up the possibility of leaving outside the scope of application of the law the actions of a person that are worthy (in terms of their dangerousness) of condemnation under criminal law. It should be underlined that the guidelines for the regulation of stalking formulated in the Model Anti-Stalking Code were based *inter alia* on an analysis of the case law of the Supreme Court of the United States of America, which guarantees the right of individuals to freedom of expression. The guarantee of freedom of expression and the protection of the individual against the perpetrator's actions that cause fear, anxiety and insecurity are identified as the two main criteria for the establishment of stalking, and both require mutual compatibility (National Institute of Justice 1993). It is the significant period of time that has passed since the initial identification of the dangerous social phenomenon under analysis that allows us to observe a change in the concept of stalking.

Indications of Stalking

The definitions of stalking in the legal texts are varied, but they all refer to premeditated, and therefore deliberate, repetitive acts of a person aimed at creating a sense of fear and insecurity. It is the latter two features, i.e., repetition and the creation of a sense of fear, that are considered to be the main criteria that distinguish stalking from other criminal offenses (Knight 2014, p.396).

As noted in the literature, stalking, unlike other criminal offenses, requires an unlawful and dangerous repetitive mental impact, which justifies the seriousness of the phenomenon and, therefore, the significant need for its criminalization. It should be pointed out that, as mentioned above, the content of stalking often consists not only of acts of a person that are regulated by criminal law, but also of acts that are not criminalized by law, and which become criminal stalking precisely because of their repetitive nature and when they are implemented against the will of a person. Repeated acts become the basis of prosecution with criminal liability (MacFarlane 1999b, p.364). It should be emphasized that a review of the regulation of stalking reveals differences not only between the acts that can be classified as forms of expression of stalking, but also between the minimum number of incidences of psychological impact that would allow the obligatory feature of stalking to be established, i.e., its repetition. It should also be noted that repetition usually refers to two or three unlawful and dangerous manifestations of a mental effect, although there are also provisions in the law requiring more than three instances of intimidating effects (Blaauw *et al.* 2002, p.137). It is this repeated exposure that forces a person to live in a constant or at least prolonged atmosphere of fear, anxiety and insecurity, which affects their health and, in particular, their mental health. The acts of stalking are systematic, which means that they are often prolonged. As studies have shown, the factors that contribute to feelings of fear and insecurity often last from a few weeks to a few months to several years (Blaauw *et al.* 2002, p.138). For example, the literature describes cases in which illegal acts of intimidation continued for 13 months, 24 months, 5 years or even 12 years (Blaauw *et al.* 2002, p.138). In assessing such a long period of mental coercion, it must also be remembered that the damage caused by prolonged mental coercion results in a disturbance to mental health. In many cases, this is also the cause of "physiological changes in the body, i.e., physical damage" (Čėsnienė and Čėsna 2006, p.29).

As discussed previously, acts of stalking vary widely in their many forms of expression and in the nature of their performance, ranging from acts that are not legally actionable, such as sending flowers or waiting outside someone's home or work, to acts that are within the scope of a criminal offense, such as threatening a person, collecting information that constitutes their private life, trespassing on private property, or disseminating information that is not true. However, irrespective of the expression of the acts carried out, what unites them all is not only their repetition, but also the creation of a sense of fear of possible harm to life, health, property, and the loss of a sense of security. An analysis of the literature reveals that the first provisions on stalking did not, in most cases, even specify the forms in which dangerous acts were to be expressed, only laconically stating that they were acts that endangered the safety, life or health of a person. In some states, the risk of endangering property was even reflected in the stalking norms (National Institute of Justice 1993, p.35).

In addition to the above-mentioned identifying features of stalking, the literature also points to unpredictability as one of the additional characteristics of the phenomenon. According to researchers, the unpredictability of stalking only adds to the sense of fear and insecurity, thereby introducing additional tension into the victim's life (MacFarlane 1997, p. 43). As noted in victims' testimonies, the unpredictability of stalking leads to the victim's constant feelings of fear and insecurity. For example: "when he called every ten minutes, I was very angry, but when he didn't, I was worried that he was somewhere nearby, watching me." In this case, the stalker's actions were repeated "without any warning and without any clear reason" (MacFarlane 1997, p. 88). In order to understand the impact of such actions on the individual, it should be remembered that, according to psychological science, the fear of undefined consequences can be as strong as the fear of death.

Acts of stalking include not only the traditional surveillance and monitoring of a person, but also many other acts, such as: repeatedly sending emails, messages, or gifts; parking near work, home, or school (Lamplugh and Infield 2003, p.854); harassing via phone calls, especially at night; taking over social networking sites; posting information on social networks that is not true (Baum *et al.* 2009, p.1); ordering various items in the name of the person being stalked (usually in cyberspace); breaking into homes and moving items from one place to another, thereby making the victim aware of the presence of a stranger in the victim's home; taking items (especially underwear) from the home; going to the same public places at the same time as the person being stalked; or going through the rubbish discarded by the stalked person and taking some of it (Hall 1998, p.131). Practical examples also show that stalkers have been known to send their victims strands of hair or even a few teeth (Hall 1998, p.133). In other cases, the stalking took the form of: the killing of domestic animals, usually by poisoning them, and the abandonment of the dead animals outside the person's home (MacFarlane, 1997, p. 206); placing a mobile home in the vicinity of the stalked person's property and monitoring them with various technical devices such as binoculars (Melton 2007, p.354); and many other acts that lead to feelings of insecurity, fear, and a lack of control over one's life.

As is well known, when assessing the dangerousness of an act, and therefore the need for criminalization, the dangerous consequences that come as an accompanying result of the phenomenon are also taken into account. The consequences of stalking are not limited to a specific list of consequences, but instead are multifaceted in their nature. Stalking is a deterrent effect of a persistent nature which can fundamentally, or at least significantly, alter the life of the stalked person.

The literature widely refers to the harm caused, in particular, to a person's mental health, which manifests itself in varying degrees of mental disturbance, such as depression and panic attacks. Post-traumatic stress disorder, or even suicidal ideation, is often the result of prolonged feelings of anxiety, fear and insecurity caused by the actions of the stalker (Blaauw *et al.* 2002, pp.139–140). Of course, we cannot forget the direct impact on the person's physical health, which often manifests itself in physical ailments such as persistent headaches and heart and digestive problems. Insomnia, extreme sensitivity and fearfulness are directly related to the experience of being stalked (Hall 1998, p.135). Studies on the phenomenon of stalking point out that this crime often affects the most diverse areas of a person's life. In order to avoid a situation that frightens them, people often quit their jobs, drop out of school, and move not only from one neighborhood to another, but even, in many cases, from one city or state to another (Doris 1998, p.134). The testimonies of stalked persons reveal that some of them change not only their appearance, for example by dyeing their hair or changing their style of dress, but also, in many cases, their names, believing that in this way they would be able to hide from their stalker. Driving a vehicle, frequently changing mobile phone numbers, using additional security measures to protect oneself from the stalker's access to private property, and many other actions show a great deal of effort to avoid possible contact. Human beings are social creatures who value contact with and support from others, but victims of stalkers often reject any social life, thus living a more closed, somewhat more solitary life. Victims stress an increased distrust of people and a sense of loss of control over their lives. However, it should be noted that the negative impact on the quality of the person's life persists even after the persecutor's actions end. According to the victims, they continue to feel fear and insecurity for a long time, and, in some cases, every time they walk down the street they have to look around and make sure that the door of their house is locked. According to one victim of stalking, this fear was relieved by one factor only: the stalker's incarceration in prison and the knowledge that they would not return, at least for a while (Hall 1998, p.135). Interestingly, many studies also focus on the indirect damage caused by the stalker's actions, i.e., the cost of additional security for the home; the cost of damage to, or theft of, property; and the cost of the medical care required for the resulting health problems (Blaauw *et al.* 2002, p.153).

Types of Definitions of Stalking

Anti-stalking measures in various countries are based on two main models of regulating stalking. The first is the so-called *list method*, where the law specifically lists the acts that constitute stalking. The Canadian and Japanese criminal laws provide legislative examples of this method. For example, the Canadian Criminal Code defines stalking as the repeated surveillance of a person, the repeated direct or indirect initiation of contact with a person against their will, and the surveillance of the home, workplace or any other place where the person being stalked is present. All of these acts are accompanied by the necessary condition of creating in the stalked person a feeling of fear or insecurity due to the actions of the stalker(s). The Japanese Criminal Code defines stalking as a somewhat broader list of acts by the stalker, including, in addition to the usual emphasis on surveillance, harassing phone calls, attempting to make contact with a person in various ways, and saying things that are aimed at possibly violating a person's honor, dignity or sexual integrity (Lamplugh and Infield 2003, p.861). As can be seen, some of the listed forms of expression of the dangerous acts of stalkers are quite broad in content. Nevertheless, the acts performed by a person must comply with the above lists of variations of the expression of stalking in order to establish the norm.

It should be noted that the list method is also subject to a fair amount of criticism. By listing possible forms of stalking, this method criminalizes only specific behaviors of a person, thus not giving the stalking norm the flexibility to respond to possible new manifestations of behavior causing insecurity and fear by the stalker. The actions performed by a person may not correspond to the forms of expression of dangerous conduct criminalized in the stalking disposition, thus leaving outside the scope of the law conduct of no less seriousness that is worthy of criminal legal condemnation. As is well known, the actions of stalkers are not static; they have a very broad dynamic, and this method excludes any possibility of identifying actions that do not specifically reflect the content of the stalking norm.

Another model that reflects the regulation of stalking is so-called *general prohibition*, where the definition of stalking does not include a specific list of the forms in which this dangerous act may be expressed, but only the main features that help to identify stalking from the range of other criminal offenses. One example of this model is the UK norm criminalizing this dangerous phenomenon. As is well known, Britain's fight against stalking gained momentum in 1997 with the Protection from Harassment Act. Although it did not formulate a specific definition of stalking, the Act refers to repeated behavior that causes anxiety, fear and insecurity, and introduces a criterion for assessing the impact of such behavior known as the "reasonable man" criterion. It is on the basis of this criterion that it is judged whether the impact on the person could actually have caused fear, insecurity and tension (Lamplugh and Infield 2003, p.863).

However, it should be noted that this model of regulating stalking has also been the subject of criticism. The main reasons for this are that the definition of the content of the Act is too abstract, which opens up the possibility of considering many acts of a person as stalking.

The British Protection from Harassment Act defines stalking as repeated, dangerous acts by a person that cause fear of violence or acts that, by reason of the danger, anxiety or distress they cause, lead to changes in everyday life. In order to show this phenomenon in as much detail as possible, the law even contains a list of representative acts that constitute stalking, such as following a person, contacting or at least attempting to contact a person by any possible means, sending messages, publishing true or false information about a person, sending messages on behalf of the person being stalked, standing in the vicinity of the person being pursued in a public or private environment, trespassing on the person's private property, or surveillance of the person (Protection from Harassment Act 1997).

Thus, although different countries choose different models for the criminalization of stalking, they all demonstrate a clear intent to use national laws to prevent deliberate, repeated exposure to feelings of fear, anxiety and insecurity, which first and foremost have a negative impact on a person's mental health, but in many cases also cause a change in their physical state, limiting the person's ability to exercise their discretion. The problem of establishing criminal responsibility and a coherent approach to stalking can also be addressed from another perspective. If the legislator decides to criminalize this negative social phenomenon as an independent criminal offense (crime), the question arises as to whether such an idea can be implemented through a special norm or through a general norm dealing with unlawful mental violence. This analysis is discussed in the following section in the context of the regulation established in Lithuania.

The Regulation of Stalking Actions in Lithuania

In Lithuania, stalking was regulated as an independent criminal offense on 14 October 2021, when the Criminal Code (2000; hereinafter – the CC) was supplemented by Article 148[1] on "Unlawful stalking." Prior to the introduction of this formulation, legal scientists had expressed concern that not all acts of stalking were subject to proper legal evaluation. Researchers had pointed out with great concern that, under the previous regulation, only certain forms of stalking entailed criminal liability for a person, their norms being found in chapters of the CC such as "Crimes endangering human health life," "Crimes against human health," "Crimes against human liberty," and "Crimes and misdemeanours against property, property rights, and property interests." Particular attention was paid to the qualification of Article 145 of the CC, i.e., "Threatening to murder or cause a severe health impairment to a person or terrorisation of a person," which criminalizes the offense of terrorizing a person with the threat to bomb, set fire to, or commit any other act dangerous to life, health, or property, or of systematically threatening a person by means of mental coercion. However, when interpreting the application of this qualified norm, researchers also noted that this article is focused on the protection of life and health, and that criminal liability should only be imposed for the threatening acts of the stalker that express a threat to life or health. Meanwhile, other acts carried out by the stalker, such as constant calling, writing insulting but non-threatening messages, or standing outside the house, were not regarded as criminal, and therefore were not subject to a reasonable legal assessment (Čėsnienė and Čėsna 2006, p.27). It is to be considered that such statements are nothing more than examples of insufficient insight into the practical interpretation of the element of systematic intimidation contained in Article 145(2) of the CC, and indicate the lack of a coherent approach to the act of stalking and its forms of expression. The case law demonstrating the practical applicability of systemic intimidation makes it possible to see a wide variety of expressions of the behavior of the person to be assessed under Article 145(2) of the CC. It should be noted that these acts performed by a person do not necessarily reflect a direct threat to life or health. The actions carried out by individuals which are especially referred to in the scientific literature as stalking – following, surveillance, writing emails, messages, loitering at work or at home, etc. (Michailovič 2018, p.86) – have been subjected to criminal legal assessment on the basis of the systematic intimidation element. The Supreme Court of Lithuania has long emphasized that "systemic intimidation may take the form not only of threats, but also of other acts that cause fear, anxiety and insecurity, such as repeated insults, intimidation, harassment, open surveillance, frightening night-time calls, or immoral SMS messages" (Ruling of 15 June 2010 of the Supreme Court of Lithuania in criminal case No. 2K-341/2010). The element of systemic intimidation is not only related to the specific actions performed by a person, as the main criterion for assessing a person's actions is the nature of the effect, which in this case is aimed at causing stress, anxiety, insecurity, and the fear that further actions or omissions will lead to certain negative consequences (Ruling of the Regional Court of Šiauliai of 11 July 2014 in criminal case No. 1A-717-116-2014). Thus, mental violence, in the context of systemic intimidation, does not only take the form of threats to kill or to cause bodily harm, but is also a process of intimidation by means of other acts of intimidation, such as the infliction of a feeling of fear on the other person

(Ruling of the Supreme Court of Lithuania of January 12, 2016 in criminal case No. 2K-65-648/2016).

The Supreme Court of Lithuania views systemic intimidation as the nature of the intimidation process, in which the actions performed are not to be viewed as random or isolated, but rather as forming a chain of criminal behavior. In its judgment of 20 March 2018, the Court noted that "the source of fear, anxiety and insecurity was not only the constant calls and threatening messages to the spouse, but also the defendant's stalking, breaking into the house, sitting in the car and following her home, passing it, using an acoustic alarm, sending obscene and indecent, abusive, threatening and intimidating messages to the letterbox, inserting an envelope containing cut-up family photographs, an angel figurine and metal money." Thus, in the totality of these acts, the implementation of systemic intimidation was established (Ruling of the Supreme Court of Lithuania of March 20, 2018 in criminal case No. 2K-90-689/2018).

Other rulings in which the Supreme Court of Lithuania recognized repeated acts of various intimidating natures as indicating systematic intimidation causing a feeling of insecurity can be observed. These behaviors include:

> informing police officers nine times by telephone and once by a statement, eleven times by contacting officials of the Children's Rights Protection Division, once by contacting the municipality [...], and twice by contacting the [...] Heat Networks about noise, drunkenness, neglect of minor children and violations of their rights in the [...] family [...] increase in the size of her apartment, the unauthorised installation of premises using district heating and the non-payment of heating fees for her apartment. [...] As a result of such false reports by the convicted person about violations, the apartment of victim [...] was systematically and unjustifiably visited by officials of various authorities. [...] The victims [...] felt great tension, stress, fear, insecurity and anxiety as a result of the constant checks. The prolonged stalking [...] had a direct impact on the mental state and health of the victim [...] who developed temporary, moderate [...] mood disorders (Ruling of the Supreme Court of Lithuania of 24 May 2016 in criminal case No. 2K-186-746/2016).

Thus, the above examples of case law demonstrate that the norm of systemic intimidation does not consist solely of a threat, the content of which clearly reflects the risk of a threat to a person's health, life, or safety. In the application of the norm of systemic intimidation, criminal liability is associated with a set of acts of various expressions that cause fear, insecurity, and uncertainty to a person. A person's actions, taken in isolation, may not represent a direct or indirect threat to another person's health or life, or may even be of a non-criminal nature, but when viewed as a whole, their intimidating nature must be recognized. These acts constitute a chain of unlawful and dangerous conduct, creating an atmosphere of insecurity and uncertainty. The repetitive and intimidating nature of them makes it possible to establish mental violence in the context of systemic intimidation. Notwithstanding the fact that systemic intimidation consists of the acts of a person in a wide variety of forms, the repetitive totality of all of them has the effect of adversely affecting another person's mental health. Therefore, it is considered that the actions carried out by a person constitute the unlawful stalking of a human being and, prior to the introduction of the new norm, were subject to legal assessment on the basis of systemic intimidation as a *delicta sui generis*.

It should be noted that during the process of drafting the legal provision on unlawful stalking as an independent act, various opinions were expressed on the need for this norm to be enshrined in the criminal law. Those opposed to the new formulation argued that the systematic intimidation enshrined in Article 145(2) of the CC encompasses acts that constitute possible forms of expression of stalking as a possible form of the unlawful and dangerous act proposed for criminalization. They based this opinion on the case law of the Supreme Court of Lithuania, which interprets the composition of systematic intimidation (Public Governance Group 2020).

In contrast, those who saw the need to regulate stalking argued to the contrary, suggesting that acts of stalking are not prevented unless they involve a "high degree of seriousness," which would be consistent with the elements of terrorizing or systematically intimidating a person under Article 145(2) of the CC. Thus, according to these authors, only some of the acts of stalking were subject to legal assessment under the elements of human terrorization or systematic intimidation, while the others, which did not constitute a "high intensity of the offence," were not subject to legal assessment. It should be noted that the representatives of this position did not provide a more detailed explanation as to what constitutes "high intensity" (Human Rights Monitoring Institute 2019). In this respect, it is worth noting that coherent legislation in the field of criminal law should ensure that there is as minimum a conflict of legal norms as possible. However, the introduction of the unlawful stalking provision in the CC has created a competition between several legal norms that is not easily resolvable.

According to case law, systematic intimidation (Art. 145(2) of the CC) is interpreted as the repeated infliction of a feeling of fear, anxiety, or insecurity (Ruling of the Supreme Court of Lithuania of October 30, 2018 in criminal case No. 2K-269-895/2018). Thus, the element of the high intensity of the offense may be linked to repeated acts of a person with intimidating content. At the same time, however, it should be noted that the new norm of unlawful stalking of a person is also linked to the systematic nature of the acts, which are repetitive. It is also important to note that case law examples show that systematic intimidation refers to a repeated act of an intimidating nature by a person which is not limited to a specific form of expression, nor is it linked solely to the risk of threatening a person's life or health (Ruling of the Supreme Court of Lithuania of November 20, 2018 in criminal case No. 2K-346-942/2018).

Consequently, on the basis of concrete examples of case law, it is easy to refute the claims made by the proponents of stalking as an independent act regarding the limited possibility of the legal assessment of the actions of the stalker in the case of the criminal offense of stalking, where the CC provides for the constituent part of the offense of systemic intimidation (Art. 145(2) of the CC) but not a criminal offense that is defined by stalking.

As already mentioned, stalking as an independent criminal offense was, however, introduced on October 14, 2021 with the addition of the new Article 148[1] on "Unlawful stalking of a person" to the chapter on "Crimes against human liberty" of the CC. The norm of unlawful stalking declares that

Whoever, against the express will of a person, without lawful grounds, systematically persecutes that person, if as a result of that persecution the victim has been forced to change his or her place of residence or work or educational institution, or if any other negative impact on the victim's social life or on the victim's emotional state has occurred, commits a criminal offense and is liable to a fine, or to a penalty of public works or a fine, or to restriction of liberty, or to imprisonment.

It should be noted that the legislator's decision to introduce the new norm of unlawful stalking in the chapter of the CC entitled "Crimes against human liberty" has given rise to further debate. The purpose of this chapter is to ensure the protection of liberty as the main legal good infringed by a criminal offense. As a dangerous act, stalking, by its very nature, involves a wide range of personal acts, which are presumably aimed primarily at creating fear, anxiety, and insecurity. Nightly phone calls, non-threatening text messages, standing outside a person's home or work, deliberately appearing in public places (Čėsnienė and Čėsna 2006, p.27), and many other acts all create a feeling of fear and insecurity.

Therefore, if the actions taken by a person are intended to have a negative impact on another person's psyche, it is the victim's mental health, not their liberty, that is the value that is primarily at stake in such actions. Of course, it is also necessary to talk about the restriction of the freedom of will when the stalker's actions force a person to change or at least adjust their decisions – for example, by taking a different route, adjusting their agenda, changing the time or place of their rest, or abandoning their usual pattern of behavior, many of which are often even necessary. However, it seems that the restriction of will should be seen as a violation of an ancillary value, not a violation of the core value. The new norm of stalking should have been included in the "Crimes endangering human health and life" chapter, and not in the "Crimes against human liberty" chapter.

The jurisprudence of the Constitutional Court emphasizes that in a democratic state governed by the rule of law, the legislator is not only obliged to prohibit acts that cause substantial damage to the interests of individuals, society, or the State or that threaten to cause such damage, but also, while ensuring the implementation of the principle of justice, to establish just and adequate penalties for the violation of the law (Ruling of the Constitutional Court of Lithuania of June 10, 2003). In this respect, it is therefore relevant to assess the new norm of unlawful stalking in the CC.

The legislator has given the new offense of stalking, as a *delicta sui generis*, the status of a misdemeanor, with the possibility of community service, a fine, a restriction of liberty, or an arrest. According to the CC, a misdemeanor is considered to be a less serious type of criminal offense compared to the category of a crime. A person may not be sentenced to imprisonment for the commission of a misdemeanor, and, if sentenced, they have no criminal record going forward (Articles 12, 55 of the CC). It should be remembered that in order to justify the need to criminalize a phenomenon, and therefore to assess the respective act performed by a person, the main criteria determining the dangerousness of the act are usually used. These criteria include the significance of the value which is endangered by the act, the real damage which is caused by the act, the significance of the forms of expression of the act, as well as the peculiarities of the forms, the nature of their features, and the negative consequences they produce.

Therefore, when looking at the criminalization of stalking as a separate norm, the question of whether the legislator has actually sufficiently assessed the seriousness of this offense by making it a misdemeanor arises. It should be recalled that stalking is primarily concerned with the repeated acts of the stalker that cause a feeling of fear, anxiety, and insecurity. These actions endanger one of the most important values protected by criminal law, i.e., the health and freedom of the individual. The stalker's actions, which last for a certain period of time, lead to a person living in a constant atmosphere of fear, insecurity, and uncertainty, which undoubtedly causes real damage to their mental and, ultimately, physical health. As a result of the continued intimidating nature of the stalker's actions, victims are diagnosed with mental health problems of varying severity, such as depression, panic attacks, and various physical health problems including heart problems, headaches, circulatory problems, and digestive disorders (Spitzberg and Cupach 2006, p.74). Stalking also causes indirect damage to the victim. This refers to the harm suffered by the individual as a result of reduced or even interrupted social contact, changed or substantially altered life patterns in order to avoid or at least limit possible encounters with the stalker, and the loss suffered when incurring the need to rebuild a deteriorated sense of well-being (Sheridan *et al.* 2003, p.153). Therefore, it is considered that – taking into account the multifaceted nature of the forms of expression of stalking as a criminal offense, its repetitive nature and the different consequences it produces for a person – the legislator did not sufficiently assess the seriousness of this offense when giving it the status of a misdemeanor.

The norm of systemic intimidation, which is set out in the qualified norm of threatening to murder or cause a severe health impairment to a person (Art. 145(2) of the CC), falls into the category of a less serious crime, with the only penalty being up to 4 years of imprisonment. It should be noted that an analysis of the CC shows that, as a rule, the legislator establishes not only the penalty of imprisonment, but also alternative penalties to imprisonment for the commission of less serious crimes. The norm of systemic intimidation refers only to the only punishment to be imposed, i.e., imprisonment. It is believed that such a sanction reflects a proper assessment of the danger of systemic intimidation, in contrast to punishments for the unlawful stalking of a person.

The newly adopted norm of unlawful stalking therefore gives rise to further debate – not only as to its necessity in the context of the preexisting norm of systematic intimidation in criminal law, but also as to the very legal construction that is used in the formulation of the elements of the offense and the penalties that may be imposed for the realization of it. The amendment of the CC with the offense of unlawful stalking has created a competition between the general (Article 145 of CC) and the special (Article 148-1 of CC) provisions. This lack of coherence has led to the special provision providing for lenient criminal responsibility, despite the contrary intention of the legislator. In conclusion, the new norm of unlawful stalking has not brought coherence to the assessment of repeated acts of intimidation. On the contrary, it has raised one of the greatest challenges in the practical application of the norms: identifying the criteria for distinguishing between cases of systemic intimidation and those of unlawful stalking.

Interim Findings

The term "stalking" refers to a wide variety of expressions of a person's behavior, which makes it difficult to provide a clear definition of this criminal phenomenon. However, despite the challenges faced by individual states in formulating their own definitions of stalking, the coherent approach that has been reached allows stalking to be seen as a repetitive act of a person that is intimidating in nature, disturbing, and unsettling. It is the repetitive nature of the acts carried out, which are geared toward creating a sense of fear and insecurity, that is considered to be the main identifying feature of stalking. The repeated actions of the stalker force the victim to live in a constant atmosphere of anxiety, which has a negative impact on their mental health in particular, but often also on their physical health.

A coherent approach to stalking is necessary not only to better understand its nature, but also in the application of criminal responsibility. Unlawful acts of stalking are usually regulated by separate norms in national criminal laws, with the names of the norms specifically referring to unlawful stalking. However, acts constituting the content of unlawful stalking may render a person criminally responsible, even if the offense specifically referred to by that name does not exist in the criminal law. The norm of systemic intimidation (Art. 145(2) of the CC) applied in Lithuanian case law is an excellent example of this. Systematic intimidation includes all repeated acts of a person that cause fear, anxiety, insecurity, and uncertainty. Thus, even before the new independent stalking norm was introduced, acts of stalking in Lithuania were subject to criminal liability as systematic intimidation. The criminal offense defined as stalking did not exist in the CC, but this did not affect the legal assessment of repeated acts of an intimidating nature in any way. The practical application of the new offense of unlawful stalking will have to identify the criteria that will enable this offense to be distinguished from the offense of systematic intimidation.

References

Blaauw, E., Sheridan, L., and Winkel, F. W., 2003. Designing Anti-stalking Legislation on the Basis of Victims Experiences and Psychopathology. *Psychiatry, Psychology, and Law*, 9 (2), 136–145. Available from: https://doi.org/10.1375/pplt.2002.9.2.136.

Baum, K., Catalano, S., Rand, M., and Rose, K., 2009. *Stalking Victimization in the United States. National Crime Victimization Survey*. Bureau of Justice Statistics Special Report, January 2009, NCJ 224527. Available from: https://www.justice.gov/sites/default/files/ovw/legacy/2012/08/15/bjs-stalking-rpt.pdf.

Human Rights Monitoring Institute to the Human Rights Committee of the Seimas of the Republic of Lithuania On the addition of Article 145[1] to the Criminal Code. July 15, 2019, No. IS-XIV-11.

Čėsnienė, I., and Čėsna, R., 2006. Asmens persekiojimas: teisinės ir psichologinės problemos [Stalking: Legal and Psychological Issues]. *Jurisprudencija*, 11 (89), 27–33.

Criminal Code of the Republic of Lithuania, 26 September 2000, No. VIII–1649. [online] Available from: https://e-seimas.lrs.lt/portal/legalAct/lt/TAD/a84fa232877611e5bca4ce385a9b7048?jfwid=q8i88l10w [Accessed 23 August 2023].

ECtHR Opuz v. Turkey, No. 33401/02, 9 June 2009.

ECtHR, Talpis v. Italy, No. 41237/14, 2 March 2017.

Fahnestock, J., 1993. All Stalk and No Action: Pending Missouri Stalking Legislation. *University of Missouri-Kansas City Law Review*, 61.

Hall, D. M., 1998. The Victims of Stalking. In: J. R. Meloy, ed. *The Psychology of Stalking: Clinical and Forensic Perspectives*. Academic Press, 113–137.

Knight, M. A., 2014. Stalking and Cyberstalking in the United States and Rural South Dakota: Twenty-Four Years after the First Legislation. *South Dakota Law Review*, 59 (2).

Lamplugh, D., and Infield, P., 2003. Harmonising Anti-Staking Laws. *The George Washington Law Review*, 34, 853–870.

Macfarlane, B., 1997. People Who Stalk People. *UBC Law Review*, 31.

Macfarlane, B., 1999a. People Who Stalk People. Part I. *The Advocate*, 57 (2).

Macfarlane, B., 1999b. People Who Stalk People. Part II. *The Advocate*, 57 (3).

Melton, H. C., 2007. Stalking in the Context of Intimate Partner Abuse: In the Victims' Words. *Feminist Criminology*, 2 (4), 347–363.

National Centre for Victims of Crime, n.d. [online]. Available from: https://victimsofcrime.org/ [Accessed 23 August 2023].

National Institute of Justice, 1993. *Project to Develop a Model Anti-Stalking Code for States*. Available from: https://www.ojp.gov/pdffiles1/Digitization/144477NCJRS.pdf

Michailović, I., 2018. Stalking and its Victims. *Information and Media*, 82, 68–96.

Mullen, P. E., and Path, M., 2002. Stalking. *Crime and Justice*, 29, 273–318.

Public Governance Group of the Chancellery of the Government of the Republic of Lithuania. Statement on the Draft Law No. XIIIP-3746 on the Supplement to the Criminal Code of the Republic of Lithuania by Article 1671 (TAP NR. TAP-20-105(3); TAIS NR. 20-1026(4)).

Ruling of the Constitutional Court of the Republic of Lithuania of 10 June 2003.

Ruling of the Regional Court of Šiauliai of 11 July 2014, Case No. 1A-717-116-2014.

Ruling of the Supreme Court of Lithuania of 15 June 2010, Case No. 2K-341/2010.

Ruling of the Supreme Court of Lithuania of 12 January 2016, Case No. 2K-65-648/2016.

Ruling of the Supreme Court of Lithuania of 24 May 2016, Case No. 2K-186-746/2016.

Ruling of the Supreme Court of Lithuania of 20 March 2018, Case No. 2K-90-689/2018.

Ruling of the Supreme Court of Lithuania of 30 October 2018, Case No. 2K-269-895/2018.

Ruling of the Supreme Court of Lithuania of 20 November 2018, Case No. 2K-346-942/2018.

Sheridan, L. P., Blaauw, E., and Davies, G. M. 2003. Stalking Knowns and Unknowns. *Trauma, Violence, and Abuse*, 4 (2), 148–162.

Spitzberg, B. H., and Cupach, W. R. 2006. The State of the Art of Stalking: Taking Stock of the Emerging Literature. *Agression and Violent Behavior*, 12 (1), 64–68.

Eglė Bilevičiūtė

Administrative and Criminal Liability: Toward Sustainability

Administrative Liability as a Separate Type of Responsibility

When examining the issues of the coherence and harmonization of administrative and criminal liability in Europe, it should be noted that the Communication of the European Commission Toward an EU Criminal Policy (European Commission 2011) states that EU criminal law policy is primarily based on the provisions of Article 83(2) of the Treaty on the Functioning of the European Union (TFEU) (2012). EU law does not provide for a consistent set of constituent elements that characterize an administrative penalty and allow it to be distinguished from criminal sanctions. Markus Kärner (2022) stated that the concept of an administrative sanction is not precisely defined in EU law, and this concept also varies greatly between Member States. In the author's opinion, the purpose of administrative sanctions is similar to the purpose of criminal sanctions: punishment for violating the law. However, criminal sanctions (such as imprisonment) have traditionally been more severe and carry greater social stigma compared to administrative sanctions. Because of the severity of potential sanctions, there are many procedural safeguards in place, and criminal sanctions are almost exclusively imposed by the courts. Administrative sanctions are applied for behavior that does not correspond to the essence of criminal law and may not require severe sanctions. Therefore, the term *administrative* is used in legal acts to indicate the non-criminal nature of sanctions and the main role of the administrative authority in sanctioning (Kärner 2022). The assessment of the administrative sanction is presented in the documents adopted based on Articles 82 and 83 of the TFEU (criminal law measures). After examining the instruments of criminal law, two examples of interaction with administrative sanctions should be presented. The PIF Directive (Directive (EU) 2017/1371, 2017) lays down the minimum rules on the definition of criminal offenses and sanctions in the fight against fraud and other illegal activities that harm the financial interests of the Union. Despite references to non-criminal sanctions and administrative fines that cannot be equated with criminal proceedings, the PIF Directive does not provide any specific guidance on how criminal sanctions differ from administrative sanctions. The Criminal Law Directives allow for non-criminal fines that penalize legal entities to be adapted to different legal systems. There are no criteria for distinguishing between criminal and administrative sanctions for legal entities. However, in 2014, the Market Abuse Regulation (Regulation (EU) No 596/2014, 2014) and the Directive on Criminal Sanctions for Market Abuse (CSMAD) (Directive 2014/57/EU, 2014) were simultaneously adopted. According to the Market Abuse Regulation, Member States can apply administrative sanctions for market abuse, while CSMAD requires criminal sanctions for serious cases of market abuse. Article 14 of the PIF Directive states that Member States shall ensure that criminal proceedings initiated on the basis of national provisions implementing this Directive do not unduly affect the proper and effective administrative application of measures, penalties, and fines, which cannot be equated to a criminal procedure established by Union law or national implementing provisions.

The European Court of Human Rights (ECtHR) has clarified that three criteria must be considered when deciding whether a person is guilty of an offense: the assessment of the offense in national law; the level of the penalty to be imposed; and the purpose of the penalty. According to the criteria laid out by the ECtHR in *Engel and Others v. The Netherlands* (1976) and the Court of Justice of the European Union (CJEU) in *Łukasz Marcin Bonda* (2012), the nature of the offense and the severity of the sanction are the most important factors in the application of the guarantees of the criminal law, rather than the formal qualification of the penalty. Therefore, the guarantees of criminal liability also apply to criminal administrative fines, which fall under the independent criminal concept. This means that the Engel-Bonda criteria cannot be used in EU law to distinguish between criminal and non-criminal administrative sanctions (Kärner 2022). The ECtHR summarizes that an administrative offense (e.g., traffic offenses, disturbance of public order and other administrative offenses) may qualify as criminal offenses within the meaning of Article 6 of the European Convention on Human Rights (ECHR), even though in some cases a light sentence is imposed. The ECtHR also considers criminal offenses within the meaning of Article 6 of the ECHR to include customs, budgetary and financial, and competition offenses. In this case, the qualification is not affected by whether the competence to punish is conferred by national law on the courts or on administrative supervisory authorities (European Court of Human Rights 2022). This means that if the process of applying administrative liability meets the criteria set out in ECtHR case law, such a process of applying administrative liability in ECtHR Member States must comply with the guarantees provided by Article 6 of the ECHR.

The CJEU has not taken a firm position on the definition of a criminal sanction in EU law. A serious problem arises from the fact that "criminal" is simply a label that can mean different things in different Member States.

Markus Kärner (2022) suggests that purely administrative fines could be understood as criminal fines for an offense imposed by an administrative authority in a non-criminal process. The author argues that three types of criminal sanctions are used in EU law: criminal sanctions, undefined sanctions, and administrative sanctions. Purely administrative fines could be understood as criminal fines for an offense imposed by an administrative authority in a non-criminal procedure.

Administrative Liability in Different European Countries

A comparative study of most European countries (ACA-Europe 2017) carried out in 2017 showed that there is no common understanding and implementation of administrative liability across Europe. In some European countries, administrative liability is defined in legislation. Some of the countries surveyed also indicated that new regulations were being drafted or were under consideration at the time of the survey, which provide for rules similar to those applicable to criminal liability. The regulatory model in Latvia was previously the most similar to Lithuania's, but in 2020 amendments came into force, creating a single law for the general rules and procedure for the application of liability, thus unifying and simplifying the application of administrative liability and bringing it into a single system. Meanwhile, Estonia has taken the decision to completely change the legal model for the regulation of administrative liability, essentially abandoning administrative offenses as a separate category and opting to classify such offenses as a less serious category of criminal offenses. The Estonian regulation is partly like the German model of legal regulation of administrative liability.

In Germany, following the adoption of the 1968 Act on Regulated Offenses, there is a distinction between offenses (*Strraftaten*) and infringements of rules (*Ordnungswidrigkeiten*) (Law Commission 2015). The German system is an example of a codified approach to administrative sanctions, which are regulated in various special administrative law acts (Andrijauskaitė 2022). In France, the differentiation is very similar. The French legal framework, compared to the Lithuanian one, draws a clearer distinction between decisions of administrative authorities which are intended to punish and those which are administrative in nature (the equivalent of public administration), and emphasizes the application of all the guarantees of Article 6 of the ECHR in cases of punishment which are intended to punish the violator. Maciej Bernatt (2016) examined the place of administrative sanctions in the Polish legal system. He pointed out that the rules for imposing penalties are rarely fully regulated in a single piece of legislation – the main reference point is the ECtHR and EU standards. The Council of Europe standards state that the design of a system for imposing administrative penalties should consider, firstly, the complexity of the specific area of administrative law and, secondly, the severity of the sanctions. Efficiency and procedural fairness must be balanced (Bernatt, 2016).

In the United Kingdom (UK), administrative offenses are not distinguished as a separate category of offense qualification. However, the UK has detailed rules on the individualization of fines. There is no general administrative offense regime in England and Wales. However, there are separate schemes for the use of such offenses in specific situations. The use of truly criminal and purely administrative offenses may lead to a dispute as to which category is most appropriate. There is a risk that political or bureaucratic expediency will lead to the classification of conduct that should be considered truly criminal as merely administrative. It is suggested that criminal law should only apply to those criminals who deserve the stigma attached to a conviction. This should not be used as the main regulatory tool. The harm or risk caused should be considered serious enough to be criminalized. Minor offenses should be abolished in all cases where the introduction of a civil penalty (or equivalent) can do as much to provide an appropriate level of punishment and deterrence (Law Commission, 2015).

Each country chooses the system of liability for breaches of public law that it wants to establish and sets its legal framework accordingly. The practice of States in this respect varies, and three different variants of the liability which in Lithuania is qualified as administrative can be distinguished: where it is not distinguished as an independent type of liability, but is integrated into the system of criminal liability of the State (e.g., administrative liability); where, although distinguished as an independent type of liability, it is integrated into the State's criminal system (e.g., Lithuania, Germany, Austria, the Czech Republic, Latvia, Montenegro, the Netherlands, Norway, Serbia, Portugal, Spain); and where it is an independent type of liability that is not criminal in nature (e.g. Cyprus, France, Hungary, Malta) (Markevičiūtė 2022). Agnė Andrijauskaitė (2022) argues that there is no single version of what an administrative sanction is and how it occurs. Legal systems may follow a centripetal (German system), centrifugal (French system) or introspective (British system) path, introducing administrative sanctions into the respective systems. For these reasons, administrative sanctions are not easily defined.

The purpose of administrative liability is essentially the same in different countries – to enforce existing legal rules, incurring criminal liability for the violation of which would be disproportionate or inappropriate, and to punish the perpetrators of such offenses. It is a common practice in foreign legal scholarship to take a broader view of administrative liability, considering it as a purposeful attempt by the state to change the behavior of individuals in a way that is beneficial to society, with the aim of ensuring that they behave in a way that is consistent with the standards set out.

Administrative and Criminal Liability According to Lithuania's Regulations

In Lithuania, administrative and criminal liability are established separately. The Criminal Code of the Republic of Lithuania (Seimas of the Republic of Lithuania 2000a) is an integral criminal law, the purpose of which is to protect the rights and freedoms of the individual and the citizen, as well as the interests of society and the state, against criminal acts by means of criminal law. Article 12 of the Criminal Code provides that a criminal offense is a dangerous act (act or omission) prohibited by the present Code, which is punishable by a penalty other than deprivation of liberty, except for arrest. Administrative liability is regulated by the Code of Administrative Offenses of the Republic of Lithuania (hereinafter – CAO) (Seimas of the Republic of Lithuania 2015), the purpose of which is to protect human rights and freedoms, the interests of society and the state against administrative offenses by means of the law, to ensure the implementation of the principle of justice, and to promote the peaceful coexistence of the state and the people and members of society. Administrative liability in Lithuania is also regulated by other laws. Article 5 of the CAO provides that an administrative offense is a dangerous act (act or omission) committed by the perpetrator, prohibited by this code, which meets the characteristics of an administrative offense for which an administrative penalty is provided. A person shall be held administratively liable under this code for an offense which meets the elements of an administrative offense provided for in this code, provided that the offense committed does not give rise to criminal liability. Article 593 of the CAO states that the provisions of the Code of Criminal Procedure shall apply *mutatis mutandis* in the case of administrative investigations of misdemeanors. Article 632 of the CAO states that, when examining the merits of a case, the court shall have the power to carry out any procedural step provided for in the Code of Criminal Procedure. In the case of such actions, the provisions of the Code of Criminal Procedure shall apply *mutatis mutandis*. Article 666 of the CAO states that the provisions of the Code of Criminal Procedure shall apply *mutatis mutandis* to the costs of proceedings before the court in cases of administrative offenses.

Thus, the CAO regulates the specific acts prohibited in respect of natural persons, as defined in the special part of the CAO, as well as the rules applicable to the imposition of penalties and the procedure for administrative offenses. By contrast, special laws, in addition to the provisions regulating activities in a specific field, generally only regulate prohibited acts and the levels of penalties, and the detail of the regulation of the investigation of infringements varies. Jurgita Paužaitė-Kulvinskienė (2021) argues that such regulation is inconsistent. Although the current Code of Administrative Offenses, which entered into force in 2017 and replaced the Code of Administrative Law Violations of the Republic of Lithuania (1984), has changed the regulation of administrative liability, it was not intended to merge administrative liability under the CAO with liability under special laws.

Milda Markevičiūtė (2022) argues that, given the abovementioned plethora of acts regulating administrative liability, it is difficult even for the courts to decide which act should be used as an analogy in a particular case of a dispute over punishment. It is considered that the inclusion of most of the rules on liability in a unified system would create greater comfort for the entities imposing administrative liability, for the entities subject to liability, and for the legislator. At present, administrative liability is closely linked to criminal liability, as both types of liability pursue the same objectives (punishment, special and general prevention). Moreover, a similar system of sanctions is provided for as a result of the application of both types of liability. Finally, the offenses themselves are of a similar nature, i.e., they apply to acts or omissions in the same areas, and the criterion for distinguishing liability is often based on features related to the expression of the specific offense (act or omission), such as the seriousness of the offense (e.g., in the case of drink-driving) or the value of the object (e.g., in the case of theft). Markevičiūtė considers that Lithuanian law emphasizes the criminal nature of administrative liability. Meanwhile, the Supreme Administrative Court of Lithuania (Supreme Administrative Court of Lithuania 2018) has expressed the opinion that to determine whether a specific violation of law qualifies as criminal within the meaning of ECtHR jurisprudence, it is necessary to assess first of all whether such a violation belongs to criminal law in the system of national law. The high level of the penalty to be imposed does not in itself determine the criminal nature of the infringement. In Lithuanian case law, the criteria for determining whether an infringement amounts to a criminal offense (the nature of the infringement and the severity of the penalty) are applied in a broad and complex manner: the presence of one of these features is sufficient for the infringement to amount to a criminal offense (Markevičiūtė 2022).

Researchers' Opinions on the Difference Between Criminal and Administrative Sanctions

The EU's criminal law competence is divided into criminal law in the narrow sense and the law of administrative sanctions. The distinction between what is and what is not criminal under the EU competence is not clear, but this should be decided on the basis of a number of factors (e.g., whether it entails imprisonment or other burdensome sanctions). Öberg (2013) proposed that there should be two concepts of criminal sanctions in EU law. He proposed a list of criteria for defining criminal sanctions and stated that individual administrative fines should not normally be criminalized (unless they are linked to the commission of a criminal offense and a criminal record), as they are not deterrents in practice and do not express serious moral condemnation.

Albertas Čaplinskas *et al.* (2004) argued that the problem of the distinction between criminal and administrative liability has become particularly acute since the new Criminal Code of the Republic of Lithuania (Seimas of the Republic of Lithuania 2000a) introduced liability not only for criminal offenses, but also for misdemeanors, which are often not easy to distinguish from administrative offenses. The criteria for distinguishing between criminal offenses and administrative offenses are based on the objective features of the offense, relating to the social importance of the object of the offense as a legal value, the nature of the offense, its social harmfulness and dangerousness, and the nature and extent of the consequences. Agnė Andrijauskaitė (2022) argued that administrative sanctions are flexible, versatile, and less costly law enforcement measures compared to criminal law measures. The use of administrative sanctions is very attractive to various policymakers who want to impose punishment quickly and economically without resorting to judicial action. However, it should be noted that a financial penalty may be small but may destroy the reputation of the applicant. Even small fines can lead to a chain of negative consequences, e.g., a traffic offense and the resulting sanction may subsequently lead to the claimant not being able to receive the full insurance benefit (Andrijauskaitė 2022).

Alan Brudner (2009) argued that none of the criteria for distinguishing between real crime and legal violations are able to distinguish between the two. Petter Asp (2013) argued that the main problem with the criminal approach is that it lacks the normative constraints on preventive measures that characterize administrative enforcement. Eithan Y. Kidron (2018) examined when a regulator should favor criminal sanctions over administrative sanctions. The author argued that administrative sanctions have evolved as a distinct sanctioning tool alongside the criminal and civil spheres. Both criminal and administrative sanctions protect public law – in both cases, the State acts as the legal representative of this right and protects it on the basis of the justification of corrective justice. Where the regulator has evidence of subjective guilt on the part of the offender, it should opt for the criminal courts. Where there is evidence of excessive future risk but no evidence of subjective fault, it should opt for an administrative court.

In other words, the administrative approach should act as a parallel rather than an alternative method of criminal enforcement (Kidron 2018). Michael Faure and Franziska Weber (2017) argued that there are significant differences between administrative and criminal procedures. In administrative proceedings, the risk of error depends on the complexity of the issues at stake and the resources, expertise, and experience of the authorities. The potential for error is more likely in administrative law enforcement compared to criminal law enforcement because the decision-making process is less complex. The high standard of proof in criminal law makes it less likely that an innocent person will be convicted. Thomas Blondiau *et al.* (2015) argued that the shift from a criminal enforcement system for environmental offenses to a combined criminal and administrative system is not necessarily positive. It should be borne in mind that there are some differences between the administrative and criminal enforcement of environmental offenses: similar offenses are punishable by lower penalties in administrative proceedings than in criminal proceedings. The authors concluded that criminal prosecution is still a more powerful tool to deter offenders. The choice between a combined approach and an enforcement system using only criminal procedures should be seen as a compromise. Markus Kärner (2022) stated that the EU law on criminal sanctions that came into force after the Treaty of Lisbon (2007; European Commission 2011) makes a distinction between criminal and non-criminal sanctions: the legislator prefers non-criminal sanctions. The regulation of such sanctions has become more precise, and the legislator has started to refer to the administrative nature of such sanctions. However, this may limit the discretion of Member States to find the most appropriate way to transpose such sanctions into national law, and may amount to a prohibition of the application of criminal law.

The Criteria for Determining Administrative and Criminal Liability in the Case Law of Various Courts

At the European level, administrative law rules are primarily shaped by the CJEU based on unwritten general principles of law common to the constitutional traditions of Member States. The CJEU jurisprudence classifies the law on administrative offenses as criminal law, as criminal law covers all acts that are punishable (Piesliakas 2008). This means that CJEU case law does not distinguish the type of liability if the administrative offense committed is criminal in nature. The imposition of criminal administrative sanctions together with criminal law measures (the so-called calibrated regulatory approach) shows that the CJEU is not prepared to identify administrative sanctions with criminal law sanctions and to prohibit their dual use. The CJEU does not talk about administrative law, let alone administrative sanctions, although it is not always easy to distinguish between administrative and criminal sanctions. It has been repeatedly stressed in case law that the CJEU cannot control the content of a State's national law through Article 6. The CJEU has reiterated that it is the task of national courts to determine the appropriate punishment in the circumstances of the case (Andrijauskaitė 2022).

In assessing whether an administrative offense committed under the national law of a Member State is criminal in nature, the CJEU applies the three so-called Engel criteria: the qualification of the offense in national law; the nature of the offense; and the severity of the sanction imposed on the offender (Opinion of Advocate General Cruz Villalón 2012). As these principles can operate independently, the fact that, for example, an offense may only be punishable by a fine does not mean that it can be classified as non-criminal. The view that minor offenses can simply be transferred to the Administrative Offenses Code may turn out to be a mistake, as the small scale of the offense is not relevant in determining whether it is truly criminal or not (Law Commission 2015).

As previously mentioned, in the Lithuanian legal system, criminal, and administrative liability are separate types of legal liability. The norms of criminal and administrative liability are similar and there are no clear criteria to distinguish between them. According to Lithuanian jurisprudence, the distinction between these types of liability is based on the seriousness of the act. When examining a criminal case, the court has to refer to the criteria formulated by the CJEU and decide whether the nature of the violation falls within the sphere of criminal law. Lithuanian case law does not distinguish between the type of liability in the case of an administrative offense of a criminal nature and in the case of an administrative offense of a non-criminal nature. The case law shows that courts sometimes do not assess whether an administrative offense is criminal at all. The most important criterion that the Lithuanian courts focus on is whether at least one essential element of the offense is identical (Supreme Court of Lithuania 2009). Lithuanian courts have also often stated, based on case law, that it is not forbidden to impose double legal liability on a person (Supreme Court of Lithuania 2006), provided that its main purpose is not punishment. However, both the ECtHR and the Lithuanian courts apply double legal liability to a person if the violations are qualified as concurrent (*Oliveira v. Switzerland* 1998).

The content of the principle of criminal liability as a measure of last resort is revealed in the jurisprudence of the Constitutional Court and the Supreme Court of Lithuania. With regard to the legality and justification of the application of administrative or criminal liability, the Constitutional Court of the Republic of Lithuania has repeatedly emphasized that, when assessing whether legal liability falls under administrative or criminal law, it should be stressed that there are a number of similarities, but also significant differences, between administrative and criminal legal liability. The gravity of administrative offenses and criminal offenses is different, as are the consequences of being held administratively or criminally liable (Constitutional Court of the Republic of Lithuania 2005). The Supreme Court of Lithuania, when speaking on the issue of the application of administrative and criminal liability, has stated that administrative offenses are dangerous acts, because their commission also violates certain values, but their seriousness is lower. Since the difference between administrative and criminal liability is also determined by the nature of administrative and criminal offenses, i.e., the greater or lesser dangerousness of these acts, the criteria for determining this increased or reduced dangerousness become crucial in distinguishing an administrative offense from a criminal offense (Supreme Court of Lithuania 2012).

On November 10, 2005, the Constitutional Court stated in its ruling that every time it is necessary to decide whether to recognize an act as a crime or another violation of the law, it is very important to assess what results can be achieved by other measures unrelated to the application of criminal penalties – *inter alia*, administrative sanctions.

The Constitutional Court, interpreting the constitutional principle of the rule of law, has stated that the imposition of legal restrictions and liability for infringements of the law must comply with the requirement of reasonableness, as well as with the principle of proportionality, according to which the legal measures imposed must be necessary in a democratic society and appropriate to the pursuit of legitimate and generally important objectives (there must be a balance between the objectives and the means), and they must not restrict a person's rights more than is necessary to achieve those objectives (Rulings of the Constitutional Court of December 13, 2004, December 29, 2004, September 29, 2005, January 16, 2006).

The Supreme Court of Lithuania, in accordance with the abovementioned interpretations of constitutional jurisprudence, has stated that both the purpose of criminal law and the general principles of law, as enshrined in the jurisprudence of democratic states governed by the rule of law, presuppose that it is impossible to establish a legal practice where criminal law norms are applied in civil, administrative or disciplinary disputes, and the behavior of a person is regarded as representing the commission of a criminal offense, exclusively in the context of the above-mentioned legal relations. Therefore, whenever it is necessary to decide whether to recognize an act as a crime or another legal offense, it is essential to assess what results can be achieved by other non-punitive measures (administrative, disciplinary, civil sanctions or measures of public influence, etc.) (Constitutional Court Resolutions of November 13, 1997, November 10, 2005, cassation rulings in criminal cases Nos. 2K-409/2011, 2K-P-267/2011) (Supreme Court of Lithuania 2021a). The Supreme Court of Lithuania (2021b), in case No. 2K-207-788/2021, stated that a criminal offense may also be recognized as a continuous offense in cases where one or several individual acts correspond to the elements of an administrative offense, but the totality of the acts must be treated as a criminal offense.

The Supreme Court of Lithuania, in its ruling of January 14, 2014, stated that in cases where both criminal and administrative liability is provided for an analogous act, when deciding on the determination of the type of legal liability, the issues of the constituent elements of a criminal act and criminal liability are considered first, and only after concluding that the seriousness of the act has not reached a level that makes it criminal are the questions of administrative liability addressed.

In the case law, it is established that the administrative penalty and the measure of administrative impact imposed must punish the offender and cause them suffer the corresponding negative consequences. The law also places the public interest of the society above the public interest in ensuring traffic safety and public security through the application of preventive measures, and not the personal interest of the person who committed the offense in avoiding negative consequences. This is also in line with constitutional jurisprudence, which has repeatedly stated that, in order to prevent unlawful acts, it is not always the case that such acts should be criminalized and that the most severe measures, namely penalties, should be applied to the perpetrators.

The Relevance of the Application of the *non bis in idem* Principle for the Qualification of Administrative and Criminal Liability

The qualification of administrative and criminal liability has important implications for the application of the *non bis in idem* principle. While the scope of this principle has traditionally been limited to criminal law, ECtHR case law has led to its extension to situations of criminal and administrative sanctions.

In the EU, the *non bis in idem* principle is enshrined in Protocol 7 of the ECHR, the Charter of Fundamental Rights of the European Union (2012), the Convention on the Schengen Agreement (2000), the Convention on the International Recognition of Criminal Sentences (1970), the European Convention on the Transfer of Criminal Proceedings (1972), and the Council of Europe Convention on Extradition (1996).

Although the autonomy and independence of administrative and criminal proceedings have traditionally been accepted in Member States, many exceptions to this principle are made (Court of Justice of the European Union 2017). Four groups of Member States can be distinguished. First, some Member States follow an autonomy approach, establishing that the initiation of criminal proceedings does not affect the course of administrative proceedings and vice versa (Germany, France). Second, other Member States, although following this traditional approach, have reduced it for many infringements by providing that the second process must be suspended or prohibited (Hungary, Poland, UK). Third, other Member States have special rules providing for the suspension of administrative proceedings after the initiation of criminal proceedings, whether during the proceedings aimed at imposing an administrative penalty (Spain) or during the enforcement phase of the imposed sanction (Italy). Fourth, in Sweden, the new system came into force in 2016. It has been established that under certain circumstances the administrative tax case is not initiated if a criminal case has been initiated.

In addition to those factors related to the connection between different processes, it can be noted that in certain states, administrative authorities are bound by the factual circumstances established during the criminal process (Spain, France) (Court of Justice of the European Union 2017). The jurisprudence of the ECtHR and the CJEU has gradually developed judicial formulations on the scope of the *non bis in idem* principle, leaving to national courts the task of applying to the various legal traditions conditions that are compatible with the ECHR, Charter of Fundamental Rights of the European Union, and CISA (The Schengen acquis; The Convention implementing the Schengen Agreement) provisions. A key issue causing tension between the jurisprudence of different courts is the question of the combination of different types of proceedings (administrative and criminal), with mutual influence between the ECtHR and the CJEU (Coffey 2023).

Giulia Lasagni and Sofia Mirandola's (2019) article observed that both the ECtHR and the CJEU have united their views – not only lowering the assessment standards, but also establishing new rules that, although partially converging, remain very unclear. Until 2016, the jurisprudence of the Strasbourg and Luxembourg courts on double jeopardy was aligned, with a higher level of protection (Simonato 2017). This pro-defendant approach can be seen in the concept of *non bis in idem*: the CJEU, and soon after the ECtHR, defined it as the same set of factual circumstances, regardless of the legal characterization of the crime or the protected legal interest (Peers *et al.* 2021). This convergence of jurisprudence, beneficial to the individual, has been extended under both the ECHR and the Charter of Fundamental Rights to cover not only criminal proceedings but also administrative criminal proceedings of a criminal nature, considering the so-called Engel criteria (*Sergey Zolotukhin v. Russia* 2009; *Åklagaren v. Hans Åkerberg Fransson* 2013). The reconciliation of the opinion of the two courts may become even more necessary, as national judges may decide to request a preliminary interpretation from both European courts for the same reason (Lasagni and Mirandola 2019).

The provision of Article 31, paragraph 5 of the Constitution of Lithuania reflects the *non bis in idem* legal principle: a person cannot be punished a second time for the same violation of the law. The principle does not mean that different types of legal responsibility cannot be applied to a person for a violation of the law in general, nor that they cannot be subject to the main and additional punishment for a crime, or the main and additional administrative penalty for an administrative violation of the law (Constitutional Court of the Republic of Lithuania 2001). The Supreme Court of Lithuania (2016) emphasized that the *non bis in idem* principle also means that if a person was held not criminally but administratively responsible for an act contrary to the law – i.e., a sanction was applied to them and the penalty was imposed not as a crime, but as an administrative violation of the law – they cannot be held criminally responsible for that act. This principle is also established in Article 592 of the Civil Code (Seimas of the Republic of Lithuania 2000b).

In ECtHR jurisprudence, criminal law includes the so-called administrative law of Lithuania. For this reason, the ECtHR, when evaluating whether, according to the Lithuanian legal system, an administrative violation of the law can be attributed to criminal law according to the ECtHR, applies three criteria: 1) the classification of the violation in national law; 2) the nature of the violation; and 3) the severity of the sanction assigned to the offender (Opinion of Advocate General Cruz Villalón 2012). When deciding whether an administrative violation of law can be attributed to criminal law, only the last two characteristics are decisive. Although the violation would be qualified as an administrative violation of the law in Lithuania, according to these criteria, the ECtHR can assess that the violation is attributable to criminal liability. In such a case, it would mean that the application of criminal liability to a person punished for the same actions with an administrative penalty violates the principle of non bis in idem.

Interim Findings

In the Lithuanian legal system, criminal, and administrative liability are separate types of legal liability. The norms of criminal and administrative liability are similar, and there are no clear criteria that would allow them to be delimited. The criminal nature of administrative liability is noted in Lithuanian law. When analyzing the prospects for the development of the legal regulation of administrative responsibility, it should be noted that the idea of defining European criminal law harmonization guidelines or common principles of special criminal law or administrative criminal law (commonly called administrative liability in Lithuanian law) has been discussed many times at the European Union level. The Lithuanian Constitutional Court (2008) supported this conclusion, indicating that economic sanctions are attributable to the institute of administrative responsibility. The Supreme Administrative Court of Lithuania (2018) relied on this practice of the Constitutional Court in subsequent cases.

After summarizing the research conducted, it can be concluded that it is necessary to consider the severity and nature of the violation of the law. Administrative sanctions imposed for certain illegal actions which are considered particularly serious may not be a strong enough response. At the same time, criminal sanctions may be chosen when it is considered important to emphasize strong disapproval to ensure deterrence. Including a conviction in a criminal record can have a particularly dissuasive effect. The type of sanction that is considered most appropriate to achieve the overall objective of an effective, proportionate, and dissuasive sanction should be chosen. An administrative sanction can often be decided on and implemented immediately, avoiding lengthy, and costly procedures. For this reason, administrative sanctions may be considered in areas where, for example, infringements are not very serious or particularly numerous, as well as in areas where administrative sanctions and procedures are appropriate and effective for other reasons (e.g., complex economic evaluations). It is not uncommon for administrative law to provide a greater variety of possible sanctions, from fines and suspension of licenses to the deprivation of the right to receive state benefits, and to adapt them to a specific situation. Therefore, in many cases, administrative sanctions can be sufficient and even more effective than criminal sanctions. It is acceptable that it is appropriate to leave two separate types of liability in Lithuanian law, more clearly demarcating administrative and criminal liability. For this, it would be appropriate to review the classification of current administrative offenses, with the aim of transferring some of the administrative offenses that cause a great danger to public safety, human health, and life – such as driving while intoxicated – to criminal offenses.

References

ACA-Europe, 2017. *Administrative Sanctions in European Law: Summary of National Reports for the Purpose of a Seminar* [online]. Available from: http://www.aca-europe.eu/images/media_kit/seminars/2017_Ljubljana/Summary-of-National-Reports-Administrative-Sanctions.pdf [Accessed 20 October 2023].

Andrijauskaitė, A., 2022. *The Principles of Administrative Punishment under the ECHR*. Thesis. (PhD). The German University of Administrative Sciences Speyer, Vilnius University [online]. Available from: https://dopus.uni-speyer.de/frontdoor/deliver/index/docId/5881/file/ivykiai.pdf [Accessed 20 September 2023].

Asp, P., 2013. Preventionism and Criminalization of Nonconsummate Offences. In: A. Ashworth *et al.*, ed. *Prevention and the Limits of the Criminal Law*. Oxford: Oxford University Press, 23–46.

Bernatt, M., 2016. Administrative Sanctions: Between Efficiency and Procedural Fairness. *Review of European Administrative Law*, 9 (1), 5–32.

Blondiau, T., Billiet, C. M., and Rousseau, S., 2015. Comparison of Criminal and Administrative Penalties for Environmental Offenses. *European Journal of Law and Economics*, 39 (1), 11–35.

Brudner, A., 2009. *Punishment and Freedom*. Oxford: Oxford University Press. Available from: https://doi.org/10.1093/acprof:oso/9780199207251.001.0001 https://global.oup.com/academic/product/punishment-and-freedom-9780199652334?cc=lt&lang=en& [Accessed 20 September 2023].

Charter of Fundamental Rights of the European Union. OJ C 326, 26.10.2012, p. 391–407. [online]. Available from: https://eur-lex.europa.eu/legal-content/EN/TXT/?uri=CELEX:12012P/TXT [Accessed 20 October 2023].

CJEU, Åklagaren v. Hans Åkerberg Fransson, Case C-617/10, 26 February 2013 [online]. Available from: https://curia.europa.eu/juris/liste.jsf?num=C-617/10 [Accessed 20 September 2023].

CJEU, Łukasz Marcin Bonda, Case C-489/10, 5 June 2012 [online]. Available from: https://curia.europa.eu/juris/liste.jsf?num=C-489/10&language=EN [Accessed 20 September 2023].

Code of Administrative Law Violations of the Republic of Lithuania, 1984. Invalid from 1 January 2017 [online]. Available from: https://www.infolex.lt/portal/start_ta.asp?act=doc&fr=pop&doc=103787&title=LR%20administracini%F8%20teis%EBs%20pa%FEeidim%F8%20kodeksas [Accessed 10 September 2023].

Coffey G., 2023. An Interpretative Analysis of the European ne bis in idem Principle Through the Lens of ECHR, CFR and CISA Provisions: Are Three Streams Flowing in the Same Channel? *New Journal of European Criminal Law*, 14 (3), 345–373.

Constitutional Court of the Republic of Lithuania, 2001. *Resolution Regarding the compliance of Article 130(2) of the Code of Administrative Offenses of the Republic of Lithuania (edition of July 18, 1994) with the Constitution of the Republic of Lithuania of May 7, 2001* [online]. Available from: https://lrkt.lt/lt/teismo-aktai/paieska/135/ta322 [Accessed 20 October 2023].

Constitutional Court of the Republic of Lithuania, 2005. *Resolution Regarding the Compliance of ATPK with the Constitution of November 10, 2005* [online]. Available from: https://lrkt.lt/lt/teismo-aktai/paieska/135/ta248/content [Accessed 20 October 2023].

Constitutional Court of the Republic of Lithuania, 2008. *Resolution Regarding the application of sanctions – deletion of the address of the place of purchase of scrap metal and waste from the license of March 15, 2008* [online]. Available from: https://lrkt.lt/lt/teismo-aktai/paieska/135/ta490/content [Accessed 20 October 2023].

Convention drawn up on the basis of Article K.3 of the Treaty on European Union, relating to extradition between the Member States of the European Union. OJ C 313, 23.10.1996, p. 12–23. Available from: https://eur-lex.europa.eu/LexUriServ/LexUriServ.do?uri=CELEX%3A41996A1023%2802%29%3AEN%3AHTML [Accessed 20 October 2023].

Court of Justice of the European Union, 2017. *Research Note. Cumulation of Administrative and Criminal Sanctions and the ne bis in idem Principle.* Available from: https://curia.europa.eu/jcms/upload/docs/application/pdf/2019-12/ndr-2017-003_synthese_en_neutralisee_finale.pdf [Accessed 20 October 2023].

Čaplinskas, A., Dapšys, A., and Misiūnas, J., 2004. Theoretical Problems of Delimitation of Criminal and Administrative Responsibility. *Teisės problemos*, 46 (4), 44–82.

European Commission, 2011. *Communication from the Commission to the European Parliament, the Council, the European Economic and Social Committee and the Committee of the Regions. Towards an EU Criminal Policy: Ensuring the effective implementation of EU policies through criminal law. COM(2011) 573 final* [online]. Available from: https://eur-lex.europa.eu/legal-content/EN/TXT/?uri=celex%3A52011DC0573 [Accessed 20 October 2023].

Directive 2014/57/EU of the European Parliament and of the Council of 16 April 2014 on criminal sanctions for market abuse (market abuse directive). OJ L 173, 12.6.2014, p. 179–189 [online]. Available from: https://eur-lex.europa.eu/legal-content/EN/TXT/?uri=celex%3A32014L0057 [Accessed 20 September 2023].

Directive (EU) 2017/1371 of the European Parliament and of the Council of 5 July 2017 on the fight against fraud to the Union's financial interests by means of criminal law (the PIF Directive). OJ L 198, 28.7.2017, p. 29–41 [online]. Available from: https://eur-lex.europa.eu/legal-content/EN/TXT/?uri=CELEX%3A32017L1371 [Accessed 20 September 2023].

European Convention on Human Rights as amended by Protocols Nos. 11, 14 and 15 supplemented by Protocols Nos. 1, 4, 6, 7, 12, 13 and 16 [online]. Available from: https://www.echr.coe.int/Pages/home.aspx?p=basictexts&c [Accessed 20 September 2023].

ECtHR, Engel and Others v. The Netherlands, Application Nos. 5100/71, 5101/71, 5102/71, 5354/72, 5370/72, 23 November 1976 [online]. Available from: https://hudoc.echr.coe.int/eng?i=001-57478 [Accessed 20 September 2023].

ECtHR, Oliveira v. Switzerland, 84/1997/868/1080, 30 July 1998 [online]. Available from: https://jurinfo.jep.gov.co/normograma/compilacion/docs/case%20of%20oliveira%20v.%20switzerland.htm [Accessed 20 September 2023].

ECtHR, Sergey Zolotukhin v. Russia, Application No. 14939/03, 10 February 2009 [online]. Available from: https://hudoc.echr.coe.int/en?i=001-91222https://hudoc.echr.coe.int/fre[Accessed 20 September 2023].

European Court of Human Rights, 2022. *Guide on Article 6 of the European Convention on Human Rights. Right to a fair trial (criminal limb). Updated on 31 August 2024* [online]. Available from: https://ks.echr.coe.int/web/echr-ks/all-case-law-guides [Accessed 20 February 2025].

Faure, M., and Weber, F., 2017. The Diversity of the EU Approach to Law Enforcement—Towards a Coherent Model Inspired by a Law and Economics Approach. *German Law Journal*, 18 (4), 823–879.

Kärner, M., 2022. Interplay Between European Union Criminal Law and Administrative Sanctions: Constituent Elements of Transposing Punitive Administrative Sanctions into National Law. *New Journal of European Criminal Law*, 13 (1), 42–68.

Kidron, E. Y., 2018. Understanding Administrative Sanctioning as Corrective Justice. *Journal of Law Reform*, 51 (2), 313–355.

Lasagni, G., and Mirandola, S., 2019. The European ne bis in idem at the Crossroads of Administrative and Criminal Law. *The European Criminal Law Associations' Forum*, 2, 126–135.

Law Commission, 2015. *Consultation Paper No 195. Criminal Liability in Regulatory Contexts* [online]. Available from: https://lawcom.gov.uk/project/criminal-liability-in-regulatory-contexts/ [Accessed 20 October 2023].

Markevičiūtė, M., 2022. *Administracinės atsakomybės samprata ir teisinio reguliavimo modelis Lietuvoje* [The Concept of Administrative Liability and its Model in Lithuania]. Thesis. (PhD). Vilnius University. [online]. Available from: https://www.google.com/url?sa=t&rct=j&q=&esrc=s&source=web&cd=&ved=2ahUKEwiYq9y6s4KCAxWE_rsIHU35BEgQFnoECA0QAQ&url=https://talpykla.elaba.lt/elaba-fedora/objects/elaba:125043656/datastreams/MAIN/content&usg=AOvVaw3vZRYZXgAkwsFoU3zXUrS&opi=89978449 [Accessed 10 September 2023].

Öberg, J., 2013. The Definition of Criminal Sanctions in the EU. *European Criminal Law Review*, 3 (3), 273–299.

Opinion of Advocate General Cruz Villalón delivered on 12 June 2012. Åklagaren v. Hans Åkerberg Fransson, Case C-617/10. ECLI:EU:C:2012:340. Available from: https://eur-lex.europa.eu/legal-content/EN/TXT/?uri=CELEX%3A62010CC0617 [Accessed 20 October 2023].

Paužaitė-Kulvinskienė, J., 2021. Administrative Liability in Lithuania: The Model of Corporate Administrative Liability. In: G. Švedas, and D. Murauskas, (eds.), *Legal Developments During 30 Years of Lithuanian Independence: Overview of Legal Accomplishments and Challenges in Lithuania*. Springer, 261–285.

Peers, S., Hervey, T., Kenner, J., and Ward, A., (eds.), 2021. *The EU Charter of Fundamental Rights. A Commentary*. Bloomsbury Publishing.

Piesliakas, V., 2008. *Lietuvos baudžiamoji teisė, Kn. 2. Aplinkybės, darančios įtaką baudžiamajai atsakomybei, ir nusikalstamos veikos teisiniai padariniai* [Lithuanian Criminal Law, Book 2. Circumstances that affect criminal liability and legal effects of criminal acts]. Vilnius: Justitia.

Regulation (EU) No 596/2014 of the European Parliament and of the Council of 16 April 2014 on market abuse (market abuse regulation) and repealing Directive 2003/6/EC of the European Parliament and of the Council and Commission Directives 2003/124/EC, 2003/125/EC and 2004/72/EC. OJ L 173, 12.6.2014, p. 1–61 [online]. Available from: https://eur-lex.europa.eu/legal-content/EN/TXT/?uri=celex%3A32014R0596 [Accessed 20 September 2023].

Seimas of the Republic of Lithuania, 2000a. *Law on the Approval and Entry into Force of the Criminal Code of the Republic of Lithuania* [online]. Available from: https://e-seimas.lrs.lt/portal/legalAct/lt/TAD/TAIS.111555/asr [Accessed 10 October 2022].

Seimas of the Republic of Lithuania, 2000b. *Law on the approval, enforcement and implementation of the Civil Code of the Republic of Lithuania* [online]. Available from: https://www.e-tar.lt/portal/lt/legalAct/TAR.8A39C83848CB [Accessed 10 September 2023].

Seimas of the Republic of Lithuania, 2015. *Law on the Procedure for Approval, Entry into Force and Implementation of the Code of Administrative Offenses. Republic of Lithuania Code of Administrative Offenses* [online]. Available from: https://www.e-tar.lt/portal/lt/legalAct/4ebe66c0262311e5bf92d6af3f6a2e8b [Accessed 10 September 2023].

Simonato, M., 2017. *Two instruments but a difficult relationship? Some upcoming decisions of the CJEU on the ne bis in idem*. European Law Blog [online]. Available from: https://europeanlawblog.eu/2017/11/15/two-instruments-but-a-difficult-relationship-some-upcoming-decisions-of-the-cjeu-on-the-ne-bis-in-idem/ [Accessed 20 October 2023].

Supreme Administrative Court of Lithuania, 2018. *Decision in administrative case no. eI-5-492/2018 of May 10, 2018* [online]. Available from: https://www.lvat.lt/data/public/uploads/2018/01/ei-5-2018-priemimo-klausimas.pdf [Accessed 20 September 2023].

Supreme Court Of Lithuania, 2006. *Ruling in criminal case no. 2K-152/2006 of March 7, 2006* [online]. Available from: https://eteismai.lt/byla/27956988274892/2K-152/2006 [Accessed 20 September 2023].

Supreme Court of Lithuania, 2009. *Ruling in criminal case no. 2K-102/2009 of April 16, 2009* [online]. Available from: https://eteismai.lt/byla/196071132630150/2K-102/2009 [Accessed 20 September 2023].

Supreme Court of Lithuania, 2012. *Ruling in criminal case no. 2K-7-76/2012 of March 13, 2012* [online]. Available from: https://eteismai.lt/byla/151425954456393/2K-7-76/2012 [Accessed 20 September 2023].

Supreme Court of Lithuania, 2016. *Ruling in criminal case no. 2K-109-788/*2016 *of March 22, 2016* [online]. Available from: https://eteismai.lt/byla/198312064267966/2K-109-788/2016 [Accessed 20 September 2023].

Supreme Court of Lithuania, 2021a. *Ruling in criminal case no. 2K-192-511/2021 of November 16, 2021* [online]. Available from: https://www.lat.lt/teismu-praktika/lat-praktika/aktuali-praktika-nuo-2015-m./61 [Accessed 20 October 2023].

Supreme Court of Lithuania, 2021b. *Ruling in criminal case no. 2K-207-788/2021 of November 30, 2021* [online]. Available from: https://www.lat.lt/veikla/teismu-praktika/lat-praktika/60 [Accessed 20 October 2023].

The Schengen acquis – Convention implementing the Schengen Agreement of 14 June 1985 between the Governments of the States of the Benelux Economic Union, the Federal Republic of Germany and the French Republic on the gradual abolition of checks at their common borders. OJ L 239, 22.9.2000, p. 19–62 [online]. Available from: https://eur-lex.europa.eu/legal-content/EN/TXT/?uri=celex%3A42000A0922%2802%29 [Accessed 20 October 2023].

Treaty of Lisbon amending the Treaty on European Union and the Treaty establishing the European Community, signed at Lisbon, 13 December 2007. OJ C 306, 17.12.2007, p. 1–271 [online]. Available from: http://data.europa.eu/eli/treaty/lis/sign [Accessed 20 September 2023].

Treaty on the Functioning of the European Union (Consolidated version). OJ C 326, 26.10.2012, p. 47–390. Available from: http://data.europa.eu/eli/treaty/tfeu_2012/oj [Accessed 20 October 2023].

Andrius Nevera

Standards for the Coherent Application of the Principles of Criminal Jurisdiction in Relation to Criminal Acts Committed by Lithuanian Citizens and Persons Permanently Resident in Lithuania Outside the Territory of Lithuania

General Remarks

The system of principles of criminal jurisdiction was designed to ensure, as far as possible, the applicability of the criminal laws of a given sovereign state and the implementation of the principle of the inevitability of liability. For this reason, in addition to the territorial principle, other principles (flag, active personality, passive personality, protection of the interests of the State, universal, and representative) have also been developed, each with specific and distinctive content which determines the grounds and limits of their application.

The awareness of these aspects and their proper implementation ensures the individuality of each jurisdictional principle and thus their coherent synergy. To hold otherwise would be to accept that the scope of application of any principle of criminal jurisdiction may be extended according to the imagination and whim of the entity applying it, based on a literal interpretation of the relevant criminal law rules. It is the beginnings of such an approach that can be identified in Lithuania, as for some time now Lithuanian citizens have been prosecuted under the Criminal Code of the Republic of Lithuania (hereinafter – Lithuanian CC, or CC) based not on the active personality principle, but on the universal principle of criminal jurisdiction for crimes committed outside the territory of Lithuania. In the case law, there are also cases where criminal acts committed by Lithuanian citizens on board a foreign vessel on the high seas are qualified as having been committed in the territory of the flag state of the vessel.

These examples demonstrate that acts committed abroad by Lithuanian citizens and persons permanently residing in Lithuania are qualified incorrectly, contradictorily, and without any appreciation of the purpose and content of jurisdictional principles. In other words, instead of ensuring the coherent application of the jurisdictional principles enshrined in the CC and thus resolving the issue of the imposition of a fair sentence, Lithuania is engaged in a fundamentally contradictory and somewhat chaotic practice. Such activities may result in the resuscitation of the concept of the territoriality of the vessel, and the recognition of the primacy of the universal principle over the active personality principle and other extraterritorial jurisdictional principles enshrined in the Lithuanian CC.

To prevent such situations and to draw very clear boundaries between the jurisdictional principles applicable to Lithuanian citizens and persons permanently resident in Lithuania in respect of criminal acts committed by them outside the territory of Lithuania, there is a need to analyze the most important and relevant aspects of the content of the flag, active personality and universal principles, and to clarify the mechanisms of their coherent interaction. In the context of this research, the analysis of the rules for determining the place of commission of a criminal act becomes an important issue in order to identify the cases where a criminal act is committed outside the territory of Lithuania.

The analysis of the rules on the place of commission of a criminal act is also relevant to the question of their relationship with the system of principles of state criminal jurisdiction. Finally, in order to fully develop the chosen topic, it is also important to clarify the substantive nature of the condition of reciprocal criminality of the act and to draw guidelines for its regulation in the CC, which would ensure the effective and consistent application of the active personality principle.

The Place of Commission of a Criminal Act and Its Relevance for the Coherent Application of the Principles of Criminal Jurisdiction

The flag principle, the active personality principle and the universal principle can be applied when a criminal act is committed outside the territory of a state. The relevance of the active personality principle for criminal acts committed abroad is clearly established in Article 5 of the Lithuanian CC. However, this is not the case either in Article 4(1) of the CC, which enshrines the flag principle, or in Article 7 of the CC, which enshrines the universal principle. Therefore, the impression may be given that these criminal acts can be punished irrespective of the place of their commission.

There is no doubt that such an interpretation of the norms enshrining the flag principle and the universal principle is impossible, as it would negate the primacy of the territorial principle, undermine the provisions of international treaties, and upset the coherence of all principles of criminal jurisdiction. At first sight, this discussion may seem pointless, since it is self-evident that criminal acts committed in the territory of any sovereign state are punishable exclusively on the basis of the territorial principle. However, in the context of the topic at hand, this emphasis is particularly important, because the explanation of any legal norm cannot be based only on a linguistic method of explanation. The Constitutional Court of the Republic of Lithuania has repeatedly addressed this issue in its jurisprudence, unambiguously emphasizing that a legal norm must be explained at least in addition to the linguistic (literal) method of explanation by applying the logical and systematic methods of interpreting legal norms (Rulings of the Constitutional Court of the Republic of Lithuania of 25 September 1996, 23 June 1999).

The systemic approach to the interpretation of legal norms is particularly important in the context of this question, as each legal norm is an integral part of a specific legal act and is linked to other norms of the relevant legal act. It is for this reason that the rules establishing the principles of jurisdiction cannot be interpreted in isolation; they must be interpreted in conjunction with the other articles of the CC in order to create a coherent pattern of jurisdictional principles.

In this respect, it should first be stressed that the issue of determining the place of commission of a criminal act is relevant to clarify the cases in which the flag principle may be applied. The flag principle in the Lithuanian CC is established together with the territorial principle in Article 4(1), which may give the impression that criminal acts committed on board vessels or aircraft flying the flag or displaying marks of registry of the State of Lithuania were committed in the territory of Lithuania.

It should be noted that, notwithstanding the construction of Article 4(1) of the CC chosen by the Lithuanian legislator, criminal acts committed on board vessels or aircraft flying the flag or displaying marks of registry of the State of Lithuania are not always committed in the territory of Lithuania. This is only the case when criminal acts are committed on board vessels or aircraft which are physically located in Lithuanian territory. Otherwise, criminal acts committed on board vessels or aircraft flying the flag or displaying marks of registry of the State of Lithuania are committed outside the territory of Lithuania, and the perpetrators must be prosecuted on the basis of the flag principle but not on the territorial principle. This emphasis is particularly important because it is only by explicitly declaring that Article 4(1) of the CC covers the flag principle that the relationship of this principle to the rule(s) of the place of commission of a criminal act can be clearly underlined.

Another peculiarity of the Lithuanian CC is that the rules for identifying the place of commission of a criminal act are established in the same Article – i.e., Article 4. For this reason, the question arises as to whether the rules for determining the place of commission of a criminal act are relevant and applicable only to the question of the liability of the perpetrator on the basis of the territorial and flag principles.

In order to understand the purpose of Article 4(2) and (3) of the CC, it should first be noted that the linguistic interpretation of these norms and their interpretation in the system show that Article 4(3) of the CC (a single criminal act committed both in the territory of the State of Lithuania and abroad shall be considered to have been committed in the territory of the Republic of Lithuania if it was commenced or completed or discontinued in this territory) is aimed at those criminal acts which are committed both in the territory of the Republic of Lithuania and abroad in a certain part. If the criminal act is confined to the territory of Lithuania, the rule laid down in this provision shall not apply, but shall be guided exclusively by Article 4(2) of the CC, which provides that "The place of commission of a criminal act shall be the place in which a person acted or ought to have acted or could have acted or the place in which the consequences provided for by a criminal law occurred. The place of commission of a criminal act by accomplices shall be the place in which the criminal act was committed or, if one of the accomplices acted elsewhere, the place where he acted."

However, in the Lithuanian case law, there are cases in which Article 4(2) of the CC is applied to determine the place of commission of a criminal act in relation to criminal acts committed in Lithuania, the consequences of which are related to the territory of a foreign state (Judgment of the Supreme Court of Lithuania No. 2K-188-489/2015). In other words, the subject of the application of the law may, as it were, choose a more appropriate CC norm for itself, notwithstanding the fact that, under the current legal regulation, it is not Article 4(2) of the CC that applies in such cases but Article 4(3) of the CC, which relates the place of commission of a criminal act to the territory of Lithuania if the same criminal act has been committed in both Lithuanian territory and abroad. If this practice is to be accepted as correct, the question arises as to the purpose of Article 4(3) of the CC, its necessity, and its relationship with Article 4(2) of the CC.

This question has been thoroughly analyzed at the academic level, and two possible solutions have been identified: (a) if the place of commission of an offence is to be determined by the application of the territorial principle alone, the rule of Article 4(3) of the CC is sufficient; (b) if the question of the place of commission of an offense is relevant to all jurisdictional principles, it should be regulated by a separate article, which would provide for the rule of Article 4(2) of the CC, without, however, the completely irrelevant rule concerning the place of the actual acts (or inactions) of the co-perpetrator (Nevera 2006, pp.156–169).

The content of the term "abroad" is also a specific aspect of Article 4(3) of the CC. A linguistic explanation of this term leads to the conclusion that "abroad" means a foreign state, i.e., the territory of another state. However, in the context of the exercise of a state's criminal jurisdiction, the meaning of this term is too narrow. This is because criminal acts may also be committed in territories or zones where no state enforces its sovereignty. Such territories are the high seas and space. Moreover, no state exercises its sovereignty over so-called *terra nullius* territories, such as Bir Tawil (Karalek 2020). Despite the fact that no state claims such a territory, criminal acts can be committed there. They can also be committed on objects that do not belong to anyone, on the high seas, or on objects that fly over them.

There is no doubt that in all such situations we cannot discuss the territory of any one country. Nor will we be able to do so if a criminal act is also committed in some part (commenced, completed, or discontinued) on a vessel or aircraft under the jurisdiction of another state which is outside Lithuanian territory.

It should be noted that in the context of the term "abroad," the Lithuanian continental shelf and exclusive economic zone are also specific territories. Article 47(5) of the Constitution of the Republic of Lithuania provides, *inter alia*, that the Republic of Lithuania has exclusive rights to its continental shelf and economic zone in the Baltic Sea. It is important that the legal status of the continental shelf and the exclusive economic zone is regulated at the international level.

The definition of an exclusive economic zone is provided in Article 55 of the Convention on the Law of the Sea (hereinafter – the 1982 Convention), and Article 56 sets out the rights, jurisdiction and obligations of the coastal state in the exclusive economic zone. The definition of the continental shelf is provided in Article 76(1) of the 1982 Convention. The main emphasis of both definitions is that these areas are beyond the territorial sea, which means that they are not integral parts of the territory of any coastal state. Therefore, when criminal acts are committed there, they must be considered to have been committed outside the territory of the coastal state. This provision must be respected, notwithstanding the fact that any state on its continental shelf or in its exclusive economic zone enjoys the rights enshrined in the relevant norms of the 1982 Convention (Chapters V and VI).

It is therefore clear that the concept of "abroad" cannot refer to the territory of another state. For this reason, it must be changed. A much more correct regulation of this question would be to replace the word "abroad" with the phrase "outside the territory of Lithuania."

The issue of determining the place of commission of so-called e-crime is becoming more and more relevant in the subject matter. The latter issue has become particularly important today, in the early 21st century, and has its origins in the late 1980s, when the computer networks of the United States of America were connected to the network of European research centers. It was then that the era of so-called electronic (virtual, Internet) space began, which not only laid the foundations for the development of traditional criminal acts, but also led to the emergence of new ones (crimes against the security of electronic data and information systems).

Given that cyberspace is a specific and non-material space, the question naturally arises as to whether, in the case of an offense committed in this space (e-crime), the same rules for determining the place of commission of the criminal act and the principle of jurisdiction apply as in the cases discussed above.

In answering this question, an important aspect may be the idea that any e-crime is characterized by its duality, i.e., although it exists in cyberspace, it is still committed using tools (information systems) in physical space, and it may also lead to dangerous consequences in physical space (Marcinauskaitė 2021, pp.203–204). In other words, according to this concept, in each case there is the possibility of attaching oneself to a specific territory (land, sea, air, or subsoil), which would also be the territory of the state concerned. This is also referred to in the scientific literature as the grounding of the e-act, which seems to be performed because of the primacy of territorial jurisdiction (Marcinauskaitė 2021, p.204).

It seems that this way of determining the place of commission of an e-crime is only relevant for those states that do not have a broad arsenal of jurisdictional principles, i.e., either they do not enshrine the necessary range of jurisdictional principles in their criminal law, or they regulate the rules of specific principles in such a way that they do not ensure their effective applicability.

Lithuania is one of these states, because the CC does not contain a passive personality principle (the protection of individual interests principle), and the active personality principle is essentially linked to the double criminality requirement, which means that it cannot be applied to an offense committed in a territory in which no state has sovereignty, or on board a ship or an aircraft in which the law of any state does not apply. It is in such cases that there is a need to link the e-crime, which concerns persons who are in Lithuania and who have been victims here, to the territory of Lithuania and to the territorial principle.

In the scientific literature, one can find the opinion that due to the fact that the rules for determining the place of commission of a criminal act in Article 4(2) and (3) have not been changed because the Lithuanian CC has incorporated a number of international treaties and legal acts of the European Union, it can be concluded that they are effective in ensuring the adaptability of the territorial principle, taking into account the dual nature of e-crime or its essential links to Lithuania (Marcinauskaitė 2021, pp.207–214). Similar conclusions can be drawn from the assessment of certain Lithuanian court decisions (Judgment of the Supreme Court of Lithuania No. 2K-188-489/2015).

This position is open to criticism for several reasons. First of all, the above arguments clearly justify that Article 4(2) of the CC cannot be applied if a criminal act (including e-crime) is committed outside the territory of Lithuania. Moreover, the rule laid down in Article 4(3) of the CC cannot be interpreted broadly and be applied to cases where an e-crime committed abroad has only a specific connection with Lithuania (e.g., the victim lives in Lithuania), but it was neither commenced, completed or discontinued in the territory of Lithuania.

The most relevant examples of such a situation are cases of fraud (Article 182 of the CC) in cyberspace, where a person acting outside the territory of Lithuania sends misleading information to a person in Lithuania on the basis of which the person makes a banking transaction leading to financial loss by e-mail or other electronic communication. However, in such cases, when the perpetrator who is outside the territory of Lithuania influences the will of the person in Lithuania to carry out a financial transaction, there is no possibility to conclude that the fraud is completed in Lithuania.

This is because the completion of the fraud is related not to the use of deception or the execution of a financial transaction, but to the acquisition of the right to the property, i.e., the moment when the perpetrator receives the money transferred by the victim to their own account or to the account of another person (Judgment of the Supreme Court of Lithuania No. 2K-682/2001; Judgment of the Supreme Court of Lithuania No. 2K-514/2014, Sinkevičius 1999, pp.70–74, 79). In other words, fraud is not complete in Lithuania when the victim, due to their credulity, transmits their identification data and these data are later used to carry out a financial transaction. The fraud will not be finished in Lithuania if the money debited from the victim's bank account is still in the process of moving to the perpetrator's account or to another person's account, which is usually not even in a bank operating in Lithuania.

Obviously, if the rules on the commission of a criminal act laid down in Article 4 of the CC are found to be wholly inappropriate for the application of the territorial principle, the question arises as to whether it is possible to modify them in such a way as to protect the interests of the persons concerned. In answering this question, it should first of all be pointed out that the problem of the application of Lithuanian criminal jurisdiction in such cases would not exist if the Lithuanian CC established a coherent system of jurisdictional principles which provided for the passive personal principle and regulated the rule on the determination of the place of the commission of a criminal act, which was separated from the territorial principle.

Failing this, Article 4(3) of the CC should certainly be improved by establishing that an offence is deemed to have been committed in Lithuania when the use of cyberspace is intended to cause damage to a natural person residing in Lithuania or to a legal entity having its registered office in Lithuania. Another possible option for improving Article 4(3) of the CC is to introduce a universal rule that a criminal act is committed in the territory of Lithuania if at least part of an e-crime is committed in its territory.

If either of these were implemented, the use of deception in Lithuania would lead to the recognition of the fact that the fraud was committed in Lithuanian territory rather than elsewhere. The same could be stated in all other problematic cases of territorial jurisdiction which are mentioned in scientific articles (Marcinauskaitė 2021, pp.207, 209).

Of course, another state (for example, the state in which the perpetrator acted) may also establish territorial jurisdiction over the acts in question. However, the establishment of so-called competing territorial jurisdiction is not a problem – the problem is only the possible violation of the *non bis in idem* principle. However, the case law of the Court of Justice of the European Union has long since provided rules which make it possible to avoid a breach of the *non bis in idem* principle (Nevera and Melničenko 2009).

On the other hand, there is certainly no need to link the possibility of punishing the perpetrator of an e-crime solely to the application of the territorial principle. However, such a solution is only possible if the sovereign state in question has established an appropriate and coherent system of jurisdictional principles in its criminal law. The relevant international treaties (2001 Convention on Cybercrime, 2003 Additional Protocol to the Convention on Cybercrime, concerning the criminalization of acts of a racist and xenophobic nature committed through computer systems) and European Union law (Council Framework Decision 2008/913/JHA of November 28, 2008 on combating certain forms and expressions of racism and xenophobia by means of criminal law, Directive 2011/93/EU of the European Parliament and of the Council of December 13, 2011 on combating the sexual abuse and sexual exploitation of children and child pornography, and replacing Council Framework Decision 2004/68/JHA, Directive 2013/40/EU of the European Parliament and of the Council of August 12, 2013 on attacks against information systems and replacing Council Framework Decision 2005/222/JHA) also address this need, as they set only minimum standards for the application of jurisdictional principles.

In the debate on the determination of the place of commission of an e-crime, one could also take the approach that cyberspace is a space that belongs to no one and that the criminality of an offense committed therein should be decided only by applying the following principles of extraterritorial jurisdiction: the active personality principle, the passive personality principle, the protection of the state's interest principle, the universal principle, and the principle of representation. This position is also endorsed in other scientific publications (Marcinauskaitė 2021, p.203).

Thus, using systematic, logical and other methods of interpretation of a legal norm, it can be concluded that, in the current wording of the norms of Article 4 of the CC, all the principles of extraterritorial jurisdiction relevant to the topic under consideration can only be applied if a specific criminal act is committed outside Lithuanian territory. In order to properly determine the place of commission of a criminal act, the independent and separate rule laid down in Article 4 of the CC stipulates that the place of commission of a criminal act is the place where the person acted or ought to have acted, or where the consequences provided for by criminal law arose or ought to have arisen. In the absence of this decision, cases of the commission of a criminal act outside the territory of Lithuania should be determined in accordance with Article 4(3) of the Lithuanian CC, the application of which is based on the following logic: if a criminal act is not committed in Lithuania, the place of its commission is the place of the areas or objects outside the Lithuanian territory.

The Concept of the Flag Principle and the Possibilities of Its Application to Criminal Acts Committed Abroad by Lithuanian Citizens and Persons Permanently Resident in Lithuania

Lithuanian citizens and persons permanently residing in Lithuania can also commit criminal acts on board vessels or aircraft located outside Lithuania. The vessels or aircraft concerned may be subject to the jurisdiction of Lithuania or a foreign state. In some cases, they may even be objects that have no nationality whatsoever, although *de facto* they carry the flag or marks of a particular state.

In such situations, the question arises as to the choice of the jurisdictional principle on the basis of which the criminal jurisdiction of Lithuania or another sovereign state may be exercised. Vessels and aircraft are registered in accordance with the rules laid down in national legislation. After registration, the law of the state of registration of the vessel or aircraft applies (also taking into account the rules of international law). It is this aspect that makes it possible to discuss the possibility of exercising criminal jurisdiction on the basis of the flag principle. On the other hand, this discussion must also identify those cases where other principles of extraterritorial jurisdiction are applicable to the legal assessment.

The flag principle, as an independent principle of state criminal jurisdiction, was first recognized at the international level at the South American Congress of Private International Law held in Montevideo (Uruguay) (hereinafter – the Montevideo Congress), as it was realized that the concept of a vessel as the territory of a state had no future. Nine treaties were signed during this Congress (August 25, 1888–February 18, 1889). One of them, signed on January 23, 1889, was the Treaty on International Criminal Law, which was devoted to questions of international criminal law (Bewes 1920). It is Article 8 of this treaty which provides that criminal acts committed on the high seas or in neutral waters on board vessels of war or merchant vessels shall be prosecuted and punished in accordance with the laws of the state whose flag the vessel is flying. This and other provisions of the above treaty were reiterated in the Treaty on International Penal Law of March 19, 1940, signed at the next Montevideo Congress.

On the other hand, the concept of the vessel as the territory of the state has not yet been fully abandoned. It was even supported by Lithuanian researchers of international law (Volsonokas 1930, p.29) and criminal law (Kavolis and Bieliackinas 1934, p.22) of the time and, sadly, can still be found in the publications of modern Lithuanian researchers (Abramavičius *et al.* 2004, p.46).

However, the majority of international and criminal law academics (Katuoka 1999, p.121; O'Connel 1970, pp.604–606; Starke 1972, pp.246–247; Jescheck and Weigend 1996, p.172; Swart 1992, p.527) were and are proponents of the fact that the acceptance of the concept of the vessel as the territory (or quasi-territory) of the flag state is essentially archaic and long overdue, especially since there has never been any serious debate on the recognition of aircraft as the territory of their state of registry.

The concept that both vessels and aircraft are not the territory of the flag state or of the state of registry is also embraced by the legislators of the most progressive states. For example, the criminal laws of the Federal Republic of Germany (Section 4), the Kingdom of the Netherlands (Section 3), the Kingdom of Denmark (Chapter 2, Section 6), the Republic of Finland (Chapter 1, Section 2), and the Kingdom of Sweden (Chapter 2, Section 3) provide that the jurisdiction of a state over offenses committed on its ships or aircraft is exercised on the basis of the principle of the independent flag. This principle is also recognized in the 1982 Convention and in some Lithuanian court decisions (Judgment of the Vilnius District Court No. 1S-334-495/2012).

Therefore, despite the fact that the flag principle in the Lithuanian CC is established in the same norm as the territorial principle, this decision of the legislator does not allow for the assertion that Lithuania recognizes the concept of a vessel or an aircraft as the territory of the state, which provides for the possibility of all criminal acts committed on a Lithuanian vessel or an aircraft outside of the territory of Lithuania to be treated as having been committed in Lithuanian territory.

The place of commission of such offenses is unambiguously a Lithuanian vessel or aircraft located outside the territory of Lithuania and where Lithuanian law is in force. Of course, if these objects are located in the territory of another state, then the perpetrator of the criminal act is subject to dual jurisdiction: the registration of the vessel or aircraft (flag principle) and the territoriality of the coastal state (territorial principle). In such cases, the allocation of jurisdiction (establishing the specific situations in which a criminal act committed on a vessel or aircraft is subject to the jurisdiction of the coastal or airspace host state and when it is subject to the jurisdiction of the state of registration of the vessel or aircraft) is carried out primarily in accordance with the rules laid down in international law. International law also lays down rules for the allocation of jurisdiction in cases where vessels or aircraft are in the exclusive economic zone of a foreign state.

For Lithuania, the most important international legal instruments regulating the jurisdiction of a particular sovereign state over a criminal act committed on a vessel or aircraft are the following: the Consular Convention between the Republic of Lithuania and Ukraine (1995); the Consular Convention between the Republic of Lithuania and the People's Republic of China (1992); the Consular Convention between the Republic of Lithuania and the Russian Federation (1992); the Consular Convention between the Republic of Lithuania and the Republic of Poland (1992); the Consular Agreement between the Republic of Lithuania and Turkey (1994); the Consular Convention between the Republic of Lithuania and Georgia (1999); the Convention on the Territorial Sea and the Contiguous Zone (1958); the Convention on Offenses and Certain Other Acts Committed on Board Aircraft (1963); the Convention for the Suppression of Unlawful Seizure of Aircraft (1970); the Convention for the Suppression of Unlawful Acts Against the Safety of Civil Aviation (1971); and the1982 Convention. Notwithstanding the fact that these international treaties are not named in the CC as having an impact on the determination of jurisdiction, their enforcement is to be ensured in accordance with Article 138(3) of the Constitution of the Republic of Lithuania (hereinafter – the Constitution), the Law on International Treaties of the Republic of Lithuania, and the principle of *pacta sunt servanda* recognized in international law.

It is true that the scientific literature also expresses the opinion that the rules of the relevant treaties cannot be applied directly because they have not been incorporated into the Lithuanian CC and there is no specific norm in the CC that would allow them to be applied (Švedas *et al.* 2017, pp.25–27). The fallacy of such a position lies in the fact that the direct applicability of unambiguously constructed international norms is sought to be denied on the basis of the principle of *nullum crimen sine lege*, although it has nothing to do with the resolution of issues falling under the principles of jurisdiction.

On the other hand, international treaties also provide for cases in which a ship or aircraft under the jurisdiction of a particular state loses its nationality. For example, in the 1982 Convention, such situations relate to piracy (Articles 100, 101, 105), slave trading (Articles 99, 110), trafficking in drugs or psychotropic substances (Article 108), and unlawful broadcasting (Articles 109, 110). Despite this, it is important to understand that, for example, the "nationality" of the vessel is not lost if one or more passengers are transporting drugs. The loss of the nationality of the vessel is linked to situations in which such a criminal act is committed by members of the crew and on an undoubtedly significant scale. In other words, situations in which the vessel or aircraft is not being used in accordance with its direct purpose (the transport of goods or passengers), but with the intention of using it for the crimes referred to in the 1982 Convention, and where the transport of goods or passengers is merely a cover for a criminal act.

In such situations, the question of the criminal liability of the perpetrator must be decided on the basis of other principles of extraterritorial jurisdiction than the flag principle. As a rule, either the active personality principle or the passive personality principle is the most appropriate, depending on the nature of the criminal act committed.

Lithuanian citizens and persons permanently resident in Lithuania can also commit criminal acts on foreign vessels or aircraft which are located neither in their country of registration nor in the territory of Lithuania. Given that foreign vessels and aircraft are under the jurisdiction of their state of registration, the criminality of offenses committed on board them is primarily based on the flag principle. It is also important that the territorial principle of the state of registration of the vessel or aircraft cannot be applied in such cases, as these objects are not the territory of any state, although in Lithuanian case law one can find other interpretations.

For example, in Judgment of the Supreme Court of Lithuania No. 2K-57-697/2018 of January 9, 2018, in deciding on the criminal liability of a Lithuanian citizen for murder committed on a Panamanian-flagged vessel located on the high seas, it was held that if it is established that the vessel of a foreign state was in neutral waters at the time of the commission of the criminal act, the criminal act was committed in the territory of the flag state of the vessel.

According to this position, it can be stated that several rules are relied on for determining the place of commission of a criminal act: 1) if the criminal act is committed on board a foreign vessel which is located on the high seas, the criminal act is committed in the territory of the state under which flag the vessel in question was flying; and 2) if the criminal act is committed on board a foreign vessel which is located in the territory of a foreign state, then the place of commission is the coastal territory of the state. In other words, in either case, a criminal act committed on board a vessel is committed either in the territory of the flag state of the vessel or in the territory of the state in whose waters (territorial sea and harbor waters) the vessel enters.

However, in such a case, it is not at all clear where a criminal act was committed if it took place while the vessel was in the exclusive economic zone of the coastal state. After all, it is common knowledge that a state's exclusive economic zone is not part of the territory of the coastal state – it is not subject to the full extent of the known rights of the high seas. It is therefore more than obvious that the theory set out in the above-mentioned judgment is misleading and cannot be followed.

On the other hand, it is more likely that in the relevant case the concept of the territoriality of the vessel was reanimated in order to resolve the issue of the criminal liability of a Lithuanian citizen for murder in accordance with the active personality principle established in Article 5 of the CC and by the application of the following provision of Article 8(1): where a person who has committed a crime abroad is prosecuted in the Republic of Lithuania but a different penalty is provided for this crime in each country, the person shall be subject to a penalty according to laws of the Republic of Lithuania; however, this may not exceed the maximum penalty specified in the criminal laws of the state of the place of commission of the crime. If the place of commission of the criminal act is not linked to the territory of the flag state of the vessel, then the double criminality requirement of Article 8 of the CC cannot apply.

There is no doubt that the problem of the construction of Article 8(1) of the CC in the context of the application of the flag principle is very relevant, as it seems to focus only on crimes committed in the territory of a foreign state. Nevertheless, there is not and cannot be any rational, modern motive for recognizing a foreign vessel as being in the territory of its state of registration and for denying the autonomy of the flag principle.

The Content and Possibilities of the Application of the Universal Principle in Relation to Criminal Acts Committed Abroad by Lithuanian Citizens and Persons Permanently Resident in Lithuania

Guidelines for the Coherence of the Universal Principle with the Flag Principle and the Active Personality Principle

After examining the most relevant problems related to the flag principle, it would be logical to analyze further the problems related to the examination of criminal acts committed abroad by Lithuanian citizens and persons permanently residing in Lithuania on the basis of the active personality principle (Article 5 of the CC). However, the choice of a different path is determined by the examples of Lithuanian practice, where the universal principle is used for the legal treatment of criminal acts committed by Lithuanian citizens outside the territory of Lithuania in order to distance oneself from the requirement of the double criminality of the act, as set out in Article 8(1) of the CC. Thus, only after the content of the universal principle has been revealed and the limits of its application have been outlined will it be possible to concentrate on the problems of the application of the active personality principle.

The universal principle of criminal jurisdiction is enshrined in Article 7 of the CC of Lithuania, providing that "Persons shall be held liable under this Code regardless of their citizenship and place of residence, also of the place of commission of a crime and whether the act committed is subject to punishment under laws of the place of commission of the crime, where they commit the following crimes subject to liability under international treaties." Article 7 of the CC also specifies those crimes for which criminality is established in international treaties ratified by the Republic of Lithuania. Such crimes are the following: crimes against humanity and war crimes (Articles 99–113^{1}); trafficking in human beings (Article 147); the purchase or sale of a child (Article 157); the production, storage or handling of counterfeit currency or securities (Article 213); property laundering (Article 216); bribery (Article 225); trading in influence (Article 226); graft (Article 227); piracy (Article 251^{1}); acts of terrorism and crimes related to terrorist activity (Article 252^{1}(1) and (2)); unlawful handling of nuclear or radioactive materials or other sources of ionizing radiation (Articles 256, 256^{1} and 257); crimes related to the possession of narcotic or psychotropic, toxic or highly active substances (Articles 259–269); and crimes against the environment (Articles 270, 270^{1}, 270^{2}, 270^{3}, 271, 272, 274).

Looking at the construction of Article 7 of the CC, it is as if one can identify the fact that only a set of conditions is required for the application of universal jurisdiction. First, an offense under one of the points set out in this article must have been committed. This clause seems to be the simplest, but its regulation and application in Lithuania has some problems.

Although Article 7 of the CC refers to the names of the crimes and the related articles, this does not mean that all of them are automatically subject to liability on the basis of the universal principle. In this context, it is important to emphasize that the universal principle is established in international treaties in two ways: directly or by the *aut dedere aut judicare* rule.

Universal jurisdiction is directly recognized for all international crimes (genocide, crimes against humanity, war crimes, and aggression) and for one crime of an international character – piracy (the 1982 Convention). However, even in these cases, international law establishes that the universality of jurisdiction as a response to such crimes is manifested in the fact that the perpetrator may be punished by a court of a state other than that of the place where the crime was committed, but also by a court of another state, or even by an international tribunal (see, for example, the Statute of the International Criminal Tribunal for the Former Yugoslavia (1993), the Rome Statute of the International Criminal Court (1998), the Convention on the Prevention and Punishment of the Crime of Genocide (1948), the International Convention on the Suppression and Punishment of the Crime of Apartheid (1974)).

Thus, despite the fact that various states and international courts have the right to punish the perpetrator for international crimes on the basis of the universal principle, the first state to exercise this right should be the one on whose territory the crime was committed (primacy of the territorial principle). Exceptions to this rule are also found not elsewhere, but in international law itself (see, for example, the Rome Statute of the International Criminal Court), and relate to a few possible situations. First, where a crime is not punished at the place where it was committed. Second, where a sovereign state is unwilling or unable to exercise its territorial jurisdiction due to possible objective and subjective circumstances. As an example of the latter situation, the events of 2020 in Belarus, where the falsified results of the country's presidential elections led to the forcible suppression of mass peaceful demonstrations, are a case in point. Another contemporary example is the aggression by the Russian Federation against Ukraine, which began on February 24, 2022, and has continued to this day, and which involves the commission of practically all broadly recognized international crimes. However, even in the latter case, it is Ukraine itself that has the primary right to exercise jurisdiction over all international crimes committed in Ukrainian territory. Other states (as well as Lithuania) have the right to launch pre-trial investigations into international crimes committed in Ukrainian territory only because the number of international crimes recorded is enormous and the state at war is certainly not in a position to either record or investigate them independently.

However, despite this procedural and concrete activity based on the national legislation of a foreign state, neither Lithuania nor other states will ultimately organize national legal proceedings, but will instead have to hand over all of their collected material to the sovereign state that can exercise its territorial jurisdiction – Ukraine. To do otherwise would be to deny the primacy of territorial jurisdiction. Doing otherwise is only possible if Ukraine is occupied.

Thus, only the total disability of a given sovereign state – which may also be due to the fact that national legislation does not provide for the criminalization of the crimes in question, or to the lack of response (or only a formal response) at the procedural level to the fact of the commission of the crimes in question – makes it possible to achieve distance from territorial jurisdiction and prosecute crimes under the universal principle. However, the application of the universal principle for the purpose of pre-trial investigation (as in Ukraine) is only possible for the purpose of investigating the enormous number of international crimes committed in the territory of another sovereign state. Of course, this model of operation does not ideally correspond to the foundations of the universal principle, but the realities of life make it necessary to modify them slightly. However, this must be done in such a way as not to distort the essence of the universal principle.

If the standards of the universal principle discussed above are linked to international crimes, it is more than obvious that they should also apply to crimes of an international character. In other words, when a crime of an international character is committed, the sovereign state on whose territory the crime was committed has the priority to prosecute and punish it. To hold otherwise would be to give crimes of an international character a more significant status than international crimes, which cannot be the case.

The problems with the universal principle that have been actualized make it clear that the conditions for its application – regardless of the place of commission of a crime and whether the act committed is subject to punishment under the laws of the place of commission of the crime – cannot be interpreted literally. This study has also shown that the law applicable at the place of commission of a crime is a crucial factor in understanding the content of the universal principle and its coherent application. This also applies to the condition of the place of commission of a crime, since it is only by establishing this condition that it is possible to identify whether the law of a state is applicable in a given territory, and whether the jurisdiction of the sovereign state concerned, based on territorial or flag principles, can be exercised in respect of a crime committed.

Moreover, the importance of determining the place of commission of a crime is also evident from the fact that the universal principle is one of the principles of the extraterritorial jurisdiction of a state, which means that a crime provided in Article 7 of the CC must have been committed outside the territory of the state applying this principle, and certainly not on board a ship or aircraft. A different interpretation of this clause would lead to a completely absurd situation: if an offense provided in Article 7 of the CC was committed in the territory of Lithuania, or on board a Lithuanian vessel or aircraft, it would be possible to apply the universal principle instead of the territorial or flag principle. Another important aspect of the connection of the offenses provided in Article 7 of the

CC with the universal principle is that not all of them (both in the previous and current wording of the Article 7 of the CC) are of such seriousness as to be necessary for the implementation of universal jurisdiction.

It is important to note that the universal principle is not intended to entitle any sovereign state that has enshrined it in national law to exercise its criminal jurisdiction over any crime. It was only in the initial phase of the principle's development, which was based on the so-called cosmopolitan theory, that it was thought that the rule of law was a value cherished by all states and that the aim of all states was therefore the maintenance of a perfect legal order, which could not be achieved by individual states confining themselves to international legal assistance alone. It is for this reason that it has been held that any state has not only the right, but also the duty to punish any crime, regardless of where it is committed (see Nevera 2006, p.127).

It is more than obvious that such goals are utopian. If we try to realize them now, then we will not be faced with the coherent application of the law for the sake of the idea of justice, but with chaos, because any sovereign state would be able to seek to impose its own criminal repression for any crime. In order to avoid this, it is necessary to follow the idea, expressed as early as the middle of the 19th century, that only those legal interests which matter to all states deserve international protection, because only then can one distance oneself from crimes which only affect national interests (Mohl 1853, p.710). Universal jurisdiction is therefore only possible in respect of crimes of a high gravity, which are clearly broadly recognized international crimes and the most dangerous crimes of an international character, for the joint and severe punishment of which the relevant international treaties are signed.

In light of these fundamental provisions of the content of the universal principle, it is easy to identify that the wording of Article 7(12) of the CC unjustifiably extends the jurisdiction of the Republic of Lithuania to minor and negligent crimes, and, in its formal application, to misdemeanor offenses (unlawful possession of narcotic or psychotropic substances for purposes other than selling or otherwise distributing them, Article 259(1) and (2) of the CC), unlawful possession of highly active or toxic substances without qualifying circumstances (Article 267(1) of the CC)). It is more than obvious that all of these crimes are not of the requisite gravity and certainly do not endanger the interests of many states, and therefore universal jurisdiction should not be available to punish them. This conclusion is confirmed even by Article 269, referred to in Article 7(12) of the CC, which does not criminalize any of these acts, but merely provides definitions of terms relevant to Chapter XXXVII of the CC.

The fact that universal jurisdiction is only available for high-risk crimes can be seen even in the 1961 Single Convention on Narcotic Drugs (hereinafter – the Convention on Narcotic Drugs) and the 1992 Convention on the Prohibition of the Development, Production, Stockpiling and Use of Chemical Weapons and on their Destruction. Finally, the principles of legality, legitimate expectations, and proportionality guide such conclusions.

Of course, opposition to this position could be based on the fact that universal jurisdiction is only available in respect of those criminal acts described in Articles 259 to 269 of the CC that fall within the definition of a crime in Article 11(1) of the CC. However, this interpretation of Article 7 of the CC does not solve the problem raised, since on April 27, 2023, criminal law act No. XIV-1925 introduced, in Chapter XXXVII of the CC, liability for smuggling narcotic or psychotropic substances (Article 260^{1} of the CC), smuggling precursors of narcotic or psychotropic substances in the first category (Article 266^{1} of the CC), smuggling potent, poisonous, or chemical substances (Article 267^{2} of the CC), and smuggling biological substances, micro-organisms, or toxins (Article 267^{3} of the CC). It should be noted that until then, these crimes were punishable under other articles of the CC (e.g., Article 199(3) of the CC (smuggling)) and had no connection with universal jurisdiction in the sense of Article 7 of the CC.

Thus, universal jurisdiction over the crimes mentioned above was instantly established in the Lithuanian CC. Although to some extent these changes seem to mirror the provisions of Articles 1 and 36 of the Convention on Narcotic Drugs, a logical question arises as to why universal jurisdiction had not been established prior to the entry into force of the changes, e.g., for smuggling nuclear or radioactive materials or other sources of ionizing radiation (Article 256^{2} of the CC), even though Article 8(2) of the 1979 Convention on the Physical Protection of Nuclear Material provides for the application of the *aut dedere aut judicare* rule in respect of such acts. There is no logical answer to this question.

It is clear that the various ways of interpreting a legal provision do not lead to any clarity regarding the content of Article 7 of the CC. On the contrary, its problems become even more acute, as universal jurisdiction becomes possible even for crimes that previously had nothing to do with universal jurisdiction. Clearly, this should not be the case, and for this reason alone, there is a clear need to amend Article 7 of the CC in such a way as to limit universal jurisdiction to those crimes which meet the criteria of this principle set out above. On the other hand, even if appropriate amendments are made, it must be clearly understood that the universal principle is not an instrument that is applied without regard to the standard of its content and its coherent interaction with other jurisdictional principles.

The latter aspect is also relevant because of the last condition for the application of the universal principle in Article 7 of the CC, which is linked to the person who committed the offense – "Persons shall be held liable under this Code regardless of their citizenship and place of residence." In interpreting this clause, it is necessary first of all to distinguish all possible categories of such persons. Since the nationality and place of residence of a person are seemingly irrelevant, the universal principle could be applied to Lithuanian citizens, foreigners permanently residing in Lithuania, and foreigners without permanent resident status. Taking into account that, according to Article 2(32) of the Law of the Republic of Lithuania on the Legal Status of Foreigners, the term "foreigner" is understood broadly, such persons include both persons holding the nationality of a foreign state and stateless persons (apatrids).

However, it is again important to understand that the interpretation of this condition of the universal principle cannot be based on a purely literal interpretation, as this is prohibited by the Constitution. Moreover, such an interpretation would also mean that Lithuanian citizens or foreigners permanently residing in Lithuania must be punished on the basis of the universal principle for crimes committed abroad and referred to in Article 7 of the CC, irrespective of whether the act committed is subject to punishment under the laws of the place of commission of the crime. In other words, the flag principle and the active personality principle should be, as it were, dissociated, although under the system of jurisdictional principles enshrined in the Lithuanian CC, they have priority over the universal principle.

Interestingly, an analysis of some decisions of the Lithuanian Prosecutor's Office shows that this is exactly what is being sought in Lithuania. In Criminal Case No. 01-1-17659-22, the indictment drawn up by the prosecutor states that the crime allegedly committed by the Lithuanian citizens J.P. and V.D. in the French Republic is qualified under Articles 7(12), 23(3), and 260(3) of the CC, as they illegally possessed a very large quantity of drugs in France. The Supreme Court of Lithuania also stated in its judgment No. 2K-526/2011 that a Lithuanian citizen may be prosecuted under Article 7 of the CC even if the state of the place of the commission of a crime does not provide for criminal liability for such an act. According to the Supreme Court of Lithuania, this would mean that the application of criminal jurisdiction based on the universal principle is not limited by the double criminality requirement.

These examples very clearly demonstrate that in Lithuania, the application of the literal interpretation of Article 7 of the CC, which is prohibited by the Constitution, can lead to a practice that exaggerates the universal principle, gives it priority over the flag principle and the active personal principle, and negates its purpose. They also show that Lithuania ignores even the provisions of Article 36(2)(a)(iv) of the Convention on Narcotic Drugs, which states that "Serious offences heretofore referred to committed either by nationals or by foreigners shall be prosecuted by the Party in whose territory the offence was committed, or by the Party in whose territory the offender is found if extradition is not acceptable in conformity with the law of the Party to which application is made, and if such offender has not already been prosecuted and judgement given."

In other words, it ignores the fact that the relevant international instrument establishes the primacy of territorial jurisdiction, and that the right of another sovereign state to punish offenses committed outside its territory and falling within the scope of the Convention on Narcotic Drugs is only conferred on it if the perpetrator is extraditable and has not yet been held liable for the relevant act (*non bis in idem* principle).

A Lithuanian citizen or any foreigner can be surrendered to another EU country under the European Arrest Warrant (hereinafter – the EAW). This possibility is provided for in Article 91 of the CC and Article 71[1] of the Code of Criminal Procedure of the Republic of Lithuania. In such a situation, the following procedure must be followed: when it becomes known that a crime has been committed in the territory of another EU state, the competent authorities of the place of commission of the crime must be informed, inviting them to decide on the exercise of territorial jurisdiction. Only if the state of the place of the offense is unwilling or unable to exercise its territorial jurisdiction (the person cannot be surrendered in accordance with the EAW due to circumstances prohibiting this (Art. 91(3) of the CC)) is the liability of the offender then to be decided on the basis of the principle of the flag or the active personality principle. Only if the national legal regulation did not allow this could the question of the perpetrator's responsibility then be decided on the basis of the universal principle.

The system of jurisdictional principles established in the Lithuanian CC clearly indicates that if a citizen of Lithuania or another person permanently residing in Lithuania is not surrendered or extradited to the state of registration of the place (vessel or aircraft) of commission of the offenses referred to in Article 7 of the CC, or if such a need has not been expressed, then they should be prosecuted on the basis of the active personality principle. However, if the crime referred to in Article 7 of the CC was committed on board a Lithuanian vessel or aircraft, then the application of the flag principle should be the first consideration.

It seems that the active personality principle should also apply in cases where the crime referred to in Article 7 of the CC is committed in territories where no state exercises its sovereignty or, if it does, does not criminalize it. However, the existing drafting of Article 8(1) of the Lithuanian CC (introducing the condition of reciprocal criminality of the act) does not yet provide for this possibility. For that reason alone, the above cases are the only ones in which the criminal liability of a Lithuanian citizen or person permanently resident in Lithuania for the crimes provided for in Article 7 of the CC should currently be implemented on the basis of the universal principle rather than on the basis of the active personality principle. However, it must be stressed that if such a crime is committed by a citizen of another state permanently residing in Lithuania and the state of their nationality seeks to exercise its criminal jurisdiction on the basis of the active personality principle, then it should act in such a way as to ensure that all the appropriate means of legal co-operation in criminal matters are used in pursuit of this goal.

However, Lithuanian court decisions focus on a different relationship between Article 5 of the CC and Article 7 of the CC. This argument is based on the fact that the applicator of the law is left with a choice, whereas in fact the specific situation has nothing to do with the essence of the universal principle and clearly points to the unequivocal necessity of applying Article 5 of the CC. On December 28, 2022, in Criminal Case No. 01-1-00696-22, the Klaipėda Regional Court passed a judgment by which, *inter alia*, K. K. was found guilty and sentenced under Article 260(3) of the CC for having transported from his flat in Ireland to the Waterville Park in Dublin 2 jars which were found to contain an extremely large amount of cocaine, and for having concealed them in the territory of the park until August 28, 2020. The judgment states, *inter alia*, that K.K. committed the offense under Article 260(3) CC in Ireland. According to the general rule, Lithuanian criminal jurisdiction and the criminal laws of Lithuania apply in the territory of the country (territorial principle, Article 4 of the CC). The accused, K.K., is a citizen of the Republic of Lithuania and is also permanently residing in Lithuania. In view of this, he is covered by the exception laid down in Article 5 of the CC of the Republic of Lithuania, which deals with the criminal liability of citizens of the Republic of Lithuania and persons permanently residing in Lithuania for criminal offenses committed abroad. […] In the present case, the criminal jurisdiction of Lithuania can also be established by applying the universal principle (Article 7 of the CC), according to which criminal liability for crimes related to the possession of narcotic drugs or psychotropic substances may be imposed irrespective of the nationality of the person, his/her place of residence, the place of the commission of the crime and whether or not the act is punishable under the law of the place of the commission of the offense (Article 7 (l) (12) of the CC).

The formulations used by the Klaipėda Regional Court, as well as the formula of qualification of a crime committed outside the territory of Lithuania, oblige us to distinguish and analyze a few more relevant problems. First of all, it should be noted that a criminal offense committed abroad must be qualified not only in accordance with the relevant norm of the special part, but also by referring to a specific norm of the criminal law establishing the principle of extraterritorial jurisdiction. This applies even to the flag principle, despite the fact that the current version of the CC regulates it together with the territorial principle. Failure to do so is equivalent to stating that the criminal act was committed in the territory of the Republic of Lithuania.

Of course, the characterization of a crime committed outside the territory of Lithuania and the application of the norm establishing the requirement of double criminality of the crime seem to correct such an error. However, in order to correctly qualify the relevant offenses (even for statistical purposes or in view of the qualification rules on preparation, attempt or aiding, and abetting), the provision of the general part of the CC, which establishes the principle of jurisdiction, should also be mentioned alongside the article of the special part of the CC.

Secondly, any principle of extraterritorial jurisdiction is no exception to the territorial principle. These principles are the result of an extension of the state's criminal jurisdiction in order to ensure the implementation of the principle of inevitability of liability. Moreover, no exception can be said to exist when the territorial and active personality principles established in the criminal code of the same state are juxtaposed. In the context of the present issue, this can only be done when comparing the laws of different states.

Thirdly, it certainly cannot be tolerated that the active personality principle and the universal principle are referred to as if they were possible alternatives to the Republic of Lithuania exercising its criminal jurisdiction over crimes committed outside its territory. The above analysis clearly demonstrates that each jurisdictional principle has its own purpose and, together with the others, forms a coherent rather than a competing system. Moreover, in the peculiar hierarchy of extraterritorial principles, the active personality principle ranks above the universal principle; it also has deeper historical roots. Thus, there can be no question of any arbitrary choice between the active personal principle and the universal principle; nor would such behavior be consistent with the Constitution's regard for the rule of law, justice, equality of persons before the courts, and other constitutional principles (Ruling of the Constitutional Court of the Republic of Lithuania March 28, 2006). Competition between these or other jurisdictional principles can only be said to exist when at least two sovereign states seek to exercise their criminal jurisdiction over the same criminal act.

Problems and Solutions for the Application of the Dual Criminality Clause to Criminal Offenses Committed Abroad by Lithuanian Citizens and Persons Permanently Resident in Lithuania

Article 8(1) of the CC establishes two aspects of the requirement of double criminality. First, it applies to those persons who are liable for crimes committed abroad under the Lithuanian CC on the basis of the active personality principle and the principle of protection of the interests of the state (Article 6 of the CC). Secondly, it is established that where a person who has committed a crime abroad is prosecuted in the Republic of Lithuania, but a different penalty is provided for this crime in each country, the person shall be subject to a penalty according to laws of the Republic of Lithuania; however, it may not exceed the maximum penalty specified in the criminal laws of the state of the place of commission of the crime. On the other hand, it is important to emphasize that Article 8(3) of the CC also provides for an exception to the condition of reciprocal criminality of the act, which applies only to Lithuanian citizens and persons permanently residing in Lithuania in respect of crimes committed by them abroad, the criminality of which is established in Articles 129, 135, 138, 148, 149, 150, 151, 151^1, 152^1, 153, 162(1), 307(3), 308(3), 309(2), and (3) of the CC.

It should be noted that the necessity of legalizing this exception is motivated by the need to implement Directive 2011/93/EU of the European Parliament and of the Council of December 13, 2011 on combating the sexual abuse and sexual exploitation of children and child pornography, and replacing Council Framework Decision 2004/68/JHA (hereinafter – Directive 2011/93/EU), as well as the provisions of the Council of Europe's Convention of 2011 on Preventing and Combating Violence against Women and Domestic Violence (hereinafter – the Istanbul Convention). There is no doubt that the requirement in Article 17(4) of Directive 2011/93/EU to ensure that a state's jurisdiction in respect of the offenses referred to in Article 3(4), (5), and (6), Article 4(2), (3), (5), (6), and (7) and Article 5(6) of Directive 2011/93/EU does not depend on the condition that the conduct constitutes a criminal act at the place where it was committed, is mandatory and ought to have been implemented. However, the question arises as to whether the requirement of Article 44(3) of the Istanbul Convention to dissociate oneself from the law of the place of commission of a crime should be implemented if this international instrument has not yet been ratified by the Seimas of the Republic of Lithuania, and is therefore not part of our legal system.

The answer to this question is not unambiguous. On the one hand, the provisions of a specific international legal act become binding on Lithuania only after they have been ratified (Article 138(3) of the Constitution) and the relevant national law has been published in the National Laws Register. On the other hand, each state has the right to implement the provisions of an international legal act of relevance to it before its ratification. This right is an expression of the sovereignty of the state and is part of its independent criminal policy, which is implemented on the basis of Article 4 and Article 67(2) of the Constitution (*inter alia* Rulings of the Constitutional Court of the Republic of Lithuania December 6, 2000, May 25, 2004). There is no doubt that such an activity of the legislator is also possible because sooner or later, the ratification of the relevant international convention will not necessitate the amendment of the criminal law.

However, in the context of the present discussion, it is important to note that the exception in Article 8(3) of the CC is not only related to the protection of persons falling under the Istanbul Convention. Victims of murder (Article 129 of the CC), severe health impairment (Article 135 of the CC), non-severe health impairment (Article 138 of the CC) and a number of other offenses under Article 8(3) of the CC may also be natural persons who have no connection with the Istanbul Convention. The question therefore arises as to the basis for the disregard of the condition of reciprocal criminality of an act when the act referred to in the Lithuanian CC provision in question is committed against persons who are not women or victims of domestic violence. There is no logical and appropriate answer to this question. On the other hand, this step by the Lithuanian legislator points in the right direction, namely that there may be more cases in which an exception to the requirement of double criminality of an act may apply.

One such case concerns the commission of a crime committed in territories where no state exercises its sovereignty. In such territories, no state's law is applicable, and the requirement of double criminality cannot be applied. Difficulties are also encountered when a criminal act is committed on the continental shelf or in the exclusive economic zone of Lithuania or of another state, or on board a vessel or aircraft of a foreign state outside its territory but not in the territory of another state.

As mentioned above, the continental shelf and the exclusive economic zone are specific areas beyond the territory of the coastal state, in which that state has only certain rights under international law within which it can exercise its jurisdiction. It is also mentioned that vessels and aircraft are not part of the territory of a state. In the context of this issue, this is particularly important in cases where Lithuanian citizens or persons permanently residing in Lithuania commit crimes on board a vessel or aircraft belonging to a foreign state, which is outside the territory of Lithuania, but not in the territory of another state. Although in such cases the law of the flag or state of registration applies to the ship or aircraft in question, these objects cannot be described as foreign, and therefore it is not possible to apply the condition of reciprocal criminality of the offense, although this should be done under the current wording of Article 8(1) of the CC.

An even more interesting situation would arise if Lithuanian citizens or persons permanently residing in Lithuania were to commit crimes on board a vessel or aircraft outside the territory of any foreign state. In such a case, the mutual criminality clause would also not be applicable, although there is no provision in the Lithuanian CC providing for such an exception.

Article 8(3) of the CC is also illogical, insofar as the exception to the requirement of double criminality is limited to specific crimes committed in the territory of another state. If Lithuanian citizens or persons permanently residing in Lithuania commit the crimes referred to in Article 8(3) of the CC outside the territory of another state, then the exception to the requirement of double criminality does not apply.

It seems that the criticized version of Article 8(3) of the CC has been constructed as a literal transposition of the rules laid down in Article 17(4) of Directive 2011/93/EU and Article 44(3) of the Istanbul Convention, without any consideration of the fact that it will only solve a part of the identified problems. It seems that the fact that such a regulation, which in some cases requires the requirement of double criminality and in others does not, is not in line with the principle of equality of all persons before the law, the courts and other public authorities, as enshrined in Article 29(1) of the Constitution.

It is therefore clear that both Article 8(1) of the CC and Article 8(3) of the CC have a number of omissions that need to be filled. A formula for filling the gaps identified and related to the requirement of double criminality was proposed in the first years of the CC's entry into force (Nevera 2006, pp.103–106) and is still relevant today. However, there is no doubt that, in view of the current state of EU law and Lithuania's independent criminal policy regarding the transposition of the provisions of international legal acts to be ratified, more formulas should be proposed. The need for them is also conditioned by the necessity of solving the problems of criminalization of offenses committed by Lithuanian citizens and persons permanently residing in Lithuania on board a vessel or aircraft belonging to a foreign state which is located outside the territory of Lithuania, but not in the territory of another state.

An important aspect of the issue at hand is whether the active personality principle should apply to all criminal acts committed outside the territory of Lithuania, in particular when committed outside the territory of a foreign state. It seems that Lithuania should seek to prosecute only those acts for which the Lithuanian CC prescribes a sentence of at least 1 year of imprisonment, i.e., only for crimes. This proposal would be guided by Article 2 of the Council Framework Decision on the European arrest warrant and the surrender procedures between Member States (2002/584/JHA) and by Article 2 of the European Convention on Extradition, which refer to acts for which persons may be surrendered under the EAW or extradited. Such a regulation would allow for the dissociation of misdemeanors and would save human and material resources.

It is clear that the question of how Article 8(3) of the CC should be modified is also relevant, as the current link to the commission of a crime in the territory of another state is not appropriate. It seems that Article 8(3) of the CC should state that a citizen of the Republic of Lithuania or a person permanently residing in Lithuania who commits one or more crimes outside the territory of Lithuania shall be punished irrespective of the whether the crime committed is punishable at that place of commission. This change would better reflect the legislator's objectives and would ensure the broader and more certain protection of victims in cases where the crimes in question are committed outside the territory of a foreign state.

Interim Findings

The coherent application of the principles of criminal jurisdiction in relation to criminal acts committed abroad by Lithuanian citizens and persons permanently residing in Lithuania can only be possible if it is understood that any principle has individual grounds for application and a specific purpose, which cannot be overturned by a literal interpretation of the norms establishing it.

The determination of the place of commission of a criminal act is also an important basis for the application of each principle of criminal jurisdiction, and the rule(s) governing it must therefore be set out in an independent article of the CC and be separate from the territorial principle. By addressing the issue of the regulation of the rule(s) on the place of commission of an offense in accordance with the guidelines proposed in the present research, the interpretations that are still common in Lithuanian case law suggesting that a ship may be granted the status of the territory of another state would be definitively prevented.

In order to achieve the objective of regulating the place of commission of a criminal act in a separate article of the CC, distinct from all jurisdictional principles, the system of jurisdictional principles currently existing in the Lithuanian CC must be expanded by introducing at least a passive personality principle, which would be very effective in solving the problem that is gaining momentum, whereby persons located in Lithuania are victimized by cyber-fraud committed outside the territory of Lithuania.

The flag principle should also be regulated in a separate article of the CC, the key aspect of which should be the understanding that international law may establish rules that allocate jurisdiction between the coastal state and the state of registration of a vessel, or between the host of the airspace and the state of registration of an aircraft of a foreign state. The direct applicability of such rules of international law is possible under Article 138(3) of the Constitution and cannot be denied on the basis of the principle of *nullum crimen sine lege*, which has nothing to do *per se* with the resolution of questions falling within the scope of the principles of jurisdiction.

Article 7 of the Lithuanian CC, stating that "Persons shall be held liable under this Code regardless of their citizenship and place of residence, also of the place of commission of a crime and whether the act committed [...]," cannot be understood literally. Its content must be revealed by delving deeper into the essence of the universal principle, which also helps to highlight the standard of its harmonious relationship with other jurisdictional principles. Using various methods of interpretation of the legal norm, it is also apparent that Lithuanian citizens and persons permanently residing in Lithuania are liable for crimes committed outside the territory of Lithuania and referred to in Article 7 of the CC on the basis of the universal principle only if it is not possible to apply the jurisdictional principles that are higher in the hierarchy (territorial, flag, or passive personal), and only in the case of crimes of high seriousness for which universal jurisdiction is established in accordance with the provisions of a specific international agreement.

The application of the universal principle must also respect the rules on the allocation of jurisdiction laid down in the relevant international treaties. Otherwise, it would be necessary to tolerate perverse situations which have nothing to do with the harmonious application of the law, in which any sovereign state which has established the universal principle in its national criminal law would be entitled to exercise jurisdiction over any crime which could be referred to in the rule governing the principle, even if it were entirely formalistic – that is to say, without an international legal basis.

According to the current wording of Article 8(1) of the CC, universal jurisdiction is to apply only to crimes committed by Lithuanian citizens or persons permanently residing in Lithuania in territories where no state exercises its sovereignty or, even if it does, does not impose criminal liability for it. However, if such a crime is committed by a citizen of another state who is permanently resident in Lithuania, and the state of their nationality seeks to exercise its criminal jurisdiction on the basis of the active personality principle, then this is precisely the direction in which it should be pursued by making use of all instruments of legal cooperation in criminal matters.

The requirement of the double criminality of an act, established in Article 8(1) of the CC of Lithuania and linked only to the law in force in the territory of the other state, blocks the more coherent application of the principle of active personality and the principle of the protection of state interests. Moreover, such a regulation does not allow for the application of the requirement of double criminality and the imposition of an appropriate penalty in cases where a Lithuanian citizen or person permanently residing in Lithuania commits a criminal act on board a vessel or an aircraft of another state, which is located outside the state of registration. In order to address these problems and to ensure the coherent interaction of the principles of extraterritorial jurisdiction, Article 8(1) of the CC should be amended as soon as possible. Article 8(3) of the CC should also be modified to provide that a Lithuanian citizen or a person permanently residing in Lithuania who commits one or more of the crimes referred to in this provision outside the territory of Lithuania shall be liable to prosecution, irrespective of whether or not the act committed is punishable at the place of the commission of the crime.

References

Abramavičius, A., *et al.*, 2004. *Lietuvos Respublikos baudžiamojo kodekso komentaras. Bendroji dalis* [A Commentary of the Lithuanian Criminal Code. General Part]. Vilnius: Teisinės informacijos centras.

Additional Protocol to the Convention on Cybercrime, concerning the criminalisation of acts of a racist and xenophobic nature committed through computer systems. ETS No. 189. [online]. Available from: https://rm.coe.int/1680081 60f [Accessed 19 July 2023].

Aiškinamasis raštas dėl Baudžiamojo kodekso 7, 8, 95, 205, 206, 207 straipsnių ir priedo pakeitimo ir kodekso papildymo 1003 straipsniu įstatymo projekto [Explanatory Memorandum to the Draft Law on the amendment of Articles 7, 8, 95, 205, 206, 207 and the Annex to the Criminal Code and the addition of Article 1003 to the Code], 17 May 2019. [online]. Available from: https:// e-seimas.lrs.lt/portal/legalAct/lt/TAK/763a4eb0786a11e99ceae2890faa4 193?jfwid=-y3rq84d8a [Accessed 19 July 2023].

Bewes, W. A., 1920. The Treaties of Montevideo (1889). *Transactions of the Grotius Society*, 6, 59–79.

Code of Criminal Procedure of the Republic of Lithuania (Consolidated version, 6 July 2023). *Official Gazette*, 2002-04-09, No. 37-1341. [online]. Available from: https://www.e-tar.lt/portal/lt/legalAct/TAR.EC588C321777/asr [Accessed 19 July 2023].

Consular Agreement between the Republic of Lithuania and Turkey, 11 July 1994. *Official Gazette*, 1998-02-19, No. 17-400. [online]. Available from: https://e-seimas.lrs.lt/portal/legalAct/lt/TAD/TAIS.50190 [Accessed 19 July 2023].

Consular Convention between the Republic of Lithuania and Georgia, 12 July 1999. *Official Gazette*, 2001-06-08, No. 49-1707 [online]. Available from: https://www.e-tar.lt/portal/lt/legalAct/TAR.996B7AE2936D [Accessed 19 July 2023]

Consular Convention between the Republic of Lithuania and the People's Republic of China, 15 August 1992. *Official Gazette*, 1993-08-06, No. 35-792. [online]. Available from: https://www.e-tar.lt/portal/lt/legalAct/TAR.90C76A97E0FE [Accessed 19 July 2023].

Consular Convention between the Republic of Lithuania and the Republic of Poland, 13 January 1992. *Official Gazette*, 1994-04-15, No. 28-494. [online]. Available from: https://www.e-tar.lt/portal/lt/legalAct/TAR.A8CC4371DFCA [Accessed 19 July 2023].

Consular Convention between the Republic of Lithuania and the Russian Federation, 8 September 1992. *Official Gazette*, 1995-12-06, No. 99-2204 [online]. Available from: https://www.e-tar.lt/portal/lt/legalAct/TAR.E7E6D8A5FAA4 [Accessed 19 July 2023].

Consular Convention between the Republic of Lithuania and the Ukraine, 28 March 1995. *Official Gazette*, 1997-11-21, No. 106-2673. [online]. Available from: https://www.e-tar.lt/portal/lt/legalAct/TAR.76BF02D85A05 [Accessed 19 July 2023].

Convention for the Suppression of Unlawful Acts against the Safety of Civil Aviation, 23 September 1971. UNTS, Vol. 974. [online]. Available from: https://treaties.un.org/doc/Publication/UNTS/Volume%20974/volume-974-I-14118-english.pdf [Accessed 19 July 2023].

Convention for the Suppression of Unlawful Seizure of Aircraft, 16 September 1970. UNTS, Vol. 860. [online]. Available from: https://treaties.un.org/doc/db/terrorism/conv2-english.pdf [Accessed 19 July 2023].

Convention on Cybercrime, 23 November 2001. ETS, No. 185. [online]. Available from: https://www.europarl.europa.eu/cmsdata/179163/20090225ATT50418EN.pdf [Accessed 19 July 2023].

Convention on Offences and Certain Other Acts Committed on Board Aircraft, 14 September 1963. UNTS, Vol. 704. [online]. Available from: https://treaties.un.org/doc/db/terrorism/conv1-english.pdf [Accessed 19 July 2023].

Convention on the Prevention and Punishment of the Crime of Genocide, General Assembly resolution 260 A (III) of 9 December 1948. UNTS, Vol. 78. [online]. Available from: https://www.un.org/en/genocideprevention/documents/atrocity-crimes/Doc.1_Convention%20on%20the%20Prevention%20and%20Punishment%20of%20the%20Crime%20of%20Genocide.pdf [Accessed 19 July 2023].

Convention on the Prohibition of the Development, Production, Stockpiling and Use of Chemical Weapons and on their Destruction, 3 September 1992.

UNTS, Vol. 1975. [online]. Available from: https://treaties.un.org/doc/Treaties/1997/04/19970429%2007-52%20PM/CTC-XXVI_03_ocred.pdf [Accessed 19 July 2023].

Convention on the Territorial Sea and the Contiguous Zone, 29 April 1958. UNTS, Vol. 516. [online]. Available from: https://treaties.un.org/doc/Treaties/1964/11/19641122%2002-14%20AM/Ch_XXI_01_2_3_4_5p.pdf [Accessed 19 July 2023].

Council Framework Decision 2008/913/JHA of 28 November 2008 on Combating Certain Forms and Expressions of Racism and Xenophobia by Means of Criminal Law. OJ L 328/55. [online]. Available from: https://eur-lex.europa.eu/legal-content/EN/TXT/PDF/?uri=CELEX:32008F0913 [Accessed 19 July 2023].

Council Framework Decision of 13 June 2002 on the European Arrest Warrant and the Surrender Procedures between Member States (2002/584/JHA). OJ L 190. [online]. Available from: https://eur-lex.europa.eu/legal-content/EN/TXT/?uri=CELEX%3A02002F0584-20090328 [Accessed 19 July 2023].

Council of Europe Convention on Preventing and Combating Violence Against Women and Domestic Violence, 11 May 2001. CETS, No. 210. [online]. Available from: https://rm.coe.int/168008482e [Accessed 19 July 2023].

Criminal Code of Denmark, 2005. [online]. Available from: https://legislationline.org/sites/default/files/documents/39/Denmark_Criminal_Code_am2005_en.pdf [Accessed 19 July 2023].

Criminal Code of the Kingdom of Netherlands, 1881, as amended in 2012. [online]. Available from: https://legislationline.org/sites/default/files/documents/f3/Netherlands_CC_am2012_en.pdf [Accessed 19 July 2023].

Criminal Code of the Republic of Finland, 1889, amendments up to 2015 included. [online] Available from: https://legislationline.org/sites/default/files/documents/a4/Finland_CC_1889_am2015_en.pdf [Accessed 19 July 2023].

Criminal Code of the Republic of Lithuania (Consolidated version of 6 July 2023). *Official Gazette*, 2000-10-25, No. 89-2741. [online]. Available from: https://www.e-tar.lt/portal/lt/legalAct/TAR.2B866DFF7D43/asr [Accessed 19 July 2023].

Directive 2011/93/EU of the European Parliament and of the Council of 13 December 2011 on Combating the Sexual Abuse and Sexual Exploitation of Children and Child Pornography, and Replacing Council Framework Decision 2004/68/JHA. OJ L 335. [online]. Available from: http://data.europa.eu/eli/dir/2011/93/oj [Accessed 19 July 2023].

Directive 2013/40/EU of the European Parliament and of the Council of 12 August 2013 on Attacks Against Information Systems and Replacing

Council Framework Decision 2005/222/JHA. OJ L 218. [online]. Available from: https://eur-lex.europa.eu/eli/dir/2013/40/oj [Accessed 19 July 2023].

European Convention on Extradition, 13 December 1957. ETS, No. 24. [online]. Available from: https://rm.coe.int/1680064587 [Accessed 19 July 2023].

German Criminal Code, 1998, last amended in 2013. [online]. Available from: https://legislationline.org/sites/default/files/documents/8c/Germany_CC_am2013_en.pdf [Accessed 19 July 2023].

International Convention on the Suppression and Punishment of the Crime of Apartheid, 1974. G.A. res. 3068 (XXVIII), 28 U.N. GAOR Supp. (No. 30) at 75, U.N. Doc. A/9030. UNTS, Vol. 1015. [online]. Available from: https://www.un.org/en/genocideprevention/documents/atrocity-crimes/Doc.10_International%20Convention%20on%20the%20Suppression%20and%20Punishment%20of%20the%20Crime%20of%20Apartheid.pdf [Accessed 19 July 2023].

Jescheck, H. H., and Weigend, T., 1996. *Lehrbuch des Strafrecht Allgemeiner Teil.* Berlin: Duncker & Humblot.

Judgment of the Supreme Court of Lithuania in Criminal Case No. 2K-514/2014. [online]. Available from: https://eteismai.lt/byla/231506973735340/2K-514/2014 [Accessed 19 July 2023].

Judgment of the Supreme Court of Lithuania in Criminal Case No. 2K-682/2001.

Judgment of the Supreme Court of Lithuania in Criminal Case No. 2K-188-489/2015. [online]. Available from: https://eteismai.lt/byla/228782047735554/2K-188-489/2015 [Accessed 19 July 2023].

Judgment of the Supreme Court of Lithuania in Criminal Case No. 2K-526/2011. [online]. Available from: https://eteismai.lt/byla/50995355157032/2K-526/2011 [Accessed 19 July 2023].

Judgment of the Supreme Court of Lithuania in Criminal Case No. 2K-57-697/2018. [online]. Available from: https://eteismai.lt/byla/192859440830595/2K-57-697/2018 [Accessed 19 July 2023].

Judgment of the Vilnius District Court in Criminal Case No. 1S-334-495/2012. [online]. Available from: https://eteismai.lt/byla/182471000191758/1S-334-495/2012 [Accessed 19 July 2023].

Karalek, D., 2020. Navigating *Terra Nullius*: The Ababda and the Case for Indigenous Land Rights in Bir Tawil. *Global Journal of Economics and Finance*, 4 (2), 41–49 [online]. Available from: http://www.gjefnet.com/images/Vol4No2/4.pdf [Accessed 19 July 2023].

Katuoka, S., 1999. Atviroji jūra: sąvoka ir laisvės [The High Seas: The Concept and the Freedoms]. *Jurisprudencija*, 13 (5), 117–125. [online]. Available from: https://cris.mruni.eu/server/api/core/bitstreams/cb8c3781-7dbc-4a65-b99a-2369720ede18/content [Accessed 19 July 2023].

Kavolis, M., and Bieliackinas, S., 1934. *Baudžiamasis statutas su papildomais baudžiamaisiais įstatymais ir komentarais* [The Criminal Statute with Additional Criminal Laws and Commentary]. Kaunas.

Law of the Republic of Lithuania on the legal status of foreigners (Consolidated version of 1 July 2023–31 December 2023). *Official Gazette*, 2004-04-30, No. 73-2539. [online]. Available from: https://www.e-tar.lt/portal/lt/legalAct/TAR.42837E5A79DD/asr [Accessed 19 July 2023].

Marcinauskaitė, R., 2021. Nusikalstamos veikos elektroninėje erdvėje ir teritorinė baudžiamoji jurisdikcija [Cybercrime and Territorial Criminal Jurisdiction]. *Jurisprudencija*, 28 (1), 200–216. [online]. https://doi.org/10.13165/JUR-21-28-1-10 [Accessed 19 July 2023].

Mohl, R., 1853. *Völkerrechtliche Lehre vom Asyle*. Tübingen: Druck von Heinrich Laupp.

Nevera, A., 2006. *Valstybės baudžiamosios jurisdikcijos principai* [Principles of State Criminal Jurisdiction]. Vilnius: Mykolo Romerio universitetas.

Nevera, A., and Melničenko, S., 2009. *Non bis in idem* principas Europos Sąjungos baudžiamojoje teisėje (I) [The non bis in idem Principle in the European Union Criminal Law (I)]. *Socialinių mokslų studijos*, 4 (4), 85–106 [online]. Available from: https://ojs.mruni.eu/ojs/societal-studies/article/view/1382 [Accessed 19 July 2023].

O'connel, D. P., 1970. *International law*, 2nd edn., 2 vols. London: Stevens & Sons.

Republic of Lithuania Law on International Treaties (Consolidated version, valid as of 1 April 2015). *Official Gazette*, 1999-07-09, No. 60-1948. [online]. Available from: https://www.e-tar.lt/portal/lt/legalAct/TAR.5BCEC9B41811/asr [Accessed 19 July 2023].

Rome Statute of the International Criminal Court, 17 July 1998. [online]. Available from: https://www.icc-cpi.int/sites/default/files/RS-Eng.pdf [Accessed 19 July 2023].

Ruling of the Constitutional Court of Republic of Lithuania 25 September 1996. [online]. Available from: https://lrkt.lt/lt/teismo-aktai/paieska/135/ta412/content [Accessed 1 October 2023].

Ruling of the Constitutional Court of Republic of Lithuania 23 June 1999. [online]. Available from: https://lrkt.lt/lt/teismo-aktai/paieska/135/ta359/content [Accessed 1 October 2023].

Ruling of the Constitutional Court of Republic of Lithuania 6 December 2000. [online]. Available from: https://lrkt.lt/lt/teismo-aktai/paieska/135/ta348/content [Accessed 1 October 2023].

Ruling of the Constitutional Court of Republic of Lithuania 25 May 2004. [online]. Available from: https://lrkt.lt/lt/teismo-aktai/paieska/135/ta265/content [Accessed 1 October 2023].

Ruling of the Constitutional Court of Republic of Lithuania 28 March 2006. [online]. Available from: https://lrkt.lt/lt/teismo-aktai/paieska/135/ta203/content [Accessed 1 October 2023].

Single Convention on Narcotic Drugs, 1961, as amended by the 1972 Protocol Amending the Single Convention on Narcotic Drugs. [online]. Available from: https://www.unodc.org/pdf/convention_1961_en.pdf [Accessed 19 July 2023].

Sinkevičius, E., 1999. *Veikos, susijusios su neteisėtu banko kredito gavimu arba panaudojimu, bei jų baudžiamojo teisinio vertinimo problemos* [Activities Related to the Unlawful Obtaining of Bank Loans or Their Use and Problems of Evaluating Such Under Criminal Law]. Thesis. (PhD). Vilnius: Lietuvos teisės akademija.

Starke, I., 1972. *Introduction to International Law*, 7th edn. London: Butterworths.

Statute of the International Tribunal for the Prosecution of Persons Responsible for Serious Violations of International Humanitarian Law Committed in the Territory of the Former Yugoslavia since 1991. [online]. Available from: https://www.icty.org/x/file/Legal%20Library/Statute/statute_sept09_en.pdf [Accessed 19 July 2023].

Swart, A. H. J., 1992. Jurisdiction in Criminal Law: Sam Reflections on the Finnish Code from a Comparative Perspective. In: R. Lahti and K. Nuotio, (eds.), *Criminal Law Theory in Transition Finish and Comparative Perspectives.* Helsinki: Finnish Lawyers Publishing Company.

Švedas, G., Veršekys, P., Levon, J., and Prapiestis, D., 2017. *Lietuvos Respublikos baudžiamojo kodekso bendrosios dalies vientisumo ir naujovių (su)derinimo iššūkiai* [Challenges in Harmonizing the Integrity and Novelties of the General Part of the Criminal Code]. Vilnius: Vilniaus universiteto leidykla.

The Swedish Criminal Code, 1965. [online]. Available from: https://legislationline.org/sites/default/files/documents/98/Sweden_CC.pdf [Accessed 19 July 2023].

Tratado de Derecho Penal Internacional. [online]. Available from: https://web.archive.org/web/20100112204828/http://www.parlamento.gub.uy/htmlstat/pl/tratados/trat10272-5.htm [Accessed 19 July 2023].

Treaty on International Penal Law of 19 March 1940. [online]. Available from: https://www.refworld.org/docid/3ae6b3a62c.html [Accessed 19 July 2023].

United Nations Convention on the Law of the Sea, 10 December 1982. UNTS, Vol. 1833. [online]. Available from: https://www.un.org/depts/los/convention_agreements/texts/unclos/unclos_e.pdf [Accessed 19 July 2023].

Volsonokas, R., 1930. Lietuvos jūros teisė [Law of the Sea in Lithuania]. *Teisė*, No. 18 (July–Dec).

Part II
The Transformation of Criminal Procedure Law in the Context of Coherence

Raimundas Jurka

The E-Evidence "Movement" in European Union Criminal Justice: Toward or Beyond Coherence?

The free "movement" of evidence without being hindered in the context of the criminal justice system of the European Union (hereinafter referred to as the "EU") and its Member States is a real challenge for both EU legislation and the platform for judicial cooperation between the Member States. The legal proceedings of collecting and transferring evidence, in particular electronic evidence, from one Member State to another not only depend on consistency within these proceedings and the interconnectivity of these processes based on cooperation established between Member States, but should be also admissible as evidence in the national court of any given Member State in criminal proceedings concerning a particular person. Thus, perceiving the whole process as an integral cross-compliance mechanism, the coherence and proportionality of EU legal instruments may also be subject to evaluation between courts of Member States in the field of collecting electronic evidence during criminal proceedings.

The optimization of legislative procedures in all matters related to gathering evidence across EU Member States for the EU criminal justice system provides an opportunity to see how attitudes toward the process of gathering electronic evidence are changing. Although this process continues to be based on the maxim of mutual recognition, which, at least theoretically, ensures the confidence of Member States in each other's legal systems and judicial decisions, the development of the legal instrumentation in question also reveals certain threats to legal assessment, the fragmentation of the regulatory framework, and the not entirely justified and reasonable differentiation of the collection of evidence depending on the type of evidence being collected.

It is therefore crucially important to understand not only what drives the changes and developments in EU legislation on electronic evidence, but also the need to maintain this legal framework as a harmonious and coherent process. However, there is nothing wrong or harmful with the notion that the modernization of social relationships also implies the need to modernize the arrangements for judicial cooperation based on the principle of mutual recognition. On the other hand, another equally important issue cannot be ignored: the recognition of electronic evidence and its admissibility in particular criminal proceedings.

This is the actual aim of the free movement of evidence among Member States in EU criminal justice.

The abovementioned insights allow for the identification of the following scientific problems that are analyzed in this research: what are the factors that cause EU legal regulation in the sphere of the evidence making procedure in criminal justice to become fragmented? Does the EU legal regulation in the sphere of e-evidence collection create preconditions to ensure the principles of the right to a fair trial in criminal justice?

Cross-Border Access to Electronic Evidence Within the European Union: Reasons and Regulatory Background

As of April 2018, when the first version of the European Commission's proposal for a Regulation of the European Parliament and of the Council on European Production and Preservation Orders for electronic evidence in criminal matters appeared, after protracted discussions and lengthy negotiations, Regulation (EU) 2023/1543 of the European Parliament and of the Council on European Production Orders and European Preservation Orders for electronic evidence in criminal proceedings and the execution of custodial sentences following criminal proceedings (hereinafter referred to as the "Regulation") was adopted on 12 July 2023. This is likely the first document of its kind that modifies the traditional model of mutual recognition and mutual legal assistance agreements (Corhay 2023b). It signals a shift from the traditional model of judicial cooperation based on mutual recognition toward substantially "operational" (European Digital Rights 2023) cooperation between the competent law enforcement authorities of a Member State and a service provider (as defined in Article 3(3) of the Regulation). The latter initiative has indeed caused considerable controversy, generating both positive and critical evaluations, as reflected in various sources. According to one source (Corhay 2023a), it institutionalizes the criminal justice paradigm – i.e., immediate and direct cooperation between law enforcement, judicial authorities and the private sector (service providers). Corhay (2023a) points out that "unlike other forms of cooperation in criminal matters regulated by EU law which involve the cooperation between judicial authorities of different Member States – like the European Arrest Warrant and the European Investigation Order – the original e-evidence proposal substitutes the traditional executing Member States by a private actor," and even expresses her concern that this new model allows the involvement of the law enforcement or judicial authorities of the executing State to be bypassed in the cooperation process. Some sources even use sarcasm, observing that such a model presupposes turning private sector companies providing electronic communications services into "private law enforcement agencies" (Petri 2018). According to Petri (2018), "criminal investigation and law enforcement are sovereign tasks. They must generally remain in the hands of government bodies in the respective country and must not be delegated to private enterprises. Likewise, the home country of the provider who is obliged to cooperate, needs to be enabled to ensure the legitimacy of the order according to its national law. This is the only way to ensure compliance with legal rules governing criminal prosecution." At the same time, there is no denying that "it should be stressed that the proposed Regulation is much more comprehensive and detailed compared to the previous legal documents in that area. The proposal targets directly the specific problem created by the volatile nature of the electronic evidence and its international dimension" (Blažič and Klobučar 2020, p.98).

These and other assessments thus show that the Regulation, which introduces a rather revolutionary model of judicial cooperation that directly involves private sector entities, is indeed met with a certain amount of mistrust. Paradoxically, the Regulation implements the principle of mutual recognition; at the same time, however, the doctrine expresses doubts as to whether the mechanism set out in the Regulation will ensure the recognition of electronic evidence as a standard of achievement to be pursued.

Indeed, as will become apparent below, the new regulatory framework on so-called cross-border access to electronic evidence is controversial, as it is interpreted and understood in different ways. It is certainly true that it would be objectively impossible to disclose all assessments in this paper due to its limited scope, but one aspect of the subject will certainly be touched upon. The question will be whether this regulation will indeed allow for the admissibility of transmitted electronic evidence and the coherence of this process in the EU criminal justice system.

When putting the emphasis on the substance of the Regulation adopted by the Council on cross-border access to electronic evidence as an innovation in the EU for the optimization of judicial cooperation in the field of criminal justice, the reasons that have led to this innovation should be identified.

Firstly, the means of receiving and storing electronic evidence are becoming increasingly important for criminal proceedings throughout the EU. Effective mechanisms for collecting electronic evidence are essential in combating crime and should be subject to conditions and safeguards that ensure full compliance with the fundamental rights and principles recognized by Article 6 of the Treaty on European Union and the Charter of Fundamental Rights of the European Union, in particular the principles of necessity and proportionality, due process, privacy and the protection of personal data, and the confidentiality of communications.

Secondly, services based on electronic communications networks can be provided from any location and do not require physical infrastructure, premises or staff in the country where the service is being offered. As a result, electronic evidence is often stored outside the borders of the investigating State or is stored by a service provider located outside the territory of that State, posing challenges for the collection of electronic evidence and obtaining proof in criminal proceedings. That implies, amongst other things, that the "globalization of criminal evidence" (Swire and Kennedy-Mayo 2017, cited in Abraha 2020, p.327) makes the territorial scope of the protection of criminal jurisdiction less relevant. Furthermore, according to Tosza (2020, pp.168–169), "investigative authorities depend much more significantly on the cooperation of service providers also for practical reasons. While a raid on a company that refuses to produce requested documents would be a viable possibility, a raid on a data center would not bring similar (if any) results, unless disproportionally significant forces are used to find the necessary data, potentially including heavy decrypting capacities if that was possible at all". This idea is echoed by Rojszczak (2022), who claims that

> the global nature of many digital services means that identifying the obliged entity may not be a straightforward task. In many cases, the service provider may have several (multiple) representative offices within the EU. On the one hand, leaving the authorities of the requesting state free to choose which office to address their request for data access to meets the objective of efficient criminal proceedings, but, on the other hand, it makes it difficult to control the decisions taken. In particular, a court order that does not allow the transfer of electronic evidence in one Member State may not prohibit the authorities of the requesting State from making an identical request to another Member State (p.1002).

Thirdly, the procedures and time limits set out in Directive 2014/41/EU of the European Parliament and of the Council of April 3, 2014 regarding the European Investigation Order in Criminal Matters (hereinafter referred to as "EIO Directive" or "EIO"), and in the Convention on mutual assistance in criminal matters between the EU Member States approved by the Council under Article 34 of the Treaty on the European Union (hereinafter referred to as the "Convention"), are not appropriate for electronic evidence, which is more volatile and can be easily and rather quickly deleted. Obtaining electronic evidence through channels for data and judicial cooperation requests is often time-consuming and may result in information being unavailable in the future. Moreover, as is pointed out in the Explanatory Memorandum to the Proposal for a regulation of electronic evidence in criminal matters, the EIO Directive, which has profoundly changed the Convention, applies to any investigative measure and includes access to electronic evidence, but the EIO Directive does not contain any specific provisions relating to this type of evidence. It is highlighted that the Regulation will not replace the EIO, which is aimed at obtaining electronic evidence, but that the Regulation provides an additional instrument available to national authorities. There may also be situations where, for example, several investigative measures need to be applied in the executing Member State and the authorities may prefer the EIO. The creation of a new instrument concerning electronic evidence is a better alternative than amending the EIO Directive when dealing with the specific challenges and problems of collecting electronic evidence, which do not affect the other investigative measures provided for in the EIO Directive (European Commission 2018). Moreover, there is no harmonized framework for cooperation with service providers, although some third-country service providers accept direct requests for such data as authorized according to their own State's national law. However, the practice employed by law enforcement authorities indicates that in reality, a number of requests to service providers/their representatives located in another EU Member State to provide the relevant electronic data remain unfulfilled because service providers are simply not obliged to comply with such requests, which has a particular impact on the work of law enforcement and the implementation of the procedural guarantees of the participants involved in criminal proceedings (Tosza 2020, p.169). Moreover, as Tosza notes, "the increasing need to obtain data for criminal investigation combined with these difficulties and the volatility of data creates the need to find a solution which would facilitate this process. The EIO may serve to acquire electronic evidence, but it is claimed that for that its deadlines are too long and create a risk that data disappears or is altered in the meantime. Nor can it resolve the question of territoriality" (p.169).

It would indeed be possible to identify more reasons for the regulation of the collection of electronic evidence in criminal proceedings. However, it has become apparent that the purpose of the new regulation is unquestionable, and it is therefore not very reasonable to limit ourselves solely to this aspect any further. What is even more important is whether the chosen regulatory model will be able to ensure the implementation of the objective of the "movement" of electronic evidence in the EU criminal justice system. In other words, whether this evidence, once it has been collected following the procedure laid down in the Regulation, will be admissible as evidence in the national court of the issuing Member State in the context of the European Production Order (hereinafter referred to as the "EPO"). Before proceeding to the analysis of this issue, it is therefore necessary to briefly summarize the substance of this Regulation.

The Regulation aims to establish a mechanism as an alternative to preexisting instruments of international cooperation and mutual legal assistance in criminal matters. In particular, it seeks to address the problems arising from the volatile nature of electronic evidence and the "non-locality" aspect by creating new procedures for rapid, efficient and effective cross-border access. The Regulation establishes the system for European Evidence Production and Preservation Orders, which can be issued by judicial authorities to obtain or preserve electronic evidence, regardless of the location of the data. These orders can be issued to any category of data, including subscriber data, traffic (flow) data, content data, etc. The Regulation governs only the collection of data stored by the service provider at the time of obtaining an EPO or a European Preservation Order, prior to a specific criminal proceeding relating to a specific criminal offense that has already been committed, based on a case-by-case assessment of the necessity and proportionality of the orders and taking into account the rights of the suspect or accused person.

The mechanism for the use of the EPO and European Preservation Order in criminal proceedings for electronic evidence is thus based on the principle of mutual trust between Member States and, at the same time, on the presumption that Member States are compliant with EU legislation, follow the rule of law and comply with fundamental rights, which are essential elements of freedom, security, and justice within EU. On the contrary, without taking into account the relationship between the powers of the state and mechanisms of protection of fundamental rights, the problem of developing a coherent model of cross-border cooperation in the transmission of electronic evidence cannot be solved (Rojszczak 2020, p.13). This mechanism allows the law enforcement and judicial authorities of Member States to issue orders directly to service providers. One point which is very important in this regard is the fact that the assessed legal mechanism must also be based on the implementation of procedural rights in criminal proceedings as laid down in Directives 2010/64/EU1, 2012/13/EU2, 2013/48/EU3, (EU) 2016/3434, (EU) 2016/8005, and (EU) 2016/19196 of the European Parliament and of the Council. In addition, it must be observed that these orders can only be issued in the light of the rights of the suspected or accused person in proceedings relating to a criminal offense, and only if such an order could be issued under the same conditions in a similar domestic case, and, consequently, if the suspected or accused person is entitled to an effective remedy in the course of criminal proceedings in which the collected data are used as evidence (the right to an effective remedy should be exercised before the court of the issuing State following its national law, and should include the possibility to challenge the legality of the measure, including its necessity and proportionality). In this respect, it should be noted that, in the context of the relationship governed by the Regulation, it is particularly important to safeguard the procedural interests not only of suspects and accused persons in the Member State of the issuing authority, but also in the State of the executing authority (Kosta and Kamara 2023, p.74). In assessing whether orders may be issued, it is necessary to consider whether the order is limited to what is necessary to fulfil a legitimate objective, i.e., to obtain data that is relevant and necessary evidence in a particular case.

To sum up very briefly, it can be considered that the new regulation on the collection of electronic evidence in criminal proceedings, which contributes to the coordination, sustainability, legal clarity, transparency, and accountability of the EU criminal justice system (Warken, van Zwieten and Svantesson 2020, p.49), is a continuation of the development of mutual recognition among Member States in EU criminal justice. The Regulation under examination establishes a new type of judicial cooperation model by avoiding the involvement of the judicial or law enforcement authorities of the executing authority in the recognition and execution of orders. Instead, it establishes a space for the issuing state to approach service providers normally belonging to the private sector directly (following the principle of direct communication (Jurka 2019, p. 322)), thus moving from a horizontal to a vertical cooperation model. At the same time, it should be noted that the aforesaid regulation which is being examined does not replace other EU legislation in matters related to gathering evidence. On the contrary, the new regulation creates a kind of differentiation in the collection of evidence in criminal proceedings.

The Relationship Between the European Investigation Order and the Regulation on Electronic Evidence

It should be recalled that the purpose and essence of the EIO Directive, unlike previous EU legislation that intends to facilitate judicial cooperation in the taking of evidence in criminal proceedings, is not only to collect, record, and transmit evidence already existing in other EU Member States, but also to carry out the actions of searching for, collecting, receiving, and transmitting evidence to the issuing State. In other words, the EIO mechanism is based on a twofold system of evidence gathering: on the one hand, it may collect and transmit existing evidence (retrospective data); at the same time, it may be used for searching, capturing, and collecting evidence of interest to a Member State's law enforcement authority in real time (prospective data). The scope of the EIO thus extends beyond the process of gathering evidence to include procedural steps (measures) to search for and collect such evidence – in particular, evidence that has not yet been gathered. The purpose of the EIO Directive is not only to collect pre-existing evidence but also to request that another EU Member State take legal proceedings to collect relevant evidence of interest to the issuing Member State (Jurka 2011, p.116). For instance, Article 5(1)(e) of the EIO Directive states that "the EIO shall, in particular, contain the following information: [...] a description of the investigative measures(s) requested and the evidence to be obtained." This is in line with the principle that "the executing authority shall comply with the formalities and procedures expressly indicated by the issuing authority unless otherwise provided in this Directive and provided that such formalities and procedures are not contrary to the fundamental principles of the law of the executing State." The executing competent authority may also have recourse to an investigative measure(s) other than that indicated in the EIO, where the investigative measure(s) selected by the executing competent authority would achieve the same result by less intrusive means than the investigative measure(s) indicated in the EIO. Thus, the Member State that requests another Member State to search for and collect the necessary evidence specifies the investigative steps that should be taken to ensure that the subsequent collection and receipt of such evidence does not create additional problems in ensuring the admissibility of such evidence, as the procedural requirements for the collection of evidence (and the procedural form for the collection of the data) may be different in the requesting State and the executing State (Belevičius 2013, p.183). This implements the requirement of *forum regit actum*, according to which a request for judicial cooperation is implemented following the national law of the requesting State.

The model of judicial cooperation created by the EIO Directive and applied in a truly effective manner does not differentiate the evidence to which the Directive applies; it does not matter whether it is personal or material evidence, whether it is tangible or digital data. In addition to these innovations (in terms of the *forum regit actum* option, which allows EU Member States not to unify the principles of data collection in their laws on criminal procedure, which, due to different legal and social traditions, could not be unified (Mangiaracina 2014, p.116); there are also opponents of this system who argue that *forum regit actum* as a consequence of the principle of mutual recognition does not resolve the issue of admissibility of evidence: "the EU, when developing the EIO Directive, did not take advantage of Article 82(2) TFEU which allows for the introduction of common EU minimum standards facilitating the admissibility of evidence. Instead of this, the EIO still relies on the *forum regit actum* principle, which has questionable potential to ensure mutual recognition of evidence in the" (Kusak

2019, p.399)), the traditional procedure for the implementation of the principle of mutual recognition has also been preserved, involving aspects such as the legal status of the issuing authority and the executing authority, the communication of these competent authorities, the procedures for the issuance, transmission, recognition, and execution of the EIO, the grounds for non-recognition and non-enforcement, the grounds and conditions for the application of alternative investigative measures, etc. Indeed, for the sake of accuracy and completeness, it should be noted that although the provisions of the EIO Directive are general in nature (it should be noted that when the proposal (draft) of this Directive was still being considered, it was strongly believed that the provisions of this legal instrument would fully cover the collection of electronic evidence (Leroux 2004, pp.193–220)) and are intended for and applicable to almost all types of evidence, Article 10(2)(e) and Article 30 of this Directive specifically provide for what investigative instruments and measures are intended for the collection of electronic evidence, i.e., the identification of persons holding a subscription of a specified phone number or IP address and the interception of telecommunications with the technical assistance of another Member State.

Regarding the relationship between the EIO and the Regulation, Corhay (2023a), analyzing the cooperation model established by the Regulation on electronic evidence in criminal proceedings and comparing it with the principle of the application of the EIO Directive, notes that "the e-evidence proposal is fundamentally different from the European Investigation Order (EIO) which require the order to be circulated between and executed by competent authorities (for a comparison between the two instruments). The competent authority receiving the order performs the necessary checks and assesses it against several grounds for refusal. While the EIO was meant to offer a comprehensive solution to cross-border gathering of evidence, it was not tailored specifically for the collection of electronic evidence which resulted in some significant shortcomings."

Thus, in the doctrinal sources, one can find a variety of assessments that reveal the relationship between the discussed evidence-collection mechanisms, including their similarities and differences. This relationship provides a basis for understanding the peculiarities of the analyzed mechanisms and the fundamental differences that led to the EU legislative decision not to combine the two mechanisms into a single one – for example, into one governed by the EIO Directive.

The two regulatory mechanisms in question, the Regulation and the EIO Directive, are essentially similar in many respects: the identical or at least very similar (Tosza 2020, p.177) objectives; the common legal basis provided for in Article 82(1) of the Treaty on the Functioning of the European Union (2012);

the traditional (customary) system of issuing orders (the requirement to issue an order following the principles of necessity and proportionality, the criterion of similar domestic cases, etc.), and so on. However, there are also substantial, even fundamental differences that allow us to answer why it was decided to regulate the relationship governed by the Regulation (the process of collecting electronic evidence) by enacting a separate piece of legislation rather than integrating these provisions into the time-tested mechanism of the EIO Directive.

The first and most fundamental difference can be found in the prerequisites for issuing an order. Whereas the EIO is based on the free movement of persons and the abolition of borders, the EPO is based on so-called cyberspace, which has no physical borders. This therefore means that the free movement of persons is not necessary for the issuing of an EPO: "There may be need for an EPO in a purely domestic case, with perpetrators, victims, place of commission and investigating authorities all from one locality, just because the data that are needed happen to be in possession of a service provider from another member state" (Tosza 2020, p.177). It is sufficient, therefore, that the data required in the criminal proceedings are managed by a service provider established or otherwise operating in another Member State.

Secondly, the Regulation establishes the principle of direct connection/communication, according to which the competent law enforcement authorities of non-EU Member States cooperate, as would be the case with the EIO. For the collection of electronic evidence, a law enforcement authority in one EU Member State directly requests a warrant from a private sector service provider, which, as Tosza (2022, p.4) argues, does not have the powers to exercise crime prevention, but which is obliged to take a proactive role in the "*prima facie*, the validity and legitimacy of these requests" by cooperating with the law enforcement authorities. In this regard, Mitsilegas (2018, pp.264–265) critically observes that this mechanism leads to the privatization of mutual trust in the field of European criminal justice, since the role of the private sector in the criminal process cannot in any way be assimilated to the powers of the law enforcement authority of the Member State. Here we cannot talk about the effective implementation of control, supervision, and responsibility functions, because the national law enforcement institution and the private sector service provider are two incomparable entities.

Thirdly, unlike the EIO, the EPO mechanism does not provide for a specific procedure for the recognition of an order submitted to an executing authority, including mandatory and optional grounds for non-recognition, etc. Various literary sources indicate that "one may question whether there is still any recognition since there is no authority to actively recognize the order" (Böse 2018). In addition, "the EPO focuses much more on the relationship between the authorities seeking electronic evidence and the service providers having it. This aspect creates a major difference between the two systems. The EPO goes in the first place to the service provider who should respond to it by delivering the requested data without engaging local authorities who could exercise some checking function from the perspective of national interest or fundamental rights" (Tosza 2020, p.177).

Fourthly, as regards EPOs and European Preservation Orders, these orders can only be issued and presented to the issuing authority, i.e., the service provider, to obtain data held by them. The mechanism of operation of these orders, unlike in the case of EIOs, does not allow the service provider to collect data that are not yet available at the time the order is being submitted. This aspect, among other things, has been criticized in the literature (Laurits 2020, p.70), as the limitations of the Regulation when it comes to obliging the service provider to collect electronic evidence in real time fundamentally undermine the effectiveness of this legal regulation.

Fifthly, there is a difference in the level of protection of the safeguards for the parties involved in the proceedings: in the case of a EPO, the service provider, as a private sector entity – unlike in the case of an EIO, where the order is recognized and executed by the law enforcement authorities of the executing State – will not look at the possible constraints on the interests of the parties to the proceedings and their safeguards "with public eye, they will do so with the private one. In other words, business interests will guide these assessments: what is more profitable, comply with the order or resist?" (Tosza 2020, p.178). Corhay (2021, p.471) pointed out in this regard that, among other things, the EU institutions still have to evaluate and resolve an extremely sensitive issue which has given rise to significant debate, i.e., whether service providers act within the limits of their respective activities and their powers that they exercise for the protection of fundamental human rights in the field. This problem is also highlighted by Rojszczak (2022, p.1023) as well as Smuha (2018, p.104), according to whom the existing provisions of the Regulation cover only those means of remedies that the suspect or the accused person can effectively exercise after the issuance of an EPO or European Preservation Order. The regulation does not provide an explicit answer as to whether remedies can be used during the process of the issuance of these orders. In addition, it is worth remembering Mitsilegas' (2018, p.264) statement on this point: if the Regulation does not foresee that the issued order must first be checked and investigated by a competent law enforcement (judicial) institution, it is difficult to talk about the effective protection of rights.

In conclusion, it appears that the principal provisions of the Regulation on cross-border access to electronic evidence are seen in a different light concerning mutual recognition as a guiding force for cooperation. Although the conceptual load of the "guiding force" principle remains the same as in the conclusions of the special EU Summit meeting in Tampere, the needs of Member States to obtain evidence in criminal proceedings located in another State, in particular electronic evidence, change the ways of thinking regarding the effectiveness of judicial cooperation. The aforementioned Regulation creates: new criteria for effective cooperation, i.e., direct connections/communication; the replacement of the law enforcement institution of another EU Member State (executive State) with a private sector entity, which is a service provider; a decrease in the number of grounds for refusal to execute orders, etc. It must be acknowledged that when analyzing the provisions of the Regulation, it was not possible to find convincing arguments in the sources of the doctrine as to why the mechanism of evidence collection established by the Regulation could not be enshrined appropriately in the EIO Directive. After all, the scope of requested electronic evidence determined by the Regulation is quite limited, i.e., only evidence that already exists can be requested. Meanwhile, a request for the collection of electronic evidence in real time can only be granted by the assistance provided by the EIO Directive. It can be assumed that this is a crucial moment which causes discussion about the diversity of the legal regulation of evidence collection in the field of criminal justice within the EU. Some authors (Brière 2021, pp.496–497, 509) even question whether it is generally true that within the EU criminal justice area there has been little discussion so far about the development of a different model that can also enhance the implementation of the principle of mutual recognition – namely, the introduction of the requirement to comply with the common procedural standards. The emergence of such common procedural standards would at least allow the fragmentation of the laws on criminal procedure which regulate judicial cooperation in the field of evidence collection within the EU Member States to be avoided. Furthermore, the fact that the analyzed regulatory framework is not established in a Directive but in a Regulation, which is binding in all its elements and directly applicable in the Member States (on the justification of direct application of the Regulation, see also in that regard the following cases: 34/73 *Variola* [1973] ECR I-981; 93/71 *Leonensio* [1972] ECR I-287), does not in itself reinforce the belief that electronic evidence obtained under the Regulation will be admitted as sufficient evidence in the national courts of the Member States without undue difficulty.

On that point, one can only completely agree with the notions provided in the doctrine. For example, emphasizing the issue of the recognition of electronic evidence in judicial cooperation, Rojszczak writes (2022, p.1001) that "in the case of electronic evidence, the reliability of information is obviously of fundamental importance, not least because digital data are particularly susceptible to modification, from direct manipulation to actual erasure. As contamination of electronic data is often irreversible, it is particularly important to maintain an appropriate work regime at each stage of collecting and processing digital evidence." At the same time, the author raises specific issues of concern "the question of the permissible use of electronic evidence transferred." The author rightly notes that

> the basic purpose of data transfer is their use in ongoing criminal proceedings. In practice, however, law enforcement agencies not only need electronic evidence during pre-trial proceedings (in personam phase) but also during early investigation – to determine whether a crime has been committed (*in rem* phase). In this case, aside from proving the guilt of a defendant, electronic evidence helps to establish the circumstances of the case – and thus to clarify whether further proceedings are necessary. The cross-border transmission of electronic evidence to be used during in rem investigation is controversial, as – in the absence of appropriate safeguards – it may deprive the data subject of a possible judicial review of the measures taken. Ongoing investigations do not necessarily lead to criminal charges being brought, and as a result, the evidence obtained may never be presented to a court (Rojszczak 2022, p.1004).

The Issue of the Admissibility of Electronic Evidence

As has already been mentioned, the issue of recognizing electronic evidence obtained by the procedure established by the Regulation as admissible in the national court of an EU Member State is one of the essential elements that make up the essence of the effective operation of the principle of mutual recognition. In general, the issue of the admissibility of evidence obtained in the field of judicial cooperation is not only a matter of mutual trust and the stability and accountability of national criminal justice across the Member States, but also cross-border criminal justice across EU Member States. After all, it is obvious that mutual legal assistance *sensu largo* mechanisms operating based on mutual recognition in the field of EU law and justice emerge from a single mission: the effective operation of the criminal justice process across the EU Member States in investigating and examining criminal cases and enforcing crime prevention. The same is true of the provisions of the Regulation and the EIO Directive governing the collection of electronic evidence. Indeed, both of the aforementioned legal acts set rather different standards for the form of taking such evidence. This is based, first of all, on the fact that the provisions of the Regulation are intended for the operative collection of electronic evidence stored by the service provider (Article 3(8) of the Regulation) in order to secure and obtain electronic evidence more quickly and effectively. In the view of the author, such an aspiration in itself is not sufficient and does not justify the electronic evidence collection model, which, in a certain sense, reduces the degree of reliability of the collected evidence. Herein, perhaps, lies the essential assumption of the issue of the admissibility of electronic evidence: if the EIO Directive, which in principle also allows for the real-time collection of electronic evidence as well as the collection of existing evidence, sets a relatively high standard for the collection of such evidence (an established system of recognition of orders, non-recognition and the abundance of grounds for non-execution, the possibility of choosing alternative means of investigation, etc.), the provisions of the Regulation appear to lower this standard quite significantly. This standard is lowered to collect only that evidence which is already stored at the time of receiving EPO or European Preservation Order certificates, i.e., existing electronic data.

Thus, both of the aforementioned legal mechanisms, combined with the principle of mutual recognition, undoubtedly seem to ensure that national courts can avoid any concerns about the unreliability of data collected in the territory of another Member State, and at the same time assuage concerns regarding the effectiveness of mutual recognition and compliance with the principles of gathering such evidence. The mutual recognition criterion is considered "a justification to EU action in the field of criminal procedure" (Öberg 2020, p.59). As Liakopolous (2020, p.347) states, mutual recognition "and therefore the direct 'circulation' between the authorities of the judicial measures, marks the abandonment of the conventional assistance system, based on the slow and cumbersome rogatory mechanism, and is based on mutual trust between the member states, thus presupposing respect for the principles of the rule of law." According to another author, Insa (2007, pp.287–288), "principles related to the effectiveness, usefulness, and legitimacy play a relevant role in the different European legislations. The need for obtaining evidence, the transparency while gathering it, and the respect for freedom of expression are principles reflected in the standards in Europe, but they have a secondary position as far as the admissibility of evidence is concerned. The principles that affect electronic evidence are basically the respect for data protection standards and the respect for the secrecy of communications and the right of freedom of expression."

Even though the Regulation is applicable only as of August 18, 2026, it is already possible to critically assess the fact that some of the principal provisions of the Regulation cast doubt on the reliability of evidence obtained from a service provider which offers services within the territory of the Union and is established in another Member State or, if not established, is represented by a legal representative in another Member State. At this point, it should be noted that only a few insights are presented below, which indicate clearly that the method of direct inquiry/communication established by the Regulation (direct contact of a Member State's law enforcement authority with a private sector entity that is a service provider or its representative) in criminal justice inadvertently causes doubts as to whether the chosen model of collecting electronic evidence is appropriate.

Firstly, Article 8(1) of the Regulation establishes that – not in all cases, but only when the aim is to access traffic data, except data requested only to determine the identity of the user or obtain content data – the issuing law enforcement authority of the Member State shall notify not only the addressee, i.e., the service provider or their representative, but also the institution ensuring enforcement (the authority in the enforcing State, which, following the national law of that State, is competent to receive an EPO and an EPOC or a European Preservation Order and an EPOC-PR transmitted by the issuing authority for notification or enforcement following this Regulation). This provision is directly related to the grounds for refusal to execute the EPO established in Article 12 of the Regulation. In other words, the grounds for refusal to execute the EPO established in Article 12(1) of the Regulation are assessed only if a notification about an EPO was delivered not only to the service provider (or their representative), but also to the enforcement authority of the Member State that received that order. Accordingly, as provided for in Article 12(2) of the Regulation, where the enforcing authority raises a ground for refusal under paragraph 1, it shall inform the addressee and the issuing authority. The addressee shall stop the execution of the EPO and not transfer the data, and the issuing authority shall withdraw the order.

This raises a discussion question as to why the provisions of the Regulation on the one hand segregate electronic data/evidence for which the notice regarding the EPO is issued to both the service provider (or their representative) and the enforcement authority, while for other electronic evidence, such as subscriber data, the EPO is addressed to the private sector entity, i.e., the service provider, only. On the other hand, there is no clear answer as to the question of why the grounds for refusal to execute an EPO are only examined if the enforcement authority also receives notification regarding this order, which means that in the case of the collection of subscriber data, the grounds for refusal will not be examined. Therefore, could the grounds for refusing to execute the order, i.e., the contradiction to the principle of *ne bis in idem*, be relevant in seeking to obtain electronic evidence of subscriber data (Article 3(9) of the Regulation)? The existing legal framework, when compared with the principal provisions of the EIO Directive, suggests that the mechanism created by the Regulation for the collection of existing (stored) electronic evidence provides for a substantially more liberal approach, which does not necessarily ensure the same standard of protection of human rights as the EIO Directive does.

Secondly, to maintain consistency and an optimum level of confidence in decisions taken in terms of judicial cooperation with another EU Member State, the grounds for refusal to execute an EIO, as set out in Article 12(1) of the Regulation, should, if not identical to those set out in Article 11(1)(c) of the EIO Directive, at least be approximate to those set out in Article 11(1). Particular attention should be drawn to Article 11(1)(b) of said Directive: in a specific case, the execution of the EIO would harm essential national security interests, jeopardize the source of information or involve the use of classified information relating to specific intelligence activities. The uniform or at least similar and systematically harmonized introduction of the above grounds for non-recognition or non-execution in EU criminal justice legislation would enable the avoidance of excessive heterogeneity and non-uniformity of the legal requirements (standards of procedural form). The harmonization of the regulatory framework (in particular the EIO Directive and the Regulation) would not only bring more legal clarity and legal certainty, but would also enhance confidence in the EU legal system. Trust in the EU legal system, accordingly, leads to the "free movement" of evidence, especially electronic evidence, across EU Member States.

Thirdly, an important issue that needs to be addressed is the admissibility of electronic evidence. However, the Regulation is silent on the procedures for recording, storing, and transferring the data stored by the service provider for which the order was issued, which may differ due to differences in territorial jurisdiction across EU Member States. Thus, even though the Regulation allows the collection of preexisting stored data only, it must therefore be held that this does not change anything in substance. Both the gathering of evidence in real-time (in the case of the application of the EIO Directive) and the process of collecting data at the time of the submission of the order should be subject to uniform provisions or, as is well chosen in the case of the EIO mechanism, the order should specify the procedural steps (methods) by which such electronic evidence should be collected, stored, recorded, and transmitted to the State that issued the order (for example, Article 5(1)(e) of the EIO Directive). Unfortunately, however, unlike in the EIO Directive, the Regulation does not contain any rules or provisions concerning this issue, which in turn may create grounds for raising doubts in a national court regarding the assessment of the admissibility of electronic evidence collected following the Regulation.

Concluding on this point, it should be noted that the model of electronic evidence collection chosen by the Regulation does not indisputably prevent discussions on the obstacles to recognizing such evidence as admissible in the national court of a Member State. The existing regulatory framework, which could indeed have been more coherent and at the same time at least minimally aligned with the model set out in the EIO Directive, has not avoided fragmentation. The aforementioned fragmentation, as well as the differentiation of the evidence collection process within the framework of EU criminal justice, could be reduced via the *Doctrine of Common Minimum Standards* proposed by some authors (Kusak 2017, p.349; Depauw 2016, p.98). According to this doctrine, all EU legal instruments that accelerate and assist Member States in cooperating in the investigation and prosecution of criminal offenses must contain at least minimum common standards to ensure uniformity in, for example, the gathering of evidence on a case-by-case basis, especially when it comes to the use of expert investigations (Depauw, 2016, p.98), procedural safeguards, the use of the same procedural form, the observance of identical principles, etc. According to the literature, the "gathering of evidence under commonly agreed minimum standards would make it easier for an issuing state to accept the way that the evidence is being gathered in the executing state. Therefore, the idea of common EU minimum standards has the potential to accommodate the problem of mutual admissibility of evidence in criminal matters in the EU" (Kusak 2017, p.349). A thorough analysis of this doctrine would, of course, require a separate study; however, it is already possible to assert that the issue of the admissibility of electronic evidence is not addressed by the provisions of the Regulation either.

Interim Findings

After unlimited efforts to look for an optimized EU criminal justice model in the context of "free movement of evidence," in 2023 Regulation (EU) 2023/1543 of the European Parliament and of the Council on European Production Orders and European Preservation Orders for electronic evidence in criminal proceedings and for the execution of custodial sentences following criminal proceedings was adopted. This legal regulation, it would seem, should have solved the problems related to the challenges that electronic data collection issues are subject to in the EU. The background to the Regulation and the paradigm of the legislative process show that the bodies involved in the legislative process – the EU Member States – sought to give a different impetus to the collection of electronic evidence than to the collection of other evidence. The aim was not only to have a fast, efficient data collection process, but also to develop a model of electronic evidence collection that would allow the law enforcement authorities of the Member States to avoid mutual contact with the law enforcement authorities of other countries, and instead to establish direct contact with the addressees, i.e., service providers (or their representatives). The parallel of this model would seem to allow the electronic evidence stored to be grasped and collected as quickly as possible.

Unfortunately, an analysis of the existing regulatory framework for the gathering of evidence (including electronic evidence) (EIO, Regulation on the Taking of Electronic Evidence) suggests that the Regulation, in order to ensure the timely and efficient gathering of evidence, lacks provisions ensuring the admissibility of such evidence before national courts.

The provisions of the Regulation on the taking of electronic evidence are characterized by their fragmentary nature, which is the result of a lack of certain safeguards that are particularly emphasized in legal practice. In particular, the selective nature of the process of refusal to recognize and execute orders for the production of electronic evidence, the lack of safeguards for the rights of the individual, the lack of procedural guarantees, and the specificity of the process of collecting, recording, and transmitting electronic evidence stored by a private body (a service provider) all mean that the admissibility of such evidence in national courts may be seriously called into question.

To avoid obstacles to the admissibility of electronic evidence collected outside the territory of the national State in which the trial is taking place, it was necessary to bring the principal provisions of the Regulation in line with those of the Directive regarding the EIO in criminal matters. At the same time, it should be emphasized that other measures have also been proposed in the academic literature that could assist in reducing the fragmentation, fundamental inconsistency, and excessive heterogeneity concerning the legal instruments of criminal justice within the EU. These include the application of the doctrine of *Common Minimum Standards* to all legal instruments on judicial cooperation without any exception.

References

Abraha, H. H., 2020. Regulating Law Enforcement Access to Electronic Evidence Across Borders: The United States Approach. *Information and Communications Technology Law*, 29 (3), 324–353.

Belevičius, L., 2013. Tarptautinis teisinis bendradarbiavimas ir Europos Sąjungos baudžiamasis procesas: aktualijos, perspektyvos, lūkesčiai [International Legal Cooperation and Criminal Proceedings of the European Union: Current Affairs, Perspectives, Expectations]. In: *Baudžiamojo proceso tarptautiškumas: patirtis ir iššūkiai.* Vilnius: Mykolo Romerio Universitetas, 170–209.

Blažič, B. J., and Klobučar, T., 2020. Investigating Crime in an Interconnected Society: Will the New and Updated EU Judicial Environment Remove the Barriers to Justice? *International Review of Law, Computers and Technology*, 34 (1), 87–107.

Böse, M., 2018. *An Assessment of the Commission's Proposals on Electronic Evidence* [online]. European Parliament. Available from: https://www.europarl.europa.eu/RegData/etudes/STUD/2018/604989/IPOL_STU(2018)604989_EN.pdf [Accessed 8 August 2023].

Brière, C., 2021. EU Criminal Procedural Law onto the Global Stage: The E-Evidence Proposals and Their Interaction With International Developments. *European Papers*, 6 (1), 493–511. Available from: https://doi.org/10.15166/2499-8249/479 [Accessed 14 August 2023].

Consolidated Version of the Treaty on the Functioning of the European Union [online]. *Official Journal*, C326. Available from: https://eur-lex.europa.eu/legal-content/EN/TXT/HTML/?uri=CELEX:12012E/TXT [Accessed 8 August 2023].

Corhay, M., 2021. Private Life, Personal Data Protection and the Role of Service Providers: The EU E-Evidence Proposal. *European Papers*, 6 (1), 441–472. Available from: https://doi.org/10.15166/2499-8249/477 [Accessed 14 August 2023].

Corhay, M., 2023a. *It is a Long Way to … E-Evidence: EU Reforms in the Collection of Electronic Evidence – Part 1* [online]. Information Law and Policy Centre. Available from: https://infolawcentre.blogs.sas.ac.uk/2023/01/24/it-is-a-long-way-to-e-evidence-eu-reforms-in-the-collection-of-electronic-evidence-part-1/ [Accessed 25 July 2023].

Corhay, M., 2023b. *It is a Long Way to… E-Evidence: EU Reforms in the Collection of Electronic Evidence Part 2 – The Role of Service Providers* [online]. Available from: https://infolawcentre.blogs.sas.ac.uk/2023/02/26/it-is-a-long-way-to-e-evidence-eu-reforms-in-the-collection-of-electronic-evidence-part-2-the-role-of-service-providers/ [Accessed 27 July 2023].

Depauw, S., 2016. A European Evidence (Air)Space? Taking Cross-Border Legal Admissibility of Forensic Evidence to a Higher Level. *European Criminal Law Review*, 6 (1), 82–98.

Directive 2014/41/EU of the European Parliament and of the Council of 3 April 2014 regarding the European Investigation Order in criminal matters [online]. *Official Journal*, L130. Available from: https://eur-lex.europa.eu/legal-content/EN/TXT/?uri=celex%3A32014L0041 [Accessed 30 July 2023].

European Commission Proposal for a regulation of the European Parliament and of the Council on European production and preservation orders for electronic evidence in criminal matters. COM/2018/225 final – 2018/0108 (COD), 2018 [online]. *EUR-Lex*. Available from: https://eur-lex.europa.eu/legal-content/EN/ALL/?uri=COM%3A2018%3A225%3AFIN [Accessed 27 July 2023].

European Digital Rights, 2023. *E-Evidence compromise blows a hole in fundamental rights safeguards*' [online]. Available from: https://edri.org/our-work/e-evidence-compromise-blows-a-hole-in-fundamental-rights-safeguards/ [Accessed 27 July 2023].

Insa, F., 2007. The Admissibility of Electronic Evidence in Court (A.E.E.C.): Fighting Against High-Tech Crime – Results of a European Study. *Journal of Digital Forensic Practice*, 1 (4), 285–289.

Jurka, R., 2011. Tarptautinis bendradarbiavimas baudžiamajame procese: įrodymai ir jų priimtinumas Europos Sąjungoje [International Cooperation in the Criminal Process: Evidence and its Admissibility in the European Union]. In: *Baudžiamasis procesas: nuo teorijos iki įrodinėjimo (prof. dr. Eugenijaus Palskio atminimui)*. Vilnius: Mykolo Romerio universitetas, 89–128.

Jurka, R., 2019. Įrodymų perdavimo Europos Sąjungos valstybių narių baudžiamojoje justicijoje iššūkiai ir atradimai [Challenges and Innovations of Evidence Transfer in European Union Member States' Criminal Justice]. *Jurisprudencija*, 26 (2), 308–325.

Kosta, E., and Kamara, I., 2023. The Right to an Effective Remedy in International Data Transfers of Electronic Evidence: Past Lessons and Future Outlook. *Review of European Administration Law*, 16 (1), 57–83.

Kusak, M., 2017. Common EU Minimum Standards for Enhancing Mutual Admissibility of Evidence Gathered in Criminal Matters. *European Journal on Criminal Policy*, 23, 337–352. https://doi.org/10.1007/s10610-017-9339-0 [Accessed 30 July 2023].

Kusak, M., 2019. Mutual Admissibility of Evidence and the European Investigation Order: Aspirations Lost in Reality. *ERA Forum*, 19, 391–400. Available from: https://doi.org/10.1007/s12027-018-0537-0 [Accessed 30 July 2023].

Laurits, E., 2020. Regulating the Unregulatable: an Estonian Perspective on the CLOUD Act and the E-Evidence Proposal. *Juridica International*, 29, 62–70.

Leroux, O., 2004. Legal Admissibility of Electronic Evidence. *International Review of Law Computers*, 18 (2), 193–220.

Liakopoulos, D., 2020. Mutual Recognition and Criminal Efficiency under Regulation (EU) 2018/1805 for the Mutual Recognition of Freezing and Confiscation Measures. *International Criminal Law Review*, 20, 346–370.

Mangiaracina, A., 2014. A New and Controversial Scenario in the Gathering of Evidence at the European Level: The Proposal for a Directive on the European Investigation Order. *Utrecht Law Review*, 10 (1), 113–133.

Mitsilegas, V., 2018. The Privatisation of Mutual Trust in Europe's Area of Criminal Justice: The Case of E-evidence. *Maastricht Journal of European and Comparative Law*, 25 (3), 263–265.

Öberg, J., 2020. Trust in the Law? Mutual Recognition as a Justification to Domestic Criminal Procedure. *European Constitutional Law Review*, 16, 33–62.

Petri, A., 2018. *No Law Enforcement by Private Corporations* [online]. Available from: https://www.telekom.com/en/company/management-unplugged/details/no-law-enforcement-by-private-corporations-544132 [Accessed 30 July 2023].

Regulation (EU) 2023/1543 of the European Parliament and of the Council of 12 July 2023 on European Production Orders and European Preservation Orders for Electronic Evidence in Criminal Proceedings and for the Execution of Custodial Sentences following Criminal Proceedings [online]. *Official Journal*, L191, 118–180. Available from: https://eur-lex.europa.eu/legal-content/EN/TXT/?uri=CELEX:32023R1543 [Accessed 8 August 2023].

Rojszczak, M., 2020. CLOUD Act Agreements from an EU Perspective. *Computer Law and Security Review*, 38, 105442.

Rojszczak, M., 2022. E-Evidence Cooperation in Criminal Matters from an EU Perspective. *The Modern Law Review*, 85 (4), 997–1028.

Smuha, N. A., 2018. Towards the EU harmonization of Access to Cross-Border E-evidence: Challenges Fundamental Rights & Consistency. *European Criminal Law Review*, 8 (1), 83–115.

Tosza, S., 2020. All Evidence is Equal, But Electronic Evidence is More Equal Than Any Other: The Relationship Between the European Investigation Order and the European Production Order. *New Journal of European Criminal Law*, 11 (2), 161–183.

Tosza, S., 2022. The Public Role of Private Actors: Internet Service Providers in the E-Evidence Proposal [online]. *European Law Blog* [blog], 22 September 2022. Available from: https://europeanlawblog.eu/2022/09/20/the-public-role-of-private-actors-internet-service-providers-in-the-e-evidence-proposal/ [Accessed 12 August 2023].

Warken, C., van Zwieten, L., and Svantesson, D., 2020. Re-thinking the Cooperation of Data in the Context of Law Enforcement Cross-Border Access of Evidence. *International Review of Law, Computers and Technology*, 34(1), 44–64.

Renata Marcinauskaitė

Electronic Evidence in Criminal Proceedings

General Remarks

The problems of proof-taking activities and proof in criminal proceedings are complex. To address these issues, it is important to identify the various aspects of the proof-taking process, define what constitutes evidence in criminal proceedings, and outline their requirements. This analysis should be seen as a starting point for unravelling the concept of electronic evidence and its peculiarities, as well as aspects of its evaluation and requirements for substantiating its reliability.

The emergence of electronic evidence in criminal proceedings is linked to the commission of cybercrime. Cyberspace is defined as "the indefinite place where individuals transact and communicate" (Britz 2009, p.3). As cyberspace activities have expanded, some activities that are considered as traditional criminal offenses (e.g., fraud, forgery of documents) have moved to cyberspace alongside the introduction of cyberspace-specific offenses (e.g., unauthorized access to an information system, unauthorized modification of electronic data). Investigating and proving these offenses is complicated by the specificity of cyberspace: "the intangible nature of computer interaction and subsequent criminality poses significant questions for investigative agents" (Britz 2009, p.6). It is also relevant that in cybercrime cases, usually "eyewitness statements and other traditional types of evidence are not available or scarce because of the digital nature of the offences" (Riekkinen 2019, p.6).

The chosen directions of analysis also underline the need for a coherent approach to this type of evidence in criminal proceedings. The legal framework should not give priority to evidence based on its form, i.e., whether it is tangible (physical) or intangible (without physical parameters). The consistency of such practice would also meet the requirements of the principle of technological neutrality. It should also be mentioned that the proper process of obtaining and managing electronic evidence is crucial for the quality of proof-taking activities and can contribute to the cost-effectiveness and speed of criminal proceedings.

The need for a coherent approach to electronic evidence is becoming an issue not only at the national but also at the international (European Union) level. This aspect is underlined by the specific cross-border nature of cybercrime. Successful cybercrime investigations often depend on cooperation between jurisdictions to facilitate access to electronic evidence while ensuring high standards of human rights protection. Obtaining access to electronic evidence in another country is complicated and burdensome for judicial authorities because of the lengthy and complex procedures that need to be followed. Legal instruments have been adopted at both the European Union and international level to address these issues. Directive (EU) 2023/1544 of the European Parliament and of the Council of July 12, 2023 laying down harmonized rules on the designation of establishments and the appointment of legal representatives for the purpose of gathering electronic evidence in criminal proceedings (hereafter – Directive 2023/1544) and Regulation (EU) 2023/1543 of the European Parliament and of the Council of July 12, 2023 on European Production Orders and European Preservation Orders for electronic evidence in criminal proceedings and for the execution of custodial sentences following criminal proceedings (hereafter – Regulation 2023/1543) have been adopted to ensure that authorities have easier and faster access to electronic evidence. At the international level, the Council of Europe Convention on Cybercrime (hereafter – Convention on Cybercrime, 2001) and its Additional Protocols, in particular the Second Additional Protocol to the Convention on Cybercrime on Enhanced Cooperation and Disclosure of Electronic Evidence (hereafter – Second Additional Protocol, 2022), should also be mentioned.

The Concept of Proof-Taking Activity and the Assessment of Evidence in Criminal Proceedings

Establishing the existence (or otherwise) of a criminal offense and other circumstances relevant to the fair disposition of a criminal case is inseparable from the proof-taking process in criminal proceedings. Proof-taking activity is the activity of the relevant entities specified in the law (suspect, defense counsel, prosecutor, court, etc.) which continues throughout all criminal proceedings and is related to obtaining, presenting, verifying, and assessing data important to the investigation of the criminal offense committed (Goda *et al.* 2005, p.171). The purpose of proof-taking activities is to clarify the circumstances relevant to the criminal case and, ultimately, to establish the truth in the criminal case. In this respect, it should be noted that "collection, verification and evaluation of evidence is a whole unit of cognitive activity, but with different intermediate tasks" (Ablamskyi and Vasko 2022, p.14).

One of the provisions of the right to a fair trial, that "everyone charged with a criminal offense shall be presumed innocent until proved guilty according to law" (European Convention for the Protection of Human Rights and Fundamental Freedoms 1950, Article 6(2)), is often reflected in the constitutional provisions of states and in legislation on criminal proceedings. Recognizing that the presumption of innocence is regarded as a guarantee to protect "accused persons from wrongful conviction" (Tadros and Tierney 2004, p.402), the Constitution of the Republic of Lithuania, for example, states that "a person shall be presumed innocent until proved guilty according to the procedure established by law and declared guilty by an effective court judgment" (Article 31(1)). These provisions have also influenced the understanding of the purpose of criminal proceedings. For example, Article 1(1) of the Criminal Procedure Code of the Republic of Lithuania states that the aim of criminal proceedings is, among other objectives, to ensure the full disclosure of a criminal offense and the proper application of the law "in order to ensure that any person who has committed a criminal act is given a fair punishment and that no one who is innocent is convicted" (Criminal Procedure Code of the Republic of Lithuania 2002, Article 1(1)). Accordingly, the discovery of the offense committed, fair punishment, and thus the determination of the truth in a criminal case is directly related to various issues of proof-taking actions and evidence.

The adoption of an evidence-based final judgment depends, *inter alia*, on the quality of the proof-taking process and the quality of obtaining, presenting, verifying, and evaluating data relevant to the investigation of the criminal offense committed. The proof-taking activity and its quality is not confined to a single stage of the criminal proceedings (e.g., trial), but is continuous, starting with the initial recording of certain data and ending with their use in the final judicial decision. For example, the case-law of the European Court of Human Rights notes that "the investigation stage may be of particular importance for the preparation of the criminal proceedings: the evidence obtained during this stage often determines the framework in which the offence charged will be considered at the trial [...]" (*Ibrahim and Others v. United Kingdom* 2016). Thus, fair trial guarantees apply to the entire criminal proceedings process, both at the pre-trial and trial stages (*Vera Fernandez-Huidobro v. Spain* 2010), and breaches of these guarantees can significantly undermine the fairness of a trial.

An important part of the proof-taking process is the examination of the evidence during the trial, its admission as evidence, and its assessment in order to arrive at a lawful and reasoned final judgment. It should be noted that, according to the case law of the European Court of Human Rights (hereinafter – ECtHR), "as a general rule, it is for the national courts to assess the evidence before them, while it is for the Court to ascertain that the proceedings considered as a whole were fair, which in case of criminal proceedings includes the observance of the presumption of innocence" (*Telfner v. Austria* 2001). According to the above-mentioned ECtHR case law, the principle of the presumption of innocence requires, *inter alia*, that "when carrying out their duties, the members of a court should not start with the preconceived idea that the accused has committed the offense charged; the burden of proof is on the prosecution, and any doubt should benefit the accused" (*Telfner v. Austria* 2001). Thus, regardless of the type of evidence, it is the prerogative of the court that renders the final judgment to assess it and draw conclusions in a criminal case. It is for the court to decide which evidence contained in the case has probative value and whether it is sufficient to establish that a person's conduct constitutes all the elements of a particular criminal offense.

It is also mentioned that evidence must be evaluated in accordance with the law. This requirement means that the court's conclusions cannot be based on data that do not meet the legal requirements. An infringement should also be established in cases where data that met the legal requirements were not admitted as evidence.

Thus, when deciding whether to accept data as evidence, the court must determine whether the data are relevant to the case, whether they were obtained in accordance with the procedure laid down by the law and were gathered by lawful means, as well as whether the reliability of the data has been verified by lawful actions of the criminal procedure.

Although the assessment of evidence is a matter for the national court, it must be consistent with, *inter alia*, the requirements of fair proceedings. The establishment and practical implementation of the latter requirements ensure coherence between international obligations and national legal regulation. Such compatibility is also a guarantee of the rights of the persons involved in criminal proceedings, including in the proof-taking process. Since one of the objectives of the proof-taking process is the establishment of facts relevant to a criminal case, the issue of evidence and its requirements become crucial. In this respect, there is also a need for a coherent approach to the evaluation of electronic evidence, especially since "evidence records vary in forms and types" (Raghavan and Raghavan 2009, p.1).

The Concept of Evidence: The Identification of Electronic Evidence

The proof-taking process, as discussed earlier, is directly concerned with obtaining, presenting, verifying, and assessing data to be admitted as evidence in criminal proceedings. The emergence of evidence in criminal proceedings and its ability to substantiate (or refute) facts relevant to the fair disposition of a criminal case is linked to the laws of cognitive theory (gnoseology). The latter laws reveal an object's defining feature: when objects interact, they can reflect the traces of the criminal offense committed. Precisely because of their interaction, the traces of all criminal acts remain as a reflection, which allows the event that occurred in the past to be identified. Accordingly, irrespective of the type of trace – material or ideal (formed in the human memory) – it must be obtained, presented, verified, and assessed by the subjects of the proof-taking process. These traces, objectively visualized, are presented in the criminal case and are verified and evaluated in the criminal proceedings in accordance with the requirements established by the law. Taking these aspects into account, both the scientific and the legal concept of evidence is formulated. From this perspective, it should also be mentioned that, in line with the dual concept of evidence, two non-identical categories are used in criminal proceedings: "data relevant to the investigation and examination of a criminal offence" and "evidence" (Juozapavičius and Leonaitė 2021, p.86). This distinction is linked to the requirements of the adversarial principle, where data become evidence only after they have been examined in the court. Hereinafter, these terms will be used interchangeably depending on the context.

According to the scientific concept of evidence, evidence is "data obtained in accordance with the law, which confirm or deny at least one circumstance that is relevant to the fair disposition of a case" (Matulienė, n.d.). The legal concept of evidence is established or derived from a systematic analysis of statutory provisions. It is the latter concept that is also used, for example, in Lithuanian case law, which states that evidence in criminal proceedings is data obtained, verified, assessed at trial and accepted by the court in accordance with the procedure established by law, on the basis of which the court draws conclusions as to the existence (or absence) of a criminal offense, the guilt (or innocence) of the person who has committed the offense and other circumstances relevant to the fair disposition of the case (Ruling of the Supreme Court of Lithuania of July 14, 2020 in criminal case No. 2K-141-303/2020). According to the legal concept of evidence, the main features of evidence are usually revealed by analyzing the specific norms establishing the requirements for data collection, presentation, verification, its admission as evidence and the assessment of evidence in criminal proceedings.

There are different classifications of evidence that complement each other. For example, evidence is divided: into personal evidence (where the information is preserved in people's minds and transmitted orally or in writing) and physical evidence (where the information is reflected and transmitted through material objects); according to the primacy of the source of the information – i.e., primary and derivative evidence; according to the relationship to the circumstances to be proved – i.e., direct and indirect evidence; and according to the relationship of the evidence to the version of the accusation – i.e., incriminating and justifying evidence (Matulienė, n.d.). The following categories of evidence do not directly mention electronic evidence. On the other hand, as far as the concept of the proof-taking process or the general concept of evidence is concerned, the exclusion of electronic evidence is not necessary, as these concepts do not change regarding the possible form of evidence (whether it is evidence with physical parameters or without such parameters – i.e., electronic evidence). However, it should be noted that the exclusion of electronic evidence is relevant in the context of justifying its admissibility in criminal proceedings, as well as in deciding on the requirements for its collection, presentation, verification, and assessment, and, accordingly, on how to ensure that it complies with the requirements of the law. The analysis of electronic evidence also provides for a better understanding of such kinds of evidence. After all, "in a digital investigation, investigators deal with acquiring digital data for examination" (Raghavan and Raghavan 2009, p.1).

As an example, Western European Codes of Criminal Procedure do not usually differentiate between physical and electronic data which may later be admitted as evidence in criminal proceedings. However, the presence of electronic evidence in the proceedings is determined by the development of technology and the possibilities it offers, as well as by the nature of the criminal offense. In this context, the view that "criminal law must respond adequately and enable the use of evidence obtained by new technologies such as satellites, GPS, GLONASS, dashcams, vehicle software, communication technologies, location, etc." is supported (Vasko and Klimek 2023, p.176). At this point, it should also be mentioned that a rather generalized approach which does not exclude electronic evidence into a separate type is also followed in foreign countries. For example, as stated in the scientific literature, there is no specific exception for computer-generated evidence in the USA; the Federal Rules of Evidence apply the same rules to electronic records as they apply to ordinary documents (Sethia 2016, p.235). On the other hand, the absence of an official concept of electronic evidence in national legislation may lead to difficulties in defining this type of evidence and identifying its characteristics.

The scientific literature defines electronic evidence as "evidence derived from data contained in or produced by any device the functioning of which depends on a software program or from data stored on or communicated over a computer system or network" (Mason, 2016, p.22). Electronic evidence can also be defined as "data (comprising the output of analogue devices or data in digital format) that is manipulated, stored, or communicated by any man-made device, computer or computer system or transmitted over a communication system, that has the potential to make the factual account of either party more probable or less probable than it would have been without the evidence" (Trigkas 2017, p.21). Accordingly, evidence may be considered e-evidence if it is stored (or transmitted) in a communication system and (or) if it was created by that system. As electronic evidence usually retains an electronic form, it is suitable for processing in an information system. Such data may be stored in the system or transmitted using communication technology. Although the concept of electronic evidence is quite clear, it is worth noting a few aspects relevant to its use in the proof-taking process:

1) The need for the collection of electronic data to prove (or disprove) at least one circumstance relevant to the fair disposition of the case should not be limited solely to the commission of criminal offenses against the security of electronic data and information systems (as understood in Chapter II, Section 1(1) of the Convention on Cybercrime). The latter offenses constitute the definition of cybercrime in the narrowest sense. It is relevant that the appearance of electronic data admissible as evidence in criminal proceedings is possible in all cases where the commission of criminal offense involves the use of information technology. In this context, various electronic evidence issues can also be addressed in cases where the use of information technology has changed the traditional criminal offense. The latter offenses fall within the category of cybercrime as defined in its broadest sense. Some of these variations are referred to, for example, in Chapter II, Section 1, Title 2 to 4 of the Convention on Cybercrime: Computer-related forgery, Computer-related fraud, Offenses related to child pornography, Offenses related to infringements of copyright and related rights. Offenses of this nature are also included in the Additional Protocol to the Convention on Cybercrime concerning the criminalization of acts of a racist and xenophobic nature committed through computer systems (ETS No. 189) and covering offenses of racist or xenophobic propaganda. It should be noted that the list of traditional offenses modified using information technology should not be considered exhaustive: "in fact, digital evidence has been utilized in cases ranging from homicide to software piracy" (Britz 2009, p.267).
2) It is proposed that the concept of electronic evidence in criminal proceedings should be as broad as possible; therefore, the terms used in the concept of electronic evidence that refer to technology (e.g., information system) should be interpreted in accordance with the requirements of the principle of technological neutrality. This principle is usually invoked to deal with the evolution of information and communication technologies and, in the most general sense, refers to the prohibition of prioritizing one technology

over another if such differentiation is not necessary (Ohm 2010). Thus "[...] legislation must be generic enough to encompass advances in technology, assuring that application to tomorrow's technology is possible" (Britz 2009, p.350). It has been stated that evidence can be considered electronic if it is stored in (or transmitted by) an information system, or it has been created by that system. Accordingly, the interpretation of what constitutes an information system should focus on its functions, i.e., the processing of data, rather than on the specific technologies that perform these functions. For example, the Convention on Cybercrime provides a technology-neutral definition of a computer system: "computer system means any device or a group of interconnected or related devices, one or more of which, pursuant to a program, performs automatic processing of data" (Chapter I Article 1(a)). It is also relevant that the reference to the information system should not only include information technology, but also communication technologies that allow the transmission of information between various devices.

3) Expertise is important for the investigation of some types of electronic evidence. In such cases, the expert must carry out the expert examination in accordance with their competence, using scientifically validated, generally accepted and reliable or accredited methods of examination. On the other hand, an expert's report is only one piece of evidence which the court must assess after a complete and impartial examination of all the circumstances of the case. The evaluation of an expert's report as evidence is subject to the requirements laid down by law. It is therefore for the court to decide in each case whether the data (including electronic data) obtained constitute evidence.

Examples of electronic evidence may include text, video, audio, photographs, network traffic captures, Random Access Memory (RAM) data, event logs, mobile device artefacts, metadata, hash values, encrypted data, malware, and many others. This data can be processed by information systems with different functions (computers, mobile phones, servers, GPS devices, cloud technologies, etc.). One example is metadata, which is defined as "structured information that describes, explains, locates, or otherwise makes it easier to retrieve, use, or manage an information resource" (National Information Standards Organization 2004, p.1). Metadata is commonly defined as "data about data" (Butterfield 2001, p.24). Metadata can reveal, for example, the origin of electronic data, relevant dates and times (creation, modification, transmission, etc.), and details of the device that generated the electronic data, and can provide the necessary context for evaluating other electronic evidence. As metadata is an integral part of electronic evidence, it is necessary to bear in mind its evidentiary value.

In the context of the analysis of electronic evidence, attention should be drawn to the need for coherence in the national legal frameworks relating to the admissibility of evidence in criminal proceedings. Firstly, the established legal framework should not reject or give priority to evidence depending on its form, whether physical or electronic. This objective can be achieved through a technology-neutral approach. According to it, electronic data, irrespective of the technology that created or processed them, should be admissible as evidence in criminal proceedings if they fulfil the purpose of evidence, its function in criminal proceedings and other requirements applicable to evidence. Secondly, it is relevant that in criminal proceedings it should be possible to present electronic evidence in its original electronic form. This would also help to ensure the economy and speed of criminal proceedings. Thirdly, the need for regulatory coherence is also linked to the transnational aspect of cybercrime. This aspect means that "evidence of [...] criminal offence is increasingly stored in electronic form on computer systems in foreign, multiple or unknown jurisdictions" (Second Additional Protocol 2022, Preamble). Accordingly, an effective criminal justice response will determine whether the States that have signed up to cooperation commitments have a coherent, harmonized approach to the collection, presentation, verification, and assessment of electronic data crucial to the fair disposition of a criminal case. The latter aspect is particularly evident in the ratification of the 2001 Convention on Cybercrime, the provisions of which also address the current issues of obtaining electronic evidence in relation to the Expedited preservation of stored computer data (Section 2 Title 2), Production order (Section 2 Title 3), the Search and seizure of stored computer data (Section 2 Title 4), and the Real-time collection of computer data (Section 2 Title 5). To achieve more effective cooperation across jurisdictional boundaries, the Second Additional Protocol was adopted in 2022. This Protocol sets out various Procedures enhancing direct co-operation with providers and entities (Section 2), Procedures enhancing international co-operation between authorities for the disclosure of stored computer data (Section 3), Procedures pertaining to emergency mutual assistance (Section 4), Procedures pertaining to international co-operation in the absence of applicable international agreements (Section 5), as well as personal data protection safeguards (Chapter III Article 14). A coherent approach at the European Union level is also important in the application of Regulation 2023/1543 related to European production and preservation orders for electronic evidence in criminal matters, and in the implementation of the provisions of Directive 2023/1544 on the appointment of legal representatives for the purposes of gathering evidence in criminal proceedings. In addition, these provisions, *inter alia*, can be seen as steps toward the harmonization of national approaches to electronic evidence.

The Requirements Applicable to Evidence

Evidence in criminal proceedings is data obtained in accordance with the law which confirm or disprove at least one circumstance that is relevant for the fair disposition of the case. Thus, data shall be considered as evidence if they meet certain requirements: 1) they prove (or disprove) at least one circumstance relevant for the fair disposition of the case; and 2) they are obtained by lawful means and may be verified by the procedural actions laid down in law. Irrespective of the form in which the data are produced (electronic or physical), they may be admitted as evidence if the prerequisites for such admission are met: the data fulfil the requirements of correlation, admissibility, and reliability.

One of the requirements for the admission of data as evidence – their correlation – is understood as a link to a fact to be proved in a criminal case. In this context, only data from which the court determines the factual circumstances of the act under investigation and other circumstances may be considered evidence. In all criminal cases, the circumstances of the act under investigation must be proven: the time, place, manner, tools and means, the type and scope of damage caused, the person who committed the act, their personal characteristics, the victim etc. It is not necessary that these circumstances be proven by direct evidence alone; they may also be substantiated by indirect evidence. According to this approach, both electronic data which are directly relevant to the matter of proof and electronic data that initially substantiate the existence of an intermediate fact – and, through that fact, the circumstances to be proved – are relevant. In such cases, it is essential that all evidence, both electronic and physical, is obtained and evaluated in accordance with the requirements laid down by law.

Another requirement for the acceptance of data as evidence is their admissibility. This means that only data obtained by lawful means and verified by actions provided by law can constitute evidence. Consequently, in deciding whether to accept the examined data as evidence, the court must verify that the way in which they were obtained does not contravene the requirements of the law and that they have been verified by actions prescribed by law. Where violations in the data obtaining procedure raise doubts and these doubts cannot be eliminated, such data shall not be admitted as evidence. Conversely, if the violations of the data collecting procedure did not affect the reliability of the data obtained, and the collection of the data did not deprive (or substantially restrict) the accused's rights guaranteed by the law, the data are usually admitted as evidence (Ruling of the Supreme Court of Lithuania of July 17, 2020 in criminal case No. 2K-164-458/2020). The requirement to comply with the law in the process of obtaining evidence is particularly important, otherwise the fairness of the criminal proceedings would not be guaranteed (Ruling of the Supreme Court of Lithuania of April 9, 2020 in criminal case No. 2K-81-895/2020). In this respect, it is also relevant that "EU and international legislation does not provide any rules for deciding the admissibility of evidence, nor has the ECtHR formulated any such rules" (Juozapavičius and Leonaitė 2021, p.81).

The final act of a court can only be based on reliable evidence. Reliability of evidence is a characteristic established by the assessment of the evidence, which means that the data relevant for the fair disposition of a criminal case correspond to the truth. The reliability of evidence shall be determined by an analysis of the way in which it was obtained, its verification by the procedures laid down by law, and its comparison with other evidence in the criminal case (Ruling of the Supreme Court of Lithuania of January 30, 2018 in criminal case No. 2K-26-689/2018). The evidence itself is assessed by the court through legal procedures, as well as by comparing evidence from different sources. For example, a conclusion on the reliability of the testimony of persons (defendants, victims, witnesses) may be reached by assessing the consistency, detail, completeness, and logic of the testimony, and by comparing it with the other evidence in the case obtained from different sources (Ruling of the Supreme Court of Lithuania of November 12, 2019 in criminal case No. 2K-264-976/2019).

The requirements discussed above are important for the analysis of the various types and forms of evidence that are relevant for the fair resolution of a case, and compliance with these requirements is fundamental to ensuring justice in criminal proceedings. On the other hand, given the specific nature of electronic evidence, there are other aspects which detail – and, at the same time, justify – the reliability of this type of evidence in criminal proceedings. The identification and proper assessment of these characteristics is relevant in order to substantiate the reliability of electronic data, and at the same time to ensure that they are truthful and properly establish the facts crucial for the fair resolution of a criminal case.

The Specifics of Electronic Evidence: The Justification of the Reliability of Electronic Evidence

As more and more criminal offenses move from the physical world to cyberspace, "more and more investigations become dependent on digital evidence"

(Grigaliūnas and Toldinas 2016, p.30). On the other hand, in the process of obtaining, presenting, verifying, and evaluating electronic data it is important that such data, compared to other types, are relatively easy to alter, both because of deliberate (or negligent) human activity and the peculiarities of the functioning of information systems themselves. As noted in the scientific literature, "digital evidence is especially volatile and voluminous, susceptible to climatic or environmental factors as well as human errors. It may be vulnerable to power surges, electromagnetic fields, or extreme temperatures" (Britz 2009, p.297). It is also important to note that the alteration of electronic data may be difficult to trace and establish in certain cases. Therefore, it should come as no surprise that "the application of traditional evidentiary rules to modern electronic content may warrant a higher degree of scrutiny in the wake of concerns regarding the trustworthiness of e-evidence" (Trigkas 2017, p.21).

Electronic data may be altered, corrupted, or destroyed if they are improperly obtained, processed, or examined. In criminal proceedings, these cases would mean that the data obtained have lost their reliability and can no longer be the basis for a final judicial decision as they no longer reflect true facts. Such electronic data shall not be admissible as evidence in criminal proceedings. In this respect, it should also be noted that "the more vulnerable computer and network-derived evidence is to exclusion, the more problematic will be the prosecution of [...] cybercrimes" (Walden 2007, p.367).

The reliability of electronic data is linked to the reliability of both the electronic data itself and the process by which the data were obtained. The requirements that electronic data must meet can be derived from the area of data security and relate, *inter alia*, to preserving their authenticity, integrity, and accountability. These aspects are also mentioned in the Guidelines on Electronic Evidence in Civil and Administrative Proceedings adopted by the Committee of Ministers to serve as a practical tool to facilitate the use of electronic evidence in court proceedings (Council of Europe 2019).

Authenticity describes the origin of electronic evidence in the most general sense. The International Electrotechnical Commission (2019a) interprets the term authenticity in the field of digital technology as a "property of data that ensures that the identity of an entity is the one claimed." Authenticity is also understood as a "state in which information is valid and known to have originated from the stated source" (International Electrotechnical Commission 2019a). In fulfilling this requirement, "the investigator must be able to persuasively show that the evidence originated from the computer under attack or the computer in the crime scene" (Kanellis *et al.* 2006, p.60). Accordingly, the authenticity of electronic data should be based on a two-fold relationship (Walden 2007, p.380):

1) the relationship between electronic data and the offender, which is described as an "identity problem" (Walden 2007, p.380). Problems related to the identification of the offender in such cases are solved in several steps: firstly, establishing a proper link between the electronic data and the virtual identity of the person who possesses them; secondly, substantiating that this virtual identity belongs to the offender. In this respect, it is important to note that this is unlike physical identity, which is "tied to social networks, legal documentation, and biological characteristics, virtual identities are, for the most part, personally constructed" (Britz 2009, p.122). Since virtual identities can be shared and information systems can have multiple users, there may be doubts in criminal proceedings as to whether it was the offender who initiated the actions using the information system.
2) the connection between electronic data and an information system, which is called "computer source" (Walden 2007, p.381). This problem of justifying authenticity arises in the context of the specificities of the information system and communication in cyberspace. An information system is usually defined as "interrelated components that collect, manipulate, store, and disseminate information and provide a feedback mechanism to achieve a goal" (Zemmouchi-Ghomari 2021, p.4). This concept is consistent with systems theory, which states that a system is a unit that functions in an environment, contributes to the achievement of common goals, and is composed of many interacting parts. The location of these parts of the system, including the electronic data they contain, depends on many factors. In this context, the source of the electronic data must be established and confirmed in the criminal proceedings.

Another requirement for establishing the reliability of electronic evidence in criminal proceedings is its integrity. In the context of digital technologies, the integrity of electronic data in the most general sense means that the data have not been altered without legitimate reason during their processing. For example, the International Electrotechnical Commission (2019b) defines the integrity of electronic data in the field of digital technology as a "property of data that have not been altered or destroyed in an unauthorized and undetected manner." As mentioned above, electronic data can easily be altered due to the peculiarities of the functioning of information systems, as well as due to inappropriate (both intentional and negligent) human activity. Accordingly, the processing of such data, for example their collection or transmission in criminal proceedings, must be carried out in accordance with procedural requirements and using the tools provided for that purpose. If electronic data have been changed for objective reasons, an “accurate and reliable method of documenting any such changes, including the reasons for any such modifications” (Mason 2016, p.23) should be followed. In this respect, it should be mentioned that different types of electronic data may be subject to different collection methods and technologies, and different methods and technologies may be used for the storage of this type of data during criminal proceedings.

Closely related to the requirement for the integrity of electronic data is the need to ensure the accountability of electronic data. Accountability implies that an appropriate mechanism for the collection and management of electronic data should be ensured. The protection of electronic data must be guaranteed through the choice of the appropriate means of obtaining the data, the processing of such data during pre-trial investigations and the presentation of the data in court. As cybercrime methods and techniques vary, “data recovery tools, data capture tools, data duplication tools, and data analysis tools may vary for every investigation” (Britz 2009, p.276). These aspects become particularly important when the circumstances in criminal proceedings are based exclusively on electronic evidence. In this context, criminal proceedings must follow procedures designed to minimize the risks to accountability and, consequently, to avoid doubts about the evidentiary value of electronic data.

In terms of accountability, it should be mentioned that “as well as identifying direct evidence of a crime, digital forensics can be used to attribute evidence to specific suspects, confirm alibis or statements, determine intent, identify sources (e.g., in social media cases), or authenticate documents” (Eoghan 2010, cited in Grigaliūnas and Toldinas 2016, p.30). Although the data contained in an expert’s report are considered evidence and are evaluated according to the same rules as other evidence, they do have some specificities. This is because the circumstances relevant to the disposition of the case are established by a person with special knowledge, not held by other participants to the criminal proceedings. For example, “an understanding of attacks is a necessary prerequisite to designing proper digital forensic methods to collect and analyse of attacks” (Kanellis *et al.* 2006, p.22). An understanding of the mechanism by which cybercrime is committed is essential for the identification and subsequent analysis of electronic evidence. For example, some investigative steps “include reading the partition table, searching existing files for relevant information such as keywords, system state changes, or text strings, retrieving information from deleted files, checking for data hidden in the boot record […] cracking passwords, and so on” (Kanellis *et al.* 2006, p.60). Therefore, when determining the circumstances relevant to a case on the basis of an expert’s report, additional circumstances must also be assessed which are related not only to the adequacy of the material submitted to the expert and the comprehensiveness of its examination, but also to the reasonableness and appropriateness of the methods used (Review of the application of the provisions of the Criminal Procedure Code on evidence in case law 2007). As stated in the scientific literature, "tested and validated tools should be used, or if other tools are used, then the investigator must ensure that the evidence is not tainted" (Kanellis *et al.* 2006, p.60).

In the case of cybercrime, the importance of substantiating the reliability of electronic evidence in criminal proceedings inevitably becomes apparent. Doubts as to whether such evidence is authentic and properly testifies to the facts arise from the very nature of the electronic data discussed above, namely the ease with which they can be altered and the difficulty of tracing such changes.

In such cases, an understanding of the specificities of electronic evidence and the development of a uniform practice of obtaining, presenting, verifying, and assessing it in criminal proceedings would ensure the development of a consistent and thus coherent approach to evidence and the emergence of good practice.

Interim Findings

A coherent approach to electronic evidence and a proper assessment of the reliability of this type of evidence is essential. In criminal cases relating to cybercrime, the quality of the proof-taking process can often be an issue when it comes to obtaining, presenting, verifying, and assessing electronic evidence. One of the main reasons for this relates to the peculiarities of such a type of evidence: 1) its instability, as electronic evidence can be altered quite easily, both due to the specificities of the operation of the information systems and intentional (or negligent) human activity; 2) the difficulty of tracing the changes made; and 3) the circumstances relevant to the case are usually determined by a person with special knowledge that is not held by the other parties involved in the criminal procedure.

The assessment of the reliability of electronic evidence in criminal proceedings is complex. Once it has been established that such evidence meets the requirements of correlation and admissibility, the assessment of its reliability also considers whether the preservation of the authenticity, integrity, and accountability of electronic evidence has been guaranteed during the proof-taking process.

In the interests of coherent regulation, legislation should not give priority to evidence based on its form. In accordance with the principle of technological neutrality, electronic data, irrespective of the technology that generated or processed them, should be admissible as evidence in criminal proceedings if they fulfil the purpose of evidence, its function in criminal proceedings and the other requirements laid down for evidence.

The speed, economy, and efficiency of criminal proceedings depend, among other aspects, on whether electronic evidence can be used seamlessly in its original electronic form in criminal proceedings. The preservation of this form may also be relevant in cases where it is necessary to implement obligations arising from international (European Union) law in the context of cooperation in criminal matters. Thus, a coherent approach to electronic data management in criminal proceedings contributes, *inter alia*, to efficient criminal proceedings.

References

Ablamskyi, S., and Vasko, A., 2022. Evidentiary Process in Ukrainian and Slovakian Criminal Proceedings: A Comparative Analysis and Implications on Criminal Proceedings. *Journal of Legal, Ethical and Regulatory Issues*, 25 (1S), 1–14.

Britz, M. T., 2009. *Computer Forensics and Cyber Crime: An Introduction*. 2nd edn. Columbus (Ohio): Pearson: Prentice Hall.

Butterfield, K., 2001. Metadata: An Overview. *AALL Spectrum*, 6 (3).

Code of Criminal Procedure of the Republic of Lithuania 2002. *Valstybės žinios*, 2002-04-09, No. 37-1341; with further amendments and supplements.

Constitution of the Republic of Lithuania (Adopted by the citizens of the Republic of Lithuania in the Referendum of 25 October 1992). Available from: https://e-seimas.lrs.lt/portal/legalAct/lt/TAD/079fcad0cf8711ecb69ea7b9ba9d787b?jfwid=-cyl92hylw [Accessed 7 August 2023]; with further amendments.

Convention on Cybercrime, 21 November 2001. ETS No. 185 [online]. Available from: https://rm.coe.int/1680081561 [Accessed 8 August 2023].

Council of Europe, 2019. *Electronic Evidence in Civil and Administrative Proceedings* [online]. Available from: https://rm.coe.int/guidelines-on-electronic-evidence-and-explanatory-memorandum/1680968ab5 [Accessed 8 August 2023].

Directive (EU) 2023/1544 of the European Parliament and of the Council of 12 July 2023 laying down harmonised rules on the designation of designated establishments and the appointment of legal representatives for the purpose of gathering electronic evidence in criminal proceedings. OJ L 191, 181–190. Available from: http://data.europa.eu/eli/dir/2023/1544/oj [Accessed 7 August 2023].

European Convention for the Protection of Human Rights and Fundamental Freedoms, as amended by Protocols Nos. 11 and 14, 4 November 1950. *ETS* 5 [online]. Available from: https://www.refworld.org/docid/3ae6b3b04.html [Accessed 7 August 2023].

ECtHR, Ibrahim and Others v. United Kingdom, 2016, Nos. 50541/08, 50571/08, 50573/08 and 40351/09 [online]. Available from: https://hudoc.echr.coe.int/fre#{%22itemid%22:[%22001-166680%22]} [Accessed 7 August 2023].

ECtHR, Vera Fernandez-Huidobro v. Spain, 2010, No. 74181/01 [online]. Available from:https://hudoc.echr.coe.int/tkp197/view.asp#{%22fulltext%22:[%22Vera%20Fernandez%22],%22itemid%22:[%22001-80608%22]} [Accessed 7 August 2023].

ECtHR, Telfner v. Austria, 2001, No. 33501/96 [online]. Available from: https://hudoc.echr.coe.int/eng#{%22itemid%22:[%22001-59347%22]} [Accessed 7 August 2023].

Eoghan, C., 2010. Handbook of Digital Forensics and Investigation. Academic Press.

Goda, G., Kazlauskas, M., and Kuconis, P., 2005. *Baudžiamojo proceso teisė [Criminal procedure law].* Vilnius: Registrų centras.

Grigaliūnas, Š., and Toldinas, J., 2016. Digital Evidence Investigation Using Habits Attribution. *The 4th International Virtual Research Conference In Technical Disciplines, 17–21 October 2016* [online]. Available from: https://www.researchgate.net/publication/311616212_Digital_Evidence_Investigation_Using_Habits_Attribution [Accessed 8 August 2023].

International Electrotechnical Commission, 2019a. *Authenticity.* [online]. Available from: https://www.electropedia.org/iev/iev.nsf/display?openform&ievref=171-08-07 [Accessed 8 August 2023].

International Electrotechnical Commission, 2019b. *Integrity <of data>*. [online]. Available from: https://www.electropedia.org/iev/iev.nsf/display?openform&ievref=171-08-05 [Accessed 8 August 2023].

Juozapavičius, A., and Leonaitė, E., 2021. Procedūriniai įrodymų leistinumo aspektai baudžiamajame procese[Procedural Aspects of the Admissibility of Evidence in Criminal Procedure]. *Teisė*, 121, 80–97. Available from: https://www.journals.vu.lt/teise/article/view/25168/24458 [Accessed 8 August 2023]

Kanellis, P., Kiountouzis, E., Kolokotronis, N., and Martakos, D. (eds.), 2006. *Digital Crime and Forensic Science in Cyberspace*. Hershey, PA: Idea Group Publishing.

Mason, S., 2016. The Concept of a Convention on Electronic Evidence. *Amicus Curiae*, 105, 21–28.

Matulienė, S., n.d. *Įrodymai* [Evidence]. Universal Lithuanian Encyclopaedia [online]. Available from: https://www.vle.lt/straipsnis/irodymai/ [Accessed 8 August 2023].

National Information Standards Organization, 2004. *Understanding Metadata* [online]. Available from: https://www.lter.uaf.edu/metadata_files/UnderstandingMetadata.pdf [Accessed 8 August 2023].

Ohm, P., 2010. The Argument Against Technology-Neutral Surveillance Laws. *Texas Law Review,* 88 (7), 1685–1714.

Raghavan, S., and Raghavan, S. V., 2009. Digital Evidence Composition in Fraud Detection. In: *Digital forensics and cyber crime: first international ICST conference, ICDF2C 2009, Albany, NY, USA, September 30-October 2009, revised selected papers.*

Regulation (EU) 2023/1543 of the European Parliament and of the Council of 12 July 2023 on European Production Orders and European Preservation Orders for electronic evidence in criminal proceedings and for the execution of custodial sentences following criminal proceedings. OJ L 191, 118–180. Available from: http://data.europa.eu/eli/reg/2023/1543/oj [Accessed 7 August 2023].

Riekkinen, J., 2019. Electronic Evidence in Criminal Procedure: On the Effects of ICT and the Development towards the Network Society on the Life-cycle of Evidence. *Digital Evidence and Electronic Signature Law Review*, 16, 6–10.

Ruling of the Supreme Court of Lithuania of 9 April 2020 in criminal case No. 2K-81-895/2020.

Ruling of the Supreme Court of Lithuania of 14 July 2020 in criminal case No. 2K-141-303/2020.

Ruling of the Supreme Court of Lithuania of 17 July 2020 in criminal case No. 2K-164-458/2020.

Ruling of the Supreme Court of Lithuania of 12 November 2019 in criminal case No. 2K-264-976/2019.

Ruling of the Supreme Court of Lithuania of 30 January 2018 in criminal case No. 2K-26-689/2018.

Second Additional Protocol to the Convention on Cybercrime on enhanced co-operation and disclosure of electronic evidence, 12 May 2022. CETS No. 224 [online]. Available from: https://www.coe.int/en/web/conventions/full-list?module=treaty-detail&treatynum=224 [Accessed 8 August 2023].

Sethia, A., 2016. Rethinking Admissibility of Electronic Evidence. *International Journal of Law and Information Technology*, 24 (3), 229–250.

Supreme Court of Lithuania, 2007. Review of the application of the provisions of the Criminal Procedure Code on evidence in case law approved by the Criminal Divisions of the Supreme Court of Lithuania. *Bulletin Court Practice*, 27.

Tadros, V., and Tierney, S., 2004. The Presumption of Innocence and the Human Rights Act. *The Modern Law Review*, 67 (3), 402–434.

Trigkas, N., 2017. The Authenticity of Electronic Evidence: First Steps Toward Improvement. *Edinburgh Student Law Review*, 3 (2), 20–27.

Vasko, A., and Klimek, L., 2023. Means of Proof in Criminal Proceedings in the Slovak Republic – New Challenges. *Access to Justice in Eastern Europe*, 1, 168–177. https://doi.org/10.33327/AJEE-18-6.1-n000106

Zemmouchi-Ghomari, L., 2021. Basic Concepts of Information Systems. In: D. Reilly (ed.). *Contemporary Issues in Information Systems – A Global Perspective*. IntechOpen. https://doi.org/10.5772/intechopen.97644

Walden, I., 2007. *Computer Crimes and Digital Investigations*. Oxford: Oxford University Press.

Rima Ažubalytė

Evidence in a Non-Conviction-Based Confiscation Procedure

General Remarks

Confiscation, as a legal tool that allows the State to acquire assets that are linked to the perpetration of a crime, can be considered as a polymorphous legal concept depending on its object and function (Milone 2017, p.151). Legal measures to seize illegal property may depend, *inter alia*, on the origins of the property. In this respect, the State may provide for such measures of controlling unlawful property as: those targeting property derived from criminal offenses – e.g., the criminalization of money laundering and the confiscation and extended confiscation of property; the civil confiscation of property, which is directed at property with an origin which is, in principle, unclear; the seizure of homeless property; and tax measures directed at property of unknown origin. These can be assets of "neutral" origin or, in fact, assets of criminal origin (Bikelis and Mikšys 2018, p.17). Thus, there are various legal measures by which the proceeds of criminal offenses, property of an unlawful origin or even property of a neutral origin may be seized and confiscated. These measures are usually broken down into: those of a criminal nature (such as criminal liability for money laundering and criminal liability for illicit enrichment); those of a mixed nature (ordinary, extended, and civil confiscation); the civil institute of the seizure of homeless property; and tax measures – tax rates, default money, and tax penalties imposed on income the sources of which the taxpayer cannot justify (Bikelis and Mikšys 2018, p.17). With regard to the confiscation of property only in the context of criminal proceedings, a distinction is made between the generations of confiscation regimes covering 1) regular;2) extended criminal confiscation; 3) non-conviction-based confiscation; and 4) the unexplained wealth mechanism (Boucht 2019, pp.529–534).

The system of national legal instruments of controlling unlawful property is not well established, and their regulatory principles differ: the "plurality of models of confiscation, very different in terms of qualification, discipline, function, object and degree of cogency, has been further accentuated almost everywhere" (Bernardi 2019, p.IX). Partly as a result of the recent increase in EU regulation on asset confiscation, States are also reviewing or adjusting asset confiscation mechanisms in addition to traditional asset confiscation (i.e., conviction-based confiscation) and other options for confiscation (non-conviction-based confiscation, hereinafter NCB confiscation, and NCB forfeiture). Directive 2014/42/EU of the European Parliament and of the Council of April 3, 2014 on the freezing and confiscation of instrumentalities and proceeds of crime in the European Union (hereinafter Directive 2014/42/EU) and Regulation (EU) 2018/1805 of the European Parliament and of the Council of November 14, 2018 on the mutual recognition of freezing orders and confiscation orders (hereinafter the Regulation) established legal bases for the freezing and confiscation of criminal assets in European Union (EU) law. Accordingly, the Court of Justice of the European Union (CJEU) has started to formulate case law on the extended confiscation of assets (CJEU C-845/19 and C-863/19).

In 2018, 26 Member States of the EU had an extended asset confiscation model that allows for the confiscation, in the context of criminal proceedings, of assets not related to the criminal offense of which the person is accused (Analysis of non-conviction-based confiscation measures in the European Union, 2019). Despite this, Member States' asset recovery systems are not well equipped to effectively address the complex *modus operandi* of criminal organizations. In May 2022, the European Commission presented a proposal for a new Confiscation Directive within the EU Strategy to tackle organized Crime 2021–2025, covering additional criminal offenses and including "a new generation of confiscation regimes": the confiscation of unexplained wealth linked to criminal activities (Proposal for a Directive of the European Parliament and of the Council on asset recovery and confiscation, 2022).

According to studies, beyond the borders of the EU, several pieces of legislation provide for NCB confiscation around the world: in the United States, the UK, South Africa, Albania, Colombia, Liechtenstein, Switzerland, Thailand, etc. (Greenberg *et al.* 2009, p.17; Bullock 2014; Cassella 2019). Numerous international acts and conventions call for States to include alternative forms of confiscation, including NCB measures, in their legislation (Alagna 2015, p.451). It is generally accepted that NCB asset recovery has become a crucial tool in the fight against organized crime over the years, especially against mafia-type issues.

On the other hand, international acts and constitutions generally establish the presumption of innocence, according to which a person is presumed innocent until proven guilty in accordance with the procedure laid down by law. At the same time, one of the most important presumptions in criminal proceedings is applicable to the procedure of proof, which obliges the State to assume onus probandi. Thus, in the context of the present issue, the question arises as to whether the presumption of innocence as a means of proof in criminal proceedings is absolute. That is to say, must the allocation of the burden of proof in relation to the seizure (confiscation) of property which is not directly linked to the criminal offense which is the subject of the criminal proceedings remain the same as when proving the guilt of the person concerned?

The regulation of the EU, the Council of Europe, the jurisprudence of supranational courts and the criminal laws of some states make it clear that the answer to this question is no. The case law has held that the right to the presumption of innocence and the consequent imperative that the burden of proof lies with the public prosecutor are, like other rights, not absolute (*Salabiaku v. France* 1988, § 28; *Krumpholz v. Austria* 2010, § 34).

Despite this trend in legal regulation, research analysis suggests that some issues of proof of the extended confiscation of assets, as well as other types of confiscation not based on a conviction, such as confiscation from third parties, remain relevant. Views on this mechanism, including the applicable standard of proof, range from harsh criticism, arguing that NCB forfeiture represents a step too far (Hendry and King 2015), to the need to further expand NCB confiscation possibilities – in particular civil confiscation, which has thus far been legalized in only a few EU countries (Bikelis 2022).

The persistence of the problems of proof in NCB confiscation proceedings is also reflected in the constitutional jurisprudence of States. Of course, as stated above, NCB confiscation in accordance with international legal standards is not illegitimate in itself. NCB confiscation *per se* has repeatedly been considered consistent with the provisions of European Convention on Human Rights (hereinafter ECHR) Article 6 (the right to a fair trial) and those of Article 1 of the First Protocol to the ECHR (the protection of property), from the European Court of Human Rights (hereinafter ECtHR). Such ECtHR case law has also been criticized as being too uncritical of the development of restrictions on the right to property (Hryniewicz-Lach 2023), or as not being fully coherent (Simonato 2017).

However, States are free to provide higher guarantees in this area. The constitutions of States often provide higher standards for the protection of human rights than international standards. Cases of constitutional justice in different states in recent years show that relatively new types of confiscation of property – usually the extended confiscation of property – raise doubts among legal practitioners as to the constitutionality of such restrictions (Ruling of the German Federal Constitutional Court of February 10, 2021; Ruling of the Constitutional Tribunal of the Portuguese Republic of February 11, 2015; Ruling of the Constitutional Court of the Republic of Romania of June 25, 2014; Ruling of the Constitutional Court of the Republic of Georgia of July 13, 2005; Ruling of the Constitutional Court of the Republic of Italy of May 10, 2019; Ruling of the Constitutional Court of the Republic of Bulgaria of

October 13, 2012) . The most recent relevant constitutional justice case was in Lithuania (Ruling of the Constitutional Court of the Republic of Lithuania of October 12, 2023). In addition to the general question of whether the regulation of extended confiscation of property complies with the substantive and procedural constitutional frameworks for restricting the right to property, the question was also raised as to whether proof in extended confiscation proceedings is compatible with the principle of the presumption of innocence. From this point of view, it is therefore necessary to consider whether and what balance exists between national, including constitutional, standards, and supranational legal practice.

It should be stressed that most scholarly sources, in particular those based on the analysis of the EU legal framework, do not consider extended confiscation as a type of NCB confiscation. For the purposes of this study, given that the object of extended asset confiscation is property that does not derive from the specific offense of which the person is accused, extended asset confiscation is also considered to be a type of confiscation of NCBs in the broadest sense (Panzavolta 2017).

Thus, this study examines, using the systematic analysis method, the problems of proof in NCB confiscation as part of a process of interference with the right to property. In order to achieve this objective, in particular, common requirements for NCB confiscation as a form of interference with the right of the respective person to the peaceful enjoyment of their possessions are laid down. Secondly, considering the different origins of the assets and the different procedural legal status of the person whose assets are confiscated, the question of which evidentiary principles are applicable to NCB confiscation proceedings is examined, and it is then analyzed whether they are consistent with the presumption of innocence inherent in criminal proceedings. Only the issue of the proof of NCB confiscation in criminal proceedings shall be investigated here. Legal measures for the confiscation of property which apply in parallel with or after criminal proceedings, or even with no link to the criminal proceedings against the defendant, are not the subject of this study.

General Requirements for the Process of Proof of NCB Confiscation

Before examining the problems of the standard of proof of NCB confiscation, it is necessary to determine whether a different standard of proof may be applied to different confiscation procedures.

First of all, the common requirements related to the protection of property and its limitation are laid down in constitutions and both international and national ordinary legal acts. They apply to all restrictions on ownership, including confiscation of assets (all types/regimes). These are, in particular: 1) the requirements under which the right to property may be restricted; 2) the proportionality of confiscation; and 3) the procedural guarantees in confiscation proceedings.

Legal regulation, case law, and research suggest that while these requirements are well established, they acquire new content as the types and scope of confiscation of assets expand. As evidenced by more recent constitutional and supranational court rulings, new questions about the constitutionality of the NCB confiscation of property and human rights doctrine continue to arise. It is therefore necessary to start with the principal grounds for the confiscation of assets before analyzing the problem of evidence raised in the process of NCB confiscation.

Firstly, the constant axiom is that a confiscation procedure represents interference with the respective person's right to the peaceful enjoyment of their possessions.

CE and EU law instruments respect the fundamental rights and observe the principles recognized by the Charter of Fundamental Rights of the European Union and the ECHR, as interpreted in the case law of the ECtHR. Directive 2014/42/EU should also be implemented in accordance with those rights and principles (Preamble, 38). The application of confiscation procedures contributes to the implementation of fundamental principles of law: the rule of law, public safety, the protection of human rights, proportionality, etc. The ECtHR states that Article 1 of Protocol No. 1 to the Convention, which guarantees in substance the right to property, comprises three distinct rules: "The first one lays down the principle of peaceful enjoyment of property in general. The second rule covers deprivation of possessions and makes it subject to certain conditions. The third recognizes that the Contracting States are entitled, among other things, to control the use of property in accordance with the general interest. The second and third rules, which are concerned with particular instances of interference with the right to peaceful enjoyment of property, must be construed in the light of the general principle laid down in the first rule" (see *Immobiliare Saffi v. Italy* [GC] 1999, § 44; *Gogitidze and others v. Georgia* 2015, § 92; *Balsamo v. San Marino* 2019, § 80; *Yordanov and others v. Bulgaria* 2023, § 97). Thus, according to ECtHR case law, confiscation measures applied to possessions are considered to represent interference with the respective person's right to the peaceful enjoyment of their possessions normally. Article 1 of Protocol No. 1 is therefore applicable. The same position is taken in constitutional doctrine when assessing the confiscation of property in the context of the constitutional right to property.

Another important premise for the further discussion of the confiscation of assets is the legal principles underlying this restriction of ownership. The applicable principles of the limitation of property rights depend on the nature of that restriction.

As already mentioned, in the common European legal area, there are two main means of confiscation: conviction-based, which is usually conditioned by the conviction of a perpetrator; and NCB. NCB confiscation may be applied both within and outside criminal proceedings (in civil or administrative proceedings). The model of the latter form of NCB confiscation is not based on the perpetrator's guilt, but on the origin of the property.

The ECtHR has also stressed that states have wide discretion to decide on appropriate measures to control the use of property, including confiscating the proceeds of crime of any kind (*Butler v. United Kingdom* 2002; *Balsamo v. San Marino* 2019, § 93). However, confiscation as interference with property rights according to the case law of constitutional and supranational courts must fulfil certain criteria. According to ECtHR case law, depending on the legal framework in Member States, such confiscation may take place in criminal proceedings, which are usually conditioned by a conviction (including extended confiscation, considered as an ancillary and auxiliary form of ordinary confiscation), or outside criminal proceedings when certain conditions are fulfilled (including preventive confiscation measures of an administrative character, in particular to combat organized crime; and a civil-law approach to confiscation, which is not based on the perpetrator's guilt, but on the origin of the property (ECtHR, 2020)).

According to the ECtHR, confiscation based on conviction is of a criminal nature: "in cases where the confiscation followed a conviction, and thus constituted a penalty, the Court found that such interference fell within the scope of the second paragraph of Article 1 of Protocol No. 1, which, *inter alia*, allows the Contracting States to control the use of property to secure the payment of penalties" (*Sofia v. San Marino* 2017; *Phillips v. the United Kingdom* 2001, § 51; *Balsamo v. San Marino* 2019, § 81). In the meantime, confiscation which is not linked to a conviction is classified by the ECtHR as the result of a civil dispute concerning the recovery of unlawful property, as evidenced by the statement that "in other cases, where a confiscation measure had been imposed independently of the existence of a criminal conviction but rather as a result of separate 'civil' (within the meaning of Article 6 § 1 of the Convention) judicial proceedings aimed at the recovery of assets deemed to have been acquired unlawfully" (*Gogitidze and Others v. Georgia* 2015, §§ 94 and 97; *Balsamo v. San Marino* 2019, § 81). This form of confiscation must comply with the principle of lawfulness and pursue a legitimate aim by means reasonably proportionate to the aim sought to be realized (*Beyeler v. Italy* [GC] 2002, §§ 108–114; *Gogitidze and others v. Georgia* 2015, §§ 94 and 97; *Balsamo v. San Marino* 2019, § 81).

Thus, the latter position of the ECtHR merely confirms the distinction between the different types of confiscation of property, which is the subject of legal research. There are scientists who consider such a position to be unjustified, arguing that such an interpretation of NCB forfeiture is an attempt "to avoid inbuilt procedural protections through a semantic mislabeling designating it as 'civil' in character, and at the very real expense of both criminal procedural and legal systemic legitimacy" (Hendry and King 2015, pp.407–408). However, this study supports the position that, depending on whether the confiscation of property is inseparable from the conviction or not directly linked to it, the distinction between confiscation *in personam* (usually conviction-based) and confiscation *in rem* (non-conviction-based) is justified. Thus, depending on the nature of the confiscation and its procedure, the object of confiscation also changes: from the three traditional elements of conviction-based confiscation – the tools and instruments of the criminal offense (*instrumentum sceleris*), the object of the criminal offense (*objectum sceleris*), and the proceeds of the criminal offense (*productum/fructum sceleris*) – to a property that is presumed to be of unlawful origin (Boucht 2019 pp.529–534; Hryniewicz-Lach 2023; Bikelis and Mikšys, 2018, p.17).

Directive 2014/42/EU directly refers to several types of confiscation of criminal assets: 1) NCB confiscation, at least if the accused or suspected person absconds or is ill; 2) extended confiscation for a specific list of criminal offenses; and 3) third-party confiscation (Report, COM(2020) 217 final), which, despite its separation in this regulatory act, is in principle regarded as a type of NCB confiscation (Panzavolta 2017, p.25; Simonato 2017, pp.367–368). For their part, Member States choose an NCB confiscation model, both before and after EU regulation, depending on their legal framework and tradition. Here, when it comes to extended confiscation, the scope of its application was initially linked with serious and organized crime, which justified – and still does, at the EU level – extensive powers in the field of legislation (Hryniewicz-Lach 2023, pp.249–250). Extended confiscation was first perceived as a tool to fight organized crime (Italy, Netherlands, Germany, Austria), terrorism (Germany and Austria), drug trafficking (Spain), serious, complex, and repetitive economic crimes (Finland), corruption (Bulgaria, Croatia), and money laundering and the smuggling of goods (Greece). As can be seen, these are serious crimes, in particular where substantial financial gains were obtained (Hryniewicz-Lach 2023, pp.249–250; also, see Country reports, Extended confiscation and its justification in light of fundamental rights and general principles of EU law). Other States, such as Lithuania, provide that extended confiscation can be applied to all criminal offenses (Article 72-3 of the Criminal Code of Lithuania), and such a wide list of offenses raises doubts about the legitimacy and proportionality of the law applicable to such a form of confiscation (Ruling of the Constitutional Court of the Republic of Lithuania of October 12, 2023).

Before examining some of the problems of the standard of proof used in confiscation proceedings, it must be said that the doctrinal and legal basis of conviction-based confiscation is well established: convicted criminals should not benefit from crime. The standard of proof for confiscated property is also clear: beyond reasonable doubt. Meanwhile, the standard of proof for the grounds of NCB confiscation (including its subject matter) tends to deviate from the classical standard of proof for criminal proceedings, which raises debate between scientists and legal practitioners.

NCB confiscation shall not be directly linked to a criminal offense which is the subject of criminal proceedings: "in the extended confiscation, some of the confiscated assets derive from crimes for which there has not been any conviction, and the third parties owning the confiscated assets are, by definition, not involved in the criminal proceedings leading to the conviction" (Panzavolta 2017, p.25; Simonato 2017, pp.367–368). Thus, the legal regulation of the grounds for NCB confiscation and proof of the origin of assets is usually based on the fact that this type of confiscation is not a penalty (or a criminal measure), but a civil measure that may be applied in criminal proceedings. Moreover, it is not linked to the guilt for a specific offense of a person whose assets may be confiscated, and is not linked to any charge against a person. On the basis of an analysis of ECtHR cases, it was concluded that "building an understanding that the recovery of illicit assets is a restorative, rather than punitive, measure contributed to the mental shift toward an approach that allowed a lower standard of proof, gave more weight to indirect evidence along with the contextual assessment of the circumstances of the case, and even allowed rebuttable presumptions of the illicit origin of the unexplained assets in some cases" (Bikelis 2022, p.56). The German Federal Constitutional Court has also recognized that the confiscation of property is not an additional punishment to which the principle of individual culpability applies, but a *sui generis* measure with a restitutionary character; it is aimed at preventing the recognition of the proceeds of crime (Ruling of the German Federal Constitutional Court of February 10, 2021, as cited in Ruling of the Constitutional Court of the Republic of Lithuania of October 12, 2023, § 16). Other constitutional courts have invoked essentially the same nature of extended confiscation in examining the constitutional standards of proof applicable in NCB confiscation.

This study takes the position that "the standard of proof, in particular, means the degree of conviction required of the judge when he makes a decision (is it enough that the judge deems one scenario (the assets stem from crime) more plausible than the other (the assets have a legal origin); secondly, this is a question related to the apportionment of the burden of proof: what should the public prosecutor prove and what can be expected from the defendant in this respect" (Vervaelle and De Zanger 2019, p.524). Although some scientists do not justify such a shift in the standard of proof from criminal to civil proceedings (Hendry and King 2015, pp.407–408), it is *de facto* happening. In such a case, it is the legal practitioners, and in particular the national courts, who are confronted with a complex situation, both theoretically and in practice. Thus, in one set of criminal proceedings, there are two probative proceedings with different objectives: both the guilt of the person and the basis for confiscating the property, the origin of which is illegal, must be proved.

The literature stresses that the treatment of NCB confiscation as a civil measure means that the standard of proof based on the "follow the money" principle can be applied to a person (even one who has not been charged, as is the case, for example, with confiscation from a third party) who is dealing with a specified property, the legitimate provenance of which they are not able to justify. Some authors are very critical of this, suggesting that "the standard of proof to be applied in such cases is the civil one, namely the lower threshold of a balance of probabilities, as opposed to the more robust criminal standard of beyond reasonable doubt. The State's hand is strengthened all the more by the lack of any requirement that the individual be convicted of a criminal offense before their property is liable to become the subject of such proceedings" (Hendry and King 2015, p.401).

Such a shift in the burden of proof in criminal proceedings is certainly problematic. Some scholars suggest that "enhanced protections such as the burden of proof and the presumption of innocence admittedly restrict the effective exercise of police power and make the task of prosecutors an onerous one, and that these procedural safeguards are necessary restrictions upon the operations of the legal system" (Hendry and King 2015, pp.407–408). As one international study points out, the scope for NCB confiscation is gradually expanding with the extension of the scope of eligible assets at the EU level, the extensive implementation of relevant EU law into national legal orders and the expansion of the territorial effectiveness of confiscation orders, which "results in the watering down of procedural safeguards (by employing a lower standard and reversed burden of proof)" (Hryniewicz-Lach 2023, p.247; also Boucht 2017, pp.119–121;), "creates tensions with the presumption of innocence (due to alleged prior criminal activity being presumed and not even having to be specified), and poses a challenge to create a firm barrier for the protection of fundamental rights, in particular, the rights to property and privacy" (Hryniewicz-Lach 2023, p.247; also Boucht 2017, pp.7–9). There are even concerns that "progressive changes in this regard have slowly accustomed the authorities in member states to the concept of confiscation of assets whose origin can neither be confirmed by the court as illicit nor proven by their owner as licit" (Hryniewicz-Lach 2023, p.247).

In order to resolve this doctrinal controversy, the courts have, among other things, invoked the principle of proportionality in the application of NCB confiscation mechanisms, as can be seen from the case law of both supranational and national courts. The State has a wide margin of appreciation with regard to political, economic, or social strategy measures aimed at recovering illegally acquired assets. Despite such discretion, "any interference with property rights should strike a fair balance between the demands of the general interest of the community and the requirements of the protection of individual rights" (*Yordanov and others v. Bulgaria* 2023, § 112). The ECtHR has repeatedly held that extended confiscation is compatible with the provisions of the Convention, *inter alia*, Article 1 of its Protocol 1, provided that the safeguards of Article 6 of the Convention are respected. It is generally accepted that confiscation measures have been proportionate to the objectives pursued, even in the absence of a conviction for a specific offense, in the case of assets presumed to have been acquired wholly or partly from the proceeds of drug trafficking offenses (*Webb v. United Kingdom* 2004; *Butler v. United Kingdom* 2002), from the activities of criminal organizations involved in drug trafficking (*Arcuri and others v. Italy* 2001), or from other illicit activities of a mafia nature (*Raimondo v. Italy* 1994).

A different situation may arise where, under national legislation, NCB confiscation (usually extended confiscation) may be applied in proceedings other than those relating to organized and other serious crimes, the seriousness of which has led to the creation of NCB confiscation mechanisms. In such cases, it is the proportionality of confiscation that may be the only effective means by which the courts can avoid the disproportionate deprivation of property rights. Some authors suggest that the principle of proportionality should be considered as the guiding principle for the application of NCB confiscation (Milone 2017, p.152). Thus, the case law of the Supreme Court of Lithuania emphasizes the importance of the proportionality of the confiscation of property – even in the case of conviction-based confiscation. The Supreme Court of Lithuania indicates that "the confiscation of property radically restricts a person's right to the protection of property, enshrined in Article 23 of the Constitution of the Republic of Lithuania and Article 1 of Protocol No. 1 of the Convention. Therefore, the application of mandatory provisions on confiscation of property has to be harmonized with the constitutional principle of proportionality" (Judgments of the Supreme Court of Lithuania in criminal cases Nos. 2K-7-130-699/2015, 2K-233-895/2019, 2K-39-495/2020, 2K-80-222/2020, 2K-288-788/2020).

In assessing the proportionality of the confiscation of property, the ECtHR and national courts take into account a number of factors, such as: the nature of the offense and its gravity; the status of confiscated property in a criminal offense; the legality of the origin and destination of the confiscated property; the significance to the applicant of the confiscated property of the convicted person from whom the property is confiscated; property damage to the State caused or potentially caused by the criminal act; and other penalties imposed on the person in addition to the confiscation of property, along with their severity and sufficiency in terms of the implementation of the objectives of the punishment in the circumstances of the specific case (Judgments of the Supreme Court of Lithuania in criminal cases Nos 2K-7-130-699/2015, 2K-39-495/2020, 2K-288-788/2020). In particular, the principle of proportionality applies to NCB confiscation, where the standard of proof is lower than that of guilt.

A third important aspect is that the confiscation of assets, as well as the process of proving it, is inseparable from the procedural guarantees in confiscation proceedings.

The ECtHR and national courts also emphasize the importance of various procedural guarantees available in confiscation proceedings, such as:

> the availability of an effective remedy, including access to courts, by which an applicant can challenge the (continuing) seizure (*Benet Czech, spol. s r.o. v. the Czech Republic*, § 49); their adversarial nature (*Yildirim v. Italy* (dec.); *Perre v. Italy* (dec.)); advance disclosure of the prosecution case (*Grayson and Barnham v. the United Kingdom*, § 45); opportunity for the party to adduce documentary and oral evidence (*Butler v. the United Kingdom (dec.)*; *Perre v. Italy (dec.)*), possibility of being legally represented by a privately hired lawyer (*Butler v. the United Kingdom* (dec.)); assumption of the criminal character of the assets can be rebutted by the party (*Geerings v. Netherlands*, § 44); a judge having the discretion not to apply the assumption if he/she considered that applying it would give rise to a serious risk of injustice (*Phillips v. the United Kingdom*, § 43); whether an individual assessment of which pieces of property should be confiscated in the light of the facts of the case has been carried out (*Rummi v. Estonia*, § 108; *Silickienė v. Lithuania*, § 68); on the whole, whether the applicant was afforded a reasonable opportunity of putting his arguments before the domestic courts (*Veits v. Estonia*, §§ 72 and 74; *Jokela v. Finland*, § 45; *Balsamo v. San Marino*, § 93) (ECtHR 2020).

The Lower Standard of Proof in the Application of NCB Confiscation: A Balance of Probabilities and/or a Reversed Burden of Proof

The desire to recover ill-gotten wealth encourages countries to develop legal mechanisms for: firstly, the confiscation of property linked to serious criminal offenses, without the prior existence of a criminal conviction; secondly, the confiscation not only of the direct proceeds of crime, but also of property, including any incomes and other indirect benefits obtained by converting or transforming the direct proceeds of crime or intermingling them with other, possibly lawful, assets; and, thirdly, the confiscation of unexplained wealth linked to unlawful activities. Thus, the requirements for proving these three forms of confiscation will be analyzed below.

According to ECtHR case law, firstly, proceedings for confiscation which do not stem from a criminal conviction or sentencing proceedings, such as civil proceedings *in rem*, should be examined under the civil head of that provision (*Gogitidze and others v. Georgia* 2015, § 121). Secondly, proof on the balance of probabilities, or a high probability of illicit origins combined with the inability of the owner to prove the contrary, was found to suffice as a standard of proof for the purposes of the proportionality test under Article 1 of Protocol No. 1 (*Balsamo v. San Marino* 2019, § 91). Thirdly, the applicants themselves may choose to waive their procedural right to take part in the proceedings (*Gogitidze and others v. Georgia* 2015, § 122). Fourthly, there can be nothing arbitrary in the reversal of the burden of proof onto the respondents in forfeiture proceedings *in rem* after the public prosecutor has submitted a substantiated claim (*Gogitidze and others v. Georgia* 2015, § 122). Finally, the forfeiture of property ordered as a result of civil proceedings *in rem* cannot give rise to the application of the provision on Article 6 § 2 (the presumption of innocence) (*Gogitidze and others v. Georgia* 2015, § 126).

However, the academic literature identifies a number of problems related to the regulation and application of NCB confiscation. It has already been mentioned that some authors take the position that such a hybrid mechanism is fundamentally inconsistent with a due process-based model of criminal procedure (Hendry and King 2015). This study takes the position that NCB confiscation *per se* can be a legitimate tool for the recovery of ill-gotten wealth, but that there are a number of challenges in its regulation and application. Here, researchers point out that the following issues are relevant when considering the legitimacy of NCB confiscation: "civil-criminal classification of law (criminal classification would lead to additional protections and criminal burden of proof); double punishment; retrospective application of NCB asset recovery laws; reversal of the onus of proof violates presumption of innocence; right against self-incrimination vis-à-vis the criminal case; interference with property rights; proportionality of confiscation to the gravity of the offence; entitlement of claimant to legal expenses" (Greenberg *et al.* 2009, p.21; Alagna 2015, p.452). The authors of this paper agree with the view that "the wide majority of these points concern specifically the way

NCB measures are established in the national legislation" (Alagna 2015, p.452), and must be decided by the national legislator. Hryniewicz-Lach (2023) also points to a number of problems related to extensions in the field of confiscation and in the EU regulation, including the EU's legislative competence in the field of confiscation.

The right to the presumption of innocence and the imperatives it implies – the right not to incriminate oneself, the rule that the burden of proof lies with the prosecutor, and the principle of *in dubio pro reo* – form the basis of evidence in criminal proceedings. "The presumption of innocence, the burden of proof resting with the prosecution, and the heightened standard of proof beyond reasonable doubt [...] are traditionally justified by reference to, *inter alia*, the relationship between the State and the individual, the imbalance of the State's and the defendant's respective resources, the potential consequences of a guilty verdict, the avoidance of wrongful convictions, and respect for individual dignity and autonomy" (Hendry and King 2015, p.398; also, see Jackson and Summers 2012, pp.199–240).

As mentioned above, a confiscation order following a conviction is normally considered as part of a sentencing procedure; thus (as far as the offender is concerned), Paragraph 1 of Article 6 of the Convention applies to confiscation proceedings under the criminal limb (e.g., *Phillips v. the United Kingdom* 2001, § 39), and this issue is therefore beyond the scope of Paragraph 2 of Article 6 (the presumption of innocence) (e.g., *Phillips v. the United Kingdom* 2001, § 34; *Van Offeren v. the Netherlands* (dec.) 2005; *Grayson and Barnham v. the United Kingdom* 2008, § 37; *Sofia v. San Marino* (dec.) 2017, § 55–56; a contrario, *Geerings v. the Netherlands* 2007, § 47).

Researchers rightly point out that "many confiscation regimes today include elements of either a lower standard of proof (a balance of probabilities rather than one that approaches the criminal standard) and/or a reversed burden of proof as regards the origin of the assets in question" (Boucht 2019). Thus, only one problematic issue related to NCB confiscation has been chosen for examination here: how the civil standard of proof applied in NCB confiscation proceedings complies with the principles governing criminal proceedings.

To begin with, the presumptions of fact and law operating in every national criminal law are not in themselves prohibited by law, but States must in all cases set reasonable limits on such presumptions, taking into account the importance of the issue at stake and the effective safeguarding of the individual's rights of defense (*Salabiaku v. France* 1988, § 28; *Krumpholz v. Austria* 2010, § 34). As already analyzed above, in the case of NCB confiscation, as in other cases of confiscation, the general guarantees of due process limiting the right to property apply. Only the consistency of the reversal of the burden of proof with the requirements of the presumption of innocence is examined below.

Article 6 of the ECHR generally does not prevent States from having recourse to presumptions. Similarly, in proceedings concerning various forms of confiscation or fiscal repression, public authorities may act on the presumption that the assets were acquired unlawfully (*Salabiaku v. France* 1988, § 28). The same approach has been used in the context of complaints about presumptions made in this context either under Article 1 of Protocol No. 1 (*Cacucci and Sabatelli v. Italy (dec.)*, § 43; *Yildrim v. Italy (dec.)*) or under Article 6 (shifting the burden of proof onto the applicant to show that their assets had been lawfully acquired (*Grayson and Barnham v. the United Kingdom* 2008, § 45; *Phillips v. the United Kingdom* 2001, § 43)). Thus, according the ECtHR, if the party has been given an opportunity to rebut the presumptions, then the use of presumptions is compatible with the presumption of innocence. At the same time, it must be emphasized that according to the case law of the ECtHR, a violation of Article 6 § 2 was found in a case where a confiscation order was given in respect of goods despite the owner having been acquitted in criminal proceedings of the crime from which the proceeds had allegedly originated (*Geerings v. Netherlands* 2007, §§ 43–51). There are further cases that illustrate this scenario.

The ECtHR, while reiterating that "every legal system recognizes presumptions of fact or of law, and that the Convention does not prohibit such presumptions in principle (*Arcuri v. Italy* 2001), cannot ignore the fact that such presumption in the particular case operated in combination with the difficulties for the applicants, namely those stemming from the wide scope of the confiscation legislation" (*Yordanov and others v. Bulgaria* 2023, § 118).

In practice, national courts are essentially confronted with two procedural situations in the context of the presumption of innocence, which requires criminal proceedings to follow the "beyond reasonable doubt" principle of proof when applying NCB confiscation mechanisms in criminal proceedings: extended confiscation and NCB confiscation from a third party. Due to the scope of this study, we do not consider the cases in which NCB confiscation is also available alongside those cases in which a person cannot be prosecuted because of procedural obstacles.

According to ECtHR case law, whenever a confiscation order was the result of proceedings related to the proceeds of crime derived from serious offenses, the Court does not require proof "beyond reasonable doubt" of the illicit origins of the property in such proceedings. Instead, proof on a balance of probabilities or a high probability of illicit origins, combined with the inability of the owner to prove the contrary, is found to suffice for the purposes of the proportionality test under Article 1 of Protocol No. 1. […] it was legitimate for the relevant domestic authorities to issue confiscation orders on the basis of a preponderance of evidence suggesting that the respondents' lawful incomes could not have sufficed for them to acquire the property in question. (*Gogitidze and others v. Georgia* 2015, § 107; *Telbis and Viziteu v. Romania* 2018, § 68)

According to Directive 2014/42/EU, Member States may also provide that it could be sufficient for the court to consider on the balance of probabilities, or to reasonably presume that it is substantially more probable, that the property in question has been obtained from criminal conduct than from other activities. As outlined in the report of the European Commission:

> Extended confiscation should be possible where a court is satisfied that the property in question is derived from criminal conduct. This does not mean that it must be established that the property in question is derived from criminal conduct. Member States may provide that it could be sufficient for the court to consider on the balance of probabilities, or to reasonably presume that it is substantially more probable, that the property in question has been obtained from criminal conduct than from other activities. The fact that the property of the person is disproportionate to his lawful income could be among those facts giving rise to a conclusion of the court that the property derives from criminal conduct (Directive, Preamble, 21; Report, COM (2020) 217 final).

CJEU case law also states that, in order to apply extended confiscation, the court must be satisfied, on the basis of the circumstances of the case and the evidence available, that the property in question belonging to the offender is derived from another offense; the court may also take into account the disproportionality of the value of the property to the legitimate income of the convicted person or a third person. The perpetrator or third party must be given an effective opportunity to challenge the attribution of the assets to the proceeds of crime (CJEU, C-845/19 and C-863/19).

The European Commission's analysis suggests that there are varying standards of evidence in the Member States. Thus, a degree of caution is necessary when comparing the formulations of the various national standards as there are different domestic interpretations. In Latvia and Lithuania, for example, the courts must reasonably believe that the property is derived from illicit activity. In Estonia, the court can presume that the assets are derived from illegal activities. In other Member States, the courts can: act when it would "be reasonable to assume"; "consider"; or "decide, based on well-founded objective evidence." Moreover, there must be "serious and concrete indications," and they can consider it "clearly more likely that it constitutes proceeds from a criminal activity than that not being the case" or "be convinced" that the property is derived from criminal conduct (Report, COM (2020) 217 final).

Thus, the new hybrid approach to the standard of proof (with some elements of civil proceedings) has become mandatory at the EU level in the form of extended confiscation in criminal proceedings (Bikelis 2022, p.56). However, the proposed EU regulation goes even further in terms of the standard of proof:

> The 2022 Proposal allows observing reduced evidentiary requirements and loosening of the link between the offence and eligible proceeds: in the 2005 Framework Decision, a court, when deciding on the confiscation of property other than instrumentalities or proceeds of criminal offences, should be fully convinced, in the 2014 Confiscation Directive – simply satisfied, that the property in question derived from (specified or similar) criminal activities of a convicted party during the period prior to their conviction (but not prior to the proven criminal offence) or that property, which value was disproportionate to the convicted party's lawful income, derived from criminal activity. Confiscation was also possible with regard to property acquired by the closest relations of the person concerned or transferred to a legal person in respect of which the person concerned had a controlling influence or received a significant part of this income. Currently, linking these assets to criminal activity is largely within the court's discretion (Hryniewicz-Lach 2023, pp.246–247).

Despite the favorable supranational legal framework and the attitudes of supranational courts toward a lower standard of proof in criminal proceedings, there have been recent constitutional disputes between countries regarding the non-application of the standard of proof guaranteed by the presumption of innocence in NCB confiscation (mostly cases of extended confiscation). An analysis of constitutional cases shows that they usually deal with the question of whether the right to property can be restricted on the basis of the presumption of the illegality of assets. The Constitutional Court of the Republic of Lithuania has analyzed the jurisprudence of some foreign constitutional courts and has concluded that the extended confiscation of property, in spite of the different constitutional provisions of foreign countries and the peculiarities of the legal regulation of the extended confiscation of property, is generally recognized as being in line with the constitutional provisions on the protection of property rights and the presumption of innocence principle. The extended confiscation of property is considered constitutionally justified, taking into account, firstly, the purpose of such confiscation and, secondly, the subjects of the burden of proving that the property has been acquired unlawfully (or by criminal means) and the distribution of the burden of proof between them (Ruling of the Constitutional Court of Republic of Lithuania of October 12, 2023).

The Romanian Constitutional Court has ruled that extended confiscation of assets is not contrary to Article 44(8) of the Romanian Constitution, which presumes the legality of the acquisition of assets. The Romanian Constitutional

Court stated, *inter alia*, that if the presumption of the lawful acquisition of property were absolute, then the judicial authorities would be subject to a legal requirement to find impossible evidence (*probatio diabolica*). At the same time, it noted that the presumption of the lawful acquisition of property is rebuttable, the burden of proof is not reversed and the principle of *actori incumbit probatio (onus probandi)* remains applicable in its entirety (Ruling of the Constitutional Court of Republic of Romania of June 25, 2014, as cited in Ruling of the Constitutional Court of the Republic of Lithuania of October 12, 2023, § 13).

The Constitutional Tribunal of the Portuguese Republic has held that the special confiscation provision, which, *inter alia*, presumes that the difference between the assets held by the convicted person and the assets that could have been acquired by legitimate means is the proceeds of crime, is not contrary to the Constitution. The Constitutional Tribunal has held that this presumption is without prejudice to the presumption of innocence, since the accused remains able to rebut it (Ruling of the Constitutional Tribunal of the Portuguese Republic of February 11, 2015, as cited in Ruling of the Constitutional Court of the Republic of Lithuania of October 12, 2023, § 14).

The Constitutional Court of the Republic of Bulgaria held that confiscation would also be applicable without a conviction for a criminal offense, "where the evidence shows explicitly that certain assets are of unlawful origin, but is at the same time insufficient for a conviction for an offence proven beyond reasonable doubt […]" (Ruling of the Constitutional Court of Republic of Bulgaria of October 13, 2012, as cited in *Yordanov and others v. Bulgaria* 2023, § 34).

The Constitutional Court of the Republic of Lithuania, also referring to the case law of the Supreme Court of Lithuania, has stated that such a legal regulation – according to which, in order to deny the origin of illegally (unlawfully) acquired property a person has to provide evidence confirming this fact – is constitutionally justified (Ruling of the Constitutional Court of the Republic of Lithuania of October 12, 2023).

Despite the change in the standard of proof, the courts remain obliged to give reasons as to why property in the case of NCB confiscation within criminal proceedings fulfils the characteristics of the property to be confiscated: "it is essential, that the domestic courts provided some particulars as to the offences, criminal, or administrative, in which the assets subject to forfeiture were alleged to have originated, and showed in a reasoned manner that there could be a link between such offences and the assets in question" (*Yordanov and others v. Bulgaria* 2023, §§ 123–124). The detailed reasoning of this judgment also relates to the fact that the national courts have to give adequate and sufficient reasons when rejecting a person's claim that they had received lawful income from various sources.

In cases where the national courts failed to discuss any criminal activity or an administrative offense which could have been the source of the assets subject to the forfeiture claim, or to establish a link between those assets and any such activity, it can be concluded that the interference with the person's possessions was not shown to be proportionate to any legitimate aim that the interference might have pursued. Thus, notwithstanding the lower standard of proof, property cannot be confiscated as unlawfully acquired only because the person has failed to prove any lawful income to justify their acquisition (*Yordanov and others v. Bulgaria* 2023, §§ 123–124).

According to the case law of the Supreme Court of Lithuania, the extended confiscation of property applies if convincing data has been collected which suggests that the property was obtained by criminal means (but not from other illegal acts or unidentified sources). In addition, it is not sufficient to establish the fact that the person did not have sufficient legal income to acquire the property, but it is necessary to establish and substantiate with convincing data that the funds were obtained in a criminal manner (Judgment of the Supreme Court in criminal case No. 2K-245-1073/2018). Moreover, data that would substantiate the criminal origin of the funds could include data on the continuity of the crime, its duration and nature, the nature of the property benefit derived from it, its adequacy to the property held by the perpetrator, the convict's repeated or long-term contacts with the perpetrators, etc. (Judgment of the Supreme Court in criminal cases Nos. 2K-245-1073/2018; 2K-295-222/2019).

Another prerequisite for the confiscation of extended property is the inability of the perpetrator to justify the legality of the acquisition of the property in their possession. According to the case law of national courts, the transfer of the burden of proving that the property has been legally acquired complies with constitutional and international standards. It is interesting to note that the Supreme Court of Lithuania also sees this transfer as a kind of procedural safeguard, observing that: "this gives the offender the opportunity to substantiate the legality of the property. Such a safeguard is necessary for persons who acquired property with essentially legal income, but these were not properly accounted for due to personal fault or other reasons (e.g., persons who received unaccounted wages, did business without a business license, etc.)" (Judgment of the Supreme Court in criminal case No 2K-245-1073/2018). However, it must be noted that the lawfulness of the source of income is not an easy matter to prove, and depends heavily on case law. For example, the domestic courts' refusal to accept witness testimony alone as proof of certain transactions increases the burden on the applicants in a situation where they had already been faced with the task of establishing their financial situation many years in the past (*Todorov and others v. Bulgaria* 2021, § 208). Evidence of the legality of the property must therefore be scrutinized in court.

Finally, where confiscation was imposed independently of a criminal charge against third parties, the authorities may apply confiscation measures not only to persons directly accused of offenses, but also to their family members and other close relatives who were presumed to possess and manage the ill-gotten property informally on behalf of the suspected offenders, or who otherwise lacked the necessary *bona fide* status (*Silickienė v. Lithuania* 2012, § 65). Such a procedure is also treated as a civil procedure, with all corresponding requirements: "in cases involving confiscation of property from applicants in the framework of criminal proceedings against third parties Article 6 § 1 of the Convention is applicable under its civil head" (*Telbis and Viziteu v. Romania* 2018).

As regards the balance between that aim and the third person's fundamental rights, where possessions are confiscated, the fair balance depends on many factors, including the owner's behavior – in particular, their degree of fault or care or, at least, the relationship between their conduct and the offenses which were committed (*Silickienė v. Lithuania* 2012, § 66; *Telbis and Viziteu v. Romania 2018*). Accordingly, the domestic procedure shall afford these persons an adequate opportunity to put their case to the courts, pleading, as the case might be, that the measure was illegal or arbitrary and that the courts had acted unreasonably (*Telbis and Viziteu v. Romania* 2018, §§ 50–51). Persons whose property is confiscated should be formally granted the status of parties to the proceedings in which the confiscation is ordered (*Silickienė v. Lithuania* 2012).

Article 6 of Directive requires Member States to enable the confiscation of the proceeds of crime transferred to, or directly acquired by, the third party from a suspected or accused person. According to Article 6 of the Directive, third party confiscation should at least be enabled in cases where the third party knew or ought to have known that the purpose of the transfer or acquisition of the property was to avoid confiscation. The requirement that the third person "knew or ought to have known [...] that the purpose of the transfer or acquisition was to avoid confiscation" has been reflected in the transposing legislation in most Member States (including Lithuania, Estonia, and Latvia).

Article 6 of the Directive refers only to the confiscation of "proceeds, directly or indirectly transferred to or acquired by a third party." Nevertheless, the transposing legislation in some Member States (including Lithuania, Estonia, and Latvia) also enables the confiscation of instrumentalities transferred to or acquired by the third party.

Article 6(2) of the Directive provides that the rights of *bona fide* third parties should not be prejudiced. According to the case law of the CJEU, it is necessary to provide for specific safeguards and judicial remedies in order to guarantee the preservation of the fundamental rights of the third parties who are not being prosecuted: "a national law which permits the confiscation [...] from the third party acting in good faith, is contrary to EU law. [...] a national law which permits the confiscation, in the context of criminal proceedings, of property belonging to a person other than the person who committed the criminal offense, without the former being afforded an effective remedy, is contrary to EU law" (CJEU, C-393/19). The Advocate General has rightly pointed out that the right of third parties to an effective remedy in proceedings for NCB confiscation cannot be lower than that guaranteed by the ECHR (e.g., *Silickienė v. Lithuania* 2012, §§ 47–50; *Veits v. Estonia* 2015, §§ 57–60; *Bokova v. Russia* 2019, §§ 55–59). Thus, the national authorities have *de facto* to afford third parties a reasonable and sufficient opportunity to protect their interests adequately (Opinion of Advocate General Pikamäe, March 24, 2021, joined cases C-845/19 and C-863/19).

Nevertheless, the evidentiary process for third-party confiscation is in practice even more complicated, and is therefore not as common as extended confiscation. In such a case, the arguments for the possible violation of the presumption of innocence against them are even more difficult to rebut. The grounds for a judgment confiscating property from a person who has not been charged with any criminal offense at all must not give the impression that the person has committed an offense.

Interim Findings

The recovery of illegally obtained property within the framework of criminal proceedings, without being linked to a criminal conviction, is based on the origin of such property, which makes the seizure of such property a civil measure rather than a punishment (a criminal measure). Nevertheless, non-conviction forfeiture as a restriction on the right to property must meet all the general requirements for such restriction.

The presumption of innocence, including the allocation of the burden of proof, which determines the proof of a person's guilt and of a conviction-based confiscation in a criminal proceeding (beyond a reasonable doubt), may not apply in a proceeding to prove an NCB confiscation. An analysis of EU law and both ECtHR and constitutional jurisprudence leads to the conclusion that the "follow-the-money" approach allows for the seizure of assets not only in the absence of a criminal conviction, but also by applying the civil standard of proof – the principle of the balance of probabilities and the rebuttable presumption of the illegality of the asset.

The grounds for extended confiscation, despite the fact that the latter is normally applied in criminal proceedings against a convicted person, may not be assessed according to the standard of proof of a criminal charge. This means that the guilt of a person will be proved according to the presumption of innocence, while the grounds for extended confiscation will be proved according to the principle of the balance of probabilities.

NCB confiscation from a third party in criminal proceedings requires not only an effective remedy for the rights of the third party, but also a particularly careful reasoning of NCB confiscation, as the final act (conviction) cannot contain statements that violate the presumption of innocence of the third party, who has not been criminally charged.

In view of the difficulty involved in a person rebutting the presumption of the illegality of assets, in particular if the national legislation provides for a wide range of NCB confiscation possibilities, courts have the duty to:

apply the principle of proportionality, both when deciding on the legitimate aim of NCB confiscation and on the scope of such confiscation;

apply the rule of evidence for NCB confiscation, according to which a person's mere inability to prove that the property was acquired by lawful means is not sufficient for the application of NCB confiscation.

References

Alagna, F., 2015. Non-Conviction-Based Confiscation: Why the EU Directive is a Missed Opportunity. *European Journal on Criminal Policy and Research*, 21 (4), 447–462.

Analysis of non-conviction-based confiscation measures in the European Union. Commission Staff working document, Brussels, 12.4.2019. (SWD(2019)1050 final). [online]. Available from: https://db.eurocrim.org/db/en/doc/3205.pdf

Bernardi, A. 2019. Presentation. In: A. Bernardi, ed. *Improving Confiscation Procedures in the European Union. Final publication of the research project "Improving Cooperation between EU Member States in confiscation procedures"*, VII–XXXIII. [online]. Available from: http://www.europeanrights.eu/public/commenti/BRONZINI7-Final-Book.pdf

Bikelis, S., 2022. Label v. Content: The Problem of Non-Recognition of Civil Confiscation Orders in Europe. *Baltic Journal of Law and Politics*, 15 (1), 54–70.

Bikelis, S., and Mikšys, S., 2018. *Civilinio turto konfiskavimo perspektyvos Lietuvoje*. Vilnius: Lietuvos teisės institutas. [online]. Available from: https://teise.org/wp-content/uploads/2023/01/Konfiskavimas-1.pdf

Boucht, J., 2017. Extended Confiscation: Criminal Assets or Criminal Owners? In: K. Ligeti, and M. Simonato, (eds.), *Chasing Criminal Money: Challenges and Perspectives on Asset Recovery in the EU*. Oxford: Hart Publishing.

Boucht, J., 2019. Asset confiscation in Europe – Past, Present, and Future Challenges. *Journal of Financial Crime*, 26, 526–548.

Bullock, K., 2014. Criminal Benefit, The Confiscation Order and the Post-Conviction Confiscation Regime. *Crime, Law and Social Change*, 62 (1), 45–64.

Cassella, S. D., 2019. Nature and Basic Problems of Non-Conviction-Based Confiscation in the United States. *Veredas do Direito*, 16 (34), 41–66.

CJEU, C-845/19 and C-863/19. ECLI:EU:C:2021:864

Country reports. Extended confiscation and its justification in light of fundamental rights and general principles of EU law. Reference number of the project: 2020/39/D/HS5/01114. [online]. Available from: https://konfiskata.web.amu.edu.pl/en/documents/

Directive 2014/42/EU of the European Parliament and of the Council of 3 April 2014 on the freezing and confiscation of instrumentalities and proceeds of crime in the European Union. OJ L 127, 29.4.2014, p. 39–50. [online]. Available from: http://data.europa.eu/eli/dir/2014/42/oj

ECtHR, *Arcuri v. Italy* (dec.), application no. 52024/99, 5 July 2001. ECLI:CE:ECHR:2001:0705DEC005202499. [online]. Available from: https://hudoc.echr.coe.int/?i=001-22586

ECtHR, *Balsamo v. San Marino*, applications nos. 20319/17 and 21414/17, 8 October 2019. ECLI:CE:ECHR:2019:1008JUD002031917. [online]. Available from: https://hudoc.echr.coe.int/?i=001-196421

ECtHR, *Beyeler v. Italy* [GC], application no. 33202/96, 28 May 2002. ECLI:CE:ECHR:2002:0528JUD003320296. [online]. Available from: https://hudoc.echr.coe.int/?i=001-60485

ECtHR, *Butler* v. *the United Kingdom*, application no. 41661/98, 27 June 2002. ECLI:CE:ECHR:2002:0627DEC004166198. [online]. Available from: https://hudoc.echr.coe.int/?i=001-22577

ECtHR, *Geerings v. the Netherlands*, application no. 30810/03, 1 March 2007. ECLI:CE:ECHR:2007:0301JUD003081003. [online]. Available from: https://hudoc.echr.coe.int/?i=001-79657 .

ECtHR, *Gogitidze and others v. Georgia*, application no. 36862/05, 12 May 2015. ECLI:CE:ECHR:2015:0512JUD003686205. [online]. Available from: https://hudoc.echr.coe.int/?i=001-154398

ECtHR, *Grayson and Barnham v. the United Kingdom*, applications nos. 19955/05 and 15085/06, 23 September 2008. ECLI:CE:ECHR:2008:0923JUD001995505. [online]. Available from: https://hudoc.echr.coe.int/?i=001-88541

ECtHR, *Immobiliare Saffi v. Italy* [GC], application no. 22774, 18 May 1998. ECLI:CE:ECHR:1998:0518DEC002277493. [online]. Available from: https://hudoc.echr.coe.int/?i=001-4240

ECtHR, *Yordanov and others v. Bulgaria*, applications nos. 265/17, 26473/18, 26 September 2023. ECLI:CE:ECHR:2023:0926JUD000026517. [online]. Available from: https://hudoc.echr.coe.int/?i=001-216617

ECtHR, *Krumpholz v. Austria*, application no. 13201/05, 18 March 2010. ECLI:CE:ECHR:2010:0318JUD001320105. [online]. Available from: https://hudoc.echr.coe.int/?i=001-97815

ECtHR, *Phillips v. the United Kingdom*, application no. 41087/98, 5 July 2001. ECLI:CE:ECHR:2001:0705JUD004108798. [online]. Available from: https://hudoc.echr.coe.int/?i=001-59558

ECtHR, *Salabiaku v. France*, application no. 10519/83, 7 October 1988. ECLI:CE:ECHR:1988:1007JUD001051983. [online]. Available from: https://hudoc.echr.coe.int/?i=001-76797

ECtHR, *Silickienė v. Lithuania*, application no. 20496/02, 10 April 2012. ECLI:CE:ECHR:2012:0410JUD002049602. [online]. Available from: https://hudoc.echr.coe.int/?i=001-110261

ECtHR, *Sofia v. San Marino* (dec.), application no. 38977/15, 2 May 2017. ECLI:CE:ECHR:2017:0502DEC003897715. [online]. Available from: https://hudoc.echr.coe.int/?i=001-174216

ECtHR, *Telbis and Viziteu v. Romania*, application no. 47911/15, 26 June 2018. ECLI:CE:ECHR:2018:0626JUD004791115. [online]. Available from: https://hudoc.echr.coe.int/?i=001-184058

ECtHR, *Todorov and Others v. Bulgaria*, applications nos. 50705/11 *and 6 others*, 13 July 2021. ECLI:CE:ECHR:2021:0713JUD00507051. [online]. Available from: https://hudoc.echr.coe.int/?i=001-211018

ECtHR, *Van Offeren v. the Netherlands* (dec.), application no. 19581/04, 5 July 2005. ECLI:CE:ECHR:2005:075DEC001958104. [online]. Available from: https://hudoc.echr.coe.int/?i=001-70070

European Court of Human Rights, 2020. Guide on Article 1 of Protocol No. 1 to the European Convention on Human Rights. Protection of property. Updated on 31 August 2020 [online]. Available from: https://rm.coe.int/guide-art-1-protocol-1-eng/1680a20cdc

Greenberg, T. S., Samuel, L. M., Grant, W., and Gray, L., 2009. *Stolen Asset Recovery: A Good Practices Guide for Non-conviction-based Asset Forfeiture.* Washington: The International Bank for Reconstruction and Development.

Hendry, J., and King, C., 2015. How Far Is Too Far – Theorising Non-Conviction-Based Asset Forfeiture. *International Journal of Law in Context*, 11 (4), 398–411.

Hryniewicz-Lach, E., 2023. Expanding Confiscation and its Dimensions in EU Criminal Law. *European Journal of Crime, Criminal Law and Criminal Justice*, 31, 243–267.

Jackson, J. D., & Summers, S. J., 2012. *The Internationalisation of Criminal Evidence: Beyond the Common Law and Civil Law Traditions*. Cambridge University Press. [online]. Available from: https://doi.org/10.1017/CBO9781139093606

Judgment of the Supreme Court of Lithuania in Criminal Case No. 2K-7-130-699/2015.

Judgment of the Supreme Court of Lithuania in Criminal Case No. 2K-233-895/2019.

Judgment of the Supreme Court of Lithuania in Criminal Case No. 2K-39-495/2020.

Judgment of the Supreme Court of Lithuania in Criminal Case No. 2K-80-222/2020.

Judgment of the Supreme Court of Lithuania in Criminal Case No. 2K-288-788/2020.

Judgment of the Supreme Court of Lithuania in Criminal Case No. 2K-7-83/2010.

Judgment of the Supreme Court of Lithuania in Criminal Case No. 2K-245-1073/2018.

Judgment of the Supreme Court of Lithuania in Criminal Case No. 2K-295-222/2019.

Milone, S., 2017. On the Borders of Criminal Law. A Tentative Assessment of Italian Non-Conviction-Based Extended Confiscation. *New Journal of European Criminal Law*, 8 (2), 150–170.

Opinion of Advocate General Pikamäe, 24 March 2021, joined Cases C-845/19 and C-863/19. ECLI:EU:C:2021:229.

Panzavolta, M. 2017. Confiscation and the Concept of Punishment: can there be a confiscation without the conviction. In: K. Ligeti, and M. Simonato, (eds.), *Chasing Criminal Money: Challenges and Perspectives on Asset Recovery in the EU*. Oxford: Hart Publishing.

Proposal for a Directive of the European Parliament and of the Council on asset recovery and confiscation. Brussels, 25.5.2022. COM/2022/245 final (2022/0167(COD)). [online]. Available from: https://eur-lex.europa.eu/legal-content/EN/TXT/?uri=CELEX%3A52022PC0245

Regulation (EU) 2018/1805 of the European Parliament and of the Council of 14 November 2018 on the mutual recognition of freezing orders and confiscation orders. OJ L 303, 28.11.2018, p. 1–38. [online]. Available from: http://data.europa.eu/eli/reg/2018/1805/oj

Report from the Commission to the European Parliament and the Council. Asset recovery and confiscation: Ensuring that crime does not pay. COM/2020/217 final. [online]. Available from: https://eur-lex.europa.eu/legal-content/EN/TXT/?uri=CELEX%3A52020DC0217

Ruling of the German Federal Constitutional Court of 10 February 2021, No. 2 BvL 8/19. [online]. Available from: https://www.bundesverfassungsgericht.de/SharedDocs/Entscheidungen/DE/2021/02/ls20210210_2bvl000819.html

Ruling of the Portuguese Constitutional Tribunal of 11 February 2015, No. 101/15. [online]. Available from: https://www.tribunalconstitucional.pt/tc/en/acordaos/20150101s.html

Ruling of the Italian Constitutional Court of 10 May 2019, No. 195 of 2019. [online]. Available from: https://www.cortecostituzionale.it/actionPronuncia.do

Ruling of the Constitutional Court of Republic of Romania of 25 June 2014, No. 356/2014. [online]. Available from https://www.scj.ro/1093/Detalii-jurisprudenta?customQuery%5B0%5D.Key=id&customQuery%5B0%5D.Value=118532#highlight=##%20%22drepturi%20de%20autor%22

Ruling of the Constitutional Court of the Republic of Lithuania of 12 October 2023 "Dėl Lietuvos Respublikos baudžiamojo kodekso 72^3 straipsnio (2010 m. gruodžio 2 d. redakcija) 1 dalies, 2 dalies 3 punkto atitikties Lietuvos Respublikos Konstitucijai [On the compliance of Article 72^3 (1) and (2)(3) of the Criminal Code of the Republic of Lithuania (of 2 December 2010) with the Constitution of the Republic of Lithuania]", No. KT86-A-N10/2023). [online]. Available from: https://lrkt.lt/lt/teismo-aktai/paieska/135/ta2908/content

Simonato, M., 2017. Confiscation and fundamental rights across criminal and non-criminal domains. *ERA Forum*, 18, 365–379. [online]. Available from: https://doi.org/10.1007/s12027-017-0485-0

Vervaelle, J. A. E., and De Zanger, W. S., 2019. Procedural Aspects of Confiscation. In: A. Bernardi, ed. *Improving Confiscation Procedures in the European Union. Final Publication of the Research Project "Improving Cooperation Between EU Member States in Confiscation Procedures"*, 513–534. [online]. Available from: http://www.europeanrights.eu/public/commenti/BRONZINI7-Final-Book.pdf

Rasa Žibaitė-Neliubšienė

Subjective Threats to the Free Evaluation of Evidence: Toward a More Coherent Legal Regulation

The Constitutional Court of the Republic of Lithuania (hereinafter also the Constitutional Court) has stated that one of the basic elements of the principle of a state under the rule of law, which is consolidated in the Constitution, is legal certainty and clarity, which presupposes certain mandatory requirements for legal regulation: it must be clear and coherent, and legal norms must be formulated precisely and not contain any ambiguities (Decisions of the Constitutional Court of May 30, 2003, January 26, 2004, December 24, 2008, and June 22 2009). As already mentioned in the introduction to this monograph, coherence itself emphasizes the need to follow not only a uniform approach to the law-making process, but also an integrated approach to the interpretation and application of law in order to ensure the predictability and stability of legal outcomes so that the law is fair to all interested parties, thus promoting public confidence in the effectiveness of the legal system (in this particular case, the courts). However, consistency is not a superior value, so it is sometimes better to have a system that is incoherent rather than a consistency that is fundamentally wrong (Sunstein *et al.* 2002, p.1203). The constitutional concept of justice implies not only a formal and nominal justice administered by the court – not only an outward appearance of justice – but also, most importantly, that such court decisions (other final court acts) must not be unjust in their content (Decision of the Constitutional Court of September 21, 2006).

Coherence is considered a minimum requirement of rationality (Sunstein *et al.* 2002, p.1203). However, it is well known that people are not actually completely rational (Jolls, Sunstein and Thaler 1998, p.14) – they are more accurately described as boundedly rational (Simon 1957, p.196–200). Thus, achieving consistency is an exceptionally difficult task for a person (including a judge). Nevertheless, consistency in law is an aspirational standard (goal), although a decentralized system itself (i.e., with many judges) may have particular difficulties in achieving this goal (Sunstein 1996, pp.50–52).

Evidence can perhaps be considered the fundamental element of criminal justice. This is because it is evidence that forms the basis for a court to adopt a final act which not only declares a person guilty or not guilty, but also has an educational effect, teaches respect for the law and obedience to it, and forms or strengthens the conviction of the inevitability of punishment. Thus, in this part of the monograph, which has been prepared on the basis of the author's dissertation research, the aim is to look at existing unforeseen threats to the legal regulation of the free evaluation of evidence with the aim of finding (or approaching) coherence between human nature and the letter of the law in force, in order to reach a fair and lawful judicial decision that does not create a false sense of certainty. After all, it is noted (albeit in the context of extraordinary law) that the judicial category itself is particularly dependent on a clear and predictable law-making process, since the requirement of consistency is directly linked with the category of coherence (for example, Trachtman 2011; Duic 2015).

After the French Revolution, the principle of free evaluation of evidence was perhaps enshrined in all criminal procedure laws of the countries of the Western European continental law tradition. This stipulates that "the court decides on the establishment or non-establishment of factual circumstances [...] on the basis of its internal conviction rather than on the basis of formal rules of evidence." The free evaluation of evidence guarantees an individual both internal freedom, without linking it to any formal requirements, and external freedom, by protecting against any external influence and pressure. This is in contrast to the formal evaluation of evidence, where the role and value of evidence are predetermined by the legislator, prohibiting any free evaluation (Pfeiffer 2005, p.9).

The shift from the formal theory of evidence to the free, independent evaluation of evidence had a multifaceted nature and, of course, caused obvious consequences: the legislator had to resolve a number of issues, including the rules of judicial examination associated with the formation of the judge's internal conviction.

When drafting the Code of Criminal Procedure of the Republic of Lithuania (hereinafter the Code of Criminal Procedure), the aim was to highlight the importance of the principle of free evaluation of evidence and to take into account the traditions of Western countries. Unfortunately, certain "non-Western" manifestations could not be avoided, and Article 20 of the Code of Criminal Procedure contained a definition of evidence – whereas the criminal procedure legislation of Western European countries does not provide for the concept of evidence. For example, Article 427(1) of the French Code of Criminal Procedure lays down that, unless the law provides otherwise, crimes may be established by any kind of evidence, and the court decides on the basis of its internal conviction. Similarly, the German Code of Criminal Procedure does not provide for a definition of evidence (Juozapavičius 2012, pp.40–43). Even in the doctrine of Western European countries with both continental and Anglo-Saxon legal traditions, it is difficult to find a definition of evidence in criminal proceedings (for example, Eisenberg 2006; Zuckerman and Roberts 2004). Perhaps the most obvious change in the

2003 Code of Criminal Procedure of the Republic of Lithuania caused by the introduction of the principle of the free evaluation of evidence was the abandonment of the statutory list of sources. This is because, as stated in the doctrine, there are no mandatory lists of sources in the codes of criminal procedure of the Western European countries, which follow the centuries-old tradition of the free evaluation of evidence (Kazlauskas and Kuconis 1998, pp.7–8). The court is not obliged to rely on any formal evidence and decides whether or not to rely on certain facts only in the light of the circumstances of the case and of the principle of free evaluation of evidence. Thus, it is obvious that the establishment of the principle of free evaluation of evidence was (and still is) a strong expression of trust in judges (Dallmeyer 2002, p.181).

The content of the principle of unfettered evaluation of evidence is defined differently throughout the Lithuanian legal literature. In the civil procedure, many authors agree that, under Article 185 of the Code of Civil Procedure of the Republic of Lithuania (hereinafter also the Code of Civil Procedure), the free evaluation of evidence is determined by the following two elements: the court evaluates the evidence on the basis of its own internal conviction, and no evidence has any predetermined power for the court.

Meanwhile, in the Lithuanian criminal procedural law doctrine and case law, when analyzing the content of the principle of free evaluation of evidence, two other elements are distinguished, noting that:

> the court bases its findings on evidence evaluated in accordance with the rules laid down in Article 20(5) of the Code of Criminal Procedure. The said Article provides that judges evaluate evidence according to their own internal conviction, based on a thorough and impartial examination of all the circumstances of the case, in accordance with the law. A necessary condition for the evaluation of evidence is that the internal conviction must be based on a thorough and impartial examination of all the circumstances of the case [...] and another condition for the evaluation of evidence is that evidence must be evaluated in accordance with the law. When evaluating the evidence from this point of view, it must first be determined whether the evidence meets the requirements provided for in Article 20 of the Code of Criminal procedure (Judgment of the Supreme Court of Lithuania of 27 March 2008 in Criminal Case No. 2K-163/2008).

Internal conviction as the basis of the free evaluation of evidence is a rather complex legal category, although it is claimed to be the main measure of evaluation. Moreover, it is also noted to be a fundamental problem of evaluation (Schmitt 1992, pp.79–85). There is no consensus in the doctrine as to what this measure is: differences of opinions are associated with a different approach to internal conviction, usually emphasizing a particular side of this multifaceted concept which covers various aspects, including legal, procedural, psychological, epistemological, moral, and ethical. Internal conviction itself, although it is a subjective category, must have an objective basis. This cannot be an arbitrary discretion, an unjustified impulse, because it is the law that obliges the court to examine carefully and thoroughly all of the circumstances of each case. A judge must always state what their convictions are, and the formation of convictions must be understandable and traceable (Schmitt 1992, pp.100–102). The only external form of the objectivity of the internal conviction is a reasoned court decision or ruling (Terebeiza 2007, p.81).

Thus, it needs to be assumed that the content of internal conviction is determined by objective and subjective factors that interact dynamically with each other and on which the outcome of the evaluation of evidence depends. The subjective aspect will be analyzed below.

The subjective aspect of internal conviction is perfectly illustrated by the structure set out in Chapter 353 of the French Code of Criminal Procedure: "The law does not require judges to report on the means by which they have reached their internal conviction, and the law does not lay down rules under which they are required to fully evaluate the completeness and sufficiency of evidence; The law obliges them to turn to themselves in silence and concentration, and to find with a clear/honest conscience the impression they think the evidence has left on them. The law raises only one question, which encompasses all their duties: are you inwardly convinced?" (Chapter 353 of the Code of Criminal Procedure Code of the Republic France) Next, the subjective aspect of internal conviction will be examined through the psychological prism. Modern legal doctrine (including psychology when analyzing judicial aspects) is under the ever-increasing influence of decision-making theories. The strengthening of the doctrine of legal realism seems to have an impact on this, as it is the legal doctrine of the Anglo-Saxon legal system which raises the following questions: "How does a judge make a decision?" and "How does a judge think?" (Posner 2010). On the contrary, in the legal doctrine of some Eastern European countries, internal conviction is more closely associated with such categories as morality, conscience and the like by noting that internal conviction as a moral, ethical category is also associated with conscience, and the latter manifests itself as a rational understanding of the moral significance of actions performed.

Manifestations of Intuitive Factors in the Process of Free Evaluation of Evidence

Traditionally, in terms of justice, the focus is on judges as neutral, rational decision-makers: the judiciary is "objective," and the prime task of the judge is to "apply" the rules (Higgins 1968, p.58). The doctrine states that judges, like most people, sincerely believe that they are making objective decisions and are open to new information, and can change their convictions when necessary. Unfortunately, studies have revealed a different picture.

Studies have shown that human decision-making, including judicial decision-making, is an activity involving two processes. Decision-making is based on one of the two different ways of processing information: 1) heuristic, also known as intuitive or experiential; and(2) step by step – logical (Tumonis 2012, p.130). Intuitive and logical systems are often perceived as conflicting. However, as Kahneman (2011, p.24) points out, these systems generally function relatively well together. The intuitive system is very effective – little effort is needed to achieve its maximum effect. Overall, the intuitive system performs its core functions very well, as initial reactions are usually very rapid. However, the intuitive system tends to produce cognitive errors in the form of systematic decision-making errors, and the intuitive system cannot be "disabled." This can be overcome by the logical system, but it gets tired easily. The logical system is a slow, rules-based and demanding system; however, the logical system is also not perfect: the validity of its decisions depends, among other factors, on legal training and reasoning skills. Moreover, fatigue and ego depletion limit decision-making (Tumonis 2012, pp.43–47).

Thus, studies conducted by psychologists (amongst other specialists) show that, in reality, judges use not only accurate, rational, and logical, but also intuitive decision-making methods when dealing with cases (Justickis, Valickas and Petkevičiūtė-Barysienė 2013). Psychologists do not deny that although judges are experienced, well-trained and motivated decision-makers, they are vulnerable to cognitive illusions (Hans and Vidmar 1986). Indeed, a further important aspect is that, in most cases, the application of these intuitive decision-making methods is not understood by the decision-makers themselves, but is instead unconscious. A person making such a decision generally understands the process as taking place spontaneously in a manner which is not clearly understandable to them; nevertheless, they make a decision which they are convinced is correct (Sowerby 2012, pp.5–12). It is interesting to note that it is argued that due to the lack of research in this area and its limited dissemination, even the most qualified judges acknowledge that they do not understand how they make decisions (Holmes 1897; Schaefer 1966, p.22).

When it comes to decision-making, there is a concept in psychology known as "bounded rationality" which implies that human cognitive abilities are not infinite, and therefore people make decisions that cannot be considered rational (Burns, 2016; Jolls, Sunstein and Thaler 1998, p.1477; Korobkin and Ulen 2000, p.1076). The reasons for making decisions involving bounded rationality include a wide range of factors, including difficulties in obtaining all the information necessary for rational decision-making, time constraints, and physical cognitive abilities (Burns 2016; Korobkin and Ulen 2000, pp.1075–1076). This is relevant in the context of the subject-matter under consideration because the specific nature of judges' work is characterized by the fact that they are not in a position to directly follow all developments in the case at hand. Theoretical legal thinking in the work of a judge is very closely linked to practical life insights. It is only on the basis of the particular facts of the case that the judge must imagine the possible versions of events and evaluate, on the basis of their internal conviction, the degree of probability of each of them (Justickis 2004, pp.270–320). It is the subjective nature of probability that determines that coherence/consistency or internal compatibility is the only valid criterion against which probabilities must be evaluated. Thus, a rational judge will seek coherence/compatibility and internal consistency. This should undoubtedly also be reflected in the grounds of the court's final act, where each of the arguments put forward in support of a particular decision is consistent with others and the specific legal decision is consistent with the fundamental principles of the particular legal system (Bertea 2005, p.372). In this way, "normative consistency" is created/maintained.

Confidence in the courts, their role in society, and an institutional sense of legality and justice are inseparable from the quality of the decisions made by judges. One of the factors of society's confidence in courts is: "*inter alia*, qualification of judges, their professionalism, ability to decide cases following not only the law, but also law, assurance of due process, respect for the persons participating in the process, rational legal argumentation (reasoning) of the final acts of the court, clarity of the final acts of the court to the persons participating in the case, etc." (Decision of the Constitutional Court of Republic of Lithuania of November 27, 2006). It is therefore essential to ensure that judicial discretion is not abused in a way that is fundamentally incompatible with the category of coherence.

Despite all of the dangers that exist, it must be borne in mind that subjective influence has its advantages and is even indispensable for a humane criminal process (Schmitt 1992, pp.427–430). Despite this, the law and the entire organization of the judicial process seek to avoid the subjectivity of the judge and to create all of the necessary conditions that would allow a judge to make objective, rational decisions free from intuitive (and therefore subjective) reasoning (Justickis, Valickas and Petkevičiūtė-Barysienė 2013). For example, the institute of removal in criminal proceedings must guarantee that, during the hearing of a case, the decision-making process cannot be influenced by participants in the proceedings who are interested in the outcome. The totality of the system of the provisions of the institute of removal determine the dual implementation of the principle of impartiality in criminal proceedings. Firstly, this principle is applied in the implementation of the right of the participants in the proceedings who are defending their legitimate substantive interests to apply for the removal of the relevant parties to the proceedings – in this case, the court (judge). Secondly, this principle is also applied in the law in respect of the respective parties, including the court (judge), which have the duty to remove themselves. Therefore, the purpose of the principle of impartiality, as stated in the doctrine, is not only to prevent the relevant parties interested in the outcome of the case from continuing to participate in the criminal proceedings, but also to predict *a priori* that such interest may arise sooner or later.

However, as Jerome Frank (1949, p.410) observed: when "all is said and done, we have to face the fact that judges are human." Therefore, it is very important to understand and recognize threats that are not visible at the declarative level and to strive for coherence (especially in the legal regulation) so that human nature does not interfere with the adoption of a fair and lawful decision.

As the doctrine bluntly states, heuristics means "decision-making short-cuts." There are many types of heuristics that can influence decision-making and risk assessment (Burns 2016). It is claimed that heuristics arise due to the fact that we have limited cognitive and motivational resources and that we need to use them efficiently to make everyday decisions. Although heuristics are highly adaptive and sometimes offer "good-enough" solutions to a problem (Peer and Gamliel 2013), they also facilitate forecasting and the performance of complex tasks – especially those related to the assessment of probabilities (Tversky and Kahneman 1974). However, in certain cases, reliance on a limited portion of the relevant information causes systemic and even predictable biases (Peer and Gamliel 2013) which interfere with correct choices and decision-making.

Next, several intuitive methods of decision-making (the heuristics of thinking) which are believed to have the greatest influence on the judge will be examined. As the judge is the decision-maker in the context of the free evaluation of evidence, these methods are directly related to the subjective element of the impartiality of the court.

Confirmation Bias

The doctrine draws attention to the fact that the greatest obstacle to solving problems is the desire to seek information that confirms our thoughts or preconceptions. Experiments have shown that people prefer information that confirms our thoughts rather than information that contradicts them (Myers 2008, pp.494–495); people tend to prefer information that is consistent with their prior beliefs. However, both information that corresponds to our opinions and that which does not can be incorrect. In both cases, new information may be insufficiently substantiated, incorrect, or distorted (Justickis, Valickas and Petkevičiūtė-Barysienė 2013). Therefore, new information should be verified. This is where confirmation bias comes into play, encouraging us to distrust information that does not match our opinion.

A classic example can be seen in the case of Rassin, Erland, and Kuijpers (2010). These scientists, when examining the evaluations made by judges and the cognitive factors influencing them, conducted a study which

> initially sought to form the judge's opinion on a particular issue, and then to determine its effect on the perception and evaluation of the information received later. In one of these studies, two groups of judges received a woman's murder case. It consisted of two parts: (a) the first part referred to the main suspect (the jealous husband of the murdered woman); (b) the second part referred to another possible murderer, namely, the first husband of the victim, who persecuted her all along, making various demands and threats. Later, the judges were also presented with 20 facts established in the case and were asked to evaluate the importance of each of them in making the final decision. The only difference between the groups of judges who participated in the study was the way the two parts of the aforementioned case were presented to them. The first group of judges was initially presented with only the first part of the case (which involved one suspect, in particular, the jealous husband), and this group evaluated the facts immediately afterwards. Later (after said evaluation of the facts) they were presented with new circumstances, the second part of the case, and were asked to reevaluate the same facts. The judges of the second group were immediately presented with both parts of the case (details about both the first and the other suspect) and were asked to evaluate the same facts. The results obtained revealed significant differences in the evaluation of the same facts by the first and the second groups of judges. It was established that the final evaluation of the facts by the first group of judges (when the participants in the study were presented with the second part of the case) compared to the first evaluation of the facts (when the participants in the study were presented with the first part of the case) changed insignificantly. This first evaluation of the facts proved to be decisive in forming the judges' opinion on the evidence presented. The evaluation of facts by the second group of judges, who were presented with both the first and second parts of the case at the same time (meaning that the evaluation of evidence was influenced by both parts of the case), was significantly different from the first group of judges (Justickis, Valickas and Petkevičiūtė-Barysienė 2013, p. 1496).

Thus, psychological studies have shown that this pattern is also reflected in the activities of judges. Like other people, judges tend to prefer information that is consistent with their previous beliefs. Specifically, judges might be biased in favor of evidence that confirms their prior hypotheses and might disregard evidence that does not correspond with their previous assumptions (Peer and Gamliel 2013). By "searching for," interpreting and evaluating information in this way, judges become cognitively biased.

In the context of the subject matter under consideration, a relevant problem that requires a wider analysis and is related to the possible formation of internal conviction (even before starting the examination and evaluation of evidence) is the requirement that obliges the chairperson of the court session to find out about the record of previous convictions of the person before beginning to examine the evidence of the criminal act. According to the doctrine, this obligation distorts the requirement of consistency of averment and legal assessment: the attention of the judge and the entire procedural audience (if any) is deliberately diverted from the main fact – i.e., the circumstances of the criminal act – and is focused on a secondary fact, i.e., the negative characteristics of the personality of the accused. This thereby reinforces the judge's internal conviction and forces the judge to psychologically position themselves against the accused (Merkevičius 2009).

Analogous debates arose a long time ago in the German criminal procedure law doctrine (Roxin 1995, pp.50–65; also, on reforms, see Henkel 1968, pp.100–120). These debates pointed out that the premature publication of unfavorable information about the accused person's personality may lead judges to form a preconceived opinion about their guilt, which is especially unacceptable considering the fact that a strong emphasis is still placed in Germany on the re-socialization of convicted persons by anticipating the further development/socialization of the convicted person's personality. Thus, in Germany, it was proposed to solve the problem by dividing the court process into two stages. In the first stage, the question of the guilt of the accused must be examined and a decision on the person's guilt must be made. In the second stage, when a positive decision is made on the guilt of the accused, all circumstances characterizing the personality of the accused are examined and the issue of the sentence imposed is resolved.

It is also worth noting that Lithuania (i.e., the Supreme Court of Lithuania) adheres to the practice that situations where a court examines a second case from the same person or examines the cases of accomplices are not considered to involve judicial bias. However, such situations also raise reasonable doubts as to the possible intuitive bias of judges.

Hindsight Bias

When people evaluate events or outcomes after they have occurred, they sometimes exhibit a hindsight bias when they judge the event as being more predictable than it was before it actually happened. This notion of "we knew it all along" or "it was clear from the beginning" has been shown to occur in many areas such as history, finance, and law, among others (Peer and Gamliel 2013).

This bias stems from the intuitive perception that the outcome that actually occurred should have been inevitable (Burns 2016; Guthrie 2007), and is particularly common in the evaluation of cases of negligence (Burns 2016) (in the context of criminal law, the most commonly considered issues are guilt by omission, criminal trust, or criminal negligence).

The most significant problem in this case is that the court is assessing outcomes, whereas the accused only had the opportunity to foresee them (LaBine and LaBine 1996). For example, in one study, judges were divided into two groups and their task was to evaluate the negligence of a psychiatrist toward his patient. Both groups received the same information about the physician's actions and the patient's behavior. The only difference was that the second group received additional information about the patient's extremely dangerous violent actions. The judges had to assess the likelihood of the patient's undesirable behavior and the degree of the psychiatrist's guilt for failing to detect and predict such actions. The group that was given additional information about the patient's highly dangerous actions rated both the likelihood of the patient's undesirable behavior and the psychiatrist's ability to predict this behavior much higher, and, accordingly, rated the physician's negligence more strictly (Justickis, Valickas and Petkevičiūtė-Barysienė 2013; Harley 2007).

A similar situation occurred when one radiologist was convicted for negligence because he failed to detect a tiny tumor in an early chest radiograph. The tumor grew larger and the patient died as a result. According to researchers, the decision to convict was made after another radiologist's testimony, which was given after the submission of all tests performed on the patient, suggested that the tumor could have been detected in the early radiograph. Clearly, the second radiologist had the benefit of knowing that the tumor was actually there, an advantage the first physician did not have at the time (Peer and Gamliel 2013).

Studies have shown that people overestimate their ability to predict and believe that others should have been able to predict events better than was possible. This happens because the learning outcome forces people to update their beliefs about the world. People then rely on these new beliefs to calculate what was predicted, and ignore the change in these beliefs (Guthrie, Rachlinski and Wistrich 2001, pp.801–807). It can therefore be said that the main result of this psychological phenomenon is the tendency of judges to overestimate the defendant's ability to foresee negative events and to correctly evaluate the probability of their occurrence during the trial (Justickis, Valickas and Petkevičiūtė-Barysienė 2013).

Although there is no consensus as to whether this should be considered a separate area of heuristics (i.e., a bias) or not, in the context of the subject matter under consideration it is important to mention the inability to ignore inadmissible evidence, or, in other words, the inability to not consider inadmissible evidence.

The susceptibility of judges to this bias, according to researchers, is worrisome because judges are often expected not to take into account information that is available to them before making their decisions. For example, judges are expected to ignore their knowledge of evidence that is presented in court but is deemed inadmissible because it was obtained illegally and is therefore not allowed (Peer and Gamliel 2013).

The European Union and international law do not contain any rules on the admissibility of evidence. However, the competence of the European Union to establish minimum standards for the admissibility of evidence, for example, could be derived from Article 82(2)(a) of the Treaty on the Functioning of the EU, which provides that "the European Parliament and the Council may, by means of directives adopted in accordance with the ordinary legislative procedure, lay down such minimum rules as are necessary to facilitate mutual recognition of judgments and judicial decisions and police and judicial cooperation in criminal matters having a cross-border dimension. Such rules shall take into account the differences between the legal traditions and systems of the Member States. They relate to: (a) the admissibility of evidence between Member States." In its case law, the European Court of Human Rights (ECtHR) also does not provide for any detailed rules regarding the recognition of illegally obtained evidence as being inadmissible, but the rules on the inadmissibility of evidence obtained by means of violence or provocation, which are laid down in the case law of the ECtHR, are of particular interest to the Member States of the European Union (*Gäfgen v. Germany*, 2010; *Ćwik v. Poland*, 2020; *Ramanauskas v. Lithuania*, 2008). However, in other cases, the ECtHR is guided by the concept of the fairness of proceedings as a whole, and does not lay down common standards regarding the evidence that needs to be regarded as being inadmissible (for example, *Ibrahim et al v. United Kingdom*, 2016) (Juozapavičius and Leonaitė 2021, pp.80–82).

It is therefore especially important to seek high-quality, coherent legal regulation which would cover not only the substantive aspects of the admissibility of evidence, but also the procedural aspects by specifying at which stage of the criminal proceedings and by which party the issue of admissibility of evidence is decided.

In this case, reference is made to a study by the Human Rights Monitoring Institute (HRMI Study Report 2021) which describes in considerable detail the procedures for the removal of unauthorized data in the Anglo-Saxon and continental countries. In summarizing these findings, it is appropriate to note the following:

> In the Anglo-Saxon jury trial model, the admissibility of evidence is decided by the judge using the *voir dire* procedure, i.e. during a special hearing held separately from the jury. If the judge decides that the exclusionary rule applies to the evidence, the evidence is considered inadmissible and cannot be presented to the jury by the parties to the proceedings during the trial. This means that only the evidence which has been recognised as being admissible (and which has not been removed by applying the rule of removal) is presented to the jury, whereas the evidence, which was not allowed by the judge to be presented by the parties to the proceedings, is not available to the jury and the jury is not even made aware of the fact of existence of such evidence [...] (HRMI Study Report 2021).

The procedure for deciding on the admissibility of evidence and the procedural legal consequences are both different in the countries belonging to the continental law tradition. In this respect, two main groups of states can be distinguished: 1) states in which the invalidation of inadmissible evidence is applied (French *nullité*), leading to its physical removal from the case; and 2) states in which the evaluation or use of inadmissible evidence is prohibited (German *Beweisverwertungsverbot*, Italian *inutilizzabilità*) (Juozapavičius and Leonaitė 2021, pp.82–84).

There is also a debate in the legal doctrine of the Lithuanian criminal procedure law on the necessity of establishing a procedure for the removal of inadmissible evidence, as inadmissible evidence is currently removed from the averment process by the same judge who adopts the final act. Lithuanian researchers do not talk about the creation of a separate institution for the resolution of the issue of the removal of unauthorized data. Instead, it is proposed to entrust such a function during the pre-trial investigation to the prosecutor and/or the pre-trial investigation judge (or to them both). This is also proposed when the grounds for the inadmissibility of the evidence collected during the pre-trial investigation become apparent later, when the case is already being heard in court, or when the court decides on the requests of the parties to the proceedings to submit new evidence (HRMI Study Report 2021). However, it is believed that this issue should be resolved after the completion of the pre-trial investigation by creating a new procedure in criminal proceedings at the stage of preparing the case for trial. It is also considered an advantage that this issue would be resolved by a judge of the same court (level) where the case will be heard. A certain concentration of responsibility and a specific duty to resolve only a specific issue (on the admissibility of evidence) would enable better work results to be achieved. Moreover, taking into account the problems arising both in the doctrine and in the case law, it is believed that the issue of compliance with (in)admissibility could be narrowed to the evaluation of evidence obtained by means of procedural coercion (or, more specifically, by secret procedural means of coercion).

The threat to impartiality posed by the inability to ignore inadmissible evidence arises even in cases where instructions have been given that certain information should be used only to establish credibility and not as evidence of guilt or innocence (or, in the case of juries, instructions by judges to disregard certain information) (Doob and Kirshenbaum 1972). Such a case is also provided for in the Lithuanian legal regulation. For example, Article 276(4) of the Code of Criminal Procedure lays down that "in order to examine the evidence available in the case, the statements given by the accused, the victim and the witness to the pre-trial investigation officer or the prosecutor can be read" taking into account the observations of a psychologist. It is clear from the data of this heuristic research that the goal of the "examination of the evidence in the case" is unlikely to be achieved, because such data will intuitively be used as evidence of guilt or innocence during the formation of internal convictions.

In summary, the wisdom over time bias is considered to be one of the most powerful cognitive illusions. As studies have shown, the ability of judges to disregard inadmissible evidence is questionable at best.

Availability Heuristic

The availability heuristic occurs when we base our decisions on information which is stored in our memory and is readily accessible (Myers 2008, p.498). Because a person usually makes decisions (judges) "on the basis of memory" (Burns 2016) – i.e., when the person does not have the data necessary to make a decision – the person tends to use previously acquired information that may be useful for that decision (Burns 2016; Hastie and Dawes 2010, p.89).

The effect of the availability heuristic in evaluating evidence is especially evident whenever the evidence under examination differs in its vividness and detail. The detail and clarity of the description of the event or fact makes one believe more in both its authenticity and significance (Fox and Birke 2002; Justickis, Valickas and Petkevičiūtė-Barysienė 2013). For example, numerous studies have provided descriptions of the same fact via different details. In one study, a first report only briefly mentioned that an injury had a negative impact on a victim's daily life, while a second report clearly and thoroughly described the limitations caused by the injury in performing work, managing a family farm, taking part in sports, communicating with children, travelling, etc. Although the effects of the same injury were described, in the case of the second report the same injury seemed much more severe to the participants in the study (Pohl, 2008, pp.363–378; Justickis, Valickas and Petkevičiūtė-Barysienė 2013). Thus, the clearer and more vividly an event is imagined, the more likely it is perceived to have occurred, although this does not mean that said fact is actually as it is described.

According to the doctrine, the availability heuristic can lead people astray because the availability of the event in one's memory does not indicate its availability in reality, since there are many factors that help restore the availability of information and allow information to "jump into memory" (Myers, 2008, p.498).

In light of the established principle of free evaluation of evidence, the legal regulation of averment is quite general and abstract in nature, with the exception of some procedures of pre-trial investigation described in detail. Thus, the letter of the law does not provide for evaluation rules (except in the case of (in)sufficiency). This is more common in the case law and legal doctrines where issues such as the detail of evidence, changes, etc., are more frequently analyzed and the rules of evaluation are discussed in detail.

It is therefore clear that intuitive methods of decision-making can be a source of various inaccuracies and errors, a hindrance to the uniform application of the law and case law, and a source of subjectivity on the part of the judge, while also stimulating the appearance of other unfair factors (Justickis, Valickas and Petkevičiūtė-Barysienė 2013, p.1503). This, in principle, hardly matches with the category of coherence, which is related not only to the uniformity of the interpretation and application of the law, but also to the predictability of legal (and specifically final) decisions and, accordingly, to the protection of legitimate expectations and legal certainty.

Possibilities to Minimize Biases

In addition to high professional qualifications, a judge is also required to be morally upright. However, the doctrine does not deny that judicial power, like any other power, can be abused. The judge must be aware that this power is intended solely for the proper exercise of the judicial function. The judge, having knowledge of the law and of the powers which it confers on them, must also understand the limitations which it imposes on them as a judge (Barak 2006, p.299). The judge must maintain a balance between the need for change and the need for stability, because stability without change is degeneration and change without stability is anarchy. The judge's function is to help bring together the needs of law and society and to prevent the legal system from degenerating or becoming anarchic. The judge must ensure stability in the face of change and change in the face of stability (Barak 2006, p.299). The aim is therefore to achieve a balance between these two categories.

Interestingly, intuitive thinking does not mean that the judge blindly rushes to make a decision. Intuition-based minds are often even superior, as the unconscious mind has more possibilities than the conscious because it has access to wider knowledge (Posner 2010, p.108, 113; Lewicki, Czyzewska and Hoffman 1987). Sometimes, conscious, coherent/consistent reasoning can even negatively affect the quality of decisions (Tumonis 2012, p.45; Wilson and Schooler 1991, p.181). On the one hand, it is not denied that intuitive decision-making methods facilitate the judge's work, allowing them to cope with obstacles such as lack of information, time pressure, etc. (for example, studies show that repetitive decisions exhaust individuals' executive function and mental resources (Vohs *et al.* 2008), and mental exhaustion increases the tendency to simplify decisions and accept the *status quo* (Danzigera, Levav, and Avnaim-Pessoa 2011, p.6992)). On the other hand, intuitive methods of decision-making can be a source of various inaccuracies and errors and a hindrance to ensuring the coherence of the application of the law and judicial practice, thus negatively affecting the quality of real decisions and the administration of justice (Pohl 2008; Justickis, Valickas and Petkevičiūtė-Barysienė 2013). Therefore, there is a need to determine what can be done to weaken the effect of these heuristics, thus potentially reducing the number of possible errors. Studies aimed at identifying ways in which to help decision-makers (in this particular case, judges) to understand and begin to control these decision-making methods are thus particularly relevant.

Levin (2016) observed that "ignorance is no blessing; a non-coherent system based on false assumptions and deficiencies is liable to make horrendous errors and cannot represent the interests of justice." Therefore, one possible option is to *inform (educate/train)* (Kelman, Rottenstreich and Tversky 1996) *judges about these factors, and to teach them to recognize these factors in their daily work.*

Unfortunately, the education and training of judges is not considered effective, as judges often continue to apply these decision-making methods even when they are aware of the threats they pose. This is because these decisions are made unconsciously and often spontaneously.

The second way that could help to reduce intuitive decision-making – and, as the doctrine notes, the only way to avoid cognitive factors – *is to limit the access of judges to certain information*. The legislator, in cooperation with courts and psychologists, could (and perhaps even should) adopt substantive and procedural norms and review the existing judicial (and non-judicial) procedures in order to reduce the harmful effects of cognitive factors on judicial decision-making. As already mentioned, this is also proposed (even with specific decisions) by participants in discussions on criminal procedure law.

Interim Findings

The category of coherence implies that a uniform approach to the interpretation and application of the law must be maintained and, accordingly, the predictability of legal decisions made by the courts must be ensured. A rational judge should seek coherence/consistency and internal compatibility in their decisions. Thus, studies conducted by psychologists (and other specialists) show that, in reality, judges use not only accurate, rational, and logical, but also intuitive decision-making methods when dealing with cases. Thus, inconsistency (through the prism of predictability) is a possible (or perhaps even inevitable) product of such a decision-making process.

It is important to seek coherence between human nature and legal regulation, i.e., to accept human imperfections and to try to optimize them by applying certain procedures or creating appropriate constructs. Forming certain general models of legislative regulation that help to ensure coherence in the evidence evaluation process is thus an institutional task. Therefore:

- the legislator, in cooperation with the courts and psychologists, should review the existing (and adopt new, if necessary) substantive and procedural norms and judicial (and non-judicial) procedures in order to reduce the harmful effects of cognitive factors on judicial decision-making.
- in the case of Lithuania, the following must be considered: 1) adjusting the procedure relating to the announcement of a person's record of previous convictions before the examination of evidence; and 2) introducing an additional procedure relating to the prior evaluation of inadmissible evidence.

References

Barak, A., 2006. Teisėjo vaidmuo demokratinėje valstybėje. *Konstitucinė jurisprudencija*, No. 1 (sausis–kovas), 291–305.

Bertea, S., 2005. The Arguments from Coherence: Analysis and Evaluation [online]. *Oxford Journal of Legal Studies*, 25 (3), 369–391. Available from: https://www.jstor.org/stable/3600675 [Accessed 27 June 2023].

Burns, K., 2016. Judges, "Common Sense" and Judicial Cognition. *Griffith Law Review*, 25 (3), 319–351.

Criminal Procedure Code of the French Republic [online]. Available from: https://legislationline.org/sites/default/files/documents/ca/France_CPC_am2006_en.pdf [Accessed 1 July 2023].

Dallmeyer, J., 2002. *Beweisführung im Strengbeweisverfahren: Die Beweisbefugnisse als Voraussetzungen der Wahrheitserforschung im Strafprozess*. Frankfurt am Main.

Danzigera, S., Levav, J., and Avnaim-Pessoa, L., 2011. Extraneous Factors in Judicial Decisions. *Proceedings of National Academy of Sciences (USA)*, 108 (17), 6889–6892.

Decision of the Constitutional Court (Lithuania) of 30 May 2003, Case No. 21/2003.

Decision of the Constitutional Court (Lithuania) of 26 January 2004, Case No. 44/03.

Decision of the Constitutional Court (Lithuania) of 21 September 2006, Case No. 24/05-04/06.

Decision of the Constitutional Court (Lithuania) of 27 November 2006, Case No. 10/04-12/04-18/04A.

Decision of Constitutional Court (Lithuania) of 24 December 2008, Case No. 09/06-30/06-01/07-30/08.

Decision of Constitutional Court (Lithuania) of 22 June 2009, Case No. 16/07-17/07-20/08.

Doob, A., and Kirshenbaum, H. M., 1972. Some Empirical Evidence on the Effect of s. 12 of the Canada Evidence Act upon an Accused. *Criminal Law Quarterly*, 15, 88–96.

Duic, D., 2015. The Concept of Coherence in EU Law [online]. *Zbornik Pravnog Fakulteta u Zagrebu*, 65, (3–4), 537–554. Available from: https://hrcak.srce.hr/clanak/219964 [Accessed 1 July 2023].

ECtHR, Ćwik v. Poland, application no. 31454/10, 5 November 2020 [online]. Available from: https://hudoc.echr.coe.int/fre#{%22itemid%22:[%22001-205536%22]} [Accessed 1 July 2023].

ECtHR, Gäfgen v. Germany, application no. 22978/05, 01 June 2010 [online]. Available from: https://hudoc.echr.coe.int/app/conversion/pdf/?library=ECHR&id=003-3151842-3499098&filename=003-3151842-3499098.pdf [Accessed 1 July 2023].

ECtHR, Ibrahim *et al.* v. United Kingdom, Applications nos. 50541/08, 50571/08, 50573/08 and 40351/09, 13 September 2016 [online]. Available from: [Accessed 1 July 2023].

ECtHR, Ramanauskas v. Lithuania, application no. 74420/01, 5 February 2008 [online]. Available from: https://hudoc.echr.coe.int/fre#{%22itemid%22:[%22002-2249%22]} [Accessed of 1 July 2023].

Eisenberg, U., 2006. *Beweisrecht der StPO: Spezialkommentar*. 5. Aufl. München.

Fox, C. R., and Birke, R., 2002. Forecasting trial outcomes: Lawyers assign higher probability to possibilities that are described in greater detail. *Law and Human Behavior*, 26 (2), 159–173.

Frank, J., 1949. Courts on Trial: Myth and Reality in American Justice. *Indiana Law Journal*, 25 (1), Article 13.

Guthrie, C., 2007. Misjudging. *Nevada Law Review*, 7 (2), 420–456.

Guthrie, C., Rachlinski, J. J., and Wistrich, A. J., 2001. Inside the Judicial Mind. *Cornell Law Review*, 86 (4), 777–830.

Hans, V. P., and Vidmar, N. 1986. *Judging the Jury*. New York: Springer.

Harley, E. M., 2007. Hindsight bias in legal decision making. *Social Cognition*, 25 (1), 48–63.

Hastie, R., and Dawes, R., 2010. *Rational Choice in an Uncertain World: The Psychology of Judgment and Decision Making*. 2nd edn. Sage Publications Inc.

Henkel, H., 1968. *Strafverfahrenrecht*, 2nd edn. Kohlhammer.

Higgins, R., 1968. Policy Considerations and the International Judicial Process. *International and Comparative Law Quarterly*, 17 (1), 58–84.

Holmes, O. W. Jr., 1897. The Path of the Law. *Harvard Law Review*, 10 (8), 457–478.

HRMI Study Report, 2021. *Gynybos teisės įrodinėjimo procese* [online]. Available from: http://hrmi.lt/tyrimo-ataskaita-gynybos-teises-irodinejimo-procese/?hilite=%27gynybos%27 [Accessed 10 July 2023].

Jolls, C., Sunstein, C., and Thaler, R., 1998. A Behavioral Approach to Law and Economics. *Stanford Law Review*, 50.

Judgment of the Supreme Court of Lithuania of 14 February 2006 in Criminal Case No. 2K-27/2006.

Judgment of the Supreme Court of Lithuania of 27 March 2008 in Criminal Case No. 2K-163/2008.

Juozapavičius, A., 2012. *Duomenų (įrodymų), gautų pažeidžiant teisę, naudojimo neleistinumas Lietuvos baudžiamajame procese*. Thesis (PhD). Vilnius University.

Juozapavičius, A., and Leonaitė, E., 2021. Procedūriniai įrodymų leistinumo aspektai baudžiamajame procese. *Teisė*, 121, 80–97.

Justickis, V., 2004. *Bendroji ir teisės psichologija*. Vilnius: Mykolo Romerio universitetas.

Justickis, V., Valickas, G., and Petkevičiūtė-Barysienė, D., 2013. Psichologiniai teisėjo priimamų sprendimų subjektyvumo veiksniai. *Jurisprudencija*, 20 (4), 1492–1509.

Kahneman, D., 2011. *Thinking, Fast and Slow*. New York: Farrar, Straus and Giroux.

Kazlauskas, M., and Kuconis, P., 1998. Nauja įrodymų samprata baudžiamojo proceso kodekso projekte. *Justitia*, No. 5.

Kelman, M., Rottenstreich, Y., and Tversky, T., 1996. Context-Dependence in Legal Decision Making. *The Journal of Legal Studies*, 25 (2), 287–318 [online]. Available at: https://www.jstor.org/stable/724508 [Accessed 10 July 2023].

Korobkin, R., and Ulen, T., 2000. Law and Behavioral Science: Removing the Rationality Assumption from Law and Economics. *California Law Review*, 88 (4), 1051–1144.

Labine, S. J., and Labine, G., 1996. Determinations of Negligence and the Hindsight Bias. *Law and Human Behavior*, 20 (5), 501–516.

Levin, B., 2016. Values and Assumptions in Criminal Adjudication. *Harvard Public Law Working Paper*, 16 [online]. Available from: https://ssrn.com/abstract=2794433 [Accessed 10 July 2023].

Lewicki, P., Czyzewska, M., and Hoffman, H., 1987. Unconscious Acquisition of Complex Procedural Knowledge. *Journal of Experimental Psychology: Learning, Memory and Cognition*, 13 (4), 523–530.

Merkevičius, R., 2009. Baudžiamojo proceso kodeksas: ar teisminio nagrinėjimo struktūra garantuoja teisingą teismą? In: Ancelis, P., *et al.*, *Sąžiningas baudžiamasis procesas: probleminiai aspektai*. Vilnius: Industrus, 135–174.

Myers, D. G., 2008. *Psichologija*.

Peer, E., and Gamliel, E., 2013. Heuristics and Biases in Judicial Decisions. *Court Review: The Journal of the American Judges Association*, 49, 114–118.

Pfeiffer, G., 2005. *Karlsruher Kommentar zur Strafprozessordnung und zum Gerichtsverfassungsgesetz*. 5. Aufl. München.

Pohl, R. F., 2008. *Cognitive Illusions: A Handbook on Fallacies and Biases in Thinking, Judgment and Memory*. New York: Psychology press.

Posner, R. A., 2010. *How Judges Think*. Harvard University Press.

Rassin, E., Eerland, A., and Kuijpers, I., 2010. Let's Find Evidence: An Analogue Study of Confirmation Bias in Criminal Investigations. *Journal of Investigative Psychology and Offender Profiling*, 7 (3), 231–246.

Roxin, C., 1995. *Strafverfahrenrecht*. Munchen.

Schaefer, W. V., 1966. Precedent and Policy. *Chicago Law Review*, 34 (1).

Schmitt, B., 1992. *Die richterliche Beweisswurdigung irn Straffprozess*. Lubeck.

Simon, H. A. 1957. Rationality and Administrative Decision Making. In: Simon, H. A., *Models of Man; Social and Rational*. Wiley, 196.

Sowerby, D. F., 2012. *Intuition and Dreams*. West Conshohocken. PA: Infinity Publishing.

Sunstein, C. R., 1996. *Legal Reasoning and Political Conflict*. Oxford University Press.

Sunstein, C. R., Kahneman, D., Schkade, D., and Ritov, I., 2002. Predictably Incoherent Judgments. *Stanford Law Review*, 54 (6), 1153–1215. https://doi.org/10.2307/1229618

Terebeiza, Ž., 2007. Laisvas įrodymų vertinimas civiliniame procese: teoriniai ir praktiniai aspektai. *Jurisprudencija*, 95 (5), 78–82.

Trachtman, J. P., 2011. Fragmentation, Coherence and Synergy in International Law. *Transnational Legal Theory*, 2 (4), 505–536. Available from: http://dx.doi.org/10.2139/ssrn.1908862 [Accessed of 17 June 2023].

Tumonis, V., 2012. *Judicial Decision-Making: Interdisciplinary Analysis with Special Reference to International Courts*. Thesis (PhD). Mykolas Romeris University.

Tversky, A., and Kahneman, D., 1974. Judgment under Uncertainty: Heuristics and Biases. *Science*, 185 (4157), 1124–1131.

Vilimoris, 2021. *Lithuanian Public Opinion poll* [online]. Available from: https://www.lrkt.lt/data/public/uploads/2021/05/visuomenes-nuomone-vilmorus-pasitikejimas-kt-2021-geguze.pdf [Accessed 10 July 2023].

Vohs, K. D., Baumeister, R. F., Schmeichel, B. J., Twenge, J. M., Nelson, N. M., and Tice, D. M., 2008. Making Choices Impairs Subsequent Self-control: A

Limited Resource Account of Decision Making, Self-regulation, and Active Initiative. *Journal of Personality and Social Psychology*, 94 (5), 883–898.

Wilson, T. D., and Schooler, J. W., 1991. Thinking Too Much: Introspection Can Reduce the Quality of Preferences and Decisions. *Journal of Personality and Social Psychology*, 60 (2), 181–192.

Zuckerman, A., and Roberts, P., 2004. *Criminal Evidence*. Oxford: Oxford University Press.

Sandra Kaija

The Trial of a Criminal Case in an Appellate Court Hearing

A Written or Oral Procedure in the Context of the Right to a Fair Trial

In modern parlance, the statement that human rights are the basis of a democratic state is used as an axiom. Among such rights is the right to a fair trial. The right to a fair trial is ensured not only in national laws, but also in many international and regional human rights documents.

The right to a fair trial is one of the most important fundamental human rights. The degree of development of these rights is largely considered a prerequisite for a person's ability to exercise or protect other rights defined in regulatory acts. When judging a case on its merits, directness, verbality, and openness (publicity) should be observed in the trial of a criminal case.

The publicity of hearings ensures the transparency of proceedings and thus provides an important safeguard for both the interest of the individual and of society at large. The requirement of a public hearing does not necessarily apply to all appellate proceedings, which may take place on the basis of written presentations, or to pre-trial decisions made by prosecutors and other public authorities (Human Rights Committee 2007).

Although the right to a fair trial is an issue that has been widely researched, the question of whether a criminal case should be tried orally during an appellate court sessions or whether a person's right to a fair trial is not limited when a written procedure applies became especially relevant during the COVID-19 pandemic, when a state of emergency was declared in many countries.

In order to clarify the provision of the right to a fair trial in the appellate court, this research examines a specific set of rights and their importance and essence – specifically, such regulatory acts as the European Convention on Human Rights (ECHR) of the Council of Europe (1950), the International Covenant on Civil and Political Rights (ICCPR) of the United Nations (1966), and the Charter of Fundamental Rights of the European Union (2012). The research also considers the limitations of the principle of openness when applied to the examination of a criminal case within a written procedure.

The Right to a Fair Trial and the Choice of Procedure

A fair trial, as a core value of a state governed by the rule of law, which characterizes every judicial process, is provided in sentence 1 of Article 6(1) of the ECHR, according to which everyone has the right to a fair and open trial conducted in a timely manner before an independent and impartial court provided for in the law when determining the validity of the accusation brought against them. In addition, Article 6 of the Convention states that anyone charged with a criminal offense shall be presumed innocent until proven guilty according to the law, and that everyone charged with a criminal offense shall have minimum rights, including: the provision of prompt information in a clear language on the charges against them, their nature and their reason; adequate time and means to prepare their defense, to defend themselves by themselves or with legal assistance of their own choice, or if there is a lack of funds for such legal assistance, to receive it for free if the interests of justice require it; to examine or have examined witnesses for the prosecution and to require the presence and examination of witnesses for the defense under the same conditions as witnesses for the prosecution; as well as the right to the services of an interpreter. The European Court of Human Rights (ECtHR) supervises the implementation of the Convention, which examines complaints from individuals and Member States regarding violations of the Convention. This, in turn, also affects the goals, modes, and forms of national law enforcement mechanisms, as they increasingly have to apply international human rights standards in their daily work.

According to sentence 2 of Article 14 of the ICCPR, everyone has the right to a fair and open hearing in a competent, independent, and impartial court established by law when determining the validity of a charge in a criminal case or rights and obligations in a civil case. Within the framework of the European Union, Article 47, part two, sentence 1 of the Charter of Fundamental Rights of the European Union stipulates that every person has the right to a fair, open and timely trial in an independent and objective court established by law.

The wording of the right to a fair trial is very similar in these documents, which is why it is relatively easy to compare them.

It is also important to point out that in accordance with section 3 of Articles 2 and 6 of the Treaty on the European Union (2012) (hereinafter – TFEU), the European Union (hereinafter – EU) was founded in compliance with the basic postulate that the Member States have common constitutional values, such as human dignity, freedom, democracy, equality, the rule of law, and respect for human rights. EU justice activities, especially in the case of criminal justice, fall under the so-called third pillar of the EU, which was established after the signing of the Maastricht Treaty in 1992. The third pillar of the EU is based on the mutual trust of the Member States, i.e., the belief that each Member State respects common values, grounds its national regulation in them and effectively protects basic human rights.

At the same time, with the EU constitutional reforms and following the signing of the Treaty of Lisbon, the EU has gained wider powers to align the criminal laws of the Member States. Article 82(2) of the TFEU provides rules that the EU legislator is entitled to adopt in order to promote the mutual recognition of court judgments and decisions, as well as police, and judicial cross-border cooperation in criminal matters. These rules also stipulate that the European Parliament and the Council, adopting directives in accordance with the ordinary legislative procedure, can determine the minimum rules on the mutual admissibility of evidence between Member States, on the rights of individuals in criminal proceedings, on the rights of victims of crime, and on any other special aspect of criminal proceedings which the Council has specified in advance with a specific decision. Having received the consent of the European Parliament, the Council adopts such a decision unanimously. The adoption of the minimum provisions referred to in this clause does not prevent Member States from maintaining or introducing a higher level of protection of personal rights.

Under EU law, secondary legislation precisely defines the scope of the right to a fair trial. For example, Directive 2012/13/EU on the right to information in criminal proceedings (2012) provides that Member States must inform suspects and accused persons of their rights, including the right to the assistance of a lawyer and the right to remain silent. According to the Directive, suspects and accused persons who are detained must also receive a notice of rights, which includes information on additional rights, including their right to access documents relating to the case held by the competent authorities, e.g., evidence, and the right to emergency medical assistance.

In the context of the current research question, the statement of preamble 41 of Directive (EU) 2016/343 of the European Parliament and of the Council on strengthening certain aspects of the presumption of innocence and the right to participate in the examination of the case in person in criminal proceedings (2016) should be emphasized. This statement provides that the right to be present at a trial can be exercised only if one or more hearings are held. This means that the right to be present at a trial cannot apply if the relevant national rules of procedure do not provide for a hearing. Such national rules should comply with the Charter and with the ECHR, as interpreted by the Court of Justice and by the ECtHR, in particular with regard to the right to a fair trial. This is the case, for example, if the proceedings are conducted in a simplified manner following, solely or in part, a written procedure or a procedure in which no hearing is provided for.

As for the principle of the right to a fair trial at the national level in the Republic of Latvia, it is defined in the first sentence of Article 92 of the Constitution of the Republic of Latvia (1922), according to which everyone can defend their rights and legal interests in a fair court. In the criminal procedural regulation, the principle of a fair trial is established in Article 15 of the Law on Criminal Procedure (2005), which stipulates that everyone has the right to a fair, objective and independent court hearing. The principle of directness and orality is established in Article 449 of the Law on Criminal Procedure, whereas that of openness is ensured in Article 550. Detailed conditions that allow a criminal case to be tried via a written procedure in the appellate court, depending on the subject under consideration, are determined in Section 4 of Article 559 of the Law on Criminal Procedure.

The Constitutional Court of the Republic of Latvia has repeatedly indicated that, under the influence of Article 89 of the Constitution, the first sentence of Article 92 of the Constitution can be specified in conjunction with Article 6 of the ECHR and the jurisprudence of the ECtHR (Constitutional Court Decision of June 14, 2018, clause 1). The Constitutional Court has also emphasized that the concept of a "fair court" includes two aspects – namely "fair court" as an independent judicial authority examining the case and "fair court" as a proper procedure conducted in accordance with the rule of law in which the case is examined. Thus, Article 92 of the Constitution obliges the state to establish a system of relevant judicial institutions and to adopt procedural norms according to which persons could effectively protect their rights and legal interests in a fair and objective court (Constitutional Court Decision of June 14, 2018, clause 12).

Furthermore, the understanding of human rights changes and develops with time. As indicated in the legal doctrine, the term used by the ECtHR regarding the ECHR could also be used as a "living instrument" that is interpreted in accordance with the spirit and requirements of the current times and is oriented toward legal knowledge contained in a modern and democratic legal system (Levits 2000, p.266). The dynamic translation of the right to a fair trial, the necessity of which is determined by the need to ensure the development of the law and compliance with the modern legal system, allows one to read the actual meaning and purpose of the right to a fair trial without amending the text of the relevant regulatory acts. This allows changes in society's life, the possibilities of available technologies and scientific achievements, and the legal thoughts of both Latvia and all democratic countries, which are contained in jurisprudence and the knowledge of legal science, to be taken into account. This, in turn, means that concepts used abstractly do not have to preserve ideas about them that existed at the time of their adoption in normative acts; instead, the content of these concepts can develop over time without changing the text itself.

The right to a fair trial also includes the right to an oral hearing. On the one hand, the consideration of a case via an oral process (court hearing) is related to the right of a person to be present at a court hearing and to express themselves personally about the circumstances of the case; on the other hand, it relates to the requirement to hear cases openly. The right to a fair trial also means that a person has the right to access a court. Namely, the fairness of the trial process does not matter if access to the trial process is not ensured.

Access to justice is an overarching principle of the right to a fair trial (Human Rights Committee 2007). Therefore, if an accused is denied access to justice, then it stands to reason that their right to a fair trial in itself has not been guaranteed (McEvoy 2023, p.143).

In a country governed by the rule of law, the right to be heard plays a vital role in the implementation of the right to a fair trial – that is, when promoting the full defense of rights and balancing the interests of the parties involved. The right to be heard is implemented in several ways – for example, as the right to receive complete information about the opinion expressed by the opposing party and the evidence and facts collected, and the right to expect the court to pass a decision containing arguments based on the opinions expressed by the parties. In addition, the right to be heard also includes the right of a person to speak about facts and legal issues (Constitutional Court Decision of February 10, 2017, Clause 33(1)). However, the Constitutional Court has also recognized that the implementation of these rights must be ensured at least in writing.

Furthermore, the right to be present at a court hearing is not absolute, and its implementation may vary depending on both the court instance and the nature of the process; specifically, direct and oral consideration of the case at a court hearing is not mandatory in all instances, and one of the most important criteria is whether the evidence and facts are evaluated at the court hearing. This means that the narrower the court's competence is in the specific case (for example, whether the court examines the case on its merits – which is traditionally done by the court of first instance and appeal – or only checks compliance with material and procedural norms, usually in the cassation instance), the wider restrictions on attendance are permissible.

The ECtHR has also recognized (*Sakhnovskiy v. Russia* 2010, paragraph 96) that an accused person should, in principle, be present in person at the hearing of the first instance court, but this requirement is no longer so strict at the appeal instance.

In addition to the classic possibility to try a case in a court session with all persons present in the courtroom, there is also the possibility to organize a court session via videoconference. The use of videoconferencing is determined by such legal acts as the Second Additional Protocol to the Council of Europe Convention on Mutual Assistance in Criminal Matters, Resolution of the EU Council of November 23, 1995, Act of the EU Council of May 29, 2000, etc. This demonstrates that the use of video conferencing does not in itself contradict the right to a fair trial.

The possibility of conducting procedural activities using technical means (video and audio conferences) by the initiator of the process, if required by the interests of the criminal process, is provided for in the first and second parts of Article 140 of the Law on Criminal Procedure in Latvia. At the same time, the same provisions stipulate that when conducting procedural activities using technical means, it must be ensured that the person in charge of the process and the persons participating in the procedural activity in different rooms or buildings hear each other during the audio conference, and hear and see each other during the videoconference. The ECtHR also recognized in *Sakhnovskiy vs. Russia* (2010, paragraph 98) that participation in court hearings using the option of video conferencing does not in itself contradict the concept of a fair and public trial, but it observed that a person must be guaranteed the capacity to follow the process and be heard without technical disturbances, and that the person must be guaranteed an environment in which to effectively and confidentially communicate with their lawyer.

Although the possibility of using video conferencing is not new, it gained special importance during the COVID-19 pandemic.

During the pandemic, countries closed courts and/or delayed some hearings to protect people's health and safety by reducing the possibility of COVID-19 transmission at in-person court hearings. Many countries turned to remote hearings, using online video or audio-conferencing technology and other similar tools alternatives to in-person hearings in the context of both pre-trial and trial proceedings (Fair Trials 2020).

In this case, the legitimate purpose of the videoconference was to ensure the epidemiological safety of society during the pandemic. However, according to the opinion of the ECtHR (*Sakhnovskiy v. Russia* 2010, paragraph 102), despite possible difficulties or limitations, the right to defense is prioritized to the degree that the right to effective legal assistance must be respected in all circumstances. In this case, the ECtHR also recognized that the accused person's right to communicate with their defense counsel without the risk of a third party eavesdropping is one of the basic conditions for a fair trial in a democratic society and derives from Sub-clause C of Article 6(3) of the ECHR. The court also recognized that if the defense attorney cannot speak to their client and receive confidential instructions from them without being overheard by others, then the assistance of the defense attorney loses much of its meaning, while the ECHR is meant to guarantee practically and effectively enforceable rights

International legal acts do not specify exactly how the right to communicate with a defender under conditions ensuring confidentiality is ensured, leaving this issue up to each country, but this right must be ensured effectively and not illusorily. As already mentioned, according to the ECtHR, legal assistance can also be provided via videoconference, but the state must take measures to ensure its effectiveness, which also includes confidentiality. For example, in *Marcello Viola v. Italy* (2006, paragraph 41), the accused was able to speak to his defense counsel in the videoconference via a phone line that was secured against any wiretapping attempt; the defense attorney of the accused could direct his assistant to the room in which the accused participated in the videoconference, or into a room in which he was able to communicate with his client personally while his assistant ensured the defense of the accused in the courtroom. Therefore, in this case, the ECtHR did not find a violation of the right to defense as an element of the right to a fair trial, as defined in Article 6 of the ECHR, as the applicants had the opportunity to effectively communicate with the defense counsel under conditions ensuring confidentiality.

Another important aspect that should be considered if a court session is held using technical means (video and audio conferences) is their quality; that is, there should not be such technical disturbances that significantly hinder the perception of a person, which could jeopardize the right to a fair trial. As indicated in the study of the Equality and Human Rights Commission, effective communication underlies the entire legal process by ensuring that everyone involved understands and is understood. Otherwise, the legal process will be impeded or derailed (Equality and Human Rights Commission 2020).

Evaluating this aspect, the ECtHR has recognized that the degree to which technical disturbances in videoconferencing are significant is related to the level of subjective perception of an individual. In the abovementioned case of *Marcello Viola v. Italy*, the ECtHR stated that there was a possibility that, for technical reasons, the transmission between the courtroom and the prison where the applicant was located might not have been perfect, thus complicating the perception of voice and images; however, neither the applicant nor his counsel had drawn the court's attention to these complications during the hearing, which is why the ECtHR did not consider the matter further. A similar opinion was expressed by the court in *Stanford v. the United Kingdom* (1994, paragraphs 27–30), where the applicant complained of poor acoustics in the courtroom. In this case, the ECtHR clearly stated that bad acoustics, without doubt, could lead to a violation of Article 6 of the ECHR; however, the court considered the acoustics level in the specific hall satisfactory, and neither the applicant nor his defenders informed the court about the applicant's hearing problems. The ECtHR also stated that the applicant's lawyers had no difficulty in understanding what was happening in the courtroom and that they had every opportunity to discuss with the applicant all matters related to the evidence.

The General Secretariat of the Council of the EU has prepared an informative material *Guide on Video Conferencing in Cross-border Proceedings* (2013), which describes quality requirements for video conferencing and technical equipment specifications. These recommendations can help to organize videoconferences without significant technical disturbances, thus avoiding the violation of the right to a fair trial.

However, it should be noted that even though the possibility of organizing a court session via video conferencing is indicated by both regulatory acts and jurisprudence, it is important to be aware that a case can be considered in a court session in such a mode only if it is required by the interests of the criminal process. Namely, the court must justify the use of such technical means for the attainment of the legitimate goal and in pertinence to the essence of this process, because, as previously mentioned, in a process in which facts are ascertained and evidence is verified, the presence of a person is a much stricter requirement.

The Possibilities of a Written Procedure in Criminal Proceedings in the Appellate Court

The ECtHR has recognized that an oral and open hearing is a fundamental principle contained in Article 6(1) and that this principle is particularly important in the criminal context, where it is usually necessary for the first instance to be a court that fully complies with the requirements of Article 6, and in which the applicant has the right to a hearing, including the opportunity to testify in their own defense, to hear the evidence against them and to ask questions of witnesses (*Talabér v. Hungar* 2009, paragraph 23).

The jurisprudence of the Constitutional Court has also recognized that the legislator has wide discretion to adopt procedural laws, to determine the categories of cases that are considered in relevant processes, and to decide on the procedure for examining cases of different categories (Constitutional Court Decision of March 15, 2018, clause 11(1)). Likewise, the ECtHR has indicated that the manner in which Article 6 of the Convention is applicable in the appellate court depends on the particularities of the particular process; in addition, the national court system as a whole and the role of the appellate court in it must be taken into account (*Hermi v. Italy* 2006).

When the written procedure is applied, the person is actually denied the opportunity to participate in the case hearing in person. However, as already mentioned, the right to an oral trial is not absolute.

Against the wishes of the applicant, the case may be examined in the appellate court via written procedure if, in the court's opinion, the type of the process does not affect the objective and fair adjudication of the case, i.e., if the circumstances of the case do not require the personal hearing of the applicant and the court can adjudicate the case after having become acquainted with the case materials and the opinion of the participants in the process in writing (*Döry v. Sweden* 2002, paragraph 37).

However, from the opinions of the ECtHR on cases that were examined in a written process, it follows that the mere fact that the legislator has provided for a written procedure for the consideration of certain categories of cases cannot in itself be considered a sufficient argument to reject a person's request to consider the case in an oral process (*Mtchedlishvili v. Georgia* 2021, paragraphs 33 and 39). This means that the cases specified in the regulatory acts do not deprive a person of the right to ask for their case to be considered in an oral process.

In Latvia, there are legally defined exemptions from the oral process in the appellate court, firstly in the Law on Criminal Procedure and secondly in the Law on the Management of the Spread of COVID-19 Infection (2020; hereinafter – COVID-19 Law). Part 1 of Article 12 of the COVID-19 Law also stipulates that a criminal case can be tried by appeal in a written process in cases that are not mentioned in the Law on Criminal Procedure. It follows from the summary of the draft of the law (Initial impact assessment 2020) that, taking into account the security measures established in the country, it is necessary to provide special regulation for certain issues in criminal proceedings in connection with the examination of criminal cases and related processes. The first part of the article envisages expanding the list of criminal cases to be considered in writing at the appeal instance. Although the fourth part of Article 559 of the Law on Criminal Procedure already provides for several circumstances in which a case can be reviewed via a written process in case of appeal, this list is too narrow and should be expanded, ensuring the smooth conduct of criminal proceedings and reducing health risks to case participants, judges, and court employees. In addition, a person has to justify their objections to the consideration of the case via a written process, while the judge has to evaluate them and choose the most suitable type of process, ensuring that the rights and interests of all parties are respected.

The norms of the COVID-19 Law allow a criminal case to be considered via a written process in the appellate court. Thus, a justified question arises as to whether the trial of a case in the appellate court during the period of validity of the first part of Article 12 of the COVID-19 Law is in itself a sufficient basis for the consideration of the case via a written process in accordance with the mentioned legal norm. This aspect was also assessed in one of the cases in the Supreme Court of the Republic of Latvia, or the Senate (Senate Decision of February 21, 2023, paragraph 6). The Senate recognized that the decision to examine the case within a written procedure in accordance with Part 1 of Article 12 of the COVID-19 Law is justified not by an opinion of the possibility to consider the case via a written process, but by an opinion that there are objective circumstances that determine the necessity of the application of the measure that is provided for in the legal provision. The limitation of the right to hearing the case via oral proceedings must be justified. The Senate also indicated that when applying Part 1 of Article 12 of the Law on COVID-19, the purpose of the law, defined in the first part of Article 1 of this law, should be considered, according to which the legal order must be set during the spread of the COVID-19 infection by providing for an appropriate set of measures that ensure public health and safety, and the scope of rights and obligations of private individuals must be commensurate with public health and safety interests as well as the effective functioning of state and local government institutions.

It clearly follows from the purpose defined in Part 1 of Article 1 of the COVID-19 Law that the possibility to examine a case in a written process established in Part 1 of Article 12 of this Law is a measure aimed at protecting the interests of public health and safety. It can also be concluded from the same article of the same law that that the abovementioned measure includes restrictions of the rights and obligations of private individuals which are proportionate to the interests of public health and safety. The general principles applied when determining the set of measures listed in the COVID-19 Law are outlined in Part 3 of Article 1 of this Law. They include the following: 1) minimization of the restriction of human rights – the rights of individuals are restricted only if there are no other alternative measures that effectively protect public health and safety; 2) mitigation of threats to public health – precautionary measures are determined by evaluating the threat of the spread of COVID-19 infection in Latvia and abroad, and are implemented by evaluating all existing risks in order to reduce the threat of the re-spread of COVID-19 infection; and 3) limitation of the availability of public and socially important services is permissible only to the extent that it is necessary to ensure public health and safety, as well as for the health and safety of persons involved in providing and receiving services.

Evaluating the purpose of the COVID-19 Law and the general principles applied when determining a set of necessary measures, it can be concluded that the existence of a legal situation in which the issue of the manner of handling a case is decided when the COVID-19 Law is applied is not in itself a sufficient basis for considering a case via a written process in accordance with Part 1 of Article 12 of this Law. The possibility to consider a case via a written process provided for in this legal norm is, firstly, an option and not an obligation; secondly, the possibility provided for in the legal norm was established with the aim of reducing risks to the health of case participants, judges, and court employees. Therefore, the existence of risks and alternative measures to reduce such risks must be evaluated – for example, by holding a case hearing as an oral process via video conferencing, if it is required by the interests of the criminal process.

Referring to the decision of the ECtHR in the case of *Andersson v. Sweden* (2010, paragraph 53), the Senate emphasized that the argumentation methodology used by the court is important in decision-making; that is, a justification for a written process is necessary as an exception to the basic principle, not as a reason for observing the basic principle or for considering a case via an oral process.

Considering the aspect of ensuring the right to a fair trial, another important question arises: the question of the form of trial in the appellate court in a situation where the case is tried via a written process in the court of first instance, referring to the COVID-19 Law, while the court of appeal is given the opportunity to review the case via a written process by the Law on Criminal Procedure. Namely, this is the question of whether it must be ensured that a person has their case heard via oral proceedings in at least one court instance, even in those cases where the Law on Criminal Procedure allows for written proceedings in the appellate court.

Part 4 of Article 559(3) of the Law on Criminal Procedure stipulates that a case can be tried via a written process if such a request is made in the appeal or protest claims only for the mitigation of the sentence and if the case was examined in the court of first instance without the examination of evidence and the sentence is not related to deprivation of freedom which is longer than five years.

Evaluating this legal issue, the Senate of the Republic of Latvia (Senate Decision of June 15, 2023, paragraph 5) drew attention to the fact that the cases provided for in Part 4 of Article 559 of the Law on Criminal Procedure are based on the provisions of the Law on Criminal Procedure. On the other hand, a case was examined in the court of first instance without examination of evidence in a written process in accordance with Part 1 of Article 12 of the Law on the Management of Spread of COVID-19 Infection; namely, a case was tried in a written process in a manner that is not mentioned in the Law on Criminal Procedure. The provision of the COVID-19 Law expands the range of cases provided for in the Law on Criminal Procedure, when the court can consider the case in the first instance via a written process. Thus, it is the duty of the court to evaluate the provisions of the Law on Criminal Procedure as a whole and in connection with other legal provisions in order to ensure a person's right to a fair trial.

According to Article 1 of the Law on Criminal Procedure, which formulates the purpose of this law, the criminal procedure must be such that it ensures the effective application of the norms of the Criminal Law and the fair settlement of criminal legal relations without unjustified interference in a person's life. Thus, compliance with the requirements of the criminal procedural form is a prerequisite for the implementation of the rights of the persons involved in the process, including the full implementation of the right to a fair trial. When evaluating the criminal proceedings procedure in the appellate court in Latvia, according to the current norms of the Law on Criminal Procedure, the basic form of trial of cases in the appellate court is the oral process. On the other hand, the trial of a case via a written process in the court of appeal is determined as an exception in the cases provided for in Part 4 of Article 559 of the Law on Criminal Procedure. This norm does not impose an obligation, but only gives the right to try a case by applying a written procedure. Thus, if the state has set a higher standard for ensuring a person's right to oral proceedings, then the court is obliged to comply with it.

The jurisprudence of the ECtHR has also recognized that the right to an open hearing arising from Part 1 of Article 6 of the Convention includes the right to an oral trial in at least one court instance that hears the case on its merits (*Gertrude Speil v. Austria* 2002, paragraph 2).

In conclusion, it should be emphasized that determining the manner of trial of a case in the appellate court primarily pertains to ensuring the right to a fair trial. The limitation of this right, unless the accused has voluntarily waived their guarantees of a fair trial, cannot be justified by considerations of the convenience and efficiency of this type of case review while ignoring the consideration of other balancing elements.

The right to a fair trial occupies such a prominent place in a democratic society that it cannot be sacrificed for the sake of expediency (*Yakhymovych v. Ukraine* 2021).

Any limitation of a person's fundamental rights must be based on the circumstances and arguments justifying this necessity. Thus, such restrictions can be applied only for a legitimate purpose.

Interim Findings

The following conclusions can be made upon the analysis of the research outcomes:

The right to a fair trial is included in international, European Union, and national law.

The right to an oral court hearing is not absolute.

The examination of criminal cases in writing is one of the limitations of the principle of openness.

The choice between an oral and written process depends on various factors, including the country's judicial system as a whole and the role of the appellate court in it, the nature and complexity of the case and the needs of the parties involved. A balanced decision can only be made by carefully evaluating the advantages and disadvantages of both written and oral procedures.

Given the importance of a fair trial in a democratic society, any limitation of the right to a fair trial must be seriously justified. If this right needs to be restricted for any reason, the most minimal possible restriction should be chosen.

Concepts used abstractly do not have to preserve ideas about them that existed at the time of their adoption in a normative act; instead, the content of these concepts can develop over time, without changing the text itself.

The appellate court, when choosing the type of case review process, must carefully evaluate whether the selected type of case review will ensure the right of the accused to a fair trial – even in extraordinary circumstances. The court must choose the type of process that both guarantees epidemiological safety and minimally restricts the rights of the persons involved in the process, including those of the accused, especially in cases when the outcome of the case may significantly worsen the condition of the accused and the involvement of the accused in the court process is much more important than deciding only on matters related to the application of the law.

The cases specified in the normative acts do not deprive a person of the right to ask for their case to be considered via an oral process.

The written procedure in the appellate court is not established as an absolute limitation of the right to an oral process. Namely, the court is given an opportunity, not an obligation, to try a criminal case via a written process. Therefore, the court must decide if the application of a written process in specific legal proceedings will be reasonable and justified.

If the state has set a higher standard for ensuring a person's right to an oral process, as stipulated by international regulations, then the court is obliged to comply with it.

If a person wishes for their case to be examined via an oral process, the person must be provided with such an opportunity in an instance that examines the case on its merits.

References

Charter of Fundamental Rights of the European Union (2012). OJ C326, 391–407. Available from: https://eur-lex.europa.eu/legal-content/EN/TXT/?uri=CELEX:12012P/TXT.

Consolidated versions of the Treaty on European Union and the Treaty on the Functioning of the European Union, 2012. OJ C326, 47–391. Available from: https://eur-lex.europa.eu/legal-content/EN/TXT/?uri=CELEX:12012E/TXT.

Constitution of the Republic of Latvia, February 15, 1922. Entry into force: November 7, 1922. *Latvijas Vēstnesis*, No. 43.

Constitutional Court Decision of February 10, 2017, in Case No. 2016-06-01.

Constitutional Court Decision of March 15, 2018, in Case No. 2017-16-01.

Constitutional Court Decision of June 14, 2018, in Case No.2017-23-0112.

Directive 2012/13/EU of the European Parliament and of the Council of 22 May 2012 on the right to information in criminal proceedings. OJ L142, 1–10. Available from: https://eur-lex.europa.eu/legal-content/EN/TXT/?uri=CELEX:32012L0013.

Directive 2016/343 of the European Parliament and of the Council of 9 March 2016 on the strengthening of certain aspects of the presumption of innocence and of the right to be present at the trial in criminal proceedings. OJ L65, 1–11. Available from: https://eur-lex.europa.eu/legal-content/EN/TXT/?uri=CELEX:32016L0343.

ECtHR, *Döry v. Sweden*, 2002, No. 28394/95.

ECtHR, *Gertrude* Speil *v. Austria*, 2002, No. 42057/98.

ECtHR, *Hermi v. Italy*, 2006, No. 18114/02.

ECtHR, *Yakhymovych v. Ukraine*, 2021, No. 23476/15.

ECtHR, *Marcello Viola v Italy*, 2006, No. 45106/04.

ECtHR, *Mtchedlishvili v. Georgia*, 2021, No.894/12.

ECtHR, *Sakhnovskiy v Russia*, 2010, No. 21272/03.

ECtHR, *Stanford v the United Kingdom*, 1994, No. 16757/90.

ECtHR, *Talabér v. Hungary*, 2009, No. 37376/05.

Equality and Human Rights Commission, 2020. *Inclusive justice: a system designed for all.* Available from: https://www.equalityhumanrights.com/sites/default/files/ehrc_inclusive_justice_a_system_designed_for_all_june_2020.pdf.

European Convention on Human Rights of the Council of Europe, 1950. Available from: https://www.echr.coe.int/documents/d/echr/Convention_ENG.

Fair Trials, 2020. *Beyond the emergency of the COVID-19 pandemic: Lessons for defence rights in Europe* [online]. July 15, 2020. Available from: https://www.fairtrials.org/articles/publications/beyond-the-emergency-of-the-covid-19-pandemic/.

General Secretariat of the Council (Council Of The European Union), 2013. *Guide on Videoconferencing in Cross-Border Proceedings – European E-Justice.* Luxembourg: EU Publications Office. Available from: https://data.europa.eu/doi/10.2860/76243.

Human Rights Committee, 2007. General Comment 32, Article 14: Right to equality before courts and tribunals and to a fair trial. U.N. Doc. CCPR/C/GC/32. Available from: https://digitallibrary.un.org/record/606075?ln=en.

Initial Impact Assessment Report of the Draft Law "Law on the Management of the Spread of COVID-19 Infection" (summary) (Likumprojekta "COVID-19 infekcijas izplatības pārvaldības likums" (reģ. No. 715/Lp13) sākotnējās ietekmes novērtējuma ziņojums (anotācija)). Available from: https://titania.saeima.lv/LIVS13/SaeimaLIVS13.nsf/0/C0F7B89859934871C22585770022A499?OpenDocument.

The International Covenant on Civil and Political Rights of the United Nations, 1966. Available from: https://www.coe.int/en/web/compass/the-international-covenant-on-civil-and-political-rights

Law on Criminal Procedure, April 21, 2005. Entry into force: October 1, 2005. *Latvijas Vēstnesis,* No. 107 (3891).

Law on the Management of the Spread of COVID-19 Infection (COVID-19 infekcijas izplatības pārvaldības likums), June 5, 2020. Entry into force: June 10, 2020. *Latvijas Vēstnesis,* No. 110A.

Levits, E., 2000. Samērīguma princips publiskajās tiesībās – jus commune europaeum un Satversmē ietvertais konstitucionāla ranga princips. *Likums un Tiesības,* 9 (13).

Mcevoy, G., 2023. Language Proficiency and the Right to an Interpreter When Accessing a Fair Trial. *The International Journal of Translation and Interpreting Research,* 15 (2), 142–156. Available from: https://www.trans-int.org/index.php/transint/article/view/1625/450

Senate Decision of February 21, 2023, No. SKK-6/2023, ECLI:LV:AT:2023:0221.16870001618.5.L.

Senate Decision of June 15, 2023, No. SKK-229/2023, ECLI:LV:AT:2023:0221.16870001618.5. L.

Inga Žukovaitė[*]

Coherence Between the Model of Remote Criminal Proceedings and the Standards Under Article 6 of the European Convention on Human Rights: The Reality of Threats to a Fair Trial

General Remarks

The focus on the person in criminal proceedings has traditionally been linked to respect for the physical presence of the parties in the proceedings. Given the exponential growth of scientific and technological progress, an inevitable person-centered approach means the need for a legislative policy that can in any case enable the application of unprecedented fact-checking methodologies and the possibility of achieving a (higher) level of safeguards (Galgani 2023). In other words, the intervention of technological progress in criminal proceedings brings about the need for a cultural approach in which technological transition, development, and diffusion are based on the typical needs of the criminal justice area rather than, conversely, being dictated by the technocratic tendencies of the market economy.

The most relevant technological intervention in proceedings in recent years concerns participation in criminal proceedings through the use of technology that transmits a person's existence or an element of it (otherwise referred to as remote participation, remote proceedings, or online proceedings). The understanding of remote criminal proceedings, as a general category, can be very broad and multi-layered – from individual examinations of witnesses, experts or accused persons by means of videoconference to a full case hearing online. Exposure to and appreciation of the increasingly expanding possibilities of remote participation in certain procedural actions and in the entire trial lead to the question of whether it is not fatal that technological innovation comes along with the identifying features of an axiologically oriented ritual, or whether it is nonetheless possible that there is a hendiadic (Galgani 2023) relationship between the two phenomena.

Discussions in academic doctrine on the impact of technological interventions on proceedings as such or on the limits of such interventions refer to the principles of criminal procedure as a point of reference. However, the notion of fair criminal

---

* This chapter has received funding from the Research Council of Lithuania (LMTLT), agreement No. S- PD- 22- 57

proceedings – which means, *inter alia*, compliance with the law, the adversarial principle, the impartiality of the judge, the equality of arms and the reasonable length of the proceedings – is more than just a set of these principles. The *logos* of proceedings is linked to the philosophical concept of ideal justice, which predates the law and is in direct relation to the inviolable, inalienable human rights of the person involved in the proceedings, which the State recognizes and undertakes to protect. Therefore, it may not be allowed for preconditions to be set in for the exercise of decision-making authority, which does not tolerate any barriers and favors the simplification of proceedings (Mazza 2020, p.80), as well as satisfies the most convenient discretion of the decision-making authority. It must not be forgotten that the equality of arms in criminal proceedings means a balance of powers rather than their equivalence (Tonini and Conti 2022, p.10).

Although active discussions on remote criminal proceedings began in the context of the COVID-19 pandemic, it should be noted that, historically, the possibilities of partial remote criminal proceedings (mostly of individual steps) have long been established in the regulation of the EU Member States and have been discussed many times in the scholarly literature for at least 30 years.

One of the first EU Member States, Italy, sought effective solutions in the trials of Mafia members to ensure the safety of both the proceedings and the public. It was on the basis of these cases that the development of the jurisprudence of the European Court of Human Rights (ECtHR) began in the context of Article 6 of the Convention for the Protection of Human Rights and Fundamental Freedoms (the Convention). The Convention is the main instrument for the protection of fundamental rights in Europe to which all Member States have acceded, although the accession of the EU to the Convention is still in the negotiation phase. Article 52(3) of the EU Charter of Fundamental Rights (the Charter) confirms that, in so far as the Charter contains rights which correspond to rights guaranteed by the Convention, the meaning and scope of those rights shall be the same, although more extensive protection may be provided. This means that the case law of the ECtHR is relevant for the interpretation of rights provided for in the Charter where these rights match, in particular in areas where it has already laid the foundations for the interpretation of the content of fundamental human rights. In the context of this topic, it should be noted that the right to justice encompasses a wide range of fundamental human rights, such as the right to a fair trial established in Article 6 of the Convention and in Article 47 of the Charter, and that the rights set out in Article 48 of the Charter correspond to the content of the rights provided for in Article 6(2) and (3) of the Convention (Explanations (*) relating to the Charter 2007). Thus, although the EU has not acceded to the Convention the doctrine of fundamental human rights in the field of criminal justice, as well as the development of standards of procedural safeguards for EU Member States, remains the task of the ECtHR, thus creating preconditions for the creation of a coherent and harmonious legal area among the EU Member States.

The development of the possibilities of remote criminal proceedings during the COVID-19 pandemic was accepted as an unavoidable necessity in the EU Member States. However, there were concerns that it would become an element of ordinary proceedings once this emergency was over. The reaction of Italian scholars to this issue was particularly sensitive (Ceresa-Gastaldo *et al.* 2023, pp.216–219). Thus, despite the experience verified by the ECtHR of the application of modifications to remote proceedings, practitioners, and scholars hold rather traditional views on the integration of technologies into criminal procedure in non-emergency situations. It should be noted that there was no development in remote procedure rules in Italy until 2022 when the justice reform, which received extensive criticism, was adopted (Dei-Cas 2023). Despite much criticism (Mazza 2023), one of the topics during the implementation of this reform (known as "*la riforma Cartabia*"), which was mostly geared toward the introduction of e-justice procedures in the post-pandemic period, was the legitimization of remote participation in criminal procedural actions and case hearings (Castronuovo *et al.* 2023, pp.86–101).

The example of this country shows, on the one hand, that criminal procedure based on orality and immediacy does not lend itself to easy modifications that pose even a slight threat of the devaluation of these principles in a society with well-established traditions of this procedure. On the other hand, such strong opposition and criticism makes us question whether we are facing the possibility of rethinking the traditional ways of understanding these safeguards in order to preserve their essence without devaluing their traditional package, or looking for new components to replace or compensate for their so-called "loss" (Corso and Peroni 2010; Chiavario 2010, pp.98, 109). The issue of the balance between safeguards is in particular distinct in the face of technological modifications or in the context of integration. Thus, reflection on technological progress in the field of criminal procedural law indicates the need to rethink, on the basis of fundamental procedural principles, the safeguards that can replace or compensate for those that are in crisis as a result of the intervention of technological progress.

In the context of the inferiority of technology, scholarly debate still addresses the issue of whether the court will not gradually become a mere site for the exercise of penal power with the resultant consequences – the deformation of the procedure itself as a physical ritual. The answer to this question is sought by exploring and discussing how the new technological instruments that litigants can use to exercise their procedural rights are compatible with the very substance, principles and purpose of criminal procedure.

In this context, the aim of this paper is to assess the challenges posed for legal regulation by the interaction of technological progress with the principles of criminal procedure. In order to achieve this goal, the following tasks are set: to identify the international human rights standards developed by the ECtHR, without which a fair trial is not possible; to analyze the main aspects of the model of regulation of remote criminal proceedings based on the example of Lithuania; and, on the basis of this analysis, to identify the directions of potential regulation by the EU Member States. For this purpose, the systematic analysis of legal acts and jurisprudence is employed, alongside the teleological and comparative methods of research.

The Interaction Between Strict Procedural Rules and the Changing Context of Technological Progress

On the one hand, judicial procedure should be regarded as a polymorphic formation with its forms adapted as far as possible to the specific subject matter entrusted to the court's appreciation, and the assumption of a uniform procedure designed to deal with all criminal offenses in an undifferentiated manner does not conform to reality (Piziali 2000, p.975). On the other hand, any criminal procedure is based on the fundamental principles of a fair trial: orality, an adversarial nature and immediacy – i.e., on the stringent procedural rules that are implemented in practice and serve as safeguards of fundamental human rights. Recent years have made it particularly clear how new technological advances have expanded the scope of procedural actions and added much relevance to the question of whether and how technological process can change the content of the fundamental criminal justice principles.

Orality is interpreted as the communication of thought through the utterance of words that are intended to be heard. The antithesis of this is the written form, which refers to communication in words using visible alphabetic signs or ideograms. Although what has been written can be read and thus expressed orally, this would be a fictional verbalism. The listener can hear, but cannot be part of the process and, most importantly, cannot ask questions or hear clarifying answers from the person questioned. As a result, orality is real and complete only when the parties are able to ask questions and receive answers from the subject with whom they are dialoguing in the present tense, with the intervention of a live voice. This ensures the right of an accused to participate directly in their own trial (Tonini and Conti 2022, pp.160, 164).

Adversarial proceedings mean the dialectical participation of the parties in the proceedings. This is a game of alternative or contextual interventions, the insertion of questions and answers, assertions, and rebuttals, which leads judicial proceedings toward an outcome (Ferrua 2012, p.100). The climate of the courtroom integrates the assumption of the potential for dialectical contestation. Adversarial proceedings can only be effective if there is a dialectical dispute between the parties who have equal rights before a third and impartial judge; therefore, the realization of a full dialectic in front of a computer raises some doubts, since it creates an intermediate link between the parties and the judge.

Creating a procedure where each of the actors participates remotely means virtualizing the communicative context, which, owing to its specific epistemic capacities, is a privileged instrument for a reliable reconstruction of facts and for a useful comparison of antagonistic theses. Radical critics of remote proceedings argue that the rituals of the adversarial principle are the backbone of evidence production in adversarial proceedings, and that this calls for a courtroom "theatre" because, as Franco Cordero has written, they "require perfect acoustics and optics" (Maiello 2020).

Such an atmosphere requires certain conditions: that the person questioned is able to sit in a place where they can easily be seen by the parties and the judge; and that the persons involved in the proceedings (witnesses, the accused, the prosecutor, the defense counsel and the judge) are able to observe and appreciate the extra-linguistic circumstances that shape non-verbal forms of communication. The tone of voice, facial expression and/or discomfort of answering, perhaps also embarrassment, are usually huge indicators of the authenticity of the source, just as a continuous sequence of questions accompanied by a glance from a witness can lead to a higher truthfulness rate or a fruitful confrontation of antagonistic theses. Therefore, according to some scholars, these are not, by any means, marginal aspects that can be attributed to the aesthetic and symbolic features of judicial activity, but rather configurations that are intertwined with the main issues of criminal court judgments (Maiello 2020). This also involves the principle of immediacy, which is treated as difficult to reconcile with remote proceedings as it is argued that even the most sophisticated videoconferencing software will never be able to reproduce the optimal immediacy of judicial proceedings required for the trial and to ensure the effectiveness of questioning.

Despite the arguments justifying the legal preference for face-to-face and physical contact in court due to considerations related to better verbal and non-verbal observation of a person, as well as better control of the person questioned, the use of videoconferencing in criminal proceedings is gradually gaining more and more supporters in an attempt to reconcile such use in criminal proceedings with the fundamental basis of the principle of immediacy (Morão and Tavares da Silva 2023, p.134). It can be noted that science is looking for arguments to develop the content of the principle of immediacy. The interaction of procedure with technology means that the key elements of immediacy – physical presence and participation – are interpreted separately, i.e., "physical presence" and "participation" are no longer elements of two poles. According to researchers, the essential element is the "participation" pole (Curtotti Nappi 2006, p.296). Physical presence is not a value in itself, but has the instrumental nature of participation, which suggests that if means can be found to ensure participation in the present tense in other ways, the element of physicality is no longer necessary. This hypothesis tends to be confirmed in sociological studies which show that younger witnesses are less stressed and less uncomfortable when giving evidence via video link. In the UK and Australia, there has been a number of pilot projects conducted in youth detention and correctional facilities where juveniles and young adults claimed that they felt more familiar, confident, and at ease when using video link (Walsh 2018). Moreover, research shows that people's habits and relation to technologies are changing quite rapidly. A testimony given through video link may even be regarded as more reliable because it offers witnesses a safer environment, which can reduce emotions and stress and thus allow them to reconstruct the facts more accurately (de Vocht 2022).

One of the most prominent progressivists in the integration of technology in legal proceedings, Richard Susskind, was overwhelmed by the outraged criticism from the English Bar Association when he wrote, back in 1990, that, in the future, lawyers would use e-mail as the main means of communication with their clients (Susskind 2019, pp.2–3). Today, this researcher makes intensive efforts to prove that the courts of the future will be virtual (Susskind 2023). Despite the fulfilment of certain predictions, such a progressive approach is viewed with a great deal of caution both in policy decisions and in the works of researchers. An analysis of the regulation of remote proceedings and the scholarly debate gives the impression that there is a reluctance to succumb to the widespread enthusiasm concerning the impact of technological innovation on the efficiency (speed) of proceedings. "The prevailing rhetoric about smart work, the digital age, about 'life 2.0' or beyond, risks overwhelming criminal procedure and turning it into a dystopian near future, a brave new world where everything is sacrificed to a misunderstood myth of progress" (Mazza 2020, p.73). "The legacy of the modernity *nomos* (Cacciari and Irti, 2019) for the storms of populist impulses and misunderstood bureaucratic-corporate demands for effective justice practice, which the frustrations of emergencies and their management threaten to make even more aggressive, may well lead to the decline of Western civilisation, if ethical indifference and witty silence prevail" (Maiello 2020).

The axioms underlying the discussions on the use of audio-visual communication in various procedural actions have always been, and still are, in practice characterized by the argument of the "inferiority of evidence." In the anticipation of future empirical and multidisciplinary research, scholars continue to rely heavily on the postulate that only the physical presence of all the different litigants in a tangible courtroom can ensure the "constitutionally required standard for both participation in the trial and the evidentiary activity" (Galgani 2023). The fact that remote proceedings are restrictive to the full participation of a person in proceedings and thus imply quality risks of evidence-taking is recognized not only by criminal procedure scholarship, but also by the ECtHR.

Thus, as criminal proceedings are faced with the inevitable challenge of integrating technology, the key issue is finding a balance. Balance in this context should be understood as the sacrifice of one right or principle for another. For legal regulation, this means the task of inputting parameters to assess the legitimacy of the sacrifice. Such an assessment could include three different elements: necessity, sufficiency, and proportionality (Morrone 2008, p.185; Alexy 2012). In this respect, it is indeed common to argue that the weakening of safeguards can only be justified if balanced against an equally ranking constitutional interest, seen as the prevailing historical-political-legal moment.

In the pandemic period, the main concern in terms of regulatory coherence was the lack of legitimization. The criminal procedure law did not contain provisions legitimizing the possibility of remote proceedings in general. Therefore, the main task was to decide and create general norms legitimizing the possibility of such proceedings because "the first error of approach is to assume that there is no need to regulate by law the conditions for the conduct of proceedings which are technological in nature" (Mazza 2020, p.75). However, it would be a mistake to assume that balance will be ensured once the foundation has been laid, and that remote proceedings can be effectively applied solely on the basis of rules governing the technology used. Neglect of the right to participation in the examination and production of evidence in order to consolidate dematerialized proceedings would be a serious betrayal of the adversarial procedure. For example, the promptness of proceedings in itself may not be considered equivalent to the interest of the right to defense. The promptness of proceedings must be linked to the reasonable length of a fair trial; therefore, the former can never lead to the abrogation of the latter interest (Dei-Cas 2022). All of this leads to the conclusion that the main challenge of the current period is the search for specific ways to guarantee procedural safeguards (both in terms of legal regulation and practical guidelines).

Encouragements, Warnings, and Boundaries Set by the European Court of Human Rights

On the assumption that EU law is in the line with the case law of the ECtHR, unless explicitly stated otherwise, the ECtHR – which substantiates its judgments in light of human rights violations rather than normative regulation cases, as derived from the general history of the case, and allows for the assessment of damage through the paradigm of proportionality in particular (Maggio 2023, p.181) – remains the guarantor of the principle of the coherence of legal regulation in the EU Member States on the subject at issue.

Although Article 6(1) of the Convention does not mention it explicitly, the established case law of the ECtHR on the object and purpose of this Article show that a person "charged with a criminal offence" has the right to be present at their trial. Moreover, paragraph 3(c), (d) and (e) guarantee "everyone charged with a criminal offence" the right to "defend himself in person", to "examine or have examined witnesses" and to "to have the free assistance of an interpreter if he cannot understand or speak the language used in court," and it is difficult to see how a person could exercise these rights without being present at their trial (*Sejdovic v. Italy* 2006, § 81; *Colozza v. Italy* 1985 § 27; *Hokkeling v. the Netherlands* 2017, § 57). Indeed, the ECtHR has recognized in a number of cases on the basis of the principles of a fair and just criminal procedure that it is of capital importance that the accused should appear at their trial and that the duty to guarantee the right of a criminal defendant to be present in the courtroom – either during the original proceedings or in a retrial – ranks as one of the essential requirements of Article 6 of the Convention (*Hermi v. Italy* 2006, § 58; *Dijkhuizen v. the Netherlands* 2021, § 59). Hence, the principle of adversarial proceedings is understood in the case law of the ECtHR as a requisite of the subjective right of the accused to be present and defend themselves in their proceedings.

The ECtHR cases which laid the foundations for the assessment of the right of the accused to participate in proceedings by means of remote procedure and established the principles for the application of such a form, as well as the safeguards necessary, can be divided into several groups: 1) cases against Italy concerning the management of mafia trials where remote proceedings were treated as an exceptional measure justified in order to protect other public security goods; 2) cases against Russia where the remote proceedings used, in principle, against the will of the accused in order to speed up case hearings were considered a repressive measure of the state, enabling the state authorities to exercise arbitrariness and the unjustified restriction of rights, starting with the right to defense; and 3) cases where it was recognized that participation in the trial by remote means (videoconferencing) could be a measure to ensure effective participation of the accused in the proceedings (*Dijkhuizen v. the Netherlands*, 2021, § 56).

The scrutiny carried out by the ECtHR is focused on the overall fairness of the proceedings. This is why the analysis of the case law developments shows that, first of all, it was necessary to express a principled position on the compatibility of remote forms of proceedings *per se* with the principles of Article 6 of the Convention. In 2006, the ECtHR confirmed that, from the perspective of the principles ensuring human rights in the proceedings, remote procedure does not violate the provisions of the Convention. The ECtHR held that the participation of an accused in a hearing by videoconferencing is not in itself contrary to the provisions of the Convention. The ECtHR also noted that though the physical presence of an accused in the courtroom is highly desirable, it is not an end (*Golubev v. Russia* 2006).

To reveal the topic under analysis, three cases against Italy stand out. Although the outcomes of the judgments in these cases were not the same as far as the violation of the Convention was concerned, the ECtHR maintained the consistent development of its reasoning. Guided by the principle of fairness, the Court set the direction by stating that recourse to remote proceedings in any given case must serve a legitimate aim and that the arrangements for the giving of evidence must be compatible with the requirements of respect for due process, as laid down in Article 6 of the Convention (*Marcello Viola v. Italy* 2006, § 67; *Zagaria v. Italy* 2007; *Asciutto v. Italy* 2007).

The case law on the interpretation of "legitimate aims" to justify remote proceedings was developed by the ECtHR in 2006 in a case where the accused, who was a member of the Mafia, participated in an appeal hearing by videoconference, as ordered by the court, because of a restricted prison regime. The ECtHR held that the participation of the accused in the appeal hearings by videoconference pursued the protection of public order, the prevention of crime, and the protection of witnesses and victims of offenses in respect of their rights to life, freedom and security (*Marcello Viola v. Italy* 2006, § 72). The Court considered the abovementioned circumstances concerning the legal status of the accused from the perspective of the aims that were essentially directed toward the security of the public and its individual members and held that the decision of the State not to bring the accused to a hearing room was justified.

The ECtHR has gone beyond this in its jurisprudence and, in the above-mentioned and other cases, has singled out the requirement of a reasonable time in judicial proceedings as a criterion for a legitimate aim (*Asciutto v. Italy* 2007). Thus, it is seen from the case law of the ECtHR that the format of videoconferencing can be considered as an appropriate measure to reduce delays caused by the transport of the accused, thereby simplifying and speeding up the criminal proceedings. Although the Court has expanded the scope of a legitimate aim to include the principle of promptness of proceedings, cases against Russia show that the mere promptness of proceedings as a justification for the use of videoconferencing under any circumstances is not compatible with the standards of Article 6 of the Convention. The weakest argument for justifying remote proceedings by a unilateral judgment of the court is, under the case law of the ECtHR, the speed of proceedings.

The jurisprudence of the ECtHR establishes the doctrine that remote proceedings are more vulnerable in terms of the use of procedural safeguards, and that this format is considered as a measure that can be applicable in exceptional cases. This means that it is not videoconferencing *per se*, but the conditions of its use that may lead to a deviation from the components of a fair trial (Corso and Peroni 2010). Therefore, the case law of the ECtHR is developed not only from the point of view of the assessment of the aims pursued, but also in terms of the compliance of the entirety of the specific conditions in which the remote proceedings were implemented with the requirements of Article 6 of the Convention.

The case law of the ECtHR expresses the position that the State cannot interpret legitimate aims narrowly in its decisions, i.e., only relying on the aims of prevention and security, all the more on promptness. In the case of the regulation of remote participation, the restriction of the inviolable right of defense must be necessary in order to ensure the legal goods of particular (constitutional) importance, but this circumstance should not apply to the principle of reasonable time as it is not comparable to the right of defense (Nappi 2006, p.104). The Court has developed case law which requires the existence of a set of conditions, i.e., in addition to legitimate aims, the relevant procedural safeguards relating to ensuring of the right of defense must be guaranteed. The ECtHR has set the requirement that the accused must be able to follow the proceedings and be heard without technical impediments, as well as communicate effectively and confidentially with a lawyer (*Grigoryevskikh v. Russia* 2009, § 83).

It is important to note that, in interpreting the rights guaranteed to the accused under Article 6 of the Convention, the case law of the ECtHR emphasizes the need to ensure effective participation in a criminal trial (*Murtazaliyeva v. Russia* [GC] 2018, § 91), which includes both the technical, organizational aspects of participation and ensuring effective representation by a defense counsel. Effective participation includes not only the right to be physically present, but also the right to hear and follow the proceedings directly through participation. Accordingly, this means that poor acoustics in the courtroom or difficulties in hearing what is going on may raise issues of a breach of Article 6 of the Convention (*Stanford v. the United Kingdom* 1994, §§ 26, 29).

According to the case law of the ECtHR, the interests of justice require that, in order to ensure a fair hearing, an applicant who appears before the court by videoconference must be represented by a lawyer, in particular when a representative of the public prosecutor is present (*Shulepov v. Russia* 2008, §§ 34–36; *Slashchev v. Russia* 2012; *Grigoryevskikh v. Russia* 2009). The ECtHR has reiterated a number of times that the exercise of the right to legal aid is of particular importance when the applicant communicates with the courtroom by video link. Moreover, the Court imposes an obligation on courts hearing cases by videoconference to verify the reasons for the absence of the defendant's counsel (*Grigoryevskikh v. Russia* 2009, § 92), and warns that failure to comply with this obligation may lead to a decision on a violation of Article 6(1) and (3)(c) of the Convention.

Thus, the case law not only emphasizes the right of an accused to communicate with a lawyer, but also highlights that unilateral decisions by authorities concerning the remote participation of an accused in a hearing should be restricted if the individual situation of the accused has not been taken into account. For example, in *Medvedev v. Russia* (2017, § 30), after finding that the applicant had been imprisoned in Moscow but had not been physically brought to a trial in Moscow by the decision of the court, and that the Government had not explained why it had been impossible to provide for different arrangements for the conduct of the appeal, the ECtHR considered that the applicant could legitimately feel ill-treated when communicating with the State-appointed counsel by video link. The ECtHR did not discern any compelling reasons to justify the authorities' decision to arrange for the applicant's participation in the appeal hearing via video link rather than ensuring his presence in the courtroom, in particular considering that both the accused and his counsel were located in the same city in which the hearing was held.

In developing its case law on ensuring the presence of a defense counsel when proceedings are organized by videoconferencing, the ECtHR draws strict limits for the formal representation of the accused. According to the Court's jurisprudence, the appointment of a defense counsel does not in itself guarantee the effectiveness of the aid that they can provide to the accused, which is why it emphasizes the need to ensure adequate facilities and time for consultations with the defense counsel (*Sakhnovskiy v. Russia* [GC] 2010). In this context, another requirement identified in the cases heard by the ECtHR is also relevant. The right of an accused to communicate with their lawyer without any risk of being monitored by a third party is regarded as one of the fundamental requirements for a fair trial under Article 6 of the Convention. The Court considers that, if a lawyer is unable to confer with their client and receive confidential instructions, their assistance would lose much of its usefulness, whereas the Convention is intended to guarantee rights that are practical and effective (*Sakhnovskiy v. Russia* [GC] 2010, §§ 97, 102 and 104; *Medvedev v. Russia* 2017, § 30; *Zagaria v. Italy* 2007).

In conclusion, the jurisprudence of the ECtHR dues not rule out the development of the use of technology in criminal proceedings. However, the search for balance should be chosen as a way forward. The Court treats remote proceedings as a means for creating preconditions for the restriction of procedural rights. Therefore, it imposes an obligation to apply strict standards of effective defense. Any safeguard that is restricted must be absolutely necessary, and where a less restrictive measure may suffice, the latter must be applied.

The Example of Lithuania: Coherence Between Regulation and Practice

The *logos* of the adversarial procedure is based on the opposite principle than authority (Filippini 2022, p.19), i.e., a dialectical opposition between the parties (prosecution and defense) based on equal rights and possibilities, where the judge is a third and impartial arbiter. According to this principle, the more the subjects with antagonistic interests share functions and are directly involved in the proceedings, the better the truth is achieved. The lack of normative typicality and the expected variations in application do not, in fact, rule out the risk that the remote procedure could turn into a formal virtual procedure or a simulacrum of a court, thus succumbing to the dangerous tendency to regard the methodological expediency of ritual forms as a mere obstacle to be removed in the interests of procedural promptness. "The step that separates the dematerialized court from the virtual court is a small one, thus, the technological monster, today welcomed by passionate futurologists, may soon turn against the very proponents of modernity" (Mazza 2020). Thus, once the emergency is over and the practice of using the remote form of criminal proceedings has been developed over almost 3 years, it is necessary to consider whether this ominous prediction is actually likely to come true, and whether there are any signs that criminal procedure is facing a technological monster that threatens its very *logos*.

The example of Lithuania is unique because, unlike in the case of Italy, the use of remote proceedings (mixed and full) has been accepted in practice without much doctrinal debate. In 2021 in Lithuania, the legislator adopted amendments to the criminal procedure law in response to the need to legalize the new practices introduced in criminal proceedings during the pandemic when some procedural steps or entire proceedings were carried out using technical equipment. With the active participation of representatives of the Bar Association, the Prosecutor General's Office and the judiciary in the legislative debate, amendments to the Code of Criminal Procedure were adopted, and the very first Chapter of the Code on the "Purpose of Criminal Procedure and the Main Rules" established new legal regulation on the "Use of information and electronic communications technologies in criminal proceedings" (Law No. XIV-270, 2021).

These provisions of the law have developed a concept of remote proceedings that is favorable for the ensuring of the rights of defense. The regulation emphasizes *expresis verbis* that remote proceedings (incidentally, the law itself does not refer to this concept, but rather uses the term "ensuring procedural actions and the participation of parties to proceedings in case hearings using information and electronic communications technologies") are only possible in exceptional cases. This means a rule of exceptional rather than ordinary procedure. This implies that the legislator does not recognize that remote procedure can be treated as a fully-fledged analogue of ordinary procedure, which is based on the principles of adversarial procedure, orality and immediacy. In light of the ECtHR's standards on compliance with the requirement of a legitimate aim, it should be noted that the criminal procedure law refers only to "reasonable grounds for believing that this will speed up the hearing of the case" as such an aim.

Despite the fact that the legitimacy of the new regulation is supported by the principle of the speed (promptness) of a case hearing, the law identifies the conditions necessary for a decision on the organization of the procedure, thus amortizing the fact that only the promptness of a case hearing is indicated as the reason for such a procedure. The legislator sets out the requirements for this set of conditions as follows: 1) such a form will not prejudice a full and objective investigation of all the circumstances of the case; and 2) this form will safeguard the rights of the parties to the proceedings. Thus, from the point of view of the ECtHR's standards, the model being developed in Lithuania is aimed not only at fast, but also at effective participation of the parties in criminal proceedings.

The main procedural safeguard of the parties is the part of the law which unequivocally obliges remote proceedings not to be applied when at least one of the parties to the proceedings objects to it (the provisions of this paragraph do not apply when the prosecutor, the victim and/or their representative, the accused, their legal representative and/or their defense counsel, the civil claimant, the civil defendant and/or their representatives object to the case hearing by means of information and electronic communication technologies – i.e., videoconferences). It should be noted that such an objection may be raised not only by the accused, their defense counsel and the prosecutor, but also by the victim, their representative, or even by the civil claimant and the defendant. The flexibility of the law and its caution with regard to remote proceedings are also confirmed by the provisions according to which, even if it becomes apparent during a hearing held using information and electronic communication technologies (via videoconferencing) that the direct participation of the parties, a witness, an expert, a specialist, an interpreter, and other persons involved in the proceedings is necessary for a particular procedural step to enable them to exercise their procedural rights in a proper manner or to have a complete and objective examination of the case circumstances, arrangements are made for the procedural step or the hearing to take place in person. Thus, it can be said that the regulation model established in the CCP does not leave any room at all for a unilateral decision of the court to organize the hearing or the procedural step remotely. Although the description of the Procedure for the Use of Videoconferencing Technologies in Criminal Proceedings states that a case heard by means of videoconference shall be organized on the court's initiative or at the request of a party to the proceedings (Order No. 1R-183, 2021), the provisions of the law which allow the vetoing of such a decision at any time without even requiring the person objecting to state their reasons confirm the supremacy of the principle of the general consensus of the parties concerning the decision to conduct the proceedings remotely. On the other hand, the question is then whether it is entirely reasonable to leave no scope for the court to take a unilateral decision on the organization of proceedings under a mixed or fully remote procedure. Such a need could be justified by the prevention of abuse of procedural rights to delay proceedings.

In view of the fact that the remote form of procedure has been established as exceptional, the provision providing that such a decision shall normally be taken by a court ruling is logical and reasonable. However, the law does not detail what "normally" includes, which brings a number of risks inherent in the interpretation and application of the practice of law. In fact, this provision is interpreted and applied in practice in a wide variety of ways, ranging from the view that a separate ruling setting out the reasons justifying exceptionality is necessary to a protocol ruling without any additional explanations of the decision. Such trends in the practice show that the "exceptionality" established by the legislator has been devalued in reality, and that the form of remote procedure (whether hybrid or full) is increasingly becoming a routine procedural decision based on the parties' agreement, rather than on the grounds of exceptionality.

In terms of procedural safeguards, several shortcomings in the regulation should be noted which threaten the right to an effective defense from the perspective of the standards established by the ECtHR. The law does not regulate cases where a defense counsel and an accused are in different places (e.g., in prison) when they connect to a hearing remotely. Neither the law nor the implementing legal act lays down rules on how confidential and effective communication between the defense counsel and the defendant is to be ensured in such cases. When the law was adopted, it was not considered that it should be possible to extend the list of cases when the participation of a defense counsel has to be mandatory by establishing that a defense counsel is required to be present when an accused participates in proceedings by videoconference.

From the perspective of the standards set in the provisions of Article 6 of the Convention, the requirement established at the level of the law that remote proceedings may be arranged only when there are appropriate technical possibilities is to be assessed positively. On the other hand, neither the law nor the implementing legal act details how the conditions of appropriateness are to be understood and what circumstances satisfy them. The statutory provision which refers to the implementing legal act where specific rules are laid down – although it requires that the reliable identification of the parties to the proceedings, the objective recording and presentation of data and evidence, access to procedural rights and the publicity of a hearing at court be ensured – is questionable (the procedure defined by the Minister of Justice has been agreed with the Judicial Council, the Prosecutor General's Office of the Republic of Lithuania and the Council of the Lithuanian Bar, and the procedure defined by the Prosecutor General of the Republic of Lithuania has been agreed with the Judicial Council and the Council of the Lithuanian Bar (Article 82(5) of the Code of Criminal Procedure)). In addition, it is questionable whether a legal act at this level can regulate legal relations of this kind which relate to the proper taking of evidence that is the first and most indispensable prerequisite for a fair trial. An analysis of the abovementioned description makes it clear that, apart from the formal declaration, there is no procedure to ensure these safeguards – even in this legal act.

Despite the safeguards relating to the regulation created by the CCP, the legal model of remote procedure where issues of considerable significance for ensuring the procedural rights of the parties are either defined in an implementing legal act or simply left to the discretion of the decision-maker can be seen as creating legal preconditions for the formation of divergent case law and for a deviation from the fundamental principles of criminal procedure. An empirical study involving interview with judges, attorneys at law and prosecutors did not confirm that the implementation of remote proceedings in practice had very negative consequences for the rights of the defense, or created negative preconditions for the principle of adversarial proceedings (the study results were presented at the international conference "European and National Criminal Policy Trends and Challenges" held in Vilnius on April 28, 2023). This is supported by the fact that, in 3 years of experience, not a single complaint concerning a procedural violation in this respect has reached the court of cassation.

In summary, it can be stated that, despite the shortcomings of regulation, legislation, and practice in Lithuania have not gone down the path of abuse of power and have chosen to seek consensus between the parties to the proceedings while maintaining respect for the importance of the adversarial procedure. The regulatory shortcomings that have been identified suggest that it is necessary to remain vigilant and not to be under the illusion that the rationality of the subjects involved in proceedings and respect for human rights alone can be a sufficient safeguard for a fair trial in the truth-seeking process.

Interim Findings

The integration of new instruments in criminal proceedings, although based on the premise of procedural efficiency, must, in light of the fundamental principles of criminal procedure, be understood first and foremost as a guarantee of fair proceedings.

Remote criminal proceedings, which do not *per se* conflict with the *logos* of criminal procedure, remain an exceptional form of organization of proceedings which may not be applied as a judicial imperative that is justified solely on the grounds of procedural promptness.

The speed of proceedings, understood only in the formal sense of procedural simplification, may not be regarded as a legitimate aim, sacrificing the safeguards of one or another party to the proceedings and paying the price for the quality of the procedural path to the truth.

The legislator's commitment to providing the best functionality to criminal proceedings through the appropriate integration of technological tools must be based on the principle of balance, where such enabling should not create preconditions for arbitrariness on the part of the decision-making body and unjustified restrictions on the rights of the parties to the proceedings.

Although remote criminal proceedings are seen as a threat to the fundamental safeguards of a fair adversarial procedure and treated as an exception in the doctrine, empirical studies show that, in the judicial practice of Lithuania, this has become a routine procedural decision of the court predetermined by an agreement reached between the parties involved in the proceedings.

The analysis of the Lithuanian case shows that the regulation model – where remote criminal procedure has been legitimized in the law but the legislator does not assume the responsibility of establishing the standards developed by the ECtHR's jurisprudence with regard to the means of safeguarding individual rights of defense at the level of a law and transfers this obligation to implementing legal acts or simply to the emerging case law – is flawed and poses risks to the safeguards of a fair trial.

References

Alexy, R., 2012. *Teoria dei diritti fondamentali.* Bologna: Il mulino.

Cacciari, M., and Irti, N., 2019. *Elogio del diritto.* La nave di Teseo.

Castronuovo, D., Donini, M., Mancuso, E. M., and Varraso, G. (eds.), 2023. *Riforma cartabia: la nuova giustizia penale.* Milano: Wolters Kluwer-CEDAM.

Ceresa-Gastaldo, M., Conso, G. B., and Grevi, V., 2023. *Compendio di procedura penale.* 11th edn. M. Bargis, (ed.). Milano: Wolters Kluwer-CEDAM.

Charter of Fundamental Rights of the European Union [online]. OL C 326, 2012 10 26, 391–407. Available from: https://eur-lex.europa.eu/legal-content/EN/TXT/PDF/?uri=CELEX:12012P/TXT [Accessed 1 September 2023].

Chiavario, M., 2010. La "videoconferenza" processuale e la Corte Europea dei diritti dell'uomo. In: *Studi in onore di Mario Pisano, vol.II – Diritto processuale penale e profili internazionali: diritto straniero e diritto comparato.* Piacenza: Casa Editrice La Tribuna, 95–109.

Corso, P., and Peroni, F. (eds.), 2010. *Studi in onore di Mario Pisani.* Casa Editrice La Tribuna.

Curtotti Nappi, D., 2006. *I collegamenti audiovisivi nel processo penale.* Milano: Giuffrè.

De Vocht, D. L. F., 2022. Trials By Video Link After the Pandemic: The Pros and Cons of the Expansion of Virtual Justice. *China-EU Law Journal*, 8 (1–2), 33–44. Available from: https://doi.org/10.1007/s12689-022-00095-9. [Accessed 10 September 2023].

Dei-Cas, E. A. A., 2022. La partecipazione a distanza, in attesa della riforma del processo penale. *Sistema penale*, 4, 5–30.

Dei-Cas, E. A. A., 2023. La partecipazione "parzialmente smaterializzata": il grimaldello del consenso a favore dell'economia processuale. *La legislazione penale*, No. 3, 88–113. Available from: https://iris.unimore.it/bitstream/11380/1302986/1/DEI-CAS-Definitivo.pdf. [Accessed 10 September 2023].

ECtHR, *Asciutto v. Italy*, application no. 35795/02, 27 November 2007 [online]. Available from: https://hudoc.echr.coe.int/?i=001-83510 [Accessed 1 September 2023].

ECtHR, *Colozza v. Italy*, application no. 9024/80, 12 February 1985 [online]. Available from: https://hudoc.echr.coe.int/?i=001-57462 [Accessed 1 September 2023].

ECtHR, Decision as to the admissibility of, application no. 26260/02, Vladimir Vitalyevich Golubev v. Russia, 9 November 2006 [online]. Available from: https://hudoc.echr.coe.int/app/conversion/pdf/?library=ECHR&id=001-78357&filename=001-78357.pdf [Accessed 1 September 2023].

ECtHR, *Dijkhuizen v. the Netherlands*, application no. 61591/16, 8 June 2021 [online]. Available from: https://hudoc.echr.coe.int/eng?i=001-210486 [Accessed 1 September 2023].

ECtHR, *Grigoryevskikh v. Russia*, application no. 22/03, 9 April 2009 [online]. Available from: https://hudoc.echr.coe.int/eng?i=001-92105 [Accessed 1 September 2023].

ECtHR, *Hermi v. Italy [GC]*, application no. 18114/02, 18 October 2006 [online]. Available from: https://hudoc.echr.coe.int/?i=001-69529 [Accessed 1 September 2023].

ECtHR, *Hokkeling v. The Netherlands*, application no. 30749/12, 14 February 2017 [online]. Available from: https://hudoc.echr.coe.int/?i=001-171096 [Accessed 1 September 2023].

ECtHR, *Marcello Viola v. Italy*, application no. 45106/04, 5 October 2006 [online]. Available from: https://hudoc.echr.coe.int/app/conversion/pdf/?library=ECHR&id=001-77246&filename=001-77246.pdf&TID=ihgdqbxnfi. [Accessed 1 September 2023].

ECtHR, *Medvedev v. Russia*, application no. 5217/06, 27 June 2017 [online]. Available from: https://hudoc.echr.coe.int/eng?i=001-174613 [Accessed 1 September 2023].

ECtHR, *Murtazaliyeva v. Russia*, application no. 36658/05, 18 December 2018 [online]. Available from: https://hudoc.echr.coe.int/eng?i=001-187932 [Accessed 1 September 2023].

ECtHR, *Sakhnovskiy v. Russia*, application no. 21272/03, 2 November 2010 [online]. Available from: https://hudoc.echr.coe.int/eng?i=001-101568 [Accessed 1 September 2023].

ECtHR, *Sejdovic v. Italy* application no. 56581/00, 1 March 2006 [online]. Available from: https://hudoc.echr.coe.int/?i=001-72629 [Accessed 1 September 2023].

ECtHR, *Stanford v. the United Kingdom,* application no. 16757/90, 23 February 1994 [online]. Available from: https://hudoc.echr.coe.int/eng?i=001-57874 [Accessed 1 September 2023].

ECtHR, *Zagaria v. Italy,* application no. 58195/00, 27 November 2007 [online]. Available from: https://hudoc.echr.coe.int/?i=001-83492 [Accessed 1 September 2023].

European Convention of Human Rights, November 4, 1950. Available from: https://www.echr.coe.int/documents/d/echr/Convention_ENG. [Accessed 1 September 2023].

Explanations (*) relating to the Charter of fundamental rights [online]. OJ C 303, 2007 12 14, 17–35. Available from: https://eur-lex.europa.eu/legal-content/EN/TXT/?uri=oj:JOC_2007_303_R_0017_01 [Accessed 1 September 2023].

Ferrua, P., 2012. *Il giusto processo.* 3rd edn. Bologna: Zanichelli.

Filippini, A., 2022. *Diritto processuale penale.* Milano: Giuffrè Francis Lefebvre.

Galgani, B., 2023. Innovazione tecnologica e tradizione personalistica. Dalla partecipazione "a distanza" alle cc.dd. "Metaverse Courtrooms"?. *Archivio Penale,* No. 2 (Maggio–Agosto), 1–18.

Lietuvos Respublikos Seimas, 2021. Lietuvos Respublikos baudžiamojo proceso kodekso 8-1, 210, 263, 269 ir 277 straipsnių pakeitimo ir Kodekso papildymo 8-2 straipsniu įstatymas Nr. XIV-270 [Law on Amendments to Articles 8-1, 210, 263, 269 and 277 of the Criminal Procedure Code of the Republic of Lithuania and Addition of Article 8-2 to the Code No.XIV-270] [online]. Available from: https://e-seimas.lrs.lt/portal/legalAct/lt/TAD/6c092531a37211ebb458f88c56e2040c?jfwid=g8m7gj7iv [Accessed 10 September 2023].

Lietuvos Respublikos Teisingumo Ministerija, 2021. Lietuvos Respublikos teisingumo ministro 2021 m. gegužės 31 d. įsakymas Nr. 1R-183 „Dėl vaizdo konferencijų technologijų naudojimo nagrinėjant baudžiamąsias bylas tvarkos aprašo patvirtinimo" [Order of the Minister of Justice of the Republic of Lithuania of 31 May 2021 No 1R-183 "On the description of the procedure for the use of videoconferencing technologies in criminal cases"] [online]. Available from: https://e-tar.lt/portal/lt/legalAct/f9151050c20e11eba2bad9a0748ee64d/asr [Accessed 10 September 2023]

Maggio, P., 2023. *Giudicato penale e diritti fondamentali in area CEDU.* Torino: Giappichelli.

Maiello, V., 2020. La smaterializzazione del processo penale e la dystopia che diventa realtà. *Archivio Penale,* No. 1 (Gennaio–Aprile), 1–3.

Mazza, O., 2020. Distopia Del Processo a Distanza [online]. *Archivio Penale,* No. 1 (Gennaio–Aprile), 73–80. Available from: https://doi.org/10.12871/97888331807316 [Accessed 11 September 2023].

Mazza, O., 2023. Ideologie della riforma Cartabia: la Procedura penale del nemico. *Diritto penale e processo*, No. 4, 481–490.

Morão, H., and Tavares Da Silva, R., 2023. *Fairness in Criminal Appeal. A Critical and Interdisciplinary Analysis of the ECtHR Case-Law*. Springer Cham. Available from: https://doi.org/10.1007/978-3-031-13001-4. [Accessed 10 September 2023].

Morrone, A., 2008. Bilanciamento (giustizia costituzionale). In: A. Giuffrè, ed. *Enciclopedia del Diritto-Annali dal 2007*, 185–204.

Piziali, G., 2000. Pluralità dei riti e giudice unico. *Rivista italiana di diritto e procedura penale*, No. 3 (Luglio–Settembre), 966–987.

Susskind, R., 2019. *Online Courts and the Future of Justice*. Oxford University Press.

Susskind, R., 2023. *Tomorrow's lawyers: An introduction to Your Future*. Oxford University Press.

Tonini, P., and Conti, C., 2022. *Lineamenti di diritto processuale penale*. 20th edn. Milano: Giuffrè Francis Lefebvre.

Walsh, T., 2018. Video Links in Youth Justice Proceedings: When Rights and Convenience Collide. *Journal of Judicial Administration*, 27 (4), 161–181. Available from: https://search.informit.org/doi/10.3316/agispt.20180925002286. [Accessed 10 September 2023].

Jolanta Zajančkauskienė, Rima Ažubalytė, Oleg Fedosiuk

Conclusions

Coherence in law, including criminal justice, is a minimum condition for rationality. Coherence is not superior to other values; however, it is believed that coherence should be pursued in every area of criminal justice to avoid arbitrariness and injustice. At the very least, efforts should be made to correct the most glaring inconsistencies, errors, or discrepancies, although it is sometimes difficult, if not impossible, to agree on what full coherence really is.

The authors of this edited volume therefore draw conclusions, make suggestions, and raise questions for discussion after researching multiple varying areas of criminal justice in the context of coherent regulation and its application.

Part I. The Search For Coherence in Substantive Criminal Law

In this part, the following essential conclusions were made:

1. The lack of certainty regarding the essential elements of trafficking in humans, such as the purposes of exploitation and the abuse of a position of vulnerability, creates the risk of the incoherent and excessive application of liability for this serious crime. Legal ambiguity in this area can lead to the over-criminalization of some social problems, such as illegal work, poor working conditions, etc. Such practices would certainly not meet the needs of a coherent fight against human trafficking. To avoid this, the determination of the legal elements in specific cases cannot be based solely on the text of the law and must instead correspond to the essence of the concept of human trafficking and the goals of its criminalization as declared in international law and European Union legal acts. Therefore, when recognizing the existence of real exploitation or such an intent, it is necessary to assess not only the formal list of areas of exploitation, but also: what real damage (discrimination, injustice, humiliation, disease) the victim has experienced or could experience as a result of the evaluated behavior; how much the exploiters benefited from it; whether this behavior correlates with the usual methods of traffickers' activities and control of victims, etc.

   The abuse of vulnerability as a legal element of human trafficking is also an extremely contextual concept, and its application must consider not only the situation of the victim and their life, but also other aspects of the case that allow the legal significance of the victim's consent to the malicious offers of traffickers to be negated.

2. The experiences of countries that have decriminalized drugs show that the consequences of such decriminalization practices are not inherently harmful, as previously thought. Countries with strict prohibitionist stances show increases in drug use, while countries with coherent decriminalization approaches show decreases in drug use, although there are discrepancies between the two scenarios that require more detailed analysis of these figures. There is growing global momentum toward a coherent approach, as countries introspectively evaluate their existing drug policies and consider more coherent and sustainable alternatives.

   The key to this dialogue is to achieve legal coherence between criminalization and decriminalization, while trying to understand the possible consequences of drug-related legislation on people's consumption habits. Legal frameworks need to be formulated in a way that is coherent with public health objectives, do not encourage drug use and do not disproportionately punish users, especially those who use light drugs occasionally without causing harm. The greatest threat is the lack of legal coherence, leading to criminal consequences and the dangers of unregulated drug markets.
3. Based on research on sentencing for offenses against justice in Lithuania, it can be observed that courts usually impose non-custodial sentences for this type of crime. Moreover, courts further dilute the penal policy against crimes against justice by combining sentences, usually by adding only a part of the sentence that is close to the legal minimum, or by over-applying the consolidation of sentences.

   A study of the laws and sentencing practices of other countries shows that the criminal policy of Lithuania in the fight against crimes against justice, in the case of obstructing the investigation or influencing the participants in the case, both at the level of legislation and case law, is considerably more lenient than that of the UK or the USA in this regard.

   Thus, in the norms providing for criminal liability for crimes against justice when obstructing the investigation of a case, the CC of Lithuania lacks coherence both with other norms of the Special Part and with the norms of the General Part. The penalties for the above-mentioned crimes are incoherent and too lenient in relation to other provisions of the Special Part of the CC, which provide for liability for similar crimes. The rules on the cumulation of punishments provided for in the General Part of the CC are not in line with the objectives of punishment and unjustifiably expand the use of cumulation of punishments, leading to a situation where, in cases of serious or very serious crimes, crimes against justice are in fact not punished.

4. The coherent approach that has been arrived at allows stalking to be seen as a repetitive act of a person that is intimidating in nature, disturbing, and unsettling. It is the repetitive nature of the acts carried out, which are geared toward creating a sense of fear and insecurity, that is the main identifying feature of stalking.

   A coherent approach to stalking is necessary to better understand its nature and the application of criminal responsibility. Unlawful acts of stalking are usually regulated by separate norms in national criminal laws, with the names of the norms specifically referring to unlawful stalking. However, acts constituting the content of unlawful stalking may render a person criminally responsible, even if the offense specifically referred to by that name does not exist in criminal law. The norm of systemic intimidation (Art. 145(2) of the CC) applied in Lithuanian case law is an excellent example of this. Systematic intimidation includes all repeated acts of a person that cause fear, anxiety, insecurity, and uncertainty. Thus, even before the new independent stalking norm was introduced, acts of stalking in Lithuania were subject to criminal liability as systematic intimidation. The criminal offense defined as stalking did not exist in the CC, but this did not affect the legal assessment of repeated acts of an intimidating nature in any way. The practical application of the new offense of unlawful stalking will have to identify the criteria that will enable this offense to be distinguished from the offense of systematic intimidation.
5. After summarizing the research conducted, it can be concluded that when separating criminal and administrative liability, it is necessary to consider the severity and nature of the violation of the law. Administrative sanctions imposed for certain illegal actions which are considered particularly serious may not be a strong enough response. At the same time, criminal sanctions may be chosen when it is considered important to emphasize strong disapproval to ensure deterrence. Including a conviction in a criminal record can have a particularly dissuasive effect. An administrative sanction can often be decided on and implemented immediately, avoiding lengthy and costly procedures. For this reason, administrative sanctions may be considered in areas where, for example, infringements are not very serious or particularly numerous, as well as in areas where administrative sanctions and procedures are appropriate and effective for other reasons (e.g., complex economic evaluations).
6. The coherent application of the principles of criminal jurisdiction in relation to criminal acts committed abroad by Lithuanian citizens and persons permanently residing in Lithuania can only be possible if it is understood that any principle has individual grounds for its application and a specific

purpose, which cannot be overturned by a literal interpretation of the norms establishing it. In summary, it is the case that:

6.1. The determination of the place of commission of a criminal act is also an important basis for the application of each principle of criminal jurisdiction, and the rule(s) governing it must therefore be set out in an independent article of the CC and be separate from the territorial principle. The system of jurisdictional principles currently existing in the Lithuanian CC must be expanded by introducing at least a passive personality principle, which would be highly effective in solving the problem that is gaining momentum, whereby persons located in Lithuania are victimized by cyber-fraud committed outside the territory of Lithuania.

6.2. The flag principle should also be regulated in a separate article of the CC, the key aspect of which should be the understanding that international law may establish rules that allocate jurisdiction between the coastal state and the state of registration of a vessel, or between the host of the airspace and the state of registration of an aircraft of a foreign state.

6.3. Using various methods of interpretation of the legal norm, it is also apparent that Lithuanian citizens and persons permanently residing in Lithuania are liable for crimes committed outside the territory of Lithuania and referred to in Article 7 of the CC on the basis of the universal principle only if it is not possible to apply jurisdictional principles that are higher in the hierarchy (territorial, flag, or passive personal), and only in the case of crimes of high seriousness for which universal jurisdiction is established in accordance with the provisions of a specific international agreement. The application of the universal principle must also respect the rules on the allocation of jurisdiction laid down in the relevant international treaties.

6.4. The requirement of the double criminality of an act, established in Article 8(1) of the CC of Lithuania and linked only to the law in force in the territory of the other state, blocks the more coherent application of the principle of active personality and the principle of the protection of state interests. To ensure the coherent interaction of the principles of extraterritorial jurisdiction, Article 8(1) of the CC should be amended as soon as possible. Article 8(3) of the CC should also be modified to provide that a Lithuanian citizen or a person permanently residing in Lithuania who commits one or more of the crimes referred to in this provision outside the territory of Lithuania shall be liable to prosecution, irrespective of whether the act committed is punishable at the place of commission of the crime.

Part II. The Transformation of Criminal Procedure Law in Context of Coherence

Procedural criminal law is more influenced by international and EU law than substantive criminal law. The consistency of procedural rights across EU countries has already been extensively studied. Meanwhile, in the area of evidence and the use of technology, the search for consistency in criminal procedure law is currently intensifying.

In this part of the monograph, the following essential conclusions were made:

7. In 2023, Regulation (EU) 2023/1543 of the European Parliament and of the Council on European Production Orders and European Preservation Orders for electronic evidence in criminal proceedings and for the execution of custodial sentences following criminal proceedings was adopted. This legal regulation, it would seem, should have solved the problems related to the challenges that electronic data collection issues are subject to in the EU. The aim was not only to create a fast, efficient data collection process, but also to develop a model of electronic evidence collection that would allow the law enforcement authorities of the Member States to avoid mutual contact with the law enforcement authorities of other countries, and instead to establish direct contact with the addressees, i.e., service providers (or their representatives).

7.1. Unfortunately, an analysis of the existing regulatory framework for the gathering of evidence (including electronic evidence) (EIO, Regulation on the Taking of Electronic Evidence) suggests that the Regulation, in order to ensure the timely and efficient gathering of evidence, lacks provisions ensuring the admissibility of such evidence before national courts.

7.2. The provisions of the Regulation on the Taking of Electronic Evidence are characterized by their fragmentary nature, which is the result of a lack of certain safeguards that are particularly emphasized in legal practice. In particular, the selective nature of the process of refusal to recognize and execute orders for the production of electronic evidence, the lack of safeguards for the rights of the individual, the lack of procedural guarantees, and the specificity of the process of collecting, recording, and transmitting electronic evidence stored by a private body (a service provider) all mean that the admissibility of such evidence in national courts may be seriously called into question.

7.3. To avoid obstacles to the admissibility of electronic evidence collected outside the territory of the national State in which the trial is taking place, it was necessary to bring the principal provisions of the Regulation in line with those of the Directive regarding EIO in criminal matters. At the same time, it should be emphasized that other measures have also been proposed in the academic literature that could assist in reducing the fragmentation, fundamental inconsistency, and excessive heterogeneity that exists concerning the legal instruments of criminal justice within the EU. These include applying the doctrine of Common Minimum Standards to all legal instruments of judicial cooperation, without exception.

8. In criminal cases relating to cybercrime, the quality of the proof-taking process can often be an issue when it comes to obtaining, presenting, verifying, and assessing electronic evidence.

8.1. One of the main reasons for this relates to the peculiarities of this type of evidence: 1) its instability, as electronic evidence can be altered easily, both due to the specificities of the operation of the information systems and intentional (or negligent) human activity; 2) the difficulty of tracking the changes made; and 3) the circumstances relevant to the case are usually determined by a person with special knowledge that is not held by the other parties involved in the criminal procedure.

8.2. The assessment of the reliability of electronic evidence in criminal proceedings is complex. Once it has been established that such evidence meets the requirements of correlation and admissibility, the assessment of its reliability also considers whether the preservation of the authenticity, integrity and accountability of electronic evidence has been guaranteed during the proof-taking process.

8.3. In the interests of coherent regulation, legislation should not give priority to evidence based on its form. In accordance with the principle of technological neutrality, electronic data, irrespective of the technology that generated or processed them, should be admissible as evidence in criminal proceedings if they fulfil the purpose of evidence, its function in criminal proceedings and the other requirements laid down for evidence.

9. The recovery of illegally obtained property within the framework of criminal proceedings, without being linked to a criminal conviction, is based on the origins of such property, which makes the seizure of such property a civil measure rather than a punishment (a criminal measure). Nevertheless, non-conviction forfeiture as a restriction on the right to property must meet all the general requirements for such restriction.

9.1. The presumption of innocence, including the allocation of the burden of proof, which determines the proof of a person's guilt and of a conviction-based confiscation in a criminal proceeding (beyond a reasonable doubt), may not apply in a proceeding to prove a non-conviction-based (NCB) confiscation. An analysis of EU law and both ECtHR and national constitutional jurisprudence leads to the conclusion that the "follow-the-money" approach allows for the seizure of assets not only in the absence of a criminal conviction, but also by applying the civil standard of proof – the principle of the balance of probabilities and the rebuttable presumption of the illegality of the asset.

9.2. The grounds for extended confiscation, despite the latter being normally applied in criminal proceedings against a convicted person, may not be assessed according to the standard of proof of a criminal charge. This means that the guilt of a person will be proved according to the presumption of innocence, while the grounds for extended confiscation will be proved according to the principle of the balance of probabilities.

9.3. NCB confiscation from a third party in criminal proceedings requires not only an effective remedy for the rights of the third party, but also a particularly careful reasoning of NCB confiscation, as the final act (conviction) cannot contain statements that violate the presumption of innocence of a third party who has not been criminally charged.

9.4. In view of the difficulty involved in a person rebutting the presumption of the illegality of assets, if the national legislation provides for a wide range of NCB confiscation possibilities, courts have the duty to:

- apply the principle of proportionality, both when deciding on the legitimate aim of NCB confiscation and on the scope of such confiscation;
- apply the rule of evidence for NCB confiscation, according to which a person's mere inability to prove that their property was acquired by lawful means is not sufficient for the application of NCB confiscation.

10. The category of coherence implies that a uniform approach to the interpretation and application of the law must be maintained and, accordingly, the predictability of legal decisions made by the courts must be ensured. A rational judge should seek coherence, consistency, and internal compatibility in their decisions. Studies conducted by psychologists and other specialists show that judges use accurate, rational, and logical, and intuitive decision-making methods when dealing with cases. Incoherence (through

the prism of predictability) is a possible (or even inevitable) product of such a decision-making process. It is important to seek coherence between human nature and legal regulation, i.e., to accept human imperfections and to try to optimize them by applying certain procedures or creating appropriate constructs. Forming certain general models of legislative regulation that help to ensure coherence in the evidence evaluation process is an institutional task. Therefore:

10.1. The legislator, in cooperation with the courts and psychologists, should review the existing substantive and procedural norms and judicial (and non-judicial) procedures in order to reduce the harmful effects of cognitive factors on judicial decision-making. If necessary, new means should be adopted to affect this change.

10.2. In the case of Lithuania, the following must be considered: 1) adjusting the procedure relating to the announcement of a person's record of previous convictions before the examination of evidence; and 2) introducing an additional procedure relating to the prior evaluation of inadmissible evidence.

11. The choice between an oral and written process depends on numerous factors, including the country's judicial system and the role of the appellate court in it, the nature and complexity of the case and the parties involved. A coherent decision can only be made by carefully evaluating the advantages and disadvantages of both written and oral procedures.

11.1. The written procedure in the appellate court is not established as an absolute limitation of the right to an oral process. Namely, the court is given an opportunity, not an obligation, to try a criminal case via a written process. Therefore, the court must decide if the application of a written process in specific legal proceedings will be reasonable and justified.

11.2. The appellate court, when choosing the type of case review process, must carefully evaluate whether the selected type of case review will ensure the right of the accused to a fair trial – even in extraordinary circumstances. The court must choose the type of process that both guarantees safety and minimally restricts the rights of the persons involved in the process, including those of the accused, especially in cases when the outcome of the case may significantly worsen the condition of the accused and the involvement of the accused in the court process is much more important than deciding only on matters related to the application of the law.

12. The coherent integration of new instruments in criminal procedure, although based on the premise of procedural efficiency, must, considering the fundamental principles of criminal procedure, be understood first and foremost as a guarantee of fair proceedings. Remote criminal procedure, which does not per se conflict with the logos of criminal procedure, remains an exceptional form of organization of proceedings which may not be applied as a judicial imperative that is justified solely on the grounds of procedural promptness. Therefore:

12.1. The legislator's commitment to providing the best functionality to criminal proceedings through the appropriate integration of technological tools must be based on the principle of balance, where such enabling should not create preconditions for arbitrariness on the part of the decision-making body and unjustified restrictions on the rights of the parties to the proceedings.

12.2. Although remote criminal proceedings are seen as a threat to the fundamental safeguards of a fair adversarial procedure and treated as an exception in the doctrine, empirical studies show that, in the judicial practice of Lithuania, this has become a routine procedural decision of the court predetermined by an agreement reached between the parties involved in the proceedings.

12.3. The analysis of the Lithuanian case shows that the regulation model – where remote criminal procedure has been legitimized in the law but the legislator does not assume the responsibility of establishing the standards developed by the ECtHR's jurisprudence with regard to the means of safeguarding individual rights of defense at the level of a law, and instead transfers this obligation to implementing legal acts or simply to the emerging case law – is flawed and poses risks to the safeguards of the right to a fair trial.

Jolanta Zajančkauskienė

Summary

Toward Coherence in Criminal Justice: Challenges, Discussions, and/or Solutions is a comprehensive study of coherence across various aspects of criminal justice. This research focuses on coherence as a principle that enhances the effectiveness of criminal justice, both as a whole and in terms of its individual components.

This monograph critically examines practical issues of coherence in various areas of criminal justice. By analyzing existing research, legal frameworks, case law, and empirical evidence, the level of coherence in various areas of criminal justice is outlined. This volume also examines whether a degree of coherence is compatible with the objectives of justice and public safety, as well as considering tensions or trade-offs between coherence and other values, such as flexibility and responsiveness to a changing social environment.

The first part of the monograph, *The Search for Coherence in Substantive Criminal Law*, addresses several key issues. These include criminalization and decriminalization, the legal framework and its interpretation, and practice within the specific areas of individual offenses (human trafficking, drug possession, offenses against justice, and unlawful stalking). It also examines the compatibility of administrative and criminal liability and the consistent application of the principles of criminal jurisdiction to offenses committed abroad by EU Member State nationals and residents.

The first chapter ("The Gray Area in the Concept of Human Trafficking: Between the Text of the Law and the Purpose of Criminalization") is dedicated to the concept of human trafficking and the correct interpretation of its ambiguous elements, thus promoting coherence in the application of this unique legal instrument in practice. The problem of defining the concept of exploitation and the limitlessness of the concept of abuse of a position of vulnerability are also analyzed in this chapter.

After this analysis, it is submitted that in order to recognize the existence of exploitation or the intent to exploit, it is necessary to assess not only the formal list of areas of exploitation, but also: what real harm (discrimination, injustice, humiliation, disease) the victim has experienced or could experience as a result of the exploiters' behavior; how much the exploiters have benefited from it; and whether this behavior correlates with traffickers' usual methods of control over victims. The application of the concept of abuse of vulnerability must consider not only the victim's situation and lived experience, but also other aspects of the case that may negate the legal significance of the victim's consent to the traffickers' malicious offers.

The second chapter ("The Search for Legal Coherence in the Criminalization or Decriminalization of Drug Possession") considers the coherence of global drug law policies and trends in the criminalization and decriminalization of drugs, seeking to identify the main factors influencing legal policy decisions and to clarify the interrelationships and implications of these decisions for society, public health, and human rights. Inevitably, the phenomenon of drug use itself, its genesis and the development of relevant legal regulation are also analyzed. This analysis aims to provide a unified understanding of the complexity and multidimensionality of global drug policy, to discuss the experiences of different countries that have adopted diametrically opposed legal solutions in the field of drugs, and to decide and reflect on the prospects for a coherent legal understanding of the issue in an increasingly globalized world.

The third chapter ("Coherence in Criminal Policy for Offenses Against Justice That Obstruct the Investigation of a Case") analyzes the law and sentencing practice of Lithuania and other countries regarding offenses against justice. This analysis shows that Lithuanian criminal policy in the fight against offenses against justice, where the investigation is obstructed or the participants in the case are influenced, is much more lenient than the criminal policy of the UK or the USA in this respect, both at the level of legislation and case law. It should be noted that the provisions of the Lithuanian Criminal Code on criminal liability for the obstruction of justice are not coherent with other special and general provisions. In addition, the penalties for the above-mentioned offenses against justice are not coherent and are too lenient in relation to other provisions of the Special Part of the Criminal Code, which provide for liability for similar offenses. Moreover, the rules on the aggregation of penalties provided for in the General Part of the Criminal Code are inconsistent with the objectives of these penalties, and unduly broaden the scope of application of the aggregation of penalties. This leads to a situation in which serious or very serious offenses against justice effectively go unpunished.

Chapter 4 ("The Unlawful Stalking of a Person") examines the definition of stalking as a criminal phenomenon. This chapter finds that, despite the difficulties faced by individual states in formulating their own definitions of stalking, a coherent approach allows stalking to be seen as constituting the repeated acts of a person which are of a frightening nature and cause disturbance and uneasiness. A coherent approach to stalking is necessary not only for a better understanding of its nature, but also for the application of criminal responsibility. Unlawful acts of stalking are usually regulated by separate norms in national criminal legislation, with the names of these norms specifically referring to unlawful stalking. However, acts constituting unlawful stalking may render a person criminally responsible even if an offense specifically referred to by that name does not exist in the criminal law of the state. The norm of systematic intimidation (Article 145(2) of the Criminal Code) applied in Lithuanian jurisprudence is an excellent example of this. Stalking as an independent criminal offense was also established in the Criminal Code of Lithuania in the chapter covering "Crimes against human freedom." However, the new norm of unlawful stalking did not bring coherence to the assessment of repeated acts of intimidation, but instead created competition between general (Article 145 of the Criminal Code) and special (Article 148-1 of the Criminal Code) norms. This norm also posed one of the most significant challenges faced in this area: to identify criteria in the practical application of the norms that would help to distinguish cases of systematic intimidation from unlawful stalking.

The fifth chapter ("Administrative and Criminal Liability: Toward Sustainability") covers the problem of coherence and harmonization between administrative and criminal liability. When examining the issues of the coherence and harmonization of administrative and criminal liability in Europe, it should be noted that EU law does not provide a consistent set of constituent elements that characterize an administrative sanction and allow it to be distinguished from criminal sanctions. The purpose of administrative sanctions is the same as criminal sanctions: to punish violations of the law. However, criminal sanctions (such as imprisonment) have traditionally been more severe and carry greater social stigma than administrative sanctions. Because of the potential severity of criminal sanctions, there are many procedural safeguards, and they are almost exclusively imposed by the courts. Administrative sanctions are used for behavior that is not criminal in nature and may not require severe sanctions. Therefore, the term "administrative" is used in legal acts to indicate the non-criminal nature of sanctions and the main role of the administrative authority in sanctioning. This study, therefore, proceeds to consider how criminal liability and administrative liability should be combined.

The sixth chapter ("Standards for the Coherent Application of the Principles of Criminal Jurisdiction in Relation to Criminal Acts Committed by Lithuanian Citizens and Persons Permanently Resident in Lithuania Outside the Territory of Lithuania") discusses the problem of the coherent interaction of the principles of state criminal jurisdiction, in particular with regard to the need for the proper application of national criminal law to offenses committed abroad by nationals and other persons residing in that state. This choice of topic was inspired by the fact that Lithuanian citizens are prosecuted under the Criminal Code of the Republic of Lithuania for criminal acts committed outside the territory of Lithuania not based on the active personality principle, but based on the universal principle. Moreover, in Lithuania it is entirely wrongly assumed that criminal acts committed by Lithuanian citizens on board a foreign vessel on the high seas must be qualified as criminal acts committed on the territory of the flag state of the vessel. In other words, the limits to the application of any principle of criminal jurisdiction are expanded on the grounds of the literal interpretation of criminal law norms. In order to avoid such situations and to draw very clear boundaries on the jurisdictional principles applicable to Lithuanian citizens and other persons permanently residing in Lithuania in respect of criminal acts committed by them abroad, the most important and relevant aspects of the content of the flag, active personal, and universal principles are analyzed, and a potential mechanism that might enable their coherent interaction with each other is outlined. The content of the double criminality clause and the rules for determining the place of commission of the crime are analyzed in connection with the elaboration of guidelines for the effective regulation and coherent application of the active personal principle.

The second part of the monograph, *The Transformation of Criminal Procedure Law in the Context of Coherence*, considers several issues, including: the movement of electronic evidence between EU Member States; the concept of electronic evidence and the assessment of its reliability; subjective threats to the free assessment of evidence; and the standard of proof in a confiscation procedure not predicated on a conviction and its compatibility with human rights, particularly the presumption of innocence. It also addresses specific issues related to the right to a fair criminal trial, such as whether a written case procedure constitutes an absolute restriction on the right to an oral hearing before an appellate court and the limits of the integration of technology into criminal procedure.

The first chapter ("The E-Evidence 'Movement' in European Union Criminal Justice: Toward or Beyond Coherence?") focuses on the coherence of the legal framework and its application to the movement of electronic evidence in EU criminal justice. In 2023, Regulation (EU) 2023/1543 of the European Parliament and of the Council on European Production Orders and European Preservation Orders for electronic evidence in criminal proceedings and for the execution of custodial sentences following criminal proceedings was adopted. This legislation should have solved problems related to the challenges of moving electronic data in the EU. Unfortunately, an analysis of the existing legal framework for the gathering of evidence (including electronic evidence, as outlined by EIOs and regulated by the Regulation on the Taking of Electronic Evidence) shows that the

Regulation lacks the provisions necessary to ensure the timely and efficient gathering of evidence and the admissibility of such evidence before national courts.

The second chapter ("Electronic Evidence in Criminal Proceedings") also addresses the issue of electronic evidence. The need for the proper evaluation of electronic evidence in criminal proceedings arises in the context of cybercrime investigations. The latter offenses are generally characterized by the fact that they tend to leave intangible traces, the proper collection, presentation, verification and assessment of which becomes crucial for establishing the truth in criminal cases. It should be noted that the characteristics of this type of evidence, such as its ease of alteration and the difficulty of detecting such alterations, make it necessary to seek criteria that can be used to establish its reliability. Therefore, a coherent approach to electronic evidence which includes the establishment of a harmonized and consistent framework for the handling of electronic data becomes important. On the one hand, the general criteria for evaluating evidence in criminal proceedings are important; on the other hand, due to its specific nature, electronic evidence may also be subject to additional requirements to establish its reliability. High-quality evidentiary activities related to obtaining, presenting, verifying and evaluating electronic evidence have an impact on the cost-effectiveness and speed of criminal proceedings, as well as on effective international (EU) cooperation in cybercrime cases. Therefore, establishing a coherent approach to electronic evidence becomes relevant at both the national and international (EU) level.

One of the most serious concerns among European countries and the EU is the protection of society against crime, especially transnational crime. For this reason, authorities, researchers, and practitioners analyze solutions that should enable them to deprive the perpetrators of crime of their profits in an effective way. Thus, the third chapter ("Evidence in Non-Conviction-Based Confiscation Proceedings") analyzes one of the most pertinent issues in confiscation proceedings – the standard of evidence in non-conviction-based confiscation proceedings and its compatibility with human rights, in particular the presumption of innocence. This chapter analyzes the coherence of international rules in non-conviction-based confiscation with national, including constitutional, standards of limitations of the right to property. International and EU approaches to asset confiscation and the jurisprudence of supranational courts are characterized by the continuous expansion of the concept and scope of non-conviction-based confiscation. On the other hand, in order to achieve effective cooperation, states must also strive for coherence, not only in regulating the grounds for confiscation, but also in ensuring the equal protection of individual rights. This includes setting an appropriate standard of proof in non-conviction-based confiscation proceedings. An analysis of the jurisprudence of constitutional courts on extended confiscation suggests that national jurisprudence also seeks coherence with that of the ECtHR and the CJEU by, *inter alia*, setting a different standard of proof. Nevertheless, the tension between the rights of the individual and the state's objective of recovering the proceeds of crime in non-conviction-based confiscation remains.

In the fourth chapter ("Subjective Threats to the Free Evaluation of Evidence: Toward a More Coherent Legal Regulation"), the ability of coherence to ensure the predictability of legal decisions made by the courts is considered. A rational judge should seek coherence, consistency and internal compatibility in their decisions. Studies conducted by psychologists and other specialists show that, in reality, judges use not only accurate, rational and logical decision-making methods when dealing with cases, but also intuitive approaches. Incoherence (through the prism of predictability) is a possible (or perhaps inevitable) product of such a decision-making process. Attention is drawn to the fact that it is important to seek coherence between human nature and legal regulation, i.e., to accept human imperfections and try to account for those by applying certain procedures or creating appropriate constructs. In addition, it is emphasized that the formation of certain general models of legal regulation which help to ensure coherence in the evidence evaluation process is an institutional task.

The fifth chapter ("The Trial of a Criminal Case in an Appellate Court Hearing: A Written or Oral Procedure in the Context of the Right to a Fair Trial") and the final chapter ("Coherence Between the Model of Remote Criminal Proceedings and the Standards Under Article 6 of the European Convention on Human Rights: The Reality of Threats to a Fair Trial") both concern the right to a fair trial, which is enshrined in regional, national, and international instruments. This right provides a number of minimum guarantees for the accused, such as the independence and impartiality of the court, the possibility for the person to participate in the proceedings, etc.

The fifth chapter analyses aspects of ensuring the right to a fair trial when considering a case at a court hearing or through a written procedure, using Latvia as a case study. When deciding whether a case should be considered by an appellate court in an oral or written procedure, it is necessary to take into account national standards for ensuring the right to a fair trial, which are more important than international or regional legal acts. Therefore, the court is obliged to act in accordance with national standards. The author concludes that the written procedure does not represent an absolute restriction of the right to an oral hearing before an appellate court; in other words, the court has the possibility, but not the obligation, to hear a criminal case through a written procedure. Therefore, the court must decide whether the application of the written procedure in the appellate court is reasonable and justified.

The final chapter analyzes the main principles of the case law of the ECtHR on the application of measures allowing remote criminal proceedings and assesses the role of the ECtHR in the framework of the EU system of human rights protection. The primary observation is that, in the context of the limits of the integration of technology into criminal proceedings, the case law of the ECtHR remains a basic unified reference point for EU countries. This allows them to avoid deviating from human rights standards in the field of criminal justice and maintains the coherence of the legal approaches of the EU Member States.

Index

www.ingramcontent.com/pod-product-compliance
Ingram Content Group UK Ltd.
Pitfield, Milton Keynes, MK11 3LW, UK
UKHW020834290926
15470UKWH00004B/1342

9 783631 929445